*W*here the river is wide, at low tide one can only see the mud flats and broad stretches of green marsh grass. But when the tide is in, it is a noble and dignified stream. There are no rapids and only a slow current, where the river from among the inland mountains flows along, finding its way to the sea, which has come part way to welcome the company of springs and brooks that have answered to its call.

—SARAH ORNE JEWETT, "RIVER DRIFTWOOD" (1881)

*Hallway, Hamilton house, South Berwick, Maine, built ca. 1787.
Photograph by Elise Tyson Vaughan, 1903. Courtesy,
Society for the Preservation of New England Antiquities.*

"A Noble and Dignified Stream"

The Piscataqua Region in the Colonial Revival, 1860–1930

Edited by

Sarah L. Giffen and Kevin D. Murphy

Old York Historical Society

York, Maine

1992

The photograph on the endpapers is Emma Coleman's *By the Third Bridge, York River,* ca. 1883–84, 4⅝ in. x 7½ in., from the collections of the Old York Historical Society. The shield on the title page has been adapted from the cover stamping on the first edition of Sarah Orne Jewett's *The Tory Lover* (1901).

Other graphic elements used in the book have been adapted from the designs of Sarah Wyman Whitman (1842–1904). Whitman was an accomplished designer of decorated trade bindings, and numbered among her friends many influential writers and publishers. Her work for Houghton Mifflin and the Merrymount Press included designs for editions of Thomas Bailey Aldrich, Robert Browning, Nathaniel Hawthorne, Oliver Wendell Holmes, William Dean Howells, Sarah Orne Jewett, Tacitus, Celia Thaxter, Henry Wadsworth Longfellow, John Greenleaf Whittier, and Kate Douglas Wiggin. The small flowers flanking the catalogue numbers are from *Deephaven* (Jewett) and *An Island Garden* (Thaxter). The larger groups of flowers are from *A Native of Winby and Other Tales* and *The Country of the Pointed Firs* (both Jewett).

Whitman's home at 77 Mount Vernon Street on Beacon Hill was long a gathering place for her literary and artistic friends. In 1936, it became the meeting place for the Club of Odd Volumes and the Society of Printers, where the ardent discussion of books continues to the present day. Bruce Rogers (1870–1957), designer of the Centaur type used in this book, was a charter member of the Society of Printers and spent many pleasant hours in Whitman's house. Rogers spent the first years of his career at the Riverside Press, the company that printed many of Houghton Mifflin's books. It is likely that Whitman and Rogers knew each other, and appropriate that their work should be brought together here.

First Edition
Copyright © 1992 by Old York Historical Society. All rights reserved.
ISBN 0–9631955–0–6

Set in Centaur, Arrighi and Minion types. Designed by Bruce Kennett.
Printed in the United States of America

Contents

Acknowledgments   VII
  Sarah L. Giffen and Kevin D. Murphy

Project Benefactors   VIII

Contributors   IX

Introduction   XI
  Kevin D. Murphy

List of Abbreviations and Frequently Cited Sources   XIII

CHAPTER 1 PROMOTING THE COLONIAL

Purchasing the Past: Summer People and the Transformation of the Piscataqua Region in the Nineteenth Century   3
  Dona Brown

Catalogue entries 1–7   15

CHAPTER 2 RESTORING THE COLONIAL HOME

The New Colonials: Restoration and Remodeling of Old Buildings Along the Piscataqua   35
  Richard M. Candee

Catalogue entries 8–17   48

CHAPTER 3 THE COLONIAL REVIVAL LANDSCAPE

"Tempus Fugit": Capturing the Past in the Landscape of the Piscataqua   81
  Lucinda A. Brockway

Catalogue entries 18–26   91

CHAPTER 4 THE COLONIAL IN ART AND ARCHITECTURE

Artistic Circles and Summer Colonies   115
  Woodard D. Openo

Catalogue entries 27–44   126

CHAPTER 5 THE LITERATURE OF THE COLONIAL REVIVAL

"Colossal in Sheet-Lead": The Native American and Piscataqua-Region Writers   165
  Karen Oakes

Catalogue entries 45–52   177

CHAPTER 6 EXHIBITING THE COLONIAL

The Politics of Preservation: Historic House Museums in the Piscataqua Region   193
  Kevin D. Murphy

Catalogue entries 53–59   205

Selected Bibliography   227
Illustration Credits   231
Index   232
Color Plates 1–8   *following* 130

Emma Coleman, Chase's Pond, York, Maine, *ca. 1883–84.*
Photograph, 7½ in. x 4⅝ in. Old York Historical Society.

Acknowledgments

The editors would like to acknowledge the assistance of a large number of individuals who contributed to this project. The genesis of this volume extends back ten years to a project jointly initiated by the Old Gaol Museum and the Society for the Preservation of Historic Landmarks in York County (now united in the Old York Historical Society) and the Brick Store Museum in Kennebunk, Maine. Under the direction of Eldridge H. Pendleton (former director of the Old Gaol Museum), Mary P. Harding (former director of the Society for the Preservation of Landmarks in York County), and Sandra S. Armentrout (former director of the Brick Store Museum), a series of exhibitions and public programs on the colonial revival was held during the summer of 1982, with the support of the Maine Humanities Council. During the intervening decade, the colonial revival has been the subject of ongoing investigation, especially since the establishment of the Elizabeth Perkins summer fellowship program at the Old York Historical Society in 1988, which has brought graduate students from around the country to York where their research efforts have provided much of the background for this book. The Elizabeth Perkins fellows who provided research incorporated into this book include Jonathan Canning, Mary Anne Caton, Vicki Chirco, Kari Federer, Amy Hufnagel, Tom Jester, Tom Johnson, Michael Kucher, Robben McAddam, Thayer Tolles Mickel, Marina Moskowitz, Alice Nash, Helen Psarakis, Jessie Ravage, Kathleen Wilson, Cindi Young, and Maria Yunis.

The staffs and volunteers of the many historic house museums in the region were especially helpful to the research that is represented in this book and worked with the Old York Historical Society staff in developing exhibitions on the colonial revival that they will host. These institutions are: the John Paul Jones House of the Portsmouth Historical Society, the Moffatt-Ladd House, the Society for the Preservation of New England Antiquities, Strawbery Banke Museum, the Warner House Association, the Wentworth-Coolidge Mansion, and the Wentworth-Gardner House. Vicki Wright and the staff of the Art Gallery of the University of New Hampshire, as well as designer Lisa Blinn, have been instrumental in planning an exhibition that will open there in September, 1992. We are particularly indebted to Sandra Armentrout and Richard Candee for their advice on all aspects of the project and their continual support.

Many people read sections of the manuscript and provided important insights that were incorporated into the final version. They include Karen Bowden, Harvey Green, Amy Hufnagel, Valencia Libby, Karal Ann Marling, Marina Moskowitz, Jane Nylander, Richard Nylander and Rodris Roth. Richard Candee was an invaluable source of information and helped us locate many of the manuscripts that are found in the bibliography. We are indebted to him for his skillful editing throughout the writing process. Richard Nylander devoted many hours to the choosing of photographs. Gerry Ward provided advice on the publishing process and copy edited the manuscript; Bruce Kennett designed the book. Several libraries provided valuable information, including the library of the Old York Historical Society (Virginia Spiller, librarian), the Portsmouth Athenæum (Carolyn Eastman), the Portsmouth Public Library (Nancy Noble), the library of the Society for the Preservation of New England Antiquities in Boston (Lorna Condon, librarian), and the Strawbery Banke Museum library (Greg Colati). The staff and trustees of the Old York Historical Society are also to be thanked for their contributions to the project. We are particularly grateful to Virginia Spiller for her relentless efforts in verifying many details in this book and to our director, Richard C. Borges, whose unflagging confidence in our work enabled the project to go forward.

Financial contributions were made to the project by the Maine Humanities Council and the York Community Initiatives Fund of the Greater Portsmouth Community Foundation. We thank Neil Rolde for his support of the project. Finally, we would like to recognize the contribution of the National Endow-ment for the Humanities for providing a planning grant (1990–91) and an implementation grant (1991–92) that have made the preparation of this book, as well as the production of accompanying exhibitions and public programs, possible.

Sarah L. Giffen and Kevin D. Murphy

Project Benefactors

Contributors

SSA
Sandra S. Armentrout
Society for the Preservation of New England Antiquities

LAB
Lucinda A. Brockway
Past Designs, Inc.

Dona Brown
University of New Hampshire

RMC
Richard M. Candee
Boston University

MAC
Mary Anne Caton
Monticello, the Home of Thomas Jefferson

SLG
Sarah L. Giffen
Old York Historical Society

PAH
Philip A. Hayden
Historical Society of Princeton

TH
Thomas Hinkle
Old York Historical Society

AWH
Amy Wilkinson Hufnagel
Lightwork

TBJ
Thomas B. Johnson
Maine Citizens for Historic Preservation

FHL
Frances Herman Lord
University of New Hampshire

TTM
Thayer Tolles Mickel
Metropolitan Museum of Art

AMM
Anne Mankin Masury
Strawbery Banke Museum

RM
Robben McAdam
Old York Historical Society

MM
Marina Moskowitz
The Lyceum, Alexandria's History Museum

KDM
Kevin D. Murphy
University of Virginia

ANN
Alice N. Nash
Columbia University

JCN
Jane C. Nylander
Strawbery Banke Museum

RCN
Richard C. Nylander
Society for the Preservation of New England Antiquities

Karen Oakes
Brandeis University

WDO
Woodard D. Openo
Portsmouth Athenaeum

JR
Jessie Ravage
Old York Historical Society

CPR
Carolyn Parsons Roy
Strawbery Banke Museum

EGS
Earle G. Shettleworth, Jr.
Maine Historic Preservation Commission

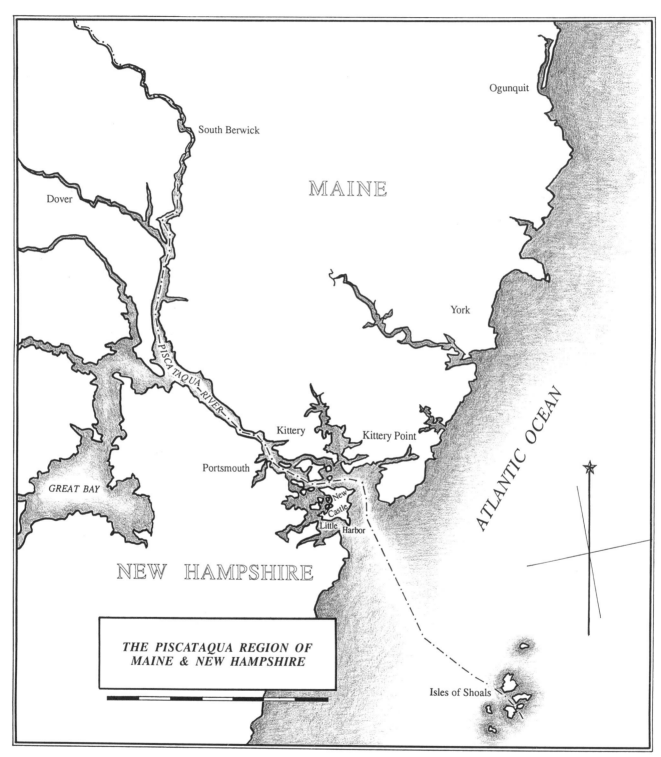

MAINE

Ogunquit

South Berwick

Dover

PISCATAQUA RIVER

York

Kittery

Kittery Point

Portsmouth

GREAT BAY

New Castle

ATLANTIC OCEAN

Little Harbor

NEW HAMPSHIRE

THE PISCATAQUA REGION OF
MAINE & NEW HAMPSHIRE

Isles of Shoals

Fig. a. Map of the Piscataqua region. Drawing, Lisa Blinn.

Introduction

Kevin D. Murphy

In "River Driftwood," published in the *Atlantic Monthly* in 1881, Sarah Orne Jewett described the eastern branch of the Piscataqua River that constitutes the border between New Hampshire and Maine as a "noble and dignified stream." Although Jewett recognized that the river was "no longer the public highway it used to be years ago, when the few roads were rough, and the railroads were not even dreamed of," this body of water provided for her a connection with the premodern era, as much as an actual transportation route between the Atlantic Ocean and inland towns.[1]

In the present study, the Piscataqua River is at the center of a group of communities first settled during the seventeenth century and renowned during much of the nineteenth century for having especially historic character (fig. a). The city of Dover, New Hampshire, was the most industrialized by the turn of the twentieth century, although Portsmouth, New Hampshire, to the east, also had extensive mills in operation by that date. The other towns covered in this book, including New Castle, New Hampshire, and Kittery, York, South Berwick, and Ogunquit, Maine, were more rural, and sustained both agriculture and small-scale industry.

The purpose of this catalogue is to document the significance of this relatively small region within the larger colonial revival movement. The renewal of interest in the material culture of the colonial period gained momentum with the celebration of the centennial of American independence in 1876 (fig. b), but as the essays and catalogue entries in this volume show, this concern with the tangible vestiges of the colonial period was already emerging in the Piscataqua region well before that date. As the national fascination with the fine art, architecture, literature, diet, dress, and domestic furnishings of the eighteenth and early nineteenth centuries—everything before 1840 being considered equally "colonial"—mounted, the Piscataqua region provided imagery of the past far out of proportion to its geographic size.[2] The historic architecture of the area was widely published, its landscape was painted by artists who exhibited in Boston and New York, and writers such as Sarah Orne Jewett and Thomas Bailey Aldrich made its history known through stories and books that claimed a large readership.

In 1881 Jewett discounted the utility of the mills along the Piscataqua, suggesting instead that "its chief use is its beauty, and that has never been as widely appreciated as it ought to be." She bemoaned the fact that "there are some who would never know who has lived beside my river unless it were told here. That says at once that their fame at best is provincial."[3] If, as Jewett asserts, the beauty and history of the Piscataqua region were known only within its

bounds in 1881, such was no longer the case by the early decades of the twentieth century. Jewett herself popularized the area in print, and even brought about the purchase of the eighteenth-century Hamilton house in South Berwick by friends from Boston. Other artists, including Aldrich and painter Marcia Oakes Woodbury, who had spent their childhood in the region, returned as adults to produce works that drew others. By this process, circles of artists, historians, collectors, and antiquarians were constituted in the region. Some members were "natives," others "outsiders," but they all belonged to a network of social relations that stretched from Portsmouth to York, from New Castle to Ogunquit.

This volume attempts to illuminate the interconnections between the men and women who took part in preserving and publicizing the history of the Piscataqua region between the 1860s and the 1930s. Moreover, it seeks to situate the production of history within a particular time and place, to question why people devoted their energies to saving old buildings and to preserving the history of the region through a variety of artistic media. No less important than understanding the motives behind the production of representations of the past is knowing more about the consumers of such images of colonial America.

To observers at the turn of the century, the Piscataqua region seemed to provide more evidence of the preindustrial era than did larger urban centers. This book attempts to explore the historical process that left the landscape of the area with an earlier appearance and the circumstances under which it became home to those who sought to promote such imagery of the past. While the social and economic motivations of the colonial revival have been addressed previously on a national level, they have yet to be detailed with respect to a geographically finite, yet nationally significant, region.[4]

The artists and others who came to the Piscataqua region at the turn of the century—with few exceptions—were not part of the development of æsthetic modernism, the cultural phenomenon that coexisted with the colonial revival. Summer and year-round residents of the Piscataqua region continued to paint using the techniques of French Impressionism, while other American artists were becoming interested in European modernism, especially after the much-discussed New York International Exhibition of Modern Art (the Armory Show) of 1913 which brought the work of avant-garde artists from the Continent to the United States. In the fields of painting and sculpture, modernists rejected traditional illusionism to produce works that took purely formal relationships as their subjects and called into question the conceits of the artistic media.

Fig. b. Detail of Louis Aubrun, Main Building, International Exhibition, 1876. *Published by Thomas Hunter; copyrighted by the Centennial Board of Finance, 1874. Old York Historical Society.*

Architects in the area were likewise outside of the development of modernism. The preservation of the early houses of the Piscataqua region, as well as the construction of new residences in the colonial revival style, continued during the early years of the twentieth century, even as Frank Lloyd Wright and other members of the Chicago School claimed to reject tradition and provided the groundwork for architectural modernism. The adherents of modernism sought an architectural solution to the problems of the industrialized West. Such a social program was not part of the work of colonial revival architects in the Piscataqua region; instead, they provided convenient summer homes for middle-class or wealthy clients.

Kenneth L. Ames has suggested that the domestic sphere was where antimodern tendencies were played out, and the one which "may well be the major focus of colonializing activity."[5] If the colonial revival home could be a retreat from the modern world, it could also serve as a space in which modernism was resisted. These conclusions seem to be born out in the colonial revival activities that took place in the Piscataqua region and can be seen in the January 1929 issue of *House Beautiful.* That month the magazine featured the Hamilton house as an example of "The House in Good Taste" (fig. c), while also publishing a debate between Chicago School architect Thomas E. Tallmadge and Gothicist architect Ralph Adams Cram on the question of "Will This Modernism Last?" Cram prophesied the demise of modernism, especially in the realm of domestic architecture which he did not believe should be subjected to any rigorously applied style: "A house is a purely personal thing and should look and act as such. You can invent a style for the skyscraper and apply it universally . . . but for heaven's sake don't try to standardize the house in which humans live."[6]

Tallmadge saw modernism differently: by 1929 the style dominated the design of skyscrapers, shops, hotels, and clubs, and he suggested that "even now you can hear it knocking on our doors and prying open the windows of our homes." Tallmadge, anticipating the proliferation of glass and steel architecture across America, concluded:

The World War changed the lives of humanity and ended an epoch. Now we are standing upon a high peak. Behind us lie the quiet and familiar groves with their gleam of white columns and their heaven-pointing spires. Before us are spread the mysterious and fearfully enchanting vistas of a new era, a new era which will surely be clothed in the garment of a new architecture.[7]

For those to whom the vision of the modern world was more "fearful" than "enchanting," the Piscataqua region offered towns like South Berwick and such traditional houses as the Hamilton house to provide a setting for the contemplation of the past. By featuring Hamilton house as an example of good taste, the editors of *House Beautiful* posed this monument of the Piscataqua region as an antimodernist solution to domestic design. This volume documents the activities of a group of people who took to the "quiet and familiar groves" to discern a glimpse of the premodern world. It also seeks to understand why they turned away from "the mysterious and fearfully enchanting vistas of a new era," in preference for the colonial period.

These questions are addressed in the essays and catalogue entries that follow. The book is composed of six chapters. The first, entitled "Promoting the Colonial," establishes the social and economic circumstances in which the history of the region was used as a tool for revitalization. The second two sections, "Restoring the Colonial Home" and "The Colonial Revival Landscape," concern those transformations of the built and natural environments that were informed by an emerging historical consciousness, and especially those that fulfilled the requirements of summer visitors. "The Colonial in Art and Architecture" and "The Literature of the Colonial Revival," the third and fourth chapters, document cultural production in the Piscataqua region that both used and disseminated its history. The last section of the book, called "Exhibiting the Colonial," treats the establishment of historic house museums, institutions that perpetuated and memorialized the history of the Piscataqua region as it was construed during the colonial revival period.

Fig. c. Hamilton house, South Berwick, Maine, built ca. 1787. Photograph by Paul J. Weber. A detail of this photograph was published in House Beautiful *(1929). Courtesy, Society for the Preservation of New England Antiquities.*

1 Sarah Orne Jewett, "River Driftwood," *Atlantic Monthly* 48 (Oct. 1881): 500.

2 Kenneth L. Ames suggests this in the introduction to Axelrod, *Colonial Revival.* He goes on to state that *colonial* "described the period before the onset of Victorianism, which in America is virtually interchangeable with modernization. In this country, *colonial* can be seen as a code word for anti- or non-Victorian, anti- or nonmodern" (11–12).

3 Jewett, "River Driftwood," 502, 504.

4 The most important works to address the colonial revival on a national level are Axelrod, *Colonial Revival;* William Rhoads, *The Colonial Revival,* 2 vols. (New York and London: Garland Publishing, 1977); and Karal Ann Marling, *George Washington Slept Here: Colonial Revivals and American Culture, 1876–1986* (Cambridge, Mass.: Harvard University Press, 1988).

5 Ames, "Introduction," in Axelrod, *Colonial Revival,* 12.

6 Ralph Adams Cram, "Will This Modernism Last?" *House Beautiful* 65 (Jan. 1929): 45.

7 Tallmadge, "Will This Modernism Last?" 88.

List of Abbreviations and Frequently Cited Sources

AAA
Archives of American Art, Smithsonian Institution, Washington, D.C.

Axelrod, *Colonial Revival*
Alan Axelrod, ed. *The Colonial Revival in America.* New York: W.W. Norton for the Henry Francis du Pont Winterthur Museum, 1985.

OTNE
Old-Time New England.

OYHS
Old York Historical Society, York, Maine.

PA
Portsmouth Athenaeum, Portsmouth, New Hampshire.

SB
Strawbery Banke Museum, Portsmouth, New Hampshire.

SPNEA
Society for the Preservation of New England Antiquities, Boston, Massachusetts.

YCRD
York County Registry of Deeds, Alfred, Maine.

I
Promoting the Colonial

Fig. 1.1. John Blunt, Portsmouth Harbor, *Portsmouth, New Hampshire, 1824. Oil on canvas; 26 in. x 33 in. Courtesy, Portsmouth Athenaeum.*

Preceding page: *Commercial photograph of the Wentworth-Gardner house, Portsmouth, New Hampshire. Photograph by Wallace Nutting, ca. 1915. Courtesy, Society for the Preservation of New England Antiquities.*

Purchasing the Past:
Summer People and the Transformation of the Piscataqua Region in the Nineteenth Century

DONA BROWN

A T FIRST GLANCE, it is not easy to distinguish the area surrounding the Piscataqua River from the rest of New England. The region has its share of aging mill towns and resort communities, of straggling second-growth woods and better-than-new restored villages. There are no clear boundaries to set the region apart from its neighbors. Even its terrain seems to be a hybrid of New England images: the typical beaches and tidal marshes of maritime New England meet the typical rocky fields of upcountry New England.

There is one way, though, that the Piscataqua region may appear distinctive to a casual observer today: it seems even older than the rest of New England. Buildings we now recognize as "colonial" dominate the landscape everywhere, from the brick seaport of Portsmouth to the old mill town of South Berwick. And in fact, those old buildings—and the appearance of stability and timelessness they create—reveal more about the region than simply its age. That distinctive landscape was produced by a common past, a history not of stability, but of generations of dramatic economic ups and downs. Twice in its history, the Piscataqua region has been the site of a lucrative but unstable trade, and twice in the region's history, wealthy men and women have made their mark on the landscape: once when ship captains and merchants first built their houses on the slopes overlooking their wharves, and once again when wealthy tourists occupied the region, recreating the landscape by restoring the same "colonial" houses.

The first industry is better known. It was in the mid eighteenth century that the Piscataqua region found its first calling as part of the lucrative West India trade, supplying the plantations of the West Indies with raw materials. Portsmouth, at the mouth of the Piscataqua, was the commercial center of the region, boasting a deep river harbor that never froze (fig. 1.1). In 1800 it employed more than a hundred ships in coastal and West Indian commercial ventures.[1] Most of the towns in the region made similar use of their protected harbors: York, Kittery, New Castle, and Berwick all launched substantial commercial fleets of their own before the American Revolution.

The West India trade was primarily a trade in raw materials and food. Lumber from the hinterlands upriver and salt fish from its own fishing fleets made up a substantial part of the region's trade with the West Indies. Even the most remote parts of the region were brought into the network of this international market: the Isles of Shoals, a cluster of small islands directly outside Portsmouth harbor, became a processing center for vast quantities of fish bound for the West Indies. Berwick, Dover, and the towns surrounding the Piscataqua's Great Bay specialized in lumber, brought from the north country down to the sea in their own vessels. During the "boom" years, the area took on an imposing and prosperous appearance: ship captains and wealthy merchants built large and elegant houses overlooking their wharves and warehouses in the towns and along the rivers.

But almost as soon as the houses were built, the sources of the fortunes that had financed them were beginning to dry up. Like most "boom" economies, this one was fragile. Economic disaster hit the region with the Embargo Act of 1807, and the War of 1812 sealed that fate with the destruction of many of the region's ships and the complete disruption of trade patterns. And that sudden shock, which the Piscataqua region shared with all of New England's seaports, was not the only blow. At least one of the region's major commodities, lumber, was already fast disappearing. By the time of Timothy Dwight's first tour through the region in 1796, he could report that the "commerce of Dover consists chiefly in lumber [which] is daily diminishing, and in a short time will probably fail." In the report of his second visit in 1810, Dwight described some parts of the region as economically devastated: the town of York in particular was almost completely deforested, "naked and bleak," with an air of "stillness and solitude," even of "antiquity."[2]

During the years following the War of 1812, the Piscataqua region was in serious decline, losing population and unable to find viable substitutes for its former trades. Some parts of the region experienced a deep downward slide in both population and business that was not arrested until the end of the nineteenth century. York, for example, lost the county courthouse to Alfred, Maine, in 1833, saw the railroad bypass its town center in 1842, and experienced a continuous loss of population from 1840 to 1890. Nearby Wells experienced the same continuous decline in population.[3]

What happened next is a little less clear. Some of the best-known nineteenth-century accounts of the region describe a place where the hand of time had completely stopped moving, as if "all the clocks . . . , and all the people with them, had stopped years ago."[4] In *The Story of a Bad*

Boy, written in 1868, Thomas Bailey Aldrich described the city of Portsmouth's decay:

> Few ships come to Rivermouth now. Commerce drifted into other ports . . . The crazy old warehouses are empty; and barnacles and eel-grass cling to the piles of the crumbling wharves, where the sunshine lies lovingly, bringing out the faint spicy odor that haunts the place—the ghost of the old dead West India trade![5]

And in 1881 Sarah Orne Jewett wrote in similar terms about her native South Berwick (fig. 1.2):

> From this inland town of mine there is no sea-faring any more, and the shipwrights' hammers are never heard now. It is only a station on the railway, and it has, after all these years, grown so little that it is hardly worth while for all the trains to stop.[6]

However, the economy of the Piscataqua region did not simply shut down in the nineteenth century, leaving its residents to live on memories. By the time Aldrich and Jewett were writing these nostalgic descriptions, the worst of the depression had come to an end in many parts of the region. Within a mile or two of the location where Jewett described the peaceful solitude of the Salmon Falls River, that same river had, as she herself put it, "made itself of great

Fig. 1.2. *South Berwick Square, South Berwick, Maine. Photograph, ca. 1880. Courtesy, Old Berwick Historical Society.*

consequence by serving to carry perhaps a dozen or twenty mills, of one kind and another."[7] Just up the river from her nostalgic revery was a modern Victorian mill town, and "little" South Berwick was actually a major junction for the Boston and Maine Railroad: its population was not declining, but increasing. Similarly, Aldrich recognized (and deplored) the fact that while Portsmouth's harbor was quiet, Portsmouth's businesses and manufactures were now being supplied by inland transportation—the railroad.

Fig. 1.3. *"Appledore House," Isles of Shoals, New Hampshire. Photograph of unsigned, undated lithograph, after Edmund Henry Garrett,* Appledore House, *1877. Courtesy, Society for the Preservation of New England Antiquities.*

By the mid nineteenth century, many parts of the region had begun the climb back into the economic mainstream. To be sure, some parts of towns that had once been busy were now deserted; the empty docks and rotting wharves that figured so prominently in reminiscences and stories were a tangible sign that the transition was not an easy one. And some parts of the region were slower to adapt to the new circumstances than others—not because of a lack of initiative, but because of simple geography. Towns that were upstream sprouted factories powered by water. Towns at the mouths of harbors found it more difficult to replace their commercial activities. At the same time, inland railroad routes left many places more isolated just a few miles from a railroad depot than they had been when their tidal rivers had given them access to a world market.

But as time went on, even the more out-of-the-way coastal towns and villages—those that could not adapt themselves to industrial uses—were finding new ways to exploit their old resource, the sea. They were becoming summer resorts. In the resort industry, at least, a location a little removed from the industrial centers of the region could be an asset rather than a liability. In fact, it was the single most isolated part of the Piscataqua region, the tiny Isles of Shoals, that led the region into the summer resort trade. The Isles of Shoals were inhabited in the early nineteenth century by a rapidly dwindling community of commercial fishers, completely cut off from other sources of income and losing out to competition from such better-equipped fishing towns as Gloucester, Massachusetts. (Rumor had it that the community was also losing touch with the finer points of mainland civilization: missionaries claimed that islanders no longer bothered with church-going or even marriage ceremonies.)

But almost overnight, these "barbaric" islanders found a new industry taking root among them. Portsmouth resident Thomas Laighton moved his family to Appledore Island, where he had taken a job as the lighthouse-keeper. There, in 1848, the family opened a hotel that soon made a reputation for itself as a rude but romantic resort of great (and soon-to-be-great) writers and artists (fig. 1.3). The Isles of Shoals profited from a new fashion among the genteel tourists of the 1840s and 1850s: the search for an experience of the "sublime" in nature—and for the proper places to show off a tourist's poetic temperament.[8] By the 1870s, their desolate landscape had become so attractive that a new and more luxurious hotel—the Oceanic—was built on nearby Star Island to accommodate the growing numbers of tourists.[9]

By that time, a veritable explosion of interest in the coast was encouraging another kind of tourist development. In the 1870s, not only "romantic" and desolate places like the Isles of Shoals were attracting tourists. Summer tourists in ever larger numbers were seeking out places along the coast simply to take in the sea breezes and play in the surf. Outside the cities, the business of providing for tourists was expanding into rural and coastal areas previously unnoticed by travelers. Whether by boarding in lodging houses,

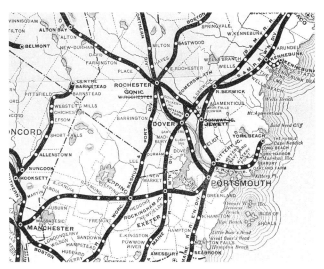

Fig. 1.4. Detail, Boston and Maine railroad map of New England, ca. 1912. Courtesy, B&O Railroad Museum.

or by erecting "tent cities" or cottage colonies, a growing number of Americans of increasingly limited means found ways to take a week or two away from the cares of their city lives. These tourists, and the people who catered to them, created entirely new tourist industries, based not so much on the thrill of wild nature as on the pursuit of health and relaxation, and suited to a new diversity of social needs and aspirations among their clients.

By the 1880s, a vacationer could choose from a veritable army of oceanfront resorts up and down the coast of New England, "an almost continued chain of hotels and summer cottages," as a *Harper's* article put it (fig. 1.4).[10] In that "continued chain," the resorts of the Piscataqua region claimed their fair share of the trade. In the 1876 edition of *Appleton's Guide to American Resorts,* the Isles of Shoals were still given preeminence as the only nationally known tourist attraction in the area. But the summer resorts of York Beach and Wells Beach were also listed, and Portsmouth itself was recommended as "a singularly venerable and tranquil-looking old place."[11] The summer trade flourished throughout the region, spreading into the oceanfront towns of Wells, Kennebunkport, and York, and the quiet harbor villages of Kittery and New Castle. Summer resorts in one form or another were bringing money, jobs, and opportunities for investment into all parts of the Piscataqua region.

The new resort businesses did not provide instant salvation for the region. Population continued to decline in many areas, and it took decades for the tourist trade to stabilize the economy of these towns. But tourist industries came to play a crucial role in the region's economy. Tourism became the second "boom" of the Piscataqua region, surpassing in many places the importance and financial impact of the factories upriver. By the last quarter of the nineteenth century, the region had become fully integrated into the contemporary resort economy, boasting the

Fig. 1.5. Trolley tracks at York Beach, Maine. Photograph, ca. 1900.
Old York Historical Society.

latest styles in cottage architecture, an efficient railroad network, and fashionable hotels with the most recent innovations in plumbing and lighting.

Two railroad companies served the Piscataqua region, and both catered to a substantial tourist trade. The Eastern Railroad was the major tourist route out of Boston to the coast, as it traveled up the North Shore of Massachusetts to Portsmouth and Kittery (following the route of today's Interstate 95). To compete with the Eastern Railroad's direct access to the shore resorts of Rye and Hampton Beach, the Boston and Maine Railroad (which ran inland through the mill cities of Lawrence and Haverhill toward Portland and its primary tourist destination in the White Mountains) extended its line above South Berwick to approach the coast more directly. By 1872 the Boston and Maine had made the beaches of Wells, Kennebunkport, and especially Old Orchard Beach the most accessible in the region, running the rails directly to the resort centers at the beach rather than passing by them a few miles inland.

Railroad companies were often able to make or break a resort town in this way. York Beach, for example, had to agitate for years—and pay a share of the costs—before it got its own branch line of the Boston and Maine in 1887 (fig. 1.5). In the meantime, at the northern edge of the Piscataqua region, the Boston and Maine Railroad established the Boston and Kennebunkport Seashore Company, a corporation designed to create a summer resort industry in Kennebunkport. During the 1870s the Seashore Company built the Ocean Bluff House, added a casino, and opened a variety of smaller boarding houses. It also subdivided seven hundred acres of shorefront property for cottage lots in a development it named Cape Arundel, creating one of the wealthiest and most exclusive summer communities in the region.[12]

Resorts were also built by local entrepreneurs using local capital. Frank Jones, a Portsmouth businessman now best remembered as a brewer (his name on the new Frank Jones

Pale Ale commemorates his role as the biggest ale-maker in the region in the late nineteenth century), used his brewing fortune to launch a venture as founder and president of the Portsmouth and Dover Railroad. But Jones was also heavily involved in local real estate speculation: he owned the Rockingham Hotel in downtown Portsmouth, invested in the Oceanic Hotel on the Isles of Shoals, and was the source of the capital that turned the Wentworth Hotel in New Castle (cat. 2) into the fabulous Wentworth-by-the-Sea, transforming it from a plain box-like hotel into an ornate and imposing landmark.[13]

On a smaller scale, local commercial families could also profit from investments in resorts. Nathaniel Grant Marshall began his career as a part-time schoolteacher and store clerk; he accumulated enough capital in 1870 to build York's most prestigious summer hotel, the Marshall House at Stage Neck (fig. 1.6). A number of men from farming and fishing families were able to convert their old-fashioned resources into modern assets: Theodore Weare built the Cliff House in 1877, on a large tract of pasture land that had belonged to his family's farm for generations; Jesse E. Frisbee, who began his career as a cook aboard a coasting ship, eventually built the luxurious Park Field Hotel at Kittery Point.[14]

All the Victorian resorts had great hotels like the Wentworth and the Marshall House: their impressive size, ornate architectural style, huge public rooms, and technological innovations made them landmarks rather than simply living quarters. Often hotel developers exerted a great deal of influence over the local government and economy. The Marshalls, for example, were leaders in the struggle to build a branch of the Boston and Maine Railroad into York. They were embroiled in a number of political disputes as well—over the building of the electric railroad and over the division of the town—both of which centered around the Marshalls' defense of the interests of their elite clientele.[15]

In many ways, the hotels were more a symbolic center than a business center for the tourist trade. Surrounding

Fig. 1.6. Marshall House, York Harbor, Maine, built 1870.
Photograph, 1907. Old York Historical Society.

them were a tremendous array of less formal, smaller-scale, but often equally profitable businesses. For some tourists, the grand hotels were too expensive. At York Beach, those who could not afford $3.50 a day at Hiram Perkins's Sea View House could opt for a much cheaper vacation: they could board in one of Perkins's smaller boarding houses, or rent one of the cottages built on his subdivided lots along the beach (fig. 1.7). Even in some of the more exclusive resort neighborhoods, boarding in a family's house could provide a less expensive, but still genteel, summer vacation for tourists short of cash. For some wealthy tourists, on the other hand, the great hotels were simply too undiscriminating. Such tourists could rent or buy one of the elegant and lavish cottages at York Harbor or York Cliffs (fig. 1.8), designed to accommodate those who found hotel life too "mixed" socially, or who wanted to bring their own staff of servants along. Local entrepreneurs catered to these groups, too.

A wide variety of trades followed in the wake of the development of a resort hotel or cottage community. In the most heavily traveled towns, there were few people left out of the reorientation of the economy. Farmers came to specialize in products for the summer visitors; town shops stocked luxury goods for urban clientele, and owners of large old farmhouses found they could make a little cash by boarding visitors during the summer. The editor of the *Old York Transcript* made a plea for support of the tourist industry in 1899 by describing its widening circle of influence: "the railroad, the newspaper, the porter, the hackman, the trader, the merchant, the bootblack, the trolley, the livery stable, the barber . . . —everyone gets some of [the summer guest's] money."[16]

What kinds of people were the tourists who provided all that money? And what brought them to the resorts of the Piscataqua region? Clearly, some people came to the beaches of York or Wells simply because they were the closest to their homes. The owners of the small cottages along

Fig. 1.8. "Cragmere" cottage, owned by George M. Conarroe, York Cliffs, Maine. Photograph, ca. 1895. Courtesy, Maine Historic Preservation Commission.

York Beach came from the inland towns of the area, from which the father of the family could commute on Sundays. They left their mark on their summer communities by naming them "Dover Bluffs" and "Concordville," after their inland homes. The working class "excursionists" or "day-trippers" who traveled to the beach on Sundays or holidays could come from no farther away than Manchester or Concord, New Hampshire.

Many of the region's vacationers, however, were wealthy and leisured people. They came from as far away as Boston and New York, and spent, not days, but months in their summer homes. These summer people had access to a wider variety of vacation experiences than did the tourists from Manchester or Dover. For salt water and fresh air they could choose from almost anywhere on the northeastern coast: they could go to Bar Harbor, Maine, and join the sporting crowd in tennis and mountain climbing; they could go to Newport, Rhode Island, and compete in the fashionable displays that provided most of the entertainment there; they could go to Swampscott, Massachusetts, the closest and most fashionable beach for the Boston elite, or Long Branch, New Jersey, one of New York City's fashionable beaches.

Nevertheless these wealthy tourists chose York Harbor, Kittery Point, and New Castle with some very specific requirements in mind. One was the experience often referred to as "privacy" or "seclusion"—which usually meant the ability to exclude vacationers of different social classes. Sometimes these requirements were expressed quite bluntly. Kennebunkport's newspaper, *The Wave*, reported in 1888 that it was the "intention of those interested in Cape Arundel to make it exclusive. Every precaution has been taken to guard against an invasion of excursionists."[17] The Seashore Company seems to have been successful in this regard: even today, their exclusive Kennebunkport development is the summer home of wealthy and well-known families (including that of President George Bush).

Fig. 1.7. "Surf Side" cottage, owned by W.B. Cole, York Beach, Maine. Photograph, August 10, 1892. Old York Historical Society.

Fig. 1.9. "Short Sands," York Beach, Maine. Photograph, ca. 1890. Old York Historical Society.

William Dean Howells, with characteristic precision, described the social stratification of his own vacation community in York a little more delicately: "Beyond our colony, which calls itself the Port, there is a far more populous watering-place, . . . known as the Beach, which is the resort of people several grades of gentility lower than ours." This next beach was "lined with rows of the humbler sort of summer cottages . . . supposed to be taken by inland people of little social importance." Down even farther along the beach were excursionists, who came to the beach by trolley, and spent "long afternoons splashing among the waves, or in lolling groups of men, women and children on the sand" (fig. 1.9).[18]

One of the most important attractions of summer resorts was their ability to sort people out in just this manner. The search for the right social niche—for one's "own kind"—was part of the problem of finding the proper summer resort. One advantage of the coastal regions of the Piscataqua was the apparently inexhaustible opportunity they provided to separate one class from another. (In fact, resort communities probably performed this function far more effectively and precisely than did most of the city neighborhoods from which tourists came. Most cities in the last quarter of the nineteenth century were not able to shield wealthy residents from their plebeian neighbors—or, for that matter, to shield respectable working people from their high-living fashionable neighbors—as well as summer resorts did.) York Harbor (fig. 1.10), for example, could cater to a clientele entirely different from those who vacationed at York Beach. Some of the region's summer people took an even safer route, preferring the built-in exclusivity of New Castle or Kittery Point, without even a beach to attract the attention of local small-time vacationers.

The search for "privacy" and homogeneity brought many wealthy vacationers to York and Ogunquit, to New Castle and Kittery, in the last quarter of the nineteenth century. But it was probably not the only attraction that kept them coming back. After all, class exclusivity was the goal of resorts everywhere on the northeastern coast. To be sure, the beaches nearest the cities might be crowded and "mixed," but discriminating tourists could still choose from places as diverse as faraway Nantucket and the exclusive "cottage" communities of Cape Ann, Massachusetts.

Fig. 1.10. York Harbor Beach, York Harbor, Maine. Photograph, 1893. Old York Historical Society.

Many of the summer communities of the Pisacataqua region came to specialize not only in a certain social class of vacationers, but in an even more precisely defined clientele: a cluster of friends and relatives who were also successful and well-to-do artists, writers, and professionals from New York and Boston. (At different times, for example, three successive editors of *Atlantic Monthly* summered in York.) The region catered increasingly to the highly educated and specialized tastes of this group of summer people. And it possessed one additional asset that made it perhaps uniquely appealing to the small but influential group of tourists who frequented it: the region's history.

In 1899 a brochure was printed advertising cottage lots for sale in a high-priced subdivision to be designated "Evanston" (after its promoter, Henry E. Evans), near York Beach. In typical resort-development fashion, one side of the brochure featured a map of the future subdivision with its numbered lots. On the other side was a series of photographs. Some of the photographs were of cottages for rent or for sale. Some were photographs of the summer cottages of wealthy or famous people in the area—those were presumably *not* for sale. Some were photographs of historic landmarks like the "Old Jail," and prominent specimens of eighteenth-century architecture in town. No distinction was made between summer housing and historic landmarks, between things for sale and things not for sale—leaving the prospective buyer with the impression that one could purchase the entire heritage of the town for summer use.[19]

And in fact, that was at least partly true. Promoters in the 1870s and 1880s increasingly sought to distinguish York and Kittery, New Castle and Portsmouth, from their competitors at Mount Desert or the White Mountains by virtue of their antiquity, the special attraction of "this historic, grandly picturesque, sombre-storied old shore."[20] In the last quarter of the nineteenth century, tourists were becoming increasingly interested in such "quaintness," increasingly turning toward the more remote parts of New England—places that, as one railroad pamphlet described it, "preserved the ancient types and customs of New England . . . [and] the original flavor and atmosphere which distinguished the region in the old colonial days."[21]

The Piscataqua region's growing tourist industry was only one of many attempts to make such "quaint bygone places" newly attractive to tourists, but the Piscataqua region had a head start in this enterprise.[22] For one thing, local promoters had already become accustomed to thinking of their region as "old" long before the fashion hit the rest of the country. Early and profound economic depression had taught many residents to celebrate the "good old days" somewhat earlier than most places. In fact, they were in the vanguard of nostalgia. Local writers had begun to memorialize the region's past as early as 1859, when Charles W. Brewster first published his *Rambles About Portsmouth*, a guided tour to the houses and history of the city. And Portsmouth led the rest of New England by a full forty years

in nostalgic celebration of its returning natives: in 1853 the "Sons of Portsmouth," a Boston group, had sponsored the first recorded reunion for the purpose of bringing those who had gone in search of greener pastures home to celebrate their heritage (cat. 3). (It was not until the 1890s that the rest of northern New England found itself in such dire straits that it hit upon the idea of "Old Home Week" to reinvigorate the region's struggling rural economy.)

For local entrepreneurs, the new interest in history quickly proved to be an effective "pitch" for promoting the region to a particular clientele. It was easy enough to advertise the region's "relics of the earliest colonial history" along with its "coast scenery of the rarest beauty."[23] Historic and "quaint" associations were used to drum up business: a hotelier might name his modern hotel the "Garrison" house, to evoke memories of the romantic "Indian-fighting" relics nearby, or the "Old Fort Inn," because it was built where an old fort used to be (cat. 5). No local publications failed to mention that York was the "oldest city in America" (even if they would not go so far as to claim, as one promoter did, that York was "the Most Famous Summer Resort on the Atlantic Coast").[24]

In addition, the Piscataqua region *was* rich in the relics of the past, and especially in the architectural relics of its short period of prosperity: its "colonial" houses and old buildings were sprinkled thickly over the region, standing among the mill houses, along abandoned highways, between the summer cottages, and in the commercial districts. As Moses Sweetser wrote in the Boston and Maine guidebook *Here and There in New England and Canada* (1889), the region was "full of fascination for the mousing antiquary or the cultivated summer-traveller" (fig. 1.11).[25]

Fig. 1.11. "Mr. Brooks in his Antique Shop," York, Maine. Photograph, ca. 1930. Old York Historical Society.

For the "cultivated summer-traveller," the Piscataqua region became a vacation destination where one could explore historical relics without giving up the more typical vacation in the mountains or at a coast resort. Even a casual visitor might stroll through the streets of Portsmouth—where in any case their railroad connections probably required them to stay overnight—to look at the house where John Paul Jones had once stayed and to see some of the "finest existing specimens of our colonial architecture."[26] With a railroad layover of a day or two, it was easy to arrange an excursion to the other towns around the harbor, to see the old Revolutionary-era forts at the mouth of the Piscataqua, the imposing Wentworth mansion in Little Harbor, or the Pepperrell houses in Kittery.

Only a little farther afield, the town of York (or "old York," as it began to be known in the late nineteenth century) presented especially fertile ground for those tourists who wanted to see the more rustic and "quaint" side of the past, yet still remain within close range of beaches and resort social life. As *Here and There in New England* put it, "only a mile from the Long Sands [York Beach] . . . slumbers the historic hamlet of York."[27] In York were to be seen the McIntire and Junkins garrison houses (cat. 5), relics of the hardy Indian-fighting pioneers. And York had an even more ancient landmark: the "old jail" (by its restoration in 1900 it had become the "Old Gaol"), which was thought to have been constructed as early as 1653. The "old jail" was York's real claim to fame; more than any other historical landmark, it seemed to be "characteristic of the early days of our colonial life and customs . . . when witches were imprisoned and a public whipping post and stocks were familiar objects in every colonial settlement."[28]

For these new historic attractions, the slow economic recovery of parts of the region began to pay off. Just as summer resorts could turn isolation into an advantage, the new historic tourist trade turned poverty and depression into an asset. If a town had not had the money to rebuild its wharves or to replace its aging building with modern substitutes, or if its people spoke with an accent or wore outdated clothes because they had so little contact with the outside world, these signs of poverty and isolation could also be seen as "quaint" reminders of bygone days. Of course, that kind of promotion could be a double-edged sword. As the Boston and Maine guide to Portsmouth somewhat anxiously put it:

> It must not be supposed that Portsmouth is dilapidated . . . The time-worn streets are lighted by electricity, the ancient mansions are furnished with modern appliances for comfort; over their mossy gables are strung telephone wires, and the minds of their occupants are wide-awake.[29]

Promoters were always aware of the need to balance the quaintness of age with the modern conveniences of a popular resort region.

But very often, it was not local promoters who set the terms for the use of the region's history. In the Piscataqua region, perhaps more than in other areas, the recreation of the region's "colonial" identity was in the hands, not of frankly commercial promoters, guide-book writers (cat. 1), and hotel keepers, but of a network of wealthy and influential visitors—editors, architects, poets, and historians. Here, unlike many other areas, the region's rediscovered history was put to use, not so much in the pursuit of profit as in the pursuit of cultural goals common to these visitors. It was the ideas and values of these "summer people" that found greatest expression in the landscape of the Piscataqua region.

Summer visitors might be in pursuit of a variety of encounters with history: like visitors to Old Deerfield, they might search for inspiration from the hardy pioneers who fought off Indian attacks; like the travelers through Salem and Marblehead, they might be moved by romantic tales of star-crossed lovers and condemned witches; like the summer people of Litchfield, Connecticut, they might search for the apparent peacefulness and serenity of the "old days." Visitors to the Piscataqua region did all these things. But most distinctively, the summer people of the Piscataqua region seem to have been in search of ancestors.

One reason for this emphasis was that many of the region's "summer people" actually did have family roots in the area. It was natural for them to see the Piscataqua region's history as in some special sense belonging to them. The family of Barrett Wendell, a Harvard historian, had summered at their cottage in New Castle since his childhood in the 1880s (cat. 27). But their connection to the Piscataqua region was older than that: the Wendells also owned a "colonial" house in Portsmouth, passed down from their ancestor Jacob Wendell, who had bought the house in 1815, and lovingly preserved and transformed in the last quarter of the nineteenth century by two generations of Wendells with money earned in New York and Cambridge (cat. 4).

In fact, some of the most influential members of the network of "summer people" are difficult to categorize either as "natives" or as visitors; they often spent substantial amounts of time in the local communities of their birth, while keeping in constant communication with the cosmopolitan world of their urban associates. Sarah Orne Jewett, for example, made a habit of spending the spring and fall of each year in her native South Berwick, but she typically wintered with her friends in Boston, and spent her summers in one of the resort towns of the Piscataqua. But whether she was ensconced in the ancestral house or visiting friends' cottages on the North Shore, Jewett belonged to a social world that included the most important editors and publishers in Boston and New York—many of whom also visited the Piscataqua region in summer.

Some "summer people" lived in their modern oceanfront cottages during the summer months and their ancestral homes in the autumn, as the Wendells did. But many visitors, even those with no such historical ties to the region, shared a common sensibility with those who were

Fig. 1.12. "Visitors at the tomb of Sir William Pepperrell at Kittery Point, Maine." Photograph by Luther Dame, 1902.
Old York Historical Society.

more literally coming "home" when they visited the region. These summer people, too, came to the area in the hope of acquiring the special sense of antiquity and permanence— of a past of one's own—that appeared to be offered by the quiet old streets and quaint houses.

Not just any past would do, of course: summer people were especially intrigued by the image of the old "aristocracy" that had dominated the region in the days of the West India trade. The search for ancestors reflected common, and increasingly urgent, preoccupations with class and "race" for the old-stock wealthy Yankees who made up the bulk of "cultivated summer travellers" in the last quarter of the nineteenth century. Many of the summer people, with or without family ties in the area, came to see in the "colonial" architecture of the region a vision of the apparent stability of a world in which the social order went unchallenged.

In its mildest form, that yearning was expressed in the gentle nostalgia of summer visitors for a past that seemed to be more gracious and orderly than the present. William Dean Howells's affection for Kittery Point, where he spent many summers, was clearly tinged with his admiration for the unchallenged elite status of its former "colonial" inhabitants: "In my personal quality I am of course averse to all

great fortunes; and in my civic capacity I am a patriot. But still I feel a sort of grace in wealth a century old" (fig. 1.12).[30] Sarah Orne Jewett's regret for the lost West India trade was clearly also tinged with regret for the apparent peace and dignity of a world where the claims of the "best families" to authority were unchallenged.

At its worst, the search for ancestry could become a way of defending deeply reactionary and racist political interests against the challenges presented by immigrants and radicals. Thomas Bailey Aldrich was perhaps best known for his *Story of a Bad Boy*, a memoir of his childhood in old Portsmouth (cat. 45). But Aldrich also found time to write an influential anti-immigrant poem, "The Unguarded Gates." Thomas Nelson Page, a York Harbor summer visitor, was best known for his nostalgic novels set in the "good old days" when a white aristocracy had ruled the south. His speech at the celebration of the 250th anniversary of the founding of York in 1902 made the politics of his summer vacations very clear: "elsewhere in the country," he argued, were "large numbers of people of other races and with other traditions" who were threatening the survival of the nation. But in York he found representatives of the "great Anglo-Saxon race" with whom he believed himself to be "of

Fig. 1.13. *Langdon house, Portsmouth, New Hampshire, built 1783–85. Photograph, 1886. Courtesy, Society for the Preservation of New England Antiquities.*

one blood." For such people as Page and Aldrich, the great houses of the Piscataqua region were representatives of earlier, purer times—and of a racial heritage of which they could be proud.[31]

Their search for a usable past gave these visitors a strong sense of ownership of the Piscataqua region's past—and it left them free to reshape that history as they saw fit. History was what they were after, but it had to be a history they could live with—at least for a summer. Although summer visitors sometimes liked to look at such relics from the barbarous past as York's old jail, for example, they usually preferred to think of the former inhabitants of the Piscataqua as comparatively enlightened. In fact, chief among the "barbaric" traits to be discarded from the region's past was apparently its religion: summer people seemed to see the Piscataqua region as a sort of "New England without the Puritans." As the author of *Down East Latch-Strings* described it, that was why Portsmouth was more attractive to tourists than, for example, Salem. Portsmouth was as "venerable and quiet" as the Massachusetts towns, but not so gloomy, because, he argued, it was not a "Puritan" town: "It was not a religious but a money-making community, and hence the picture of the earliest civilization here has a brightness that does not belong to that of its Pilgrim neighbors."[32] Sarah Orne Jewett took pains to distinguish the builder of her favorite Hamilton house from the inhabitants of those other New England shores: "I have heard that he came from Plymouth in Massachusetts, and was a minis-

ter's son, but if ever a man's heart gloried in the good things of this life it was his, and there was not a trace of Puritan asceticism in his character."[33]

As strong as their sense of ownership was, the claims of the summer people to the heritage of the Piscataqua region did not always go unchallenged. The "natives" of the region may have shared with the summer people some assumptions about race and history, but they might also disagree about who "owned" that history. In 1899, for example, the editor of the *Old York Transcript* set down in no uncertain terms the contest over who owned "Old York's" Anglo-Saxon heritage. "Of the men one meets in York nine out of every ten can tell you of their father, their grandfather, and—yes their ancestors way back to the founding of this republic," he wrote, "yet not one of them will thrust a coat of arms before your gaze or send you a note of invitation adorned by a family crest."[34]

But, whether or not these summer people had a better claim to the region's heritage, they were generally in a better position to make use of at least one of the material remnants of it: the old houses strewn all over the region. Increasingly, near the end of the nineteenth century, summer people began to concern themselves with the preservation and restoration of the old buildings in their summer communities. Sometimes they restored houses that had belonged to their own families. Woodbury Langdon, a New York merchant, purchased and restored a Portsmouth house in 1877 that had originally belonged to

Fig. 1.14. "Old Historic Mansions, Kittery Point, Me." From Attractive Bits Along Shore *(ca. 1900). Old York Historical Society.*

his family (fig. 1.13). Sometimes the houses were bought from farm families no longer able to make a profit on the old place. The Hamilton house in South Berwick was bought at the suggestion of Sarah Orne Jewett by her friends Elizabeth and Elise Tyson, a mother-daughter team who created something of their own "colonial revival" community through their elaborate restoration of the house and gardens. The circle of summer people who carried out these private restorations were often also prominent in efforts to restore and claim historic landmarks for public use. By the early twentieth century, eighteenth-century buildings all over the region were being preserved in larger and larger numbers by such efforts as these, both as private houses and as museums.

Finally, the summer people were more than "consumers" of the region's past. They were also its primary "producers." Samuel Adams Drake wrote the region's history. Sarah Orne Jewett created loving depictions of the remnants of colonial high society, and Thomas Bailey Aldrich evoked its simplicity and charm. Emma Coleman photographed nostalgic portrayals of colonial life in the Pepperell houses. Edmund Tarbell and his friends painted domestic scenes of life in New Castle's colonial mansions. Boston architects made careful studies of the region's architecture and reproduced it in their own designs, and a host

of others with emotional roots in the region made certain that the old houses belonging to them survived to be reinterpreted to fit their own needs. In the process, they helped to create the national movement we know as the "colonial revival."

At the same time, all these loving preservationists helped to create a region different from the one they had found. When writers and painters used the Piscataqua region to create the colonial revival, they also fueled the tourist industry of the region perhaps even more effectively than the writers of the Boston and Maine Railroad pamphlets. Their version of the region's history was not the same version as that of local promoters; it was not even exactly the same as that of writers and artists in other parts of New England. But it was the version that stuck, and its impact on the region was enormous.

The published images of the region produced by its summer people had a lasting effect both on the public perception of America's "colonial" past and on the region that provided them with their material (fig. 1.14). They preserved and transformed the eighteenth-century architecture of the region, guaranteeing that the appearance that had attracted them to the region would become an ever more prominent part of the landscape in the twentieth century. Even in death, summer people (albeit inadvertently) promoted tourism in the region: they became themselves a part of the tourist's landscape. The "Nutter House" in which Thomas Bailey Aldrich grew up became the "Thomas Bailey Aldrich Memorial" in 1908 (cat. 54); tourists in the region can now visit the homes of Aldrich and Sarah Orne Jewett along with that of John Paul Jones.

By the last quarter of the nineteenth century, the region of the Piscataqua had become a thoroughly modern place. From its textile mills to its vacation resorts it offered the latest in technology, business, and social arrangements. And yet its most "modern" innovation may have been the recreation of its history. In the long run, the nostalgic interests of the summer tourists of the Piscataqua region changed the landscape of the region much more than did the other modern industries that replaced the West India trade. The great hotels of the era have almost all disappeared. The ambitious development schemes most often came to nothing, and the tourist trains of the period no longer carry their trainloads of excursionists to York Beach. Today in the Piscataqua region, the restored buildings of the eighteenth century are often the twentieth century's most visible reminders of the tourist industry of the nineteenth century. Colonial architecture—the relic of the region's first "boom" economy—by the end of the nineteenth century had become the most lasting product of its second era of prosperity.

1 Timothy Dwight, *Travels in New England and New York* (Cambridge, Mass.: Harvard University Press, 1969), 1:312–13.

2 Dwight, *Travels*, 2:138–39.

3 The coastal towns of York and Wells showed the steepest and most longlasting population declines for the decades after 1850: York declined from 2,980 in 1850 to 2,444 in 1890, while Wells declined in the same period from 2,945 to 2,029. Portsmouth also experienced a loss of population between 1850 and 1870, from 9,738 to 9,211, but had begun to recover by the 1880 census. On the other hand, towns with significant manufacturing interests showed a different pattern during the same years: the mill town of South Berwick had a fluctuating population that grew very quickly between 1880 and 1890; the town of Kittery, which housed workers in the Portsmouth Naval Yard, saw a substantial population increase between 1850 and 1870, followed by equally substantial losses between 1870 and 1890. See Edmund S. Hoyt, *Maine State Year-Book* (Portland, Me.: Hoyt and Fogg, 1891).

4 Sarah Orne Jewett, "Deephaven," in *Deephaven and Other Stories* (New Haven, Conn.: College and University Press, 1966), 71.

5 Thomas Bailey Aldrich, *The Story of a Bad Boy* (Boston: Houghton Mifflin Co., 1923), 28.

6 Jewett, "River Driftwood," in *Deephaven and Other Stories*, 510.

7 Jewett, "River Driftwood," 502.

8 The daughter of the lighthouse-keeper had ensured the islands' future by marrying Levi Thaxter, a man whose extensive connections among the Boston literary elite helped to provide their clientele. Celia Thaxter also contributed in another way to the success of the Isles of Shoals as a resort: she wrote a series of essays, poems, and sketches, collected in 1873 as *Among the Isles of Shoals*, which gave her islands national recognition.

9 William M. Varrell, *Summer-By-The-Sea* (Portsmouth, N.H.: Strawberry Bank Print Shop, 1972), 92–101.

10 Charles Dudley Warner, "Their Pilgrimage," *Harper's New Monthly Magazine* 73 (July 1886): 170.

11 *Appleton's Hand-Book of American Summer Resorts* (New York: D. Appleton & Co., 1876), 97–99.

12 Varrell, *Summer-By-The-Sea*, 27–28, 126–27.

13 Varrell, *Summer-By-The-Sea*, 60–62.

14 *Biographical Review* (Boston: Biographical Review Publishing Co., 1896), 352–53.

15 John D. Bardwell, *The Diary of the Portsmouth, Kittery, and York Electric Railroad* (Portsmouth, N.H.: Portsmouth Marine Society, 1986), 37.

16 E.D. Twombly, *Old York Transcript*, Nov. 16, 1899, 2.

17 *The Wave*, July 18, 1888, 3.

18 William Dean Howells, "Confessions of a Summer Tourist," in *Literature and Life: Studies* (1902; reprint, Port Washington, N.Y.: Kennikat Press, 1968), 52–53.

19 H.E. Evans, *Plan of Evanston and Evans Park, Property of H.E. Evans, York, Maine* (York, Me.: York Bureau of Information and Real Estate Agency, 1897).

20 Ernest Ingersoll, *Down East Latch-Strings, or Sea Shore, Lakes and Mountains by the Boston and Maine Railroad* (Boston: Boston and Maine Railroad, 1887), 35–36.

21 Old Colony Railroad, *The Old Colony: or Pilgrim Land, Past and Present* (Boston: Old Colony Railroad, 1887), 52.

22 Many sorts of tourists, from a variety of social backgrounds and with differing motives, planned their vacations to include an imagined experience of the past. For examples, see William Butler, "Another City upon a Hill: Litchfield, Connecticut, and the Colonial Revival," in Axelrod, *Colonial Revival*, 15–51; David C. Bryan, "The Past as a Place to Visit: Reinventing the Colonial in Deerfield, Massachusetts (senior honors thesis, Amherst College, 1989); and Dona Brown, "The Tourist's New England" (Ph.D. diss., University of Massachusetts, 1989).

23 Ingersoll, *Down East Latch-Strings*, 32.

24 [H.E. Evans], *York, Maine* (York, Me.: York Bureau of Information, 1896), front cover.

25 Moses F. Sweetser, *Here and There in New England and Canada: All Along Shore* (Boston: Passenger Department, Boston and Maine Railroad, 1889), 94.

26 Ingersoll, *Down East Latch-Strings*, 233.

27 Sweetser, *Here and There*, 192.

28 *Old York Transcript*, July 27, 1899, 2.

29 Ingersoll, *Down East Latch-Strings*, 235.

30 Howells, "Staccato Notes of a Vanished Summer," in *Literature and Life*, 258–59.

31 *Agamenticus, Bristol, Gorgeana, York: An Oration Delivered by the Hon. James Phinney Baxter . . . on the Two Hundred and Fiftieth Anniversary of the Town* (York, Me.: Old York Historical and Improvement Society, 1904), 113–17.

32 Ingersoll, *Down East Latch-Strings*, 232–35.

33 Jewett, "River Driftwood," 179.

34 *Old York Transcript*, June 8, 1899.

I

GUIDEBOOKS TO THE PISCATAQUA REGION

Samuel Adams Drake (1833–1905)
The Pine-Tree Coast (1891)

Sarah Haven Foster (1827–1900)
The Portsmouth Guide Book (1896)

Caleb Stevens Gurney (1848–1924)
Portsmouth Historic and Picturesque (1902)

G. Alex Emery
Ancient City of Gorgeana and Modern Town of York (1873)

John F. Sears, in *Sacred Places: American Tourist Attractions in the Nineteenth Century* (1989), argues that people react most strongly to places connected with stories or historical events.[1] Guidebooks and the historical buildings, events, and characters they portray were integral to the promotion of the historic Piscataqua region as a tourist destination. The early guidebooks of the 1870s expressed the same nostalgic view of the area as the writers and artists who visited and brought many sightseers in search of an escape from city life. Samuel Adams Drake began *The Pine-Tree Coast* (cat. 1) by describing Portsmouth as an "historic vestibule" through which all travelers should pass.[2] As the majority of summer visitors to the Piscataqua changed from wealthy urbanites to the middle class, the region's guidebooks began to focus less on fine examples of architecture and

Cat. 1. "Wentworth Mansion and Mouth of the Piscataqua." From Samuel Adams Drake, The Pine-Tree Coast *(1891). Old York Historical Society.*

more on natural features and sites associated with sensational stories such as the Nubble Lighthouse, the Old Gaol, and the "Devil's Kitchen," a rock formation along the shore in York.

As early as 1839 Portsmouth had turned to tourism as a source of income to supplement its waning shipping industry. In that year the *Portsmouth City Directory* claimed that the city's quietness, proximity to the sea and neighboring beaches, and delightful surrounding countryside made it a remarkably pleasant summer resort.[3] Year after year Portsmouth's absent sons and daughters returned to visit their home during the summer. Throughout the nineteenth century, as nostalgia for Portsmouth's glorious past grew, real estate agents and promoters of tourism began to capitalize upon the city's historic landmarks that became just as important to visitors as the beaches.

In 1876 Joseph Foster, a local printer and bookseller, published his daughter Sarah's *Portsmouth Guide Book* which described a series of walking tours around the city. The *Portsmouth Daily Chronicle* for June 10, 1876, reported that the book "is a neat volume of 150 pages, bound in flexible covers, and of a handy size to carry in the pocket. The author's preface is signed with the initials of a lady of culture, taste, talent and marked ability as a writer."[4] It was written for "strangers" but also for sons and daughters who "return[ed] to see the houses of their forefathers."[5] The format of the book was based on European guidebooks that focused on convenient walks past historic sites. Foster was also influenced by Charles W. Brewster, who published *Rambles About Portsmouth* in 1859 and 1869. Brewster had intended "to collect the incidents of unwritten history and to connect incidents and localities" so that readers, as they passed through the streets, might "at the turn of almost every corner be reminded of some early historical event."[6] Through Brewster, and later Foster, buildings became visible links to a seemingly better time.

In 1896 Sarah Haven Foster republished *The Portsmouth Guide Book.* On the cover she placed a quotation from the Bible (Psalms 48:12–13) which symbolized to her the importance of Portsmouth's historical edifices: "Walk about Zion and go round about her; tell the towers therof. Mark ye well her bulwarks, consider her palaces; that ye may tell it to the generation following."[7] In an addenda she discussed Portsmouth's progress during the last quarter of the nineteenth century and mentioned the improvements to the Navy Yard, new parks, and the opening of the electric railroads which had increased trade.

In 1902 Caleb Stevens Gurney entered the field with *Portsmouth Historic and Picturesque* (cat. 1a). Although Gurney was heavily influenced by Foster, he did not focus primarily on Portsmouth's historic sites. Instead, he created a complete photographic record of Portsmouth, including scenes of older, residential streets as well as views of more modern commercial buildings such as the Eldredge Brewery. Contemporary events such as the blizzard of 1898, numerous parades, and the arrival of the Spanish–American

Cat. 1a. Ursula Cutt farm, Portsmouth, New Hampshire. From Caleb Stevens Gurney, Portsmouth Historic and Picturesque *(1902). Courtesy, Portsmouth Athenaeum.*

War prisoners were also included. Gurney was one of Portsmouth's earliest photographers. In 1892 he established the Acme Portrait Company, and five years later he organized the "Company International de Belles Artes."[8] His photographs and glass-plate negatives provide one of the earliest and most complete portraits of the city. Gurney's choice of the more straightforward medium of photography corresponded to a less romanticized view of the city.

Although guidebooks to York exhibit a similar change from discreet discussions of history to more sensational depictions of the town's sites, from the beginning they seem to have been commercially oriented and aimed primarily at potential tourists. In 1873 Alex Emery, a native of York and a schoolteacher, published the *Ancient City of Gorgeana and Modern Town of York* with the intention of interesting "the thousands who will be brought to know it [York] through its associations [and] as a place of summer residence."[9] Emery's book is arranged chronologically, beginning with early explorers and ending with a discussion of seaside resorts. Unlike Foster in *The Portsmouth Guide Book,* Emery does not focus his guide on historical sites; instead he provides a thematic history of such subjects as early schools, commerce, and religion, as well as more sensational issues such as earthquakes, haunted houses, and witches. In 1896 the York Bureau of Information further commercialized the book by condensing the historical sections and including information on train schedules and places to stay.[10]

Tourism played a powerful role in America's invention of itself as a culture. The Piscataqua's guidebooks were crucial to the promotion of the area as an important cultural region through the use of key images of the colonial revival. Garrison houses, churches, and other historical sites are illustrated in the Piscataqua guidebooks and drew increasing numbers of visitors to the area. As the region moved from a place dedicated to those of genteel taste to catering for tourists, the commercialization of the region through guidebooks increased. Guidebooks transformed the Piscataqua's historic and natural sites into a commodity for tourists, often creating romantic historical myths which to this day are drawing cards for the region.

SLG

1 John F. Sears, *Sacred Places: American Tourist Attractions in the Nineteenth Century* (New York: Oxford University Press, 1989), 61.

2 Samuel Adams Drake, *The Pine-Tree Coast* (Boston: Estes and Lauriat, 1891), 17.

3 *Portsmouth City Directory* (Portsmouth, N.H.: Joseph M. Edmonds, 1839), 2.

4 "Book Notices," *Portsmouth Daily Chronicle*, June 10, 1876, clipping, Sarah Haven Foster file, Portsmouth Public Library.

5 Sarah Haven Foster, *Portsmouth Guide Book* (Portsmouth, N.H.: Joseph N. Foster, 1876), 3.

6 The contents of *Rambles About Portsmouth* first appeared as individual newspaper columns. They were collected and published in two volumes in 1859 (first series) and 1869 (second series). Both volumes were reprinted in 1971–72. Charles W. Brewster, *Rambles About Portsmouth,* first series (Portsmouth, N.H.: C.W. Brewster & Son, 1859), 5.

7 Sarah Haven Foster, *Portsmouth Guide Book* (1876; reprint, Portsmouth, N.H.: Joseph N. Foster, 1896), n.p.

8 Caleb S. Gurney, *Portsmouth Historic and Picturesque* (1902; reprint, Portsmouth, N.H.: Strawbery Banke, 1982), xii.

9 George Alex Emery, *Ancient City of Gorgeana and Modern Town of York* (1873; reprint, Boston: G. Alex Emery, 1894), vi.

10 The resulting publication was entitled *York, Maine, Bureau of Information and Illustrated History of the Most Famous Summer Resort on the Atlantic Coast.*

Cat. 2. The Rockingham Hotel, Portsmouth, New Hampshire. Photograph, 1890. Courtesy, Patch Collection, Strawbery Banke Museum.

2

ROCKINGHAM HOTEL
Portsmouth, New Hampshire, ca. 1785
Renovation Jabez H. Sears, 1885–87

WENTWORTH HOTEL
New Castle, New Hampshire, 1873
Additions Jesse B. Edwards, 1879–80

The expanding railroad system and the establishment of hotels were inextricably intertwined, especially in Portsmouth and its island neighbor of New Castle. Here between 1870 and 1900 its leading industrial magnate and millionaire brewer, Frank Jones (1832–1902), rebuilt a series of hotels for both the commercial traveler and the summer tourist. A near Horatio Alger-type career transformed this New Hampshire farm boy into the "King of the Alemakers," mayor of Portsmouth, Democratic congressman, director of the Eastern Railroad, and ultimately president of the Boston and Maine Railroad.[1] Jones's hotels promoted his ale and railroads while providing an opportunity for lavish entertainments expected of the richest man in the area.

Jones purchased the Rockingham House in 1870. The brick State Street edifice, built about 1785 as the home of Woodbury Langdon, was a hotel for boarders throughout much of the mid nineteenth century. Jones hired the Boston architectural office of Bryant and Rogers to produce designs for a "French" or Mansard roof, enlarged it to 130 rooms with new Victorian interior appointments, and reopened the Rockingham in 1871 as a commercial hotel. While serving in Congress in 1874, he placed the Rockingham under the professional management of Frank W. Hilton, formerly of the Pullman Company and the Oceanic Hotel at the Isles of Shoals.[2]

The Wentworth Hotel, begun at New Castle in 1873 by Boston distiller Daniel Chase, was constructed during a flurry of hotel-building along the northern New England coast, including the Isles of Shoals (where in 1876 Jones became a stockholder in the expanded Oceanic House), Rye, and Kittery.[3] The simple three-story building, with a front porch facing the ocean and a monitor on top of a hipped roof, was designed by Erastus G. Mansfield of Somerville, Massachusetts, one of Chase's distillery investors who is not otherwise known as an architect or builder.[4]

For his part in helping acquire the land, local historian John Albee (cat. 13) was given the honor of naming the new hotel. "The Wentworth," as it was initially known, memorialized eighteenth-century Governor Benning Wentworth, whose mansion stands across the harbor; the new hotel boasted a massive framed mirror in the parlor "surmounted with a statue of Governor Wentworth."[5]

Frank Jones and Frank Hilton acquired The Wentworth in 1878, Jones providing the capital and Hilton the hotel management until his untimely death in 1882. Over the next two years they enlarged the hotel, transforming the facade by doubling its length, adding three towers, and building a new Mansard roof. The design of the new hotel (as well

Cat. 2a. "Views in the New Rockingham Hotel at Portsmouth, N.H." From
The Decorator and Furnisher *(1887). Courtesy, Earle G. Shettleworth, Jr.*

Cat. 2b. *The Wentworth Hotel, New Castle, New Hampshire, built 1873–1900. Photograph, ca. 1923. Private collection.*

Cat. 2c. *"Parlor of the Colonial Annex, Hotel Wentworth, New Castle, New Hampshire." Photograph, ca. 1900. Courtesy, Portsmouth Athenaeum.*

as Jones's new Portsmouth Maplewood Farm estate) was apparently supplied by Jesse B. Edwards of Salem, Massachusetts, an industrial contractor who specialized in moving buildings, including those along the Eastern Railroad's right of way.[6] Inside, painted plaster walls and ceilings of "Eastlake frescoing and aesthetic dados" by "Fresco artist and designer" Philip Butler of Boston (who had earlier painted the Rockingham) decorated the stick-style hotel with an Eastlake geometry in dozens of brilliant colors.[7]

After Hilton's death in 1882 Jones considered elaborate plans by Frederick N. Footman, a young Boston-trained architect from nearby Somersworth, New Hampshire. Never executed, presumably because the work could not be accomplished between seasons, these plans would have quadrupled the hotel in length (making it 646 feet across), and they called for five towers and a grand staircase rising from an open hall in the central tower to be heated by "an immense, old-fashioned fireplace of elaborate design."[8]

In September 1884 the Rockingham was nearly destroyed by fire, and Jones turned to another Boston architect, Jabez H. Sears, to enlarge and remodel the hotel (cat. 2). The result of this more than $300,000 rebuilding was "the most elegant and superbly furnished establishment . . . outside Boston," described by its architect as "a palace open to the traveling public." For the first time in the hotel's remodelings, the design attempted to echo its location in an historic town. The dining room from the original Woodbury Langdon house "was saved from the fire by great exertion," and its woodwork was now "painted white, with abundance of gold decoration" picking out its old neoclassical detailing. Furnished with "beautiful and artistic" furniture, the room was then "used as a private dining room for social parties, whose convivial enjoyments are increased and heightened by the historical reminiscences clustering about its ancient and time honored walls."[9]

Jones's association with Langdon was made even more explicit in the two facade gables above a new fifth story. These were embellished with "two busts in terra-cotta of heroic size," depicting Woodbury Langdon and Frank Jones, by Professor F. Mortimer Lamb of Stoughton, Massachusetts. Lamb, whose drawing of the new Rockingham interiors was published in *The Decorator and Furnisher* in May 1887 (cat. 2a), was also responsible for the "hunting scene in terra-cotta around a massive horseshoe" fireplace in the registration lobby. The "artistic" embellishment of the striking fireplace for this commercial living hall owes much to the American version of the aesthetic movement. Yet Sears proclaimed of this room's seven-foot-high mahogany wainscoting and fireplace, "the architectural treatment . . . partakes of the Colonial, with its small moldings and carvings" compared to the Queen Anne details elsewhere in the hotel. The room's reference to the colonial was also "in reminding one of 'ye olden days,' with its yule logs, cheery fires, and weary travelers refreshing themselves from tankards of fur [*sic*] or mugs of 'flip.'"[10]

A decade later, between 1895 and 1899, Jones finally enlarged The Wentworth Hotel in a neoclassical vernacular that reflected many popular elements of the colonial revival. The exterior, originally green and then yellow, became white. Its lobby was expanded with a circular one-story addition beneath a shallow dome painted with swags and cherubs.[11] A new chimney with a "colonial" enframement was built opposite the main entrance and the walls paneled with mahogany dados. At the same time the elaborate Eastlake-style painted decoration of the old lobby was replaced by a white decorated plasterwork ceiling of Adamesque detail within the structural organization of large boxed beams.

In 1896 a huge wing replaced the 1880 dining room. The new first-floor dining room was articulated by a series of plate-glass Palladian window openings along its facade and decorated with false-grained plaster columns and pilasters with elaborate composite capitals. Modern improvements in the summer hotel, perhaps designed to attract a more affluent clientele, were advertised when the wing was completed. Upper floors of this wing, unlike the earlier hotel, offered suites of two, three, or four rooms with connecting baths.[12]

In the fall of 1898 the last major addition to The Wentworth was begun. In September, unnamed architects examined the hotel for a 175-foot addition "which will be a separate hotel by itself and connected to the present house by a bridge." Like many new urban hotels, the kitchen and dining room were placed on the upper story, both to expel cooking odors and to provide aerial views of the ocean and harbor. Designed to permit an expanded season, serving a smaller number of off-season visitors with reduced staff, this was later known as the "Colonial Annex" (cat. 2b).[13] The name derived, at least in part, from colonial revival detailing composed of readily available manufactured building parts. These included a fan-lit doorway with entrance settle beneath the semicircular tower, the colonial interior staircase and Ambassador's Parlor (used by the Russian delegation during the 1905 Russo-Japanese Peace Conference) (cat. 2c), and the white paneling of the dining room—like the Rockingham's Langdon room—with white boxing and cornices picked out in gold to accent the trompe l'oeil coffered-ceiling decoration.[14]

The Rockingham and Wentworth hotels under Frank Jones's ownership illustrate the evolution of colonial allusion in commercial architecture from the 1870s to the turn of the century. The white and gold finish of the Langdon Dining Room in the Rockingham stands out as a particularly early expression of "colonial" reuse in the mid-1880s, especially amidst commercial decoration derived from English Queen Anne and other sources in this urban commercial palace. The Wentworth, while deriving its name from the nearby colonial governor's mansion, retained its Eastlake-style decoration until the major changes of the late 1890s. By then, many New England architects were designing public buildings based on New England's colonial relics or generic Georgian details of eighteenth-century Anglo-American classicism. The colonial revival redecoration of the hotel's public spaces and construction of its Colonial Annex was a commercial example of this widespread phenomenon.

RMC

1 Ray Brighton, *Frank Jones, King of the Alemakers* (Portsmouth, N.H.: Peter Randall Publisher, 1976). I wish to thank Brighton for sharing an unpublished history of the Wentworth Hotel and for carefully combing the local newspapers for many of the excerpts cited here.

2 Brighton, *Frank Jones*, 145–55; "Around Home," *Portsmouth Journal*, Sept. 6 and 11, 1873; also see William H. Withey, *The Rockingham: The House that Jones Built* (Portsmouth, N.H.: Rockingham Condominium Assoc., 1985), 17–46, 89. Gridley Bryant was well known as a hotel architect, whose last major work was the expansion of the Parker House in Boston. Bryant had already designed at least one Portsmouth home, the brick mansard double house on Middle Street for William F. Parrott in 1864.

3 "Around Home," *Portsmouth Journal*, Sept. 27, 1873; Rockingham County Registry of Deeds, Exeter, N.H., 446:66; "Death of Daniel E. Chase," *Somerville Journal* (Massachusetts), July 19, 1907, 2; "Oceanic Hotel Company," *Hotel World*, Sept. 21, 1876, 5.

4 "Around Home," *Portsmouth Journal*, June 27, 1874, 2; R.G. Dun collection, Baker Library, Harvard Business School, Cambridge, Mass., 54:52 (D.E. Chase & Co., Distillers).

5 "Laconics," *Portsmouth Chronicle*, May 8 and 13, 1874, 3; John Albee, *New Castle, Historic and Picturesque* (Boston, Mass.: Rand Avery Supply Company, 1884), 69; "Around Home," *Portsmouth Journal*, June 27, 1874, 2.

6 Brighton, *Frank Jones*, pp. 156–65; obituary of Jesse B. Edwards, *States & Union* (Portsmouth, N.H.), Feb. 13, 1896, 3.

7 Interior brackets and painted designs were discovered under later ceilings and recorded by Gregory Clancey, Adams and Roy, Consultants, working for The Henley Group in 1988, the current owners of The Wentworth-by-the-Sea. Dun collection, 79:223; "Around Home," *Portsmouth Journal*, July 12, Aug. 16, 1874, 3; "Around Home," Jan. 17, 1880, 3. "The Wentworth," *White Mountain Echo*, July 28, 1883, 6; Philip A. Butler bill head courtesy, Downs Manuscript and Microfilm Collection, Winterthur Museum, Winterthur, Del., 68x124.97.

8 *Portsmouth Chronicle*, Oct. 12, 1882; May 24, 26, July 14, 1883. Footman's later design for Frank Jones's 1886 shingled Queen Anne-style summer home, "Ledgemere," at Sorrento, Me., may have been Jones's way of compensating the architect for not using his plans to enlarge the Wentworth. See advertisement, New England [wall plaster] Co., Boston, June 15, 1892, in *Frenchman's Bay and Mt. Desert Land and Water Co. Proprietors of Sorrento, Maine* (ca. 1894), courtesy of Earle G. Shettleworth, Jr., collection.

9 Susan Mackiewicz Evans, *F. Mortimer Lamb (1861–1936), A Master from our Midst* (Brockton, Mass.: Brockton Art Center, 1975); Jabez H. Sears, "The Rockingham House at Portsmouth, N.H.," *Decorator and Furnisher* 10, no. 2 (May 1887): 48.

10 Sears, "Rockingham House," 48. Sears's redesign of the Rockingham combined a variety of sources not only for the first-floor public rooms, but "the rooms occupied by Mr. Jones en suite" as a second-story private residence. The parlor cornice of this apartment was said to be "modeled from an example in the Louvre" while the painted ceilings were "frescoed in designs of the romantic school." James D. Kornwolf, "American Architecture and the Aesthetic Movement," in Doreen Bolger Burke et al., *In Pursuit of Beauty: Americans and the Aesthetic Movement* (New York: Rizzoli International Publications in association with the Metropolitan Museum of Art, 1986), 370, argues that the colonial revival only gained momentum in the late 1880s, when the influence of the aesthetic movement had begun to wane.

11 "Local Affairs," *Portsmouth Chronicle*, July 27, 1895, 2.

12 *New England's Summer and America's Leading Winter Resorts* (New York: G. Frederick Kalhoff, 1897), "Wentworth Hotel," n.p.

13 "Local Affairs," *Portsmouth Chronicle*, Sept. 17, 1898, 2.

14 The addition was erected by W.G. Edwards, son of Jesse Edwards, and contractor of Boston's Union Station. The painted dining-room ceilings, as well as fragments of the plasterwork and architectural woodwork of the Ambassador's Parlor, were recorded by Adams and Roy, Consultants, in 1988 prior to the demolition of the 1890 wings of the hotel.

Cat. 3. J.H. Bufford, Market St. Portsmouth, N.H., *1853. Lithograph; 18 in. x 14½ in. Courtesy, Portsmouth Athenaeum.*

⤳ 3 ⤳

HISTORICAL CELEBRATIONS IN THE PISCATAQUA REGION

Return of the Sons, Portsmouth, 1853
York Tercentenary, 1902
York County Tercentenary, 1936

As early as the 1850s, towns in New England were beginning to experience economic decline as a result of the Industrial Revolution. Portsmouth, which had relied heavily on its shipping business, was one of the first towns in the Piscataqua area to be affected as men followed the path of the railroad to the larger cities of Boston and Portland. By 1853 the leaders of Portsmouth recognized that this heavy drain upon the human resources of the town would be fatal to its growth and development.[1] In that year the "Return of the Sons" gathering was established as the first in a series of efforts which lasted through the turn of the century to bring people back to the less industrialized areas of New England. There were two goals in these "Old Home Day" celebrations, as they came to be called. The first was to create a sentiment for coming home; it was hoped that visiting natives would give money to the communities for worthy projects such as new libraries and hospitals. The second goal of the organizers was to help local residents gain a sense of pride in their community. By emphasizing the historic character and the natural beauty of the towns, they attempted to persuade local residents not to move away.

In 1853 an announcement appeared in the *Boston Globe* stating that a reunion of "Portsmouth Boys" would occur on July 4.[2] Word spread throughout New England and groups from as far away as New York City formed to organize visits to their old homes. More than one thousand people returned to a city which was decorated with flags, evergreens, and flowers for historical exercises and parades (cat. 3).[3] The 1853 event was so successful that it was decided to hold it again every ten years; after the Civil War, the "Return" was held in 1873, 1883, and 1910, when over two thousand former residents returned.[4]

Smaller towns, such as York, followed the example of Portsmouth and began to lure former residents back through community celebrations. A columnist writing in the *York Transcript* in 1899 projected that a visiting native would spend more money in town during a brief visit than would be expended by a farmer's family in the entire year. The columnist went on to say that the visitors would not only aid the town financially, but would also inspire the local population to higher cultural and educational aspirations.[5] Apparently, while the idea was to promote rural life, the columnist saw the urban inhabitants as having the cultural knowledge to raise the "moral character" of the declining town of York—a typical attitude of the reformers which frequently created tension between natives and summer visitors.

The idea of an Old Home Week was first conceived of in 1897 by New Hampshire Governor Frank Rollins in the *New England Magazine* where he "exhorted the sons and daughters of the granite state to listen to the call of their homeland and revisit the spot where they were born." He hoped that every visitor would go to the place of his or her birth and see what he or she could do to assist in the "improvement and beautifying of the place and its general upbuilding and uplifting."[6] The last week in August 1898 was designated Old Home Week, and during that summer sixty-five Old Home Week associations were formed throughout New Hampshire. Each town made up a list of its former residents living outside the state, sent invitations to all, and that summer "thousands of New Hampshire's absent children returned."[7] The hopes of the Old Home Week originators were achieved as libraries were endowed, new public buildings erected, and old farms repurchased for seasonal use.[8]

In July 1900 an editorial appeared in the *York Transcript* urging the town to participate in the movement, suggesting that "Old Home Week not only affords an opportunity to meet old friends in their native state, it also gives back the upward looking and the light, rebuilds the music and the dream, and makes the returning wanderers better and happier."[9] A stern editorial written one month later reveals that the town did not celebrate Old Home Week that year, an admission that was a "very embarrassing acknowledgement, especially since the father of [the] Old Home Week idea [Governor Rollins] is a summer resident of York."[10]

Perhaps York did not celebrate Old Home Week in 1900 because it was preparing for its Tercentenary, which would take place in 1902. The commemoration was sponsored jointly by the town of York and the Old York Improvement Society. The day began with a parade which consisted of a series of historical tableaux on floats, officials, schoolchildren in costume, and fire department members dressed as minutemen (cat. 3a). Town officials, guests, and Improvement Society officers delivered numerous speeches. Included in the list of speakers were Samuel Clemens, Thomas Nelson Page, and Joshua Chamberlain, a former governor of Maine. The rather patronizing goal of helping local residents gain pride in their community was expressed by Portland lawyer Frank Marshall, who stated that "this commemoration day, so singularly beautiful . . . cannot but have an enduring influence for good in the community, stimulating a healthy pride in this old municipality."[11]

In his speech at the anniversary celebration, John Stewart, a doctor and lawyer in York—the only year-round resident asked to speak—thanked the summer visitors for "improving our schools, repairing our churches, giving us roads equal to any in the country towns of our state, bringing the markets of the world to our doors, and establishing libraries for our use. Whatever of prejudice there may have been in the past is gone. You have been our friends. We are yours."[12] In *The Pine-Tree Coast*, Samuel Adams Drake comments on the relations between the year-round resident and the summer visitors:

> Old York was located with reference to the serious business of life; recent York, with regard to its idle pleasures only. Two constituents have thus come in contact, so completely antagonistic in their outward and inward aspects, that, like the ancient auguries, they can scarcely confront each other without laughing.[13]

Although Stewart's speech indicates a hoped-for cordiality between year-round and summer residents, the proposal to divide the town in 1907 between the eastern and western sections indicates that a certain degree of tension persisted between the groups.

During the Depression, York County residents decided to celebrate the county's Tercentenary. While the overall agenda of the York County Tercentenary was derived from earlier celebrations such as the Sons of Portsmouth and early Old Home Weeks, the goal of the 1936 organizers was oriented toward commercializing the area's historic qualities to attract tourists rather than estranged sons and daughters. Articles in the *Boston Globe* and specially printed brochures on the county's historic landmarks brought a new, larger audience to the area than earlier promoters would have ever imagined.

That summer, throughout York County, towns planned Old Home Days with historical exercises, parades, musters,

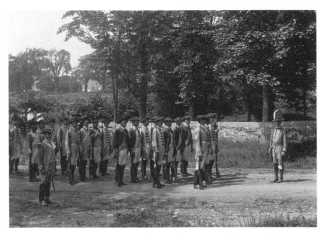

Cat. 3a. Tercentenary Parade, York, Maine. Photograph, 1902. Old York Historical Society.

orations, and tableaux. The three Berwick towns joined together to celebrate "Old Berwick Day." The celebration featured an historical parade, band concert, baseball game, and historical address. Eliot's historical exercises began with the singing of "Auld Lang Syne" and then moved on to the presentation of pageants of local historical events such as the "Submission of Maine to Massachusetts." Many former residents also came back to Kittery. They gathered to hear the Sanford, Maine, band which played at various spots throughout York County in memory of historic events and persons. Kittery's nautical parade consisted of floats pulled by sailors in "old-fashioned" uniforms. A series of vignettes depicting scenes from Kittery's history was displayed along the main road in Kittery Point. These included a statue of the first selectmen of Kittery and a figure of John Smith with a group of Indians. A display of relics and local literature filled the community house until "the sensation of pride in Maine's first town became indelible."[14]

The historical celebrations with their elaborate orations, pageants, and parades were an effort, often on the part of visitors, to define a community identity and to promote a sense of common moral purpose among native residents.[15] The promotion of a nostalgic version of history, emphasizing a preindustrial past, brought many urbanites to the country in search of what many thought was missing in the city. The dual purposes of moral and economic reform, first identified by the organizers of the 1853 "Return of the Sons," continued to be inculcated by historical celebrations in the Piscataqua region throughout the early twentieth century.

SLG

1 *Return of the Sons and Daughters of Portsmouth, 1873* (Portsmouth, N.H.: Charles Gardner, 1873), 5. The population of Portsmouth at this time was approximately 10,000. *Portsmouth City Directory, 1851* (Portsmouth, N.H.: Joseph M. Edmonds, 1851), 7.

2 *Return of the Sons and Daughters of Portsmouth, 1873,* 6.

3 *The Reception of the Sons of Portsmouth Residents Abroad, July 4, 1853* (Portsmouth, N. H.: C.W. Brewster & Son, 1853), 80.

4 Raymond A. Brighton, *They Came to Fish* (Portsmouth, N.H.: Portsmouth 350, Inc., 1973), 1:155.

5 "The Chimney Corner," *Old York Transcript,* Aug. 10, 1899, 2.

6 N.J. Bachelder, *Report of Old Home Week in New Hampshire* (Manchester, N.H.: Arthur E. Clark, 1900), 3.

7 Frank W. Rollins, *Old Home Week Addresses* (Concord, N.H.: Rumford Press, 1900), v.

8 Rollins, "Address at Portland, Maine," in *Old Home Week Addresses,* 125.

9 *The York Transcript,* July 19, 1900, 3.

10 *The York Transcript,* Aug. 2, 1900, 2.

11 *Agamenticus, Bristol, Gorgeana, York: An Oration Delivered by the Hon. James Phinney Baxter . . . on the Two Hundred and Fiftieth Anniversary of the Town* (York, Me.: Old York Historical and Improvement Society, 1904), 82.

12 *Agamenticus, Bristol, Gorgeana, York,* 101.

13 Samuel Adams Drake, *The Pine-Tree Coast* (Boston: Estes and Lauriat, 1891), 47.

14 "Kittery's Celebration," *The Kittery Press,* Sept. 4, 1936, 2.

15 See David Glassberg, *American Historical Pageantry: The Uses of Tradition in the Early Twentieth Century* (Chapel Hill: University of North Carolina Press, 1990).

4

Jacob Wendell House
Portsmouth, New Hampshire, 1789

During the summer of 1910, Mr. and Mrs. Barrett Wendell came up to Portsmouth from Cambridge where he was on the faculty at Harvard College and took up residence in his grandfather's old house on Pleasant Street (cat. 4). They spent the summer "cleaning it of rubbish and restoring it to life." By October, Wendell could write "there is more of our old times than I dared hope: furniture of anywhere from 1750 to 1825—hardly any later; papers, of one and another kind, by the hundred—the oldest I have yet found was 1709 . . . a good deal of old glass, a little old china, and so on. In New England the old order passes so swiftly that I know hardly any other place so wholly of the olden time."[1] Always interested in family history, Wendell delved happily into the thousands of family manuscripts which he discovered in the house, and Edith began the reorganization of the interior to create "the desired effect of a century of comfortable living."[2] Gradually this became more self-conscious and the process of cataloging manuscripts, documenting an illustrious ancestry, and refining and rearranging the furnishings continued throughout the remaining years of family ownership of the house—a process that included the consideration of establishing it as a house museum in the 1980s.[3]

Barrett Wendell's fondness for the house had been encouraged by his father and by his own boyhood visits. At the time of his marriage to Edith Greenough in 1880, the

Cat. 4. Jacob Wendell house, Portsmouth, New Hampshire, built 1789. From American Homes and Gardens *(1914). Photograph by Mary Northend, 1914. Courtesy, Portsmouth Athenaeum.*

house was occupied by his Aunt Caroline, who made the house available to the young couple. Certainly the fact that the old family house was the setting for their blissful honeymoon secured it in their lifelong affections.

Barrett Wendell's father, Jacob Wendell II, was a prosperous New York merchant who had helped to relieve his own father of financial trouble and took over responsibility for the care and maintenance of the Portsmouth house and its occupants, even though he never lived there as an adult. Always feeling a call to the city of his birth, "the moribund old Yankee seaport," as he called it, he returned in 1873 as the chief marshall of the New York delegation for the Return of the Sons of Portsmouth (cat. 3), when "the old town was genuinely cordial, and so was the old house."[4] The New York family summered first at Appledore Island and later at New Castle, where in 1883 they built "Frostfields" (cat. 27), which they enjoyed for many summers.[5] From Frostfields, Jacob Wendell "hovered over the family homestead, caring for those within it and providing funds for the maintenance of it and them."[6] His son wrote in 1918, "really, I can see now, this remote but firm centre was the most secure of all. In time, even the furniture grew so much a part of it that no one was quite disposed to break things up. That is why, after my grandfather [Jacob I] died, it was left intact in Aunt Carry's hands; and then, by friendly consent, in my father's, who let James Stanwood live on there and treat it as his own."[7]

To those family members who did not live in the house, there may well have been a sense that it was essentially unchanged, even though it was they who paid the bills and may even have instigated some significant changes in the architecture and decoration. Soon after her father died in 1865, Caroline installed a black-marble mantel in the parlor fireplace, as well as fresh wallpapers and new carpets in some of the rooms. During the next three decades there were improvements in plumbing and heating as well as the introduction of gas light. Some radiators were added before

1902 and electricity soon followed. These changes are documented by four interior photographs taken by Arthur T. Greenough in August 1887, workmen's bills, and surviving samples of the wallpaper.[8] In the 1890s, soon after Caroline died, there were architectural changes which were designed to enhance the "colonial" feeling of the house, notably a new parlor mantel in the colonial revival style, Dutch blue-and-white delft tiles depicting ships which were installed around the dining-room fireplace in 1890, and a section of the original cornice from the nearby Haven house which was installed in 1912 as a chair rail in the room which had been the best parlor.[9]

Fourteen more photographs of the Wendell house are bound in an album entitled "An Old Homestead in 1902."[10] Seven of these were published the same year in C.S. Gurney's *Portsmouth Historic and Picturesque.* Gurney described the Wendell house as "one of the comparatively rare instances of an interesting collection of antiques which have been well kept together, amid many changes, during the passage of a century . . . That the original equipment of this house should have been retained almost in its entirety, rendering a visit to it always a pleasant experience."[11] The 1902 photographs show the books and papers of the antiquarian James Rindge Stanwood and strong evidence of filiopietism in the display of family pictures, military relics, coats of arms, and framed documents (cat. 4a). Gurney particularly admired the Chippendale-style furniture and 138 pieces of what he called "Flemish" glass, and he was sufficiently impressed by the Sherburne family decanter with its engraved coat of arms to illustrate it in the only picture of an individual object in his entire book.[12]

When Barrett Wendell came into full possession of the house after Stanwood's death in 1910, it was in good physical condition but piled high with Stanwood's antiquarian collections and large quantities of other things which were condemned as "trash." After clearing away things of little value or interest, the Wendells began to study and rearrange the contents of the house and barn. Wendell proposed to write about the house, to compile "a record of what tradition makes old New England seem to have been."[13] Perhaps in preparation for this book, which he never wrote, another series of fifteen photographs was taken in 1912, and a description of each room with detailed notes on the provenance of individual objects was prepared by William Greenough Wendell.[14]

Like others of their time and class, the Barrett Wendells were interested in their ancestral home and its old family furniture as evidence of exclusivity and colonial origins. The 1912 catalogue of the house takes care to mention furnishings which were thought to have belonged to New Hampshire's last colonial governor, John Wentworth, and a strong sense of family ties was observed even in the selection of the family colors of blue and white for the ribbon from which John Wendell's miniature portrait was hung. Such things served to document the family's status and to set them apart from people with "new money." Barrett

Cat. 4a. Parlor, Jacob Wendell house, Portsmouth, New Hampshire. Photograph, 1902. Courtesy, Wendell Collection, Strawbery Banke Museum.

Wendell wrote that no family in Portsmouth "combined honestly professed belief in democratic principles with unbroken persistence in aristocratic feeling," and he recognized that "family pride had become an element of self-respect, and consequently less a vanity than a moral support."[15]

Edith Wendell's historical interests ranged far beyond the Portsmouth house. She was president of the Massachusetts Society of Colonial Dames from 1903 to 1923, serving on the Jamestown Committee in 1907, as chairman of the committee which supported the publication of E. Alfred Jones's *Old Silver of American Churches* in 1913, and was the leader in the restoration of the Dorothy Quincy house which became the society's headquarters.[16] Active in the movement against women's suffrage, she opened her "old colonial home" at Portsmouth, served tea, and "made $161.50 for 'the cause.'" Later, she came to the rescue of another historic Portsmouth house, as founder of the Warner House Association (cat. 58).[17]

Barrett and Edith Wendell entertained frequently during their annual spring and fall residency in Portsmouth, often inviting people whom they knew would appreciate the old family homestead and its contents. The remarkable quantity of early furnishings preserved in the Wendell house and the high quality of individual pieces attracted the attention of early antiquarians and collectors. Luke Vincent Lockwood, for example, illustrated several objects in *Colonial Furniture in America* in 1913, including an unusual eighteenth-century couch.[18] Although this remarkable piece was used in the parlor chamber throughout much of the nineteenth century, it was moved downstairs in 1933 at the urging of Henry Francis du Pont. Once the couch had been installed in the parlor in place of Aunt Carry's square piano, du Pont wrote to Mrs. Wendell, "I was perfectly thrilled to hear that you had moved the piano, and it was all I could do not to jump in an airplane and rush to see the result . . . Your house must now be perfectly superb."[19]

Margaret Deland summed up the effect which Mrs. Wendell had created as "a quality very unusual in American houses, of being intensely interesting, *and* a habitation. I don't know anything just like it in this country. And there was, too, a sense of *rare permanence,* which one doesn't meet very often in this land of the free where freedom seems to consist in spinning around a good deal!"[20]

JCN

1 Barrett Wendell to Sir Robert White-Thomson, Boston, Oct. 16, 1910, in M.A. DeWolfe Howe, *Barrett Wendell and His Letters* (Boston: Atlantic Monthly Press, 1924), 207.

2 William Greenough Wendell, "The Jacob Wendell House" (typescript, PA, 1940), 1.

3 After the death of Mrs. William G. Wendell in 1988, the Wendell heirs decided to break up the house and its contents. Through the generosity of Gerrit van der Woude, SB was able to select more than two hundred pieces of furniture and furnishings for its collection. The manuscript collections were donated by the heirs to the PA. The remaining contents of the house were sold at Sotheby's in New York City in January 1989, and the house was sold privately. Since the sales, additional Wendell objects have been added to the SB collections through the kindness of Ronald Bourgeault.

4 Barrett Wendell, "Recollections of My Father Jacob Wendell, 1826–1898" (typescript, PA, 1918), 95–96.

5 The Wendell family continued to summer at Frostfields until 1910, when James Stanwood died and Barrett Wendell began summer occupancy of the house on Pleasant Street.

6 B. Wendell, "Recollections," 128. After Jacob Wendell's death in 1865, the house was occupied by his daughter, Caroline Quincy Wendell (Aunt Carry) (1820–90), and by her nephew, James Rindge Stanwood (d. 1910), son of Mehitable Rindge Wendell and Isaac Henry Stanwood. Jacob Wendell II provided for the support of the house, giving Stanwood a right of tenancy in the house for his lifetime.

7 B. Wendell, "Recollections," 23.

8 The photographs, now owned by Ronald Bourgeault, were published in Robert F. Trent, "The Wendell Couch," *Maine Antique Digest* (Feb. 1991): 34–D; the bills are in the Wendell Papers at the PA; and the wallpaper samples are at SB.

9 W.G. Wendell, "Jacob Wendell House," 1; a pencil drawing of a design for the mantel is at SB.

10 One copy is now at SB.

11 C.S. Gurney, *Portsmouth Historic and Picturesque* (1902; reprint, Portsmouth, N.H.: Peter E. Randall for SB, 1981), 82.

12 Gurney, *Portsmouth Historic and Picturesque*, 83. The decanter is now in the SB collection. Like many authors of his time, Gurney was imprecise in his use of the term *colonial*, for the Wendell house was not built until 1789, and many of the furnishings which he so admired were in fact those purchased by Jacob Wendell I at the time of his marriage in 1816. Perhaps he was misled by the presence of some distinguished examples of Portsmouth furniture in the Chippendale style which had come from earlier generations and other branches of the family or were purchased locally at auction.

13 Howe, *Letters of Barrett Wendell*, 251.

14 Two more sets of interior photographs of the Wendell house were made, one by Douglas Armsden in 1940 and another by Samuel Chamberlain in 1966. Some of the latter were published in Samuel and Narcissa G. Chamberlain, *The Chamberlain Selection of New England Rooms, 1639–1863* (New York: Hastings House, 1972), 136–37. It is remarkable that there are at least five sets of interior photographs taken during the occupancy of the Wendell family, ranging in date from 1877 to 1966. Additional documentary photographs were taken by SB in 1988.

15 B. Wendell, "Recollections," 16–17.

16 All this despite Barrett Wendell's opinion of the Colonial Dames as "the rather comical name by which a society of women is described who occupy themselves pleasantly and not uselessly in preserving the older traditions of America. In several instances, for example, they have rescued and restored old houses, keeping them as museums of our colonial history"; see Barrett Wendell to Sir Robert White-Thomson, Boston, May 6, 1908, in Howe, *Letters of Barrett Wendell*, 196.

17 [William G. Wendell], *Edith Greenough Wendell (1859–1938)* (ca. 1938), esp. pp. 5–6.

18 Trent, "Wendell Couch," 34–37D.

19 Henry Francis du Pont to Edith Greenough Wendell, Winterthur, Del., Aug. 22, 1933, Wendell Papers, PA.

20 Letter dated July 14, [ca. 1925–35], Wendell Papers, PA. Author Margaret Deland was a summer resident of Kennebunkport, Me.

5

"LOGG" HOUSES OF THE PISCATAQUA REGION

McIntire Garrison
York, Maine, ca. 1710

Junkins Garrison
York, Maine, ca. 1710; burned, ca. 1896
(see plate 1)

Dam Garrison
Dover, New Hampshire, ca. 1680

Frost Garrison
Eliot, Maine, ca. 1730

The towns of southern Maine and New Hampshire were unique during the late nineteenth century for the concentration of surviving dwellings constructed of sawn "logg" walls, now known to have been produced as a by-product of the early colonial water-powered sawmill industry along the Piscataqua's tributaries. Local historians and antiquarians, believing that these "logg" houses were hand-hewn in the tradition of the American log cabin, identified this special building type as a defensive or military construction method required by the northern frontier's vulnerability to Indian attack. Physical evidence of gun-ports, portcullis doors, and other features of some buildings suggested that they were especially designed to "garrison" colonial militia and act as neighborhood houses of refuge.[1]

Charles W. Brewster, perhaps the first writer to draw special attention to the log garrison phenomenon, devoted a chapter of *Rambles About Portsmouth* (1859) to the construction and use of the Whipple garrison house in Kittery. Brewster defined the building type and helped establish several myths repeated by generations of later writers:

> The garrison part of this house was constructed of hemlock timber hewed square, dove-tailed together at the corners . . . This house, like nearly all garrison houses, was built with the upper story projecting beyond the lower about eight or ten inches on every side . . .[which] with its loop holes and scuttles, was intended to give the women of the house a chance to pour down boiling water, at once to scald the Indians.

Brewster correctly surmised that the overhanging story "was doubtless copied by the colonists from European houses, in which projecting upper stories were common."[2] However, his belief that it was designed to permit boiling water to be poured on attackers was not. Edward Emerson Bourne of Kennebunk, repeating this tale in 1876, noted, "I do not remember any instance from books or tradition in which the former mode of defence was resorted to."[3]

Bourne, among all who wrote on garrisons in York

Cat. 5. Winslow Homer, The Junkins Garrison, York, Maine, *ca. 1880. Oil on canvas; 6³⁄₁₆ in. x 8⅞ in. Courtesy, Cooper-Hewitt Museum.*

County, was unique in describing sawn rather than hewn timbers. He wrote from personal knowledge (and memories of a man born in 1737) of a form "once found all along the sea-board" and easily "distinguished from other dwellings."[4] Like all early historians, Bourne accepted conventional wisdom that log walls and four-sided overhangs were synonymous with garrison use.

Among the half dozen houses whose construction details and history of conflict he memorialized were two in the outlying Scotland section of York. The Junkins and McIntire "garrisons" were structurally identical houses built in the first decade of the eighteenth century, but thought by some antiquarians to date "between 1640 and 1660."[5] Neither of them was ever garrisoned with troops; they were farmhouses incidentally defensive through the use of log walls.

The Junkins "garrison" was the log house most often drawn, painted, and photographed during the colonial revival. Its steady decay between 1872 and 1889 (when it burned) was documented by such artists as Edwin Whitefield, Frank S. Church, Winslow Homer (cat. 5), Charles Woodbury (see pl. 1), and others.[6] While they were attracted to its picturesque ruinous state, antiquarians like Samuel Adams Drake appealed for someone to repair it "as

a memorial of the dark days when the settler fought the savage." In his *Nooks and Corners of the New England Coast* Drake lamented:

> It can not survive much longer. It is dilapidated inside and out to a degree that every blast searches it through and through. The doors stood ajar; the floors were littered with corn-fodder, and a hen was brooding in a corner of the best room . . . and where the timbers were ten inches thick, they have rotted away under their long exposure to the weather.[7]

Emma Coleman, who illustrated *New England Captives Carried to Canada* (1925) with Susan Minot Lane's painting of the Junkins house, reveals that one of its panels was reused by C. Alice Baker as a china-closet door in the 1890 "restoration" of the Frary house in Deerfield, Massachusetts. Writing of the 1880s when Baker, Lane, and Coleman summered in York, she recalled that the tenantless farmhouse

> was deserted except by hens when Miss Baker rescued the panel in a very filthy condition. At our boarding-house . . . she scrubbed it and in Cambridge she treasured it to be ready when needed.[8]

Cat. 5a. Parlor, McIntire garrison, York, Maine, built ca. 1710. Photograph by W.F. McIntire, ca. 1890. Courtesy, Society for the Preservation of New England Antiquities.

Cat. 5b. William Dam garrison, Dover, New Hampshire, built ca. 1680. Photograph, 1915. Courtesy, Society for the Preservation of New England Antiquities.

Stealing relics to remodel other historic homes was only one way to memorialize colonial pioneers. Unlike its neighbor, the McIntire garrison, "occupied by the richest man in York" in the 1870s, still remained in the family.[9] When William Sumner Appleton visited this, "the most interesting of our remaining garrisons" in 1913, he found it had been "unfortunately over-restored in 1909" by its owner:

> At that time the original chimney was taken out and a new one put in its place, but the accuracy of the restoration is open to serious question, partly because to suit Mr. McIntyre's son, Mr. John McIntyre, the fireplaces were arched in two of the rooms.

A later addition was also removed in 1909 and much of the interior trim replaced; new doors were hung "with ultra-modern hinges." But Appleton was delighted with the way the house was "fitted up with McIntyre ancestral relics of all kinds. Not a piece has been brought in from outside sources" (cat. 5a).[10]

The William Dam garrison (cat. 5b), originally begun in the 1680s and enlarged about 1712, was located in the Back River district of Dover, New Hampshire. This relic was saved by one of the most unusual colonial revival preservation solutions. Mrs. Holmes B. Rounds inherited and repaired the house, and then "commenced collecting antique articles of historic interest." Rounds eventually acquired eight hundred objects with the help of many friends and opened the house to interested visitors. After thirty-two years of this stewardship, however, she offered the house and collections to be moved to Dover's newly established Annie B. Woodman Institute, if the trustees would "permit her to arrange the articles . . . as she saw fit."[11]

For a week in October 1915 the one-story log house was slowly rolled into town and placed behind two adjoining brick mansions recently purchased with a bequest from Miss Woodman, creating an institute "for the preservation and exhibition of works of art, antiquities, books, manuscripts, historical collections, scientific cabinets, etc." The prominent Dover architect, J. Edward Richardson, provided plans for the remodeling of the early nineteenth-century brick mansion into a natural history museum and a public hall and for laying out the grounds. Richardson also designed a classical envelope of latticework to hold the log house, which protected the relic under a roof through which the rebuilt central chimney was extended. The columned portico of this shrine to New England pioneer life was connected to the brick mansions by a semicircular beaux-arts colonnade (cat. 5c).[12]

Richardson may have drawn his ideas from the recent Louisiana Purchase Exposition (St. Louis, 1904), where no less than four log cabins had been exhibited—including one purported to be Lincoln's birthplace. In 1911, in fact, one log cabin reputed to be the "real" Lincoln birthplace was installed inside a masonry "Temple to Patriotism" promoted by Theodore Roosevelt and Collier's magazine. Just as the preservation of Dover's Dam garrison was a faint echo of the country's continuing fascination with the "log cabin," its odd formal placement behind a classical colonnade was a distant reflection of the "White City" ideals of urban propriety.

The special character of the "Logg" buildings of the Piscataqua continued to interest architects and antiquarians. For example, William Sumner Appleton helped focus attention on them in the Bulletin of the Society for the Preservation of New England Antiquities.[13] While the Dam garrison was being moved to the Woodman Institute, William E. Barry of Kennebunk privately published a monograph on The Blockhouse and Stockade Fort with his own drawings of colonial military log structures including the McIntire and Dam houses.[14]

As late as 1933 these houses and the log barn at the 1730s Frost garrison in Eliot, Maine, were described and illustrated in a national series designed especially for colonial revival architects.[15] The overhanging form lingers on today in modern "garrison colonial" tract homes. Totally disasso-

Cat. 5c. Woodman Institute, Dover, New Hampshire. From Dedication Ceremonies *(1916). Private collection.*

ciated from their ancient "logg" prototypes, the name be-speaks a continuing fascination with images and myths of New England's colonial pioneer life.

RMC

1 Richard M. Candee, "Wooden Building in Early Maine and New Hampshire: A Technological and Cultural History, 1600–1720" (Ph.D. diss., University of Pennsylvania, 1976), 103–59, 247–346. See also Abbott L. Cummings, "The Garrison House Myth," *Historical New Hampshire* 22, no. 1 (Spring 1967): 2–17, and Richard M. Candee, "The Architecture of Maine's Settlement," in *Maine Forms of American Architecture,* ed. Deborah Thompson (Camden, Me.: Downeast Magazine, 1976), 27, 33.

2 Charles W. Brewster, *Rambles About Portsmouth,* first series (Portsmouth, N.H.: C.W. Brewster & Son, 1859), 157.

3 Edward Emerson Bourne, "Garrison Houses in York County," *Maine Historical Society Collections* 7 (1876): 110.

4 Bourne, "Garrison Houses," 113.

5 George Henry Preble, "The Garrison Houses of York County, Maine," *New England Historic and Genealogical Register* 28 (1874): 270–72. Samuel Adams Drake, *Nooks and Corners of the New England Coast* (New York: Harper Brothers, 1875), 140, notes that any date before 1650 is "not to be credited."

6 Edwin Whitefield, Maine sketchbook, SPNEA Archives, and lithograph in his *The Homes of our Forefathers: Maine, New Hampshire, Vermont* (Reading, Mass.: By the author, 1886), 1, as "The Jenkins Garrison." For Church, see Preble, "Garrison Houses," engraving, 269; for Woodbury, see OYHS collection.

7 Drake, *Nooks and Corners,* 139–40. He "observed a loop-hole or two" to confirm his garrison association.

8 For Lane's painting, see frontispiece in Emma Coleman, *New England Captives Carried to Canada* (Portland, Me.: By the author, 1925). Emma Lewis Coleman, "Concerning Frary House" (typescript, Pocumtuck Valley Memorial Association Library, Deerfield, Mass., 1940).

9 Bourne, "Garrisons," 111; Preble, "Garrison Houses," 272, notes in 1874 that John McIntire has built a "modern mansion" and the garrison was then occupied by his unmarried sister. Drake adds that Mr. McIntire also owned the Junkins garrison, although Whitefield noted a few years later that Mr. Junkins, its owner, worked in a shoe factory in Salmon Falls.

10 William Sumner Appleton, "McIntyre garrison house, York Corner, Me. Owned by John R. McIntyre" (typescript, York, Me., correspondence file, SPNEA Archives, July 1913).

11 *Catalogue of Articles in ye William Dam Garrison at the Woodman Institute* (Dover, N.H.: Charles F. Whitehouse, 1917), 4–5.

12 *Dedication Ceremonies on July 26, 1916: The Annie B. Woodman Institute* (Concord, N.H.: Rumford Press, 1916), 3–6.

13 *Bulletin of the Society for the Preservation of New England Antiquities* (later OTNE) 1, no. 2 (Feb. 1911): 1–7; 5, no. 1 (April 1914): 14–15.

14 William E. Barry, *The Blockhouse and Stockade Fort* (Kennebunk, Me.: Enterprise Press, 1915).

15 Stuart Bartlett, "Garrison Houses Along the New England Frontier," *Monograph Series* 19:33–48 in *Pencil Points* 14 (June 1933): 253–68.

Cat. 6. Passaconaway Inn, Cape Neddick, Maine, built 1893. Photograph, 1892. Old York Historical Society.

6

PASSACONAWAY INN
Cape Neddick, Maine, 1893; demolished, 1937
E.B. Blaisdell (1845–1924), architect

York Harbor and York Beach were thriving resort communities by the last decade of the nineteenth century, and more cottages and hotels appeared with every season. Yet there remained a large tract of undeveloped shorefront on the north side of the Cape Neddick River, about a mile from York Beach; the land was part of the holdings of the Weare family who had owned it since before 1652.[1]

In 1890 two brothers from New Jersey decided to create a new summer resort on this property. Cornelius Vermeule was an accomplished civil engineer. His brother John was a banker and president of the Goodyear India Rubber Company. Cornelius Vermeule negotiated purchases of

land with several members of the Weare family, amounting to approximately 150 acres.[2] Later purchases increased the total holdings to about 300 acres and included a scenic pond which was dubbed "Lake Carolyn." The use of the land as a resort was made possible by Cornelius Vermeule's design of a municipal water system, a bridge over the Cape Neddick River that linked York Cliffs with the railway at York Beach, and a pier that provided access to deep water.

In the first of a series of publicity brochures for the development, known as "York Cliffs," its promoters claimed that the resort offered more amenities "than Bar Harbor or any other locality upon the coast of Maine, yet it is as conveniently located as is famed Newport." York Cliffs boasted, among other qualities, proximity to wooded forest, rocky coastline, and sandy beaches; the 1893 brochure styled the surrounding landscape "as rich in rural loveliness, historical associations, traditions and romance as any in New England."[3]

The centerpiece of the development was the expansive Passaconaway Inn (cat. 6), said by local historian Ralph

Winn to have catered to a "very swanky clientele."[4] The newly completed inn was described in 1893 as having been "built substantially, equipped with the best modern appliances, steam laundry, cold storage, model cooking, lighting and heating apparatus, a passenger elevator," and every room had an open fireplace and marble-topped lavatory.[5]

The first brochure went to press before construction of the inn was completed. It contains the only known views of the interior of the Passaconaway Inn which was both rustic and colonial in feeling. The lobby or "office" was dominated by a large stone fireplace, the lintel bearing the inscription "WAPANACHEEN," apparently a native American word whose meaning has been lost. Around the walls was a seascape frieze painted by New York artist Frank DeHaven. Before the fireplace was spread an oriental carpet, and a tall-case clock and a number of pressed-back rocking chairs accounted for most of the visible furniture.

The 1893 brochure also illustrates three of the cottages built as part of the York Cliffs development. "Rockhaven," which was the summer home of Frank DeHaven, stands on the northern edge of the tract. Built in 1892, its exterior combined locally available rubblestone with wood shingles in a treatment characteristic of summer cottages of the period. Nearby, the former Weare homestead was transformed into "Pinehurst Cottage" (cat. 7). The third York Cliffs building shown in the brochure was the cottage of Joseph N. Kinney of New York, vice president of the York Cliffs Improvement Company. Kinney had quickly chosen as the site for his own cottage a desirable seven-acre tract at the mouth of the harbor called "Weare Point." The *York Transcript* described the property thus:

> Now we emerge on a wide spreading lawn that slopes down to the very water's edge where the white foam washes up among the pebbles and rocks. On this spot stands a beautiful cottage, "Greystone." It is without exception the finest summer residence anywhere along this section of the coast. Its quaint style is most pleasing and its magnificent location unsurpassed.[6]

Greystone has the settled, rambling quality of an English country house (cat. 6a). English-inspired elements include the low Gothic porch, the patterned brickwork, and, originally, the half-timbering in the gable over the entry. Otherwise, the house has a typical shingle-style gambrel roof broken by dormers.

Both Greystone and the Passaconaway Inn were designed by architect Joseph H. Taft of New York City, but only the design for Greystone was executed. The York Cliffs Improvement Company had set a limit of $100,000 for construction of the inn, and Taft's design was rejected as too costly. The company instead accepted a design by the local architect and builder E.B. Blaisdell.[7] Blaisdell completed the construction of the inn in ninety days.

Built in the same year as Greystone, but not included in the first York Cliffs brochure, was a small shingle-style cottage perched on the rocks at the ocean's edge north

Cat. 6a. Greystone, Cape Neddick, Maine. Photograph, 1892. Old York Historical Society.

of the larger cottage. Its original owner, Elizabeth Blackwell, has been called "the first American woman doctor," but it is more likely that she was the first woman to receive a medical degree from an American university. Born February 3, 1821, she was awarded an M.D. by Syracuse University in 1849.[8]

Eleven more cottages were built at York Cliffs between 1894 and 1902, of which all but three survive. Most of these summer houses were commissioned by officers of the York Cliffs Improvement Company for their own use, or served the company as rentals; only four were for people without connections to the development, like Elizabeth Blackwell. The company eventually built a golf club, bathhouses, and a large carriage house and stable. Several cottage owners built private stables at a remove from their residences on the western side of Shore Road. Despite the grandiose projections of its promotional brochures, this was the extent of the development at York Cliffs.

TH

1   In 1872 Theodore and Elsie Jane Weare, descendants of Peter Weare, the earliest known member of the family to settle in Cape Neddick, built the famous Cliff House summer hotel overlooking Bald Head Cliff, between York and Oqunquit. It continues to be run under Weare ownership, much altered and expanded.

2   YCRD, 435:292, 442:492, 446:226.

3   *York Cliffs, Coast of Maine* (New York: York Cliffs Improvement Society, 1893).

4   Ralph Winn, *Legends of Cape Neddick* (Freeport, Me.: Bond Wheelwright Co., 1964), 65.

5   *York Cliffs*, 10–11.

6   *York Transcript*, June 22, 1899.

7   Taft is credited with the design of the Passaconaway Inn in an article that appeared in the *Industrial Journal* (Bangor, Me.), Jan. 13, 1893. Taft showed his design for Greystone in the 1893 annual exhibition of the Architectural League of New York; see *Catalogue of the Eighth Annual Exhibition of the Architectural League of New York* (New York: Architectural League of New York, 1893). Earle G. Shettleworth, Jr., kindly brought these references to my attention.

8   *York County Coast Star*, Feb. 2, 1966. I am grateful to Dr. Roberta S. Batt of Portland, Me., for further information on Dr. Blackwell.

Cat. 7. "Pinehurst Cottage," Cape Neddick, Maine. From promotional brochure by Harvey and Wood Hotels, "Passaconaway Inn, York Cliffs, Maine," ca. 1895. Old York Historical Society.

✧ 7 ✧

PINEHURST COTTAGE
Cape Neddick, Maine, ca. 1800
Remodeled, ca. 1895

"Pinehurst Cottage" was originally built for the Weare family around 1800 and remained in their possession until it was sold in 1890, as part of a larger land transaction, to the brothers Cornelius and John Vermeule of New Jersey and New York, founders of the York Cliffs Improvement Company. The three hundred or more acres sold to these resort developers were only a small part of the Weare holdings.[1] Much of this shoreland parcel had been used for grazing livestock, and contemporary photographs show the area almost barren of trees. The Weare family developed their own resort at Bald Head Cliff which they continue to operate as the Cliff House.

The York Cliffs Improvement Company laid out an extensive summer colony with a system of roads and some three hundred cottage lots; most of this scheme was never realized. Twelve large "cottages" were built, for officers of the company, as rentals, or as private commissions. The former Weare homestead (cat. 7a) became one of these cottages, through a total remodeling which transformed the simple federal-style house into a striking example of what was then called "colonial style" architecture. Pinehurst Cottage (cat. 7) represents the turn-of-the-century practice of enlarging and embellishing old buildings, and in the process transforming vernacular structures by adding a variety of classical details.[2] In the course of its remodeling, the simple farmhouse became a fashionable summer residence.

Among the additions to the Weare house was a heavy exterior cornice rising above the existing roof line and combining dentil and other moldings. Resting on this cor-

nice was a roof-line balustrade that has since been removed. To each of the principal facades a porch was added with slender classical columns, as were balustrades at both the first and second stories, the posts topped with urn finials. Most of the windows and doors of the original house were left intact or in their original locations. In the course of remodeling, all of the original interior features were removed, with the exception of the boxed beams and corner posts.

The remodeling of Pinehurst Cottage was completed in 1895. To its east stood the towering Passaconaway Inn (see cat. 6), built by the York Cliffs Improvement Company in 1893. Pinehurst Cottage was intended as deluxe guest quarters for patrons of the inn and the York Cliffs brochure for 1900 states that "While it [Pinehurst Cottage] is fitted complete for housekeeping, its close proximity to the Inn renders it possible for meals to be obtained there with perfect ease."[3]

TH

1 YCRD, 435:292, 442:492, 446:226.

2 See Richard M. Candee's essay in chap. 2 of this volume and J. Seabury, *New Houses Under Old Roofs* (New York: F.A. Stokes, 1916).

3 *York Cliffs, Coast of Maine* (New York: York Cliffs Improvement Company, 1900), 25.

Cat. 7a. "Weare Homestead," Cape Neddick, Maine. Photograph, ca. 1860. Private collection.

II
Restoring the
Colonial Home

Fig. 2.1. Sophia Sewall Wood Monroe, Barrell Homestead, *York, Maine, ca. 1800. Pen and ink and watercolor on paper; 5¾ in. x 8⅜ in. Private collection; courtesy, Frick Art Reference Library.*

Preceding page: *"Hanging a Reproduction Architecture Paper," Hamilton house, South Berwick, Maine. Photograph by Elise Tyson Vaughan, 1898. Courtesy, Society for the Preservation of New England Antiquities.*

The New Colonials:
Restoration and Remodeling of Old Buildings Along the Piscataqua

Richard M. Candee

At the turn of the twentieth century, colonial American architecture inspired many sorts of contemporary architectural projects. Large Victorian shingled "cottages" built along the New England seacoast after the 1880s sported Palladian-style windows, balustrades based on eighteenth-century prototypes, and other historicizing details. Commodious turn-of-the-century suburban homes were modeled after Georgian mansions, and even small tract houses built during and after World War I (cat. 44) were dressed up with ornament drawn from early American sources. At the same time, "real" historic houses were transformed through remodelings, additions, and renovations, liberally termed "restorations." Such projects were undertaken during the decades around 1900 to make the old buildings of the Piscataqua suitable summer homes or permanent residences. Many of these renovations brought modern facilities to houses that had been untouched for decades, but an increasing interest in the past made it important for the renovators to retain old elements and add new ones in an historic style.

Remodeling old buildings and the design of new "colonial" homes became the staple of many professionally trained architects at the turn of the century. Drawing and photographing old buildings made some architects into historians of America's earlier architecture (cat. 8). One such practitioner, R. Clipston Sturgis, explored Portsmouth in 1899 and identified two kinds of architecture. Sturgis saw the old as representative of "the best of a vigorous period," while the new was "the careless product" of ignorant and uncaring people "little in touch with the old and having scant sympathy with its point of view." In this context it became "customary to call the old work colonial" whether it was the vernacular timber-framed constructions of the earliest settlers, the formal architecture of the eighteenth century, or the three-story mansions of the early nineteenth century. "All these dwellings," Sturgis reported, "and the churches and public buildings which accompanied them, are called colonial." To many educated Americans of similar antimodern biases the colonial was "a precious heritage" continually eroded by new buildings "out of harmony with the old town" or endangered by remodeling, like Portsmouth's "quiet business buildings . . . bedizened with cheap show of copper ornament" and "gaudy paint." While the city already had "good examples" of remodeling that respected a building's historic character,

such as architect William A. Ashe's 1895–96 conversion of the old Academy into a public library, "each year one wonders whether the Athenaeum [cat. 11] will escape destruction or renovation."[1]

In fact, traditional methods of remodeling meant the total transformation of an old house into a "new" one embellished in the style of the day. This had happened to many seventeenth-century homes, like the Sherburne house in Portsmouth; only forty years after its construction about 1695, the old-fashioned character of the house was masked by a completely new plan and finish in the fashionable Georgian style. Such a process of continued enlargement and alteration over many generations is also evident at Barrell Grove in York. Begun about 1720 as a modest hip-roofed rural farmhouse, enlarged in the 1760s to an L-shaped plan (fig. 2.1), the house entered the nineteenth century as the estate of the eccentric Nathaniel Barrell who died in 1831. His son and heir, Charles C. Barrell, continued this pattern to produce a model of rural improvement. In 1841 he unified old and new rooms beneath a huge gable roof that created a new third story and attic (fig. 2.2). The exterior was ornamented with vernacular Greek revival trim, while the interior gained a circular staircase.[2]

The practice of total transformation not only persisted in the building trade, but was actively promoted by professional architects seeking to "reform" the American landscape into conformity with new aesthetic ideals. As early as 1846, A.J. Downing, in the first volume of the *Horticulturist*, illustrated the way "a plain country house, common in almost every neighborhood," could be turned into a Gothic revival cottage (fig. 2.3) through the kind of alteration that "confers a character of taste and picturesqueness on what was before a very ordinary and stupid building."[3]

In the design of public and commercial buildings, too, both the mid-nineteenth-century architectural community and its clients sought to elevate aesthetic taste. Portsmouth's leaders sought to symbolize its new status as a city and assert its economic vitality through extensive construction in the Italianate style around Market Square. The decade of the 1850s saw the removal and replacement of its eighteenth-century meetinghouse with a new North Church (Towle and Foster, architects, 1854–55), a new home for the Rockingham Bank (S.S. Woodcock, architect, ca. 1857), and the construction of a new United States

Fig. 2.2. Barrell Grove, York, Maine, begun 1720. Photograph, 1886. Old York Historical Society.

Customs House (Ammi B. Young, architect, 1857–60). A campaign was mounted to replace the public market, a building which had won the praise of Timothy Dwight as the handsomest of its kind after it was erected in 1800. Jefferson Hall, as the market became known, was modified in 1849, when a steeply pitched roof replaced its original low hip roof, but it still retained a severe classicism. A decade later the building was described as "that miserable abortion of a building on Market Square, which disgraces the name of Jefferson," in efforts to promote its remodeling or removal to make way for a new city hall.[4]

Older commercial buildings, visual reminders of Portsmouth before the arrival of the railroad, were not considered sufficiently modern for the city's Victorian business leaders. Efforts to alter the federal-style facades of the commercial district can be seen in unexecuted plans to add an Italianate bracketed balcony to the Athenaeum (William Tucker, architect, 1848) and the extensive "improvements" to shopfronts or whole facades after the 1850s. Several old buildings, like their modern counterparts around Market Square, were covered with stucco scored and painted in im-

itation of the brownstone construction then fashionable in Boston and other American cities.[5] Portsmouth had not yet discovered its identity as an historic seaport rich in fine examples of earlier architecture.

But in the years preceding the Civil War, New England's most well-known authors and local antiquarians began to identify the region's colonial heritage with the homes of the eighteenth-century elite. The continued loss of buildings not yet seen as "historic" to modern rebuilding and commercialism became a major theme of the next generation of writers. Moreover, architectural thinking about appropriate sources for new American designs was greatly influenced by contemporary historicism in England. In the 1860s and 1870s younger British architects began to derive inspiration from the vernacular buildings of their country's hitherto despised eighteenth-century past. The style of their designs for new urban buildings that were inspired by the old became known as "Queen Anne."[6]

In 1877, Boston architect Robert Swain Peabody worried in print that if American architects followed the lead of these English architects "without any native Jacobean or

Queen Anne models of importance to inspire us, we shall be adding one more fashion to our already rather long list" of imported revival styles. He called for architects to draw inspiration instead from the Georgian houses of New England and to create a distinctive American architecture. In citing the Sparhawk house in Kittery, the Wentworth mansion in Little Harbor, and the Ladd and Langdon houses in Portsmouth among the key monuments of early New England whose form and details might be appropriate sources for the new style, Peabody drew attention to the role that the historic architecture of the Piscataqua region would play in the development of the revival aesthetic he advocated.[7]

Peabody's fear that Americans would apply the English Queen Anne by merely adopting its stylistic features was often realized. For example, in his book *The Old House Altered* (1878), Newport, Rhode Island, architect George C. Mason called for remodeling older homes to meet the new Queen Anne taste. Written as a series of letters from a young city architect to his sister who had inherited their parents' old home, Mason's book takes his imaginary female client through a series of steps that help her turn a simple, four-square Georgian block into a most up-to-date dwelling. Changes in plan, additions, near total exterior and interior resurfacing, and the installation of modern conveniences are all presented as methods that readers could use to remake an old family house into a Queen Anne dream home with the help of the local builder.[8]

In 1879 William M. Woollett, an architect practicing in Albany and nearby parts of Connecticut, published a volume of drawings and photographs called *Old Homes Made New . . . Illustrating the Alteration and Remodeling of Several Suburban Residences.* Typical of much self-promotional architectural publishing, Woollett suggested hiring an architect rather than a mere builder. Like Mason's, Woollett's remodelings sought to provide all the technological and spatial necessities that supported the cult of domesticity. Nor were all of his designs hypothetical; photographs show actual farmhouses converted into the exuberant Queen Anne dwellings he advocated. Arguing that a "large number of buildings are yearly remodeled at great expense, without a result commensurate," he suggested two criteria for deciding whether or not to remodel. The first was economic: one should remodel where condition and materials would "render its destruction unadvisable." But the other was something new; this was

> when, although perhaps in a dilapidated condition, its preservation is in the highest degree desirable, owing to the associations of family, its peculiar phase or style of architecture, or the historical interest that may attach itself.

The first prescription was for the "motley crowd of dwellings" built since the 1840s; the latter Woollett reserved for "the homes of colonial times" because:

FIG. 2. VIEW OF A COMMON COUNTRY HOUSE.

FIG. 3. VIEW OF THE SAME, IMPROVED.

Fig. 2.3. Gothic revival cottage. From Horticulturist *(1846). Courtesy, Boston Public Library.*

In this phase of architecture there are many things that are quaint, interesting and, in an artistic light, good. How generally this is believed, is shown in the fact that many of the new dwellings that are being erected at present are based on this style of architecture.

Woollett even supplied a set of rules, by no means evident in any of his own designs, to guide such careful alterations: "everything should be done to preserve that which is already built"; in changing, "doing away with as little as possible of the old"; while in adding-on "the same style should be employed." The goal was not to lose desirable features, but to change the building "merely enough" to meet modern requirements for domestic life.[9]

Woollett's ideas about how the interests of both history and comfort could be respected in renovating an old house were circulating elsewhere in the architectural community as well. Charles F. McKim's 1875 renovation of and addition to the 1725 Robinson-Smith house in Newport, Rhode Island, included a widely published remodeling of the old kitchen with a new fireplace employing tiles, overmantel panels, and other elements only loosely derived from colonial design sources. Clarence Cook, advocate of the aesthetic movement, praised McKim for his:

> uncommon skill in finding out what there is left in an old house to build up for modern comfort and elegance . . . the old kept wherever it was sound enough, and suited to a new lease on life, and whatever new was added kept true to the spirit of the old time, though without any antiquarian slavishness.[10]

Such a liberal attitude toward the remodeling of colonial houses was characteristic of the decade immediately following the Civil War. However, along the Piscataqua, the concept of preservation was already surfacing and one early "restoration" signaled the first stirrings of a sentiment that would later become more widespread. The combination of old and new work (including a corner cupboard carved by John Haley Bellamy) in the 1867 remodeling of Sparhawk

house at Kittery Point predates the ideas of McKim or Woollett by almost a decade. Apparently directed by the owner without the help of an architect, this "restoration" combined salvaged paneling of different dates (perhaps from two eighteenth-century buildings) to create a large dining hall that completely fooled all the subsequent architects who sketched, measured, and photographed the room (cat. 9).

A precursor to the work of architects who valued new design in the "spirit of the old" over antiquarian copying, the restoration of Sparhawk house may have grown out of the English background of its owner, Walter R. Brown of Toronto. As a member of the Church of England before his emigration to Canada, Brown may have been familiar with the heavy-handed practices of Anglican parish church restorers or the renovation of country homes by the English gentry. It is possible, therefore, that he brought the concept of restoration with him from England. Brown clearly valued this house, sometimes called "Pepperrell house" after its connection with the region's only colonial baronet, for both its aristocratic association and its eighteenth-century elegance.[11] Similarly, in 1874 Oliver Cutts, owner of the Lady Pepperrell house in Kittery Point (cat. 10), had that building "thoroughly repaired, preserving and restoring all of its rich and grand old style of architecture," although

Fig. 2.4. Sunset cottage, York Harbor, Maine. Photograph, ca. 1890. Old York Historical Society.

removing the original flocked wallpaper that still looked "good as new."[12]

Before the 1890s, acquiring a colonial house for permanent or summer use did not always lead to substantial restoration or remodeling. For example, when J. Templeman Coolidge purchased the Wentworth mansion at Little Harbor in 1886, he retained the mixture of antiques and historical portraits, as well as early wallpapers and carpeting, that had been in place when the "romantic premises" were promoted as a tourist attraction by a former owner.[13] The number of new owners consciously opting to preserve old houses in the Piscataqua, as elsewhere in New England, was actually quite small until the 1890s. In fact, most old houses still in the hands of local families displayed a decor that mixed heirloom furniture with the clutter of Victorian life, including new technologies like gas lighting. Perhaps for this reason, few household furnishings are shown in Arthur Little's sketches of Piscataqua-region houses published as *Early New England Interiors* (1878). Contemporary photographs from the 1870s through the end of the century illustrate both antiquarian survival and modern aesthetic ideals about "artistic" interiors (fig. 2.4). These houses contained important groups of fine and decorative arts that made them important to the antique collectors then trying to place early American furniture into an understandable stylistic and chronological sequence. Popular house biographies and tourist guides regularly noted family heirlooms, and the first collector's books frequently cited or illustrated furnishings of Sir William Pepperrell (in the Ladd house), Governor Benning Wentworth, and Jonathan Warner still in private hands.[14]

When colonial homes changed owners at the turn of the century, they sometimes returned to those who could claim a genealogical relationship with the original occupants. As the editors of the *Old York Transcript* noted in 1899, upper-class city dwellers increasingly sought to spend the summers in their own homes rather than "herding together . . . in large numbers in great hotels." New Englanders who had made their money elsewhere were "coming back to the old home . . . and restoring them to a greater degree of grandeur than even their occupants had ever aspired to."[15] In Portsmouth, Woodbury Langdon, who had acquired the John Langdon mansion in 1877 for his mother's residence, took over the house and expanded it in 1905 (cat. 12) and Barrett Wendell purchased his own family home as a summer place in 1910 (cat. 4). York's most elaborate federal-period house, Coventry Hall, was occupied throughout the summers of the 1890s by descendants of the second wife of Judge Sewall, the original owner. But the best example of what the editor may have had in mind would soon occur across the street from Coventry Hall, at the eighteenth-century homestead of the Emerson family.

Edward Octavius Emerson (1834–1912), an oil salesman from Titusville, Pennsylvania, brought his family to summer with his mother in York annually from 1878. His son later recalled:

In the earliest days of our visits to York, our whole family would board the [railroad] cars at Titusville, ride to Buffalo and change; ride to Albany and change to Boston and change, and on to Portsmouth where we would all spend the night . . . at the Rockingham. The next morning Father would . . . hire a team of horses and a double and usually a single carriage (the latter to be brought over later) and we would all pile in bag and baggage for York. In later years Father always sent down his own team and carriages from Titusville in a freight car, with a hostler and man-of-all-work accompanying.

In 1878, the white house stood directly on the edge of the road with its columned front porch painted and sanded in imitation of brownstone. Behind the main building was a chaise house where the senior Mrs. Emerson, "who was very modern in her taste and wanted everything in the best and latest style," had discarded old family furniture.[16]

Edward acquired the family home following his mother's death in 1890; after the carriage house burned in 1892, he began to make a series of changes which culminated in substantial alterations between 1899 and 1900. Over that winter Emerson had the rear ell and side porch removed, and the house moved back from Woodbridge Road several yards "so carefully that none of the plastering showed a single crack." Early in March 1900, local builders E.B. and S.T. Blaisdell began the carpentry for a large new addition and "the reconstruction of the Old Colonial Mansion." Drawings were prepared by Fred Crowell Watson, "a prominent architect of New York City" trained in Massachusetts who soon joined the Blaisdell firm as an in-house designer for the contractor's summer cottages. The plans called for a new dining room in the original eighteenth-century kitchen, a new service wing behind, and extensive new stables (figs. 2.5a, 2.5b).[17]

In 1913 the General John Sullivan house at Durham was also reported to have "recently come into the hands of a direct descendant." Such repurchases of familial homesteads coincided with state government campaigns to attract summer residents to bolster a declining agricultural economy through their adoptions of the thousands of abandoned farms throughout the region. From 1891 to World War I, for example, the state agriculture board published works like *New Hampshire Farms for Summer Homes* to attract wealthy buyers by advertising available farms and, in ancient towns of the seacoast at least, promoting success stories like the return of General Sullivan's colonial home to his family.[18]

During the 1890s Kate Sanborn (1839–1917) wrote two popular books, *Adopting an Abandoned Farm* (1891) and *Abandoning an Adopted Farm* (1894), that give human substance to this movement. The stories record the comic tribulations of the New Hampshire–born single woman, a former English professor at Smith College and now a New York newspaper correspondent, literary lecturer and author, who leased an old farm in Holliston, Massachusetts.

Fig. 2.5a. Emerson house, York, Maine, begun ca. 1759. Photograph, ca. 1880. Courtesy, Mr. and Mrs. S. Thompson Viele.

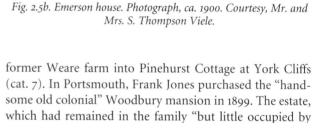

Fig. 2.5b. Emerson house. Photograph, ca. 1900. Courtesy, Mr. and Mrs. S. Thompson Viele.

After taking the old farm for three years, she attended local auctions to furnish her house with antiques and cast-offs within her hundred-dollar budget. "Finding after one or two trials that the interested parties raised rapidly on anything I desired," she sent her hired maid and gardener to do her bidding. She raised poultry on the farm and even acquired two elegant peacocks at a poultry show. After their arrival, the simplicity of the farm appeared

> shabby, inappropriate, and unendurable. It became evident that the entire place must be raised, and at once, to the level of the peacocks.
>
> The house and barn were painted (colonial yellow) without a moment's delay. An ornamental piazza was added, all the paths broadened and graveled, and even terraces were dreamed of.

Although the annual rent was only $40, the cost of her improvements the first year totaled $5,713.85.[19]

Imbued with a keen sense of progressive feminism that might have appealed to C. Alice Baker and Elizabeth Perkins, and a self-deprecating humor about a city woman learning the mores of the country, Sanborn found her new life a delight. Her personal transformation from "invalidism" and "mental depression" (common complaints among many late nineteenth-century upper-class women) to health and "exuberant spirits" were the compensations Sanborn found in amateur farming. Thus, when her lease ran out she abandoned her improved farm and purchased another nearby 1815 farmhouse with eighty acres of land to continue her rural life as well as her writing career.[20]

Through popular stories like Sanborn's, the idea of remodeling a country farmhouse spread beyond houses associated with family, colonial heroes, or possessing elaborate architecture. The growing popularity of private remodelings that enhanced the "colonial" character of an early dwelling can be seen in the 1895 transformation of the former Weare farm into Pinehurst Cottage at York Cliffs (cat. 7). In Portsmouth, Frank Jones purchased the "handsome old colonial" Woodbury mansion in 1899. The estate, which had remained in the family "but little occupied by the Woodburys," was to be "beautified and restored to its old time glory" although Jones died in 1902 before this was accomplished.[21]

The Piscataqua region was by no means alone in this activity. Throughout rural New England old farms were reclaimed, old houses remodeled or restored, and historic communities preserved through an influx of summer residents. Old towns like Hadley and Deerfield, Massachusetts, Litchfield, Connecticut, or the suburban communities surrounding Boston and the North Shore all saw similar renovations. The mixture of old families, returning descendants, and new artistic circles had a distinct impact on the architectural and decorative treatment used in the old houses in these places.[22]

The particular methods for modernizing colonial homes were codified through books and magazine articles that appeared before World War I. Among the books on the subject were Charles Edward Hooper's *The Country House* (1904) and his *Reclaiming the Old House* (1913), which documented a single Connecticut remodeling project.[23] Starting with the existing frame, Hooper explored "the most plausible ways of addition," enlargement, and alteration to common New England plan-types. These changes were usually needed to add service functions and install modern heating, plumbing, and lighting. By this date many "reproductions" of period hardware, wallpaper, and furniture were available and thought to be appropriate for old houses. This sort of practical advice would have been particularly useful in planning additions to the eighteenth- and early nineteenth-century buildings of the Piscataqua region.

Hooper's contemporary, Mary Harrod Northend

(1850–1926), the daughter of a prominent North Shore, Massachusetts, family, became known as "a famous authority and writer of American historical and colonial homes, their settings and their furniture." After her father's death in 1902 she took up the typewriter to cure her "semi-invalidism." What began "first through ill health and the desire for occupation" became a career. Realizing that "photographs would enhance her success," she bought a Kodak Brownie, but quickly learned to hire professional photographers "to accompany her on copy-producing excursions." Northend used her family social connections to gain access to historic homes, country houses, and summer estates that might otherwise never have been photographed. She once estimated she took between two thousand and three thousand pictures a year and, by 1912, she had a photographic archive of more than thirty thousand negatives and a file of over a million clippings. She also established a cottage industry of genteel women (including Elizabeth Perkins and her friends [cats. 15, 52]) who ghosted magazine articles for her. From her archives Northend sold thousands of photographs to illustrate the stories of other journalists in addition to illustrating hundreds of her own articles in *Country Life* and women's magazines. Between 1912 and her death in 1926 she also wrote nearly a dozen books on historic houses, antique collecting, home decoration, and architecture.[24]

In *Remodeled Farmhouses* (1915), Northend explores these subjects through twenty-two examples that range geographically from Cape Cod in Massachusetts to Hollis, Maine. Informally written, Northend's book describes the nature of each renovation and the reasons behind "necessary" changes; her photographs show large homes (one built around a core of an old barn to provide character for the living room), stately saltboxes with central chimneys, as well as small cottages doubled in size by new additions.

But it is the variety of interior treatments illustrated in her photographs that makes these stories so valuable as a record of contemporary taste. Certain conventions are clearly in vogue: sun porches and pergolas extend the old houses in various directions outdoors, and several variants of the colonial kitchen are seen as a new "living room," with exposed ceiling beams, white woodwork, and cupboards with small-paned glass doors to display old china. "Another room, showing wainscot and a quiet yellow and white Colonial paper," she writes of one house, "has a Field bed with white spread and white muslin canopy." She also illustrates several interiors influenced by the arts and craft movement that show hand-painted murals, exposed brick in craftsman-style fireplaces, and mixtures of antique and contemporary mission-style furniture.[25] The interior treatments recorded by Northend illustrate the overlap between the colonial revival and arts and crafts movements at the turn of the century: renewed interest in preindustrial methods of production were integral to both camps and were evident in the furnishings their adherents selected or made.

The style of decoration popularized by Mary Northend

can be seen in many Piscataqua-region interiors, but especially in Elizabeth Perkins's dining room in York—with its beams, paneling, and wide hearth—and in the Tysons's airy decorating style at Hamilton house in South Berwick. Nearby, Sarah Orne Jewett's interest in the contemporary arts was manifested in the bold wallpaper she used to redecorate the central entrance hall of her family's eighteenth-century South Berwick home (fig. 2.6). While Jewett's writing has often been described as an effort to secure an image of her native town against change, her introduction of an arts and crafts wallpaper into her colonial house demonstrates a sympathy with contemporary artistic developments.

Like Sarah Orne Jewett, many renovators of historic houses near the Piscataqua were writers or visual artists. But Joseph Stowe Seabury, a Boston real estate salesman, proposed in *New Homes Under Old Roofs* (1916), that such homes were not just for "historians and antiquarians and artists and poets," the primary clients of an earlier era, but for "captains of industry, those little lords of finance" to whom such a country house was a symbol of success.[26] As such, the renovated colonial house could hardly do without the latest in domestic improvements. Both Northend and Seabury show how the introduction of new heating, cooking, plumbing, and lighting technologies played an important role in renovation projects designed by architects (whose involvement Seabury emphasized) and owners alike. The fear of tuberculosis likewise led reformers to add sun rooms and sleeping porches to the list of requirements for a healthful and modern early twentieth-century home. At the same time, a leisured life-style was hardly possible without servants who were put up in made-over attics, or in added service wings. Summer homes also required guest quarters and shaded porches. Gardens needed summer houses as well as potting sheds; stables made way for the new automobile.

Such practical considerations are evident in the colonial homes along the Piscataqua remodeled between the late 1890s through the 1920s. Major service additions (kitchens, pantries, servant's quarters, and bathrooms) were made to the Emerson and Perkins houses in York, the Hamilton house in South Berwick (since removed; see figs. 2.7, 2.7a), the Langdon mansion in Portsmouth, and the "Jaffrey"-Albee-Niles house formerly on Wild Rose Lane in New Castle (cat. 13). Hamilton house also had sun rooms and sleeping porches, Elizabeth Perkins added a well-ventilated bedroom over her shaded porch, and the Coolidges added a new service wing, a guest suite with modern baths, and a swimming pool to the Wentworth mansion. Alterations also occurred to the plan and finish of the old interiors as small rooms were combined to create larger, more convenient spaces. For example, Elizabeth Tyson Vaughan removed a side hallway at Hamilton house to permit direct access to the gardens from the enlarged dining room.

The newness of these changes was often masked by the use of old woodwork. To Mary Northend, like C. Alice

Fig. 2.6. Hall, Sarah Orne Jewett house, South Berwick, Maine, built 1774. Photograph by Elise Tyson Vaughan, ca. 1890. Courtesy, Society for the Preservation of New England Antiquities.

Baker before her (cat. 40), this was a form of preservation. "In these old houses . . . that are past complete restoration, the architect of today finds choice old woodwork . . . Often some of these details are introduced into another remodeled farmhouse to replace parts too far gone to be used."[27] As old beams, paneling, and other fragments were incorporated into new summer homes (cat. 15), so Elizabeth Perkins reused old woodwork for her 1920 bedroom addition. In Portsmouth, Barrett Wendell preserved cornice moldings (reused as a parlor dado) from the Samuel Haven house, destroyed in 1900 to create Haven Park. Mrs. Wendell created a new summer sitting room with an open ceiling of rough-hewn beams, and a screened porch overlooking a garden entered through a reused colonial doorway (fig. 2.8).

Harriet Richardson captured the impact of modern technologies, new functional demands, and arts and crafts ideas of appropriate interior decoration on the "vigorously renewed" Bray house in Kittery Point for *House Beautiful* in 1929 (fig. 2.9; see also fig. 1.14). Purchased by the Pepperrell Family Association's realty company in 1910 with hopes of restoring the dilapidated home, the house, because of insufficient funds, was resold to Boston lithographer and artist Raymond Moreau Crosby and his wife. In 1916, the

Fig. 2.7. Hamilton house, South Berwick, Maine, built ca. 1787. Photograph by Elise Tyson Vaughan during renovation, ca. 1900. Courtesy, Society for the Preservation of New England Antiquities.

Crosbys completely renovated the house, adding a new one-story ell with guest room and bath, part of an enlarged modern kitchen, and a screened porch or "open sitting room":

Fig. 2.7a. Hamilton house. Photograph by Elise Tyson Vaughan, May 30, 1901. Courtesy, Society for the Preservation of New England Antiquities.

Fig. 2.8. Sitting room in the barn, Jacob Wendell house, Portsmouth, New Hampshire. Photograph by Douglas Armsden, ca. 1940. Courtesy, Portsmouth Athenaeum.

Sound from sill to rafter and modern through its electric kitchen, constant supply of hot and cold water, its bath, and open-air living-room, the structure has become an example to all ancient houses as to how they, too, may harmonize under one roof the regard for the old and the demands for home comfort required by the courageous pioneer and the leisure-loving summer people of today.

For this writer, "new life enters an old house" through the water pipe and electric wire which feed the modernized kitchen. "It is in this active region that the influence of woman has overshadowed the architect" and arranged the room "for maximum ease in kitchen work for the single worker." The former attic "lined with beaver board, lighted, and divided into sewing and trunk rooms" conveys the same modern message. The old kitchen was "now raised to the dignity of dining-room," the colonial staircase preserved with its "carved" spindles of three different turnings, but "it is in the white-paneled drawing-room that the gracious character of the house is felt." Here the owner,"an artist, has painted a series of frescoes depicting Italian scenes."[28] Murals of classical or Mediterranean scenes, the artistic remodeler's answer to scenic wallpapers preserved in several Portsmouth houses, were also added to Arthur Hill's old Sheafe farm and to the walls of the Hamilton

house (cat. 17). Such murals expressed the artistic sensibilities of the owners, and made visual the connections that were perceived between the classical world and its revivals in America during the early years of both the nineteenth and twentieth centuries.

The publications of Hooper and Northend, among others, documented and disseminated an approach to renovation that sacrificed authenticity to convenience. In contrast, the writings of architect Joseph Everett Chandler (1864–1945) promoted a more historically accurate attitude toward historic houses and criticized many of the measures featured in Hooper's and Northend's books. Chandler, whose *Colonial House* appeared in 1916, not only was one of those Boston architects who could "display before you his drawings of concrete examples" of remodeled colonial houses, but he also was responsible for some of the most important restorations of the previous decade. A native of Plymouth, Massachusetts, Chandler worked in McKim, Mead and White's Boston office while attending the Massachusetts Institute of Technology, where he earned his architectural degree in 1889. After a brief stint as a draftsman with the firm of Rotch and Tilden, he established his own office in 1892 and published his first book, a folio of photographs of *The Colonial Houses of Maryland, Pennsylvania and Virginia*. His earliest known commissions were around Plymouth, where in 1898 he converted the 1754

Winthrop house into a summer home for a Chicago client. By 1906, however, Chandler began to specialize as the architect for some of the most important early restorations in Massachusetts; his museum restoration work continued into the 1920s with projects such as the removal of architect William Ralph Emerson's porch from the John Paul Jones house (cat. 57) in Portsmouth.[29]

Chandler's practice emphasized remodeling projects, but with a novel attitude toward the relationship between history and design. He was convinced that "when it comes to alterations and additions to existing Colonial houses . . . it is all the more important that things that were not done and features that were not used at the time the structure was built should not be embodied in the new dress." He railed against much of the so-called Georgian work that, since the 1880s, "bristled with features with the sad inclination to be unstudied, badly proportioned, and generally uncomfortable in disposition." He thought the "Palladian" window was "used in excess and in places where it rarely looks the least at home," and he considered the pergola "a recent and apparently contagious disease" to be "assiduously avoided." He expected colonial architecture to be quiet and dignified. Inside, for example, the use of gold, "as in the elaborately gilded details of that modernly decorated once-beautiful octagonal room of the Rockingham Mansion [sic] in Portsmouth—now embodied in a hotel— consorts but ill with the purity of the style, which is best when it is simple" (cat. 2). While an owner had a right to do as he or she wished to a building, "as a Colonial house, it easily lapses, and one more authentic and worthy example may be lost" to inappropriate renovation.[30] Indeed, extensive loss of original architectural elements during such renovations led William Sumner Appleton in 1910 to found the Society for the Preservation of New England Antiquities as a regional organization devoted to preserving key buildings intact, documenting those about to be lost, and advising the owners on those about to be restored or altered.

After World War I, as interest in the use of colonial houses for private residences increased, it soon became clear that many good old buildings were not located in the best locations. This was apparently true for the eighteenth-century Moulton farmhouse which originally stood on Scituate Road in York and which was moved to York Harbor to become the core of "Four Acres" (fig. 2.10). The early building was nearly lost in new "colonial" additions after being moved to the site of the former Albraca Hotel in Norwood Farms about 1926.

During the two decades following the war and especially after the restoration of Williamsburg began in 1926, the interiors of many Piscataqua houses that had long remained in family ownership took on a new, more "colonial" appearance. Some were restored to an historic "period" because they were preserved as historical or literary memorials (see Chapter 6). The evolutions of others were edited to rid them of Victorian decor and furniture, replaced by "historic" paint colors and "colonial" wall-

Fig. 2.9. John Bray house, Kittery Point, Maine. From House Beautiful (1929). Courtesy, University of New Hampshire.

papers. By the 1930s John Mead Howells's room portraits in *The Architectural Heritage of the Piscataqua* (1937) no longer show the eclectic mixture seen in nineteenth-century photographs. Rather, he portrays restored "period rooms" of local historic house museums and private homes whose formal antique furniture arrangement, light-painted woodwork, and reproduction wallpapers share a stylistic interpretation of the colonial common to the 1930s. The museum room style as popularized in decorating books and magazines helped new owners transform the Langley Boardman house (figs. 2.11a, 2.11b), for example, authenticating their understanding of a genteel colonial past.

As the old homes of the Piscataqua region were restored as period settings for antique collections consistent with new attitudes about stylistic "correctness," they became revised documents of the past. While much of their eighteenth- and early nineteenth-century architecture remains, the murals, wallpapers, and other interior redecoration of the colonial revival era presented later museum and private owners difficult choices of retention or removal. As documents of social and artistic history, their primary evidence is

Fig. 2.10. Four Acres, York, Maine, moved to York Harbor ca. 1926. Photograph, 1930. Old York Historical Society.

Fig. 2.11a. Langley Boardman house, Portsmouth, New Hampshire, built 1800. Photograph, ca. 1898. Courtesy, Society for the Preservation of New England Antiquities.

no longer that of preindustrial life but of the introduction of modern mechanical systems and the variety of decorative treatments that emerged over more than a half century of restoration and remodeling. Paint and wallpaper, ephemeral in nature and often of poorer quality than earlier materials, were usually the first to go. Sun rooms and sleeping porches, as well as the labor-intensive gardens and garden architecture of this period, have been removed from many properties. Bathrooms, kitchens, and other elements of service wings have been upgraded and remodeled. Although a battery of scientific techniques now makes it possible for museums to recover and recreate more accurately the lost physical attributes of eighteenth- and nineteenth-century buildings, the fragile and outmoded products of earlier restorers and re-modelers are often lost to modern reproductions in our continuing desire to preserve old homes as private residences.

Only in those few large summer homes bequeathed by house-proud owners to charitable museum institutions can the collections, interior decor, architecture, and colonial revival belief in the "spirit of the old" be retained or recovered. Because so many individuals in the Piscataqua region

participated so early and so fully in this phenomenon, there are few better places to experience the many complex ways Americans a century ago tried to invent a more physically comfortable and socially satisfying past by preserving, re-modeling, or restoring the buildings of an earlier era.

1 R. Clipston Sturgis, "Architecture of Portsmouth," *The Portsmouth Book* (Boston: George H. Ellis, [1899]), 5–8. William A. Ashe, manuscript memorandum book, PA, 42-45.

2 Richard Candee, "The Appearance of Enterprise and Improvement: Architecture and the Colonial Elite of Southern Maine," in *Agreeable Situations: Society, Commerce, and Art in Southern Maine, 1780–1830*, ed. Laura Fecych Sprague (Kennebunk, Me.: The Brick Store Museum, 1987), 73–74.

3 A.J. Downing, *The Horticulturist* 1 (July 1846): 14–15, figs. 2, 3.

4 "Local," *Portsmouth Chronicle*, June 18, 1859, 3.

5 William Tucker, manuscript bill, elevation and balcony section, 1848, PA Archives; "Market Square," *Portsmouth Chronicle*, Aug. 29, 1857, 2; see James L. Garvin, *Historic Portsmouth: Early Photographs from the Collection of Strawbery Banke, Inc.* (Somersworth, N.H.: New Hampshire Publishing Co., 1974), 20, 59.

6 For the beginnings of the English Queen Anne style and its American

Fig. 2.11b. Langley Boardman house. Photograph by Douglas Armsden, 1950. Courtesy, Portsmouth Athenaeum.

counterpart, see Mark Girouard, *Sweetness and Light: The Queen Anne Movement 1860–1900* (Oxford: Clarendon Press, 1977; reprint, New Haven, Conn.: Yale University Press, 1984); James D. Kornwolf, "American Architecture and the Aesthetic Movement," in Doreen Bolger Burke et al., *In Pursuit of Beauty: Americans and the Aesthetic Movement* (New York: Rizzoli International Publications in association with the Metropolitan Museum of Art, 1986), 342–83.

7 [Robert S. Peabody], "Georgian Houses of New England," *American Architect and Building News* 2, no. 45 (Oct. 28, 1877): 338. His list may have been influenced by the sketches of Arthur Little, then a young architect in his office with whom he may have sketched colonial buildings during the summer of 1877.

8 George C. Mason, *The Old House Altered* (New York: G.P. Putnam's Sons, 1878). This book was purchased by the PA soon after its publication.

9 William M. Woollett, *Old Homes Made New: Collection of Plans, Exterior and Interior Views, Illustrating the Alteration and Remodeling of Several Suburban Residences* (New York: Bicknell & Comstock, 1879), 1, 5–7.

10 Clarence Cook, *The House Beautiful: Essays on Beds and Tables and Candlesticks* (New York: Scribner Armstrong & Co., 1878), 189–90, illustrates the Robinson-Smith house fireplace. McKim also published a photograph of his renovation and fireplace in the *New York Sketch Book* 2 (Oct. 1875): pl. 37; see Leland M. Roth, *McKim, Mead & White, Architects* (New York: Harper & Row, 1983): 44–45, 377n.

11 For another example of the impact of English interest in restoration on a New England architect, see Margaret H. Floyd, "Measured Drawings of the Hancock House by John Hubbard Sturgis: A Legacy to the Colonial Revival," in *Architecture in Colonial Massachusetts,* ed. Abbott Lowell Cummings (Boston: Colonial Society of Massachusetts, 1979), 87–111. Sturgis, who had trained in England and had a demonstrable interest in historic elements, might be a candidate for architect of Sparhawk Hall's renovations had he not returned to England from 1868 to 1870.

12 *Portsmouth Journal,* June 6 and 13, 1874, 2; "Around Home," *Portsmouth Journal,* Oct. 26, 1872.

13 Samuel Adams Drake, *Nooks and Corners of the New England Coast* (New York: Harper & Brothers, 1875), 202–3; Charles W. Brewster, *Rambles About Portsmouth,* first series (Portsmouth, N.H.: By the author, 1859); broadside, New Hampshire Historical Society, Concord.

14 "New Houses," *Portsmouth Journal,* Nov. 15, 1862, 2; see James M. Corner and E.E. Soderholtz, *Examples of Domestic Colonial Architecture in New England* (Boston: Boston Architectural Club, 1891), 2, pls. 19–23; see also photographs of Portsmouth homes in Newton W. Ellwell, *Colonial Furniture and Interiors* (Boston: Geo. H. Polley & Co., 1896) and various interiors by the Davis Brothers, photographers of Portsmouth, 1870s–1900.

15 "The Chimney Corner," *Old York Transcript,* June 29, 1899, 2.

16 "Rambling Recollections of John L. Emerson . . ." (typescript, 1938), 1; courtesy of Mr. and Mrs. S. Thompson Viele of York.

17 I thank Mr. and Mrs. Viele for Emerson genealogical data and am indebted to them for providing the following citations on the moving and remodeling of their home from the *Old York Transcript:* Sept. 28, Nov. 16 and 30, 1899; Feb. 8, Mar. 1 and 8, 1900. Watson's association with the Blaisdell firm first appeared in the July 13, 1899, *Old York Transcript.* In leaving Blaisdell to establish his own practice two years later, Watson

claimed design credit for not only the renovation of the Emerson house, but Blaisdell-built York summer residences for George L. Cheney of N.Y., H.B. Dominic of N.Y., and M.W.R. Mercer; private stables for J.D. Vermeule and Mr. Emerson, the Roaring Rock Inn and the clubhouse of the York Country Club; as well as plans for Miss F. Cocharan at York Cliffs, a seashore house for Miss Thaxter at New Castle, two at "Biddeford Pool for Miss Marjorie Brown and Mrs. Harper of New York." Watson also did a 1901 cottage for the Emersons on Long Sands; see *Old York Transcript*, Apr. 4 and 11, 1901. A Watson design for "A Shingled House at Portsmouth, N.H.," located at 622 Middle Street and employing a variety of colonial elements, was published in *Carpentry and Building* 29, no. 11 (Nov. 1907): 343–45. At that date Watson was listed as practicing at Bar Harbor, Me.

18 *New Hampshire Farms for Summer Homes*, 11th ed. (Concord: State Board of Agriculture, 1913); the 1902–16 series, edited by N.J. Batchelder, was preceded in 1891 by Commissioner of Agriculture and Immigration, N.J. Batchelder, comp., *Secure a Home in New Hampshire, Where Health, Comfort, and Prosperity Abound* (Manchester, N.H.: J.B. Clark, public printer, 1891).

19 Kate Sanborn, *Adopting an Abandoned Farm* (New York: D. Appleton & Co., 1891), 1–10, 18, 129–30.

20 Sanborn, *Adopting an Abandoned Farm*, 168; Kate Sanborn, *Abandoning an Adopted Farm* (New York: D. Appleton & Co., 1894); Sanborn later became interested in scenic wallpapers and published both a 1902 article in *House Beautiful* and *Old Time Wall Papers* (New York: Literary Collector Press, 1905) on the subject.

21 "Around Home," *Portsmouth Journal*, Aug. 12, 1899, 5; "The Governor Woodbury Mansion," *Portsmouth Journal*, Aug. 19, 1899, 7; Levi Woodbury's son, Charles Levi Woodbury of Washington, D.C., had bought the Woodbury family farm in Salem, N.H., in 1896 as a summer place; see *New Hampshire Farms for Summer Homes* (Concord, N.H.: State Board of Agriculture, 1902), 52–54. Two York Harbor examples of this phenomenon are the Caswell cottage (built ca. 1780, remodeled ca. 1890) and the Nancy Philbrick cottage (built 1837, remodeled 1893).

22 John Stilgoe, *Metropolitan Corridor* (New Haven, Conn.: Yale University Press, 1983), 315–33; William Butler, "Another City upon a Hill: Litchfield, Connecticut, and the Colonial Revival," in Axelrod, *Colonial Revival*, 15–51; Huntington, *Under a Colonial Roof-Tree* (Syracuse, N.Y.: Wolcott & West, 1892).

23 Charles Edward Hooper, *The Country House* (Garden City, N.Y.: Doubleday Page & Co., 1904); *Reclaiming the Old House* (New York: McBride, Nast & Co., 1913); "Nuttinghame Again Remodeled," with photographs by Wallace Nutting, *Country Life in America* 30, no. 6 (Oct. 1916): 31–33; "The Reclamation of the Old Colonial Farmhouse," *Country Life in America* 16, no. 6 (Oct. 1909): 617–20.

24 Mary H. Northend, *Remodeled Farmhouses* (Boston: Little Brown & Co., 1915), 196, *passim*. For the use of data from her unpublished paper (Boston University, 1989) on Mary Northend I must thank Maureen Phillips; see also Charles A. Higgins, "Mary Harrod Northend," *Massachusetts Magazine* (Jan. 1915): 23–26; "Hampered by Illness, Work Has Made Her Well," *Boston Sunday Herald*, Aug. 25, 1912; Karal Ann Marling, *George Washington Slept Here* (Cambridge and London: Harvard University Press, 1988), 166–71 (although she errs over the size of Northend's collection of photographs). Northend's other titles included *Colonial Homes and Their Furnishings* (1912), *Historic Homes of New England* (1914), *The Art of Home Decoration* (1921), and *We Visit Old Inns* (1925).

25 Northend, *Remodeled Farmhouses*, 121.

26 Joseph Stowe Seabury, *New Homes Under Old Roofs* (New York: Frederick A. Stokes, 1916), 11–13.

27 Northend, *Remodeled Farmhouses*, 4. An example of this practice is the "restoration" by the New Hampshire Colonial Dames of their headquarters in Exeter which incorporated decorative details from the John Haven house.

28 Harriet T. Richardson, "The John Bray House in Kittery, Maine," *House Beautiful* 65 (May 1929): 704–12.

29 I am indebted to Mark Landry's unpublished study (Boston University, 1989) of Chandler, from which much of this sketch is drawn. Seabury, *New Homes*, 11.

30 Joseph Everett Chandler, *The Colonial House* (1916; rev. ed., New York: Robert McBride & Co., 1924), 1, 4, 9, 176–77, 186–89.

8

PUBLICATIONS OF PISCATAQUA COLONIAL ARCHITECTURE
1877–1937

The emergence of the American architect as historian followed the establishment of architectural schools at the Massachusetts Institute of Technology (1865) and Columbia University (1881), where the curriculum placed special emphasis on both drawing and historical sources. This focus created a market for books in both professional training and architectural practice. Until the 1890s Boston was the country's leading publishing center, and interest in New England's colonial buildings benefited from the presence of two major architectural book and magazine publishers, James R. Osgood and George H. Polley. A growing market and changes in publishing technology combined to encourage the publication of some 1,100 architectural books written by American architect-historians between 1870 and 1940.[1]

Many of these publications included drawings and photographs of historic buildings along the Piscataqua as sources for modern designs. Architects first began to explore the Piscataqua for outstanding colonial homes soon after the centennial. In the summer of 1877 Arthur Little and his employer, the eminent Boston architect Robert Swain Peabody, sketched several eighteenth-century homes in the area to inspire their modern domestic designs. The first major architectural publication to emerge from these studies was Little's *Early New England Interiors* (1878), "the result of a Summer's work . . . to preserve a style fast disappearing . . . [owing to] a national love of new things in preference to old" (cat. 8).[2]

Many private homes that Little recorded along the Piscataqua, as in the old towns of Boston's North Shore, were generally unknown to either the tourist or the professional. For example, he did not include the Sir William Pepperrell house at Kittery Point, the only local building treated in Martha J. Lamb's *The Homes of America* (1879) inspired by the literary efforts of Longfellow, Hawthorne, and antebellum antiquarians.[3] Rather, Little's book helped establish a canon of architecturally important colonial buildings: the recently "restored" Sparhawk house (cat. 9), as well as elaborate Portsmouth homes of the Jaffrey, Lord, Ladd, Langdon, and Wentworth families. And while he apparently did not gain access to the Governor Benning Wentworth mansion, both he and Peabody sketched its complex exterior composition and established it as an influential icon of the early colonial revival.

The next folio to include a few details of Portsmouth buildings was *Old Colonial Architecture and Furniture* (1887) by Frank E. Wallis, a Maine-born architect who had just left the Peabody and Stearns office in Boston where he was dubbed "Colonial Wallis." He also illustrated a few Portsmouth building details in *American Architecture,*

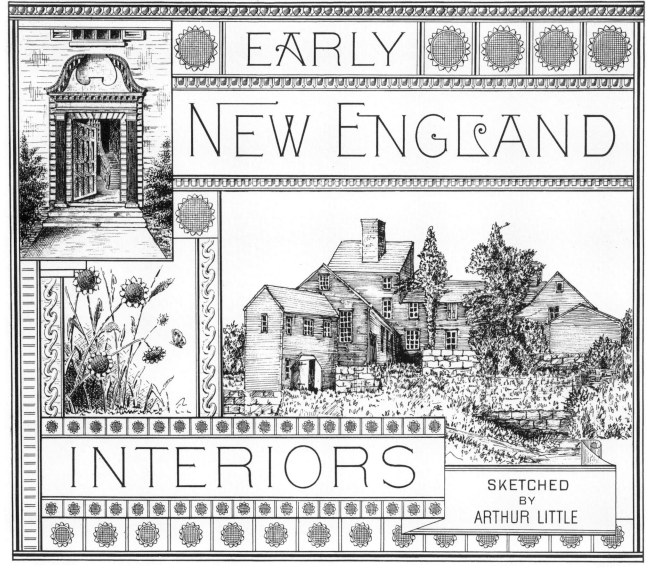

Cat. 8. Arthur Little, cover illustration from *Early New England Interiors: Sketches in Salem, Marblehead, Portsmouth, and Kittery (1878).*
Courtesy, Society for the Preservation of New England Antiquities.

Decoration, and Furniture (1896). Many of Wallis's drawings were unscaled perspective sketches much like Little's earlier work, but adorned with figures in colonial costume. Others were precise elevations or details measured and drawn to scale.[4] The former reflects the first generation of architects who sought picturesque forms or evocative details for their new summer houses; the latter appealed to architects of new "colonial" homes for a growing suburban clientele.

Photography also offered a new means of building documentation, providing architects with more exact models than the freehand sketches of a decade earlier. The first book composed entirely of architectural photographs was Corner and Soderholtz's *Examples of Domestic Colonial Architecture in New England* (1891) published by the Boston Architectural Club and illustrating the Pepperrell house, as well as Portsmouth's Warner, Ladd, and Langdon man-

sions. Architectural photography quickly appeared in many other forms of publication, from postcards and souvenir booklets to women's magazines and the professional architectural press during the 1890s. It often blurred distinctions between popular and technical books. For example, *The Portsmouth Book* (1899) includes an essay on the city's historic architecture written by Boston architect R. Clipston Sturgis, who summered at Little Harbor; other chapters, illustrated with photographs of historic buildings, are literary biographies of the city's churches, taverns, and other social institutions.

Increasing interest in accurate proportion and detailing among architects at the turn of the century can be seen also in the evolution of *The Georgian Period,* twelve folios of measured drawings and photographs edited by William Rotch Ware and published between 1898 and 1902. The first volumes present material previously printed in Ware's

Cat. 8a. Parlor, Moffatt-Ladd house, Portsmouth, New Hampshire, built 1764. Photograph, ca. 1886. Courtesy, Portsmouth Athenaeum.

magazine, *The American Architect and Building News,* with illustrations redrawn in the pictorial style of Frank Wallis. Later volumes published the work of M.I.T. architectural summer school students and include several Portsmouth buildings carefully measured and drawn in elevation, section, or in details such as molding profiles. Buildings of the Piscataqua's colonial and early national elite continued to be measured, drawn, and published as sources of colonial revival design over the next thirty years, including Lois Lily Howe and Constance Fuller's *Details from Old New England Houses* (1913), the Architects' Emergency Committee's *Great Georgian Houses of America* (1933), and the Metropolitan Museum of Art's *Measured Drawings of Woodwork Displayed in the American Wing* (1935).

After twenty years of books and journalism about America's architectural past, several architects offered the first general surveys—many of which drew upon the Piscataqua canon to illustrate the stylistic evolution of architecture in the nation or region. Both Joy Wheeler Dow's *American Renaissance* (1904) and Harold Donaldson Eberlein's *Architecture of Colonial America* (1915) illustrated the Warner house; Aymar Embury used Portsmouth's St. John's Church to illustrate his *Early American Churches* (1914). Boston architect, remodeler, and restorer Joseph Everett Chandler showed a half-dozen Portsmouth homes in *The Colonial House* (1916), one of a series of books on domestic styles for those wanting to build or design a modern colonial home. The best synthesis of America's stylistic development, however, was Fiske Kimball's *Domestic Architecture of the American Colonies and of the Early Republic* (1922), which helped place the region's finest examples into a national historical perspective.

The White Pine Series, short monographs on thematic aspects of colonial architecture, began in 1915. Combining drawings and photographs like the architectural magazines, the series was initially subsidized by the lumber industry to promote the use of white pine among architects designing new colonial houses. Among the early titles, Frank C. Brown illustrated "Three-story Colonial Houses of New England" (1917) with federal examples from Portsmouth, C. Howard Walker devoted his 1918 monograph to "Some Houses Along the Southern Coast of Maine," while Aymar Embury used several Portsmouth houses in his 1921–22 studies of doorways and cornices.

Traveling fellowships established in the earliest architectural schools had encouraged talented students to continue their education through European travel. When World War I prevented students from measuring monuments in Europe, some young architects were encouraged to explore colonial New England. In fact, the most extensive study of the colonial and federal buildings of the Piscataqua for almost two decades was the survey of Maine architecture made by John Hutchinson Porter, winner of the 1918 *Architectural Review* traveling scholarship. Measured drawings, photographs, and descriptive text were printed in the sponsoring journal from 1918 to 1922 as one of the first comprehensive records of Maine's buildings. During the

Cat. 8b. Parlor, Moffatt-Ladd house. Photograph, ca. 1915. Courtesy, The National Society of The Colonial Dames of America in the State of New Hampshire.

Great Depression the Works Progress Administration developed a similar program for unemployed architects, later continued as the Historic American Buildings Survey. Eight separate essays using many of the W.P.A. drawings and photographs of Piscataqua sources were written for *The Monograph Series* (continuing the former White Pine Series) and published in *Pencil Points,* a magazine for artists and draftsmen.

A wide range of books containing architectural photography was directed toward professional and popular audiences during the 1920s and 1930s. Leigh French, Jr., organized *Colonial Interiors* (1923) around ornamental features of interest to architects and decorators. John Mead Howells published selected historic photographs of *Lost Examples of Colonial Architecture* (1931), recording images of old buildings destroyed or badly altered. But the most successful photographer of New England's image was Samuel Chamberlain, an artist whose photography of New England's traditional architecture won a wide popular audience.

Chamberlain captured enduring images of New England's historic and vernacular landscapes and buildings. Published in a vast array of nearly wordless picture books large and small, beginning with *A Small House in the Sun* (1936), the artist helped redefine New England's regional character to a new generation. In *Beyond New England Thresholds* and *Open House in New England* (both

1937), as well as in *New England Doorways* (1939), he took advantage of the region's many museums, including those along the Piscataqua, to illustrate both colonial architectural forms and period-room settings of broad interest to tourists, collectors, designers, and homeowners alike. From these broad strokes Chamberlain moved to local studies, including *Portsmouth, N.H.: A Camera Impression* (1940) which combines images of the landscape, streetscape, building portraits, and interior details to demonstrate the city's "Colonial atmosphere," and *The Coast of Maine* (1941) which follows the jagged coast down east from the buildings and shoreline of Kittery Point and York.

The culminating historical work about Portsmouth and its architectural hinterland was that of John Mead Howells. The son of author William Dean Howells, the New York architect was also drawn to the city's "stately mansions which stand under the arching elms, with their gardens sloping, or dropping by easy terraces."[5] *The Architectural Heritage of the Piscataqua* (1937) captured not only the facades, interiors, and landscapes of the area's major architectural monuments but, through exterior photographs, its "lesser" colonial and federal homes. It is useful to compare the interior photographs of homes still occupied by old families, as well as those restored for country estates or historic house museums, in *The Architectural Heritage of the Piscataqua* with the same rooms in older architectural publications (cats. 8a,

Cat. 9. "Sparhawk House, Kittery Point, Maine." Photograph by Luther Dame, 1902. Old York Historical Society.

8b). Howells's visual record of the 1930s shows that most homeowners had adopted colonial revival ideas of interior decoration. Their rooms had become as much the product as the source of the colonial revival.

RMC

1 See Keith N. Morgan and Richard Cheek, "History in the Service of Design: American Architect-Historians, 1870–1940," and William B. Rhoads, "The Discovery of America's Architectural Past, 1874–1914," in *The Architectural Historian in America,* ed. Elisabeth Blair MacDougal (Washington, D.C.: National Gallery of Art, 1990), 23–39, 61–75.

2 William B. Rhoads, *The Colonial Revival* (New York: Garland Publishing, 1977), 1:76–81; Georgian [pseudonym for R.S. Peabody], "Georgian Houses of New England," *American Architect and Building News* 2 (Oct. 20, 1877): 338–39; Arthur Little, *Early New England Interiors* (Boston: A. Williams and Co., 1878), preface. Walter Knight Sturgis, "Arthur Little and the Colonial Revival," *Journal of the Society of Architectural Historians* 32, no. 2 (May 1973): 147–62; for Peabody, see Wheaton Holden, "The Peabody Touch: Peabody and Stearns of Boston, 1870–1917" in the same issue, 114–31.

3 For a more complete analysis of the literary genre of the house biography, see Jan Cohn, *The Palace or the Poorhouse: The American House as a Cultural Symbol* (East Lansing: Michigan State University Press, 1979), 193–212.

4 The only study of Wallis is Kevin D. Murphy, "'A Stroll Thro' the Past': Three Architects of the Colonial Revival" (M.A. thesis, Boston University, 1985).

5 W.D. Howells, "From New York into New England," *Life and Literature: Studies* (New York and London: Harper & Brothers, 1902), 235. Murphy, "'A Stroll Thro' the Past.'"

 9

SPARHAWK HOUSE
Kittery Point, Maine, ca. 1742
Restored, 1867–88; demolished, 1953
(see plate 2)

Sparhawk house (cat. 9) was a Georgian mansion built by Sir William Pepperrell for his daughter about the time of her marriage to Nathaniel Sparhawk in 1742. Remodeled between 1867 and 1868 for Mr. and Mrs. Walter Brown of Toronto, it may have been the first colonial private home in America to be consciously "restored." Its new owners sought not only to preserve its remaining eighteenth-century details but also to embellish it with additions in its own historic style. This renovation predates the major repair work at George Washington's Mount Vernon and architect William R. Emerson's 1869 restoration of the Old Ship Meetinghouse in Hingham, Massachusetts, generally considered the first instances of architectural restoration in America.[1]

The Sparhawk family held the farm until 1817, after which time it passed though several hands before being sold to the Penhallows of Portsmouth in 1853. Agents for Pearce Penhallow offered the ten-acre property for sale or lease in

1866, describing the house as containing thirteen "splendid rooms with spacious [stair] hall." Noting its association with the daughter of Sir William Pepperrell, it was said to be "in very good condition, and worth renewal, according to the taste and inclination of the owner." The advertisement was seen by Walter R. Brown, Esq., of Toronto and "he purchased it by telegraph," sight unseen, "influenced in no small degree by the historical association of the mansion" with the baronet who won Canada for England. The deed was signed in September 1866.[2]

Born in England about 1826, Brown was recorded in an 1861 Canadian census as a gentleman and a member of the Church of England; his English-born wife, Jane Selina Akril Brown, was a year older and a Wesleyan Methodist. During the late 1850s Brown appeared in Toronto as the publisher of its city directory, a real estate auctioneer, and money broker. He built a cottage called "Idlewold," the second house in a new middle-class suburb, Rose Park (later Rosedale), outside Toronto. From 1862 to 1868 he was described as a banker, apparently parlaying his assets into a partnership with a later publisher of city directories to form Brown's Bank, a small unchartered private bank on Toronto's King Street. The Browns remained in Toronto until 1868 when they moved to Kittery Point. He bought a yacht in September 1868 and transferred ownership of the house to his wife in January 1869. In 1871 the Browns were recorded as residing in Brooklyn, New York, suggesting that the Sparhawk house may have initially functioned as a country place.[3]

When Arthur Little visited the mansion in the summer of 1877, he sketched the unusual stairhall with "a small room under the rear staircase. The latter winds up from the kitchen with numerous turns, and is seen through the landing window" (cat. 9a). Also recorded was what he (and presumably the Browns) called the "Banquet Hall," a large room that occupied the full depth of the main block east of the stairhall. In *Early New England Interiors* Little noted that this east room, completely wainscotted with fielded paneling, "was in a state of dilapidation, most of the panels being gone, but the present owner has restored it fully."[4] The restoration work was done by Charles G. Bellamy and his son, John Haley Bellamy, the noted ship carver of Kittery Point. Also attributed to the younger Bellamy is a carved pineapple (said to be from the Pepperrell coat of arms) installed on the newel post of the front staircase before 1895 and a separate carving of a hawk sitting on a spar.[5]

The major interior features of the Sparhawk house were removed in 1953. At this time, an inscription written on the back of the large overmantel in this east room was discovered. It read: "This panel removed by Robert Stafford. Replaced by Charles G. Bellamy, January 27, 1868." Other pencil notations indicated that Walter R. Brown, the new owner, had directed the work. Panels on the west wall showed evidence of having formerly been removed and replaced by lath and plaster. Moreover, one of the two shell-headed corner cupboards flanking the fireplace was found

to have its shell hand-carved from a single block (and thus attributable to the younger Bellamy), rather than being fashioned with the eighteenth-century methods used on the front cupboard shell.[6]

Writing in 1893, Moses A. Safford noted that the east room "had been for many years divided into several smaller ones" and that Brown restored it "to its original size and finish." It is believed that materials from the nearby 1730 meetinghouse, removed by the senior Bellamy in 1838, may have been reused in the remodeling of the Sparhawk east room. The physical evidence suggests that the Bellamys and the Browns may have actually reconfigured the room, opening up what might have been two original rooms with corner fireplaces and identical ornate finish—altered in later years—into a single space thirty-four-feet deep.[7] The resulting hall provided the Browns, in good Victorian fashion, a huge public room to impress their guests.

Until a 1934 fire seriously damaged the interior, an eighteenth-century dome-and-pillar wallpaper remained in the stairhall. It was described variously as "a peculiar allegorical paper in black and white," an "old English landscape design," and "specially made, with the fair lady and her happy lover as the principal figures." Modern scholars can now date this English architectural paper to sometime after 1759; perhaps it was installed when the Lady Pepperrell house was built nearby.[8] This redating of the paper to after Sir William's death in 1759 may suggest the date of the stop-fluted pilasters which flanked the east-room fireplace.

Other modifications also helped transform the house into a fine country estate for the English couple drawn to its aristocratic associations. The old one-story kitchen ell was replaced by a larger one with gables angled to form a Greek revival temple projecting over columned porches on each side. A new and oversized cupola was built in the center of the large gambrel roof of the main block; window pediments identical to the originals above first-floor windows on the facade were added to those on the side walls. Overall, the exterior restoration of Sparhawk house was less drastic and more guided by historical precedent than might be expected for this era.

The Browns led a private and exclusive life, unsuccessfully trying to teach the locals proper respect for gentry. After the death of an adopted daughter and of her husband, Mrs. Brown became insane and from 1890 until her own death in 1899 she lived with a guardian. During these nine years the house was well maintained and occasionally illustrated in print. Photographs published under the name "Pepperill House" appear in the first book of American architectural photographs (1891). In 1895 the stair and fireplace wall were measured and drawn by architect Frank C. Adams, whose exterior sketches and detailed drawings appeared in the *Inland Architect* the next year; a measured plan and elevation was first prepared in 1918 by Frederic Hutchinson Porter.[9]

In 1902 the property was sold to Horace Mitchell of

Cat. 9a. Arthur Little, stairhall, Sparhawk Hall. From Early New England Interiors: Sketches in Salem, Marblehead, Portsmouth, and Kittery (1878). Courtesy, Society for the Preservation of New England Antiquities.

Kittery, the proprietor of the Pocahontas and Champernowne hotels as well as a Sparhawk descendent. Given "the never ending summer procession of people who . . . ask to see the house" he told Virginia Robie, "an historic house is public property." A local political figure, Mitchell treated his home as a special attraction. President Taft and several other prominent government dignitaries, for example, visited Sparhawk in 1912. Despite Safford's earlier statement that it contained "no furniture . . . that belonged to its original proprietors," the editor of *House Beautiful* claimed in 1904 that not only was "the wall paper the same, the furniture is unchanged."[10]

But the best colonial revival myth, perhaps relayed to this gullible visitor by the genial Mitchell, was that Sir William himself designed the grand staircase. For "it was he who drew every spindle, thus proving himself as great a master of the draughting-board as with the musket . . . It pleased Sir William when he designed it and it pleases the most critical pilgrim to day."[11] Typical of the many myths that grew up around colonial homes at the turn of the century, this story invested the house with a direct and physical association to its key historical figure.

RMC

1   Charles B. Hosmer, Jr., *Presence of the Past: A History of the Preservation Movement in the United States Before Williamsburg* (New York: G.P. Putnam's, 1965), 53; Roger G. Reed, *A Delight to All Who Know It: The Maine Summer Architecture of William R. Emerson* (Augusta, Me.: Maine Historic Preservation Commission, 1990), 12.

2   The deed was signed in Sept. 1866. Land title and newspaper clippings from a scrapbook about Sparhawk Hall in the possession of Mrs. Horace Mitchell, Jr., of Kittery Point. YCRD 99:91 (1817), 301:45 (1866); see also John E. Frost, *Colonial Village* (Kittery Point, Me.: Gundalow Club, 1948), 27–35.

3   I am grateful for the excellent biographical detective-work of Mrs. J.C. Douglas of Toronto, Canada, for tax, census, directory, and topographic citations about Walter R. Brown and his wife in Toronto; Patricia McHugh, *Toronto Architecture: A City Guide* (Toronto: McClelland & Stewart, 1986), 245–50; YCRD 314:14 (1869), 324:422–23 (1871; Jane S. Brown vs. Caldwell Ashworth, court case, PA files. It was rumored that Brown "had to leave Canada fast" for unspecified reasons; see "Bellamies Active in Life of the Sparhawk," *The Kittery Times*, Feb. 6, 1953, 3. Probate records indicate Mrs. Brown's investments were in a mining company; see Sparhawk Hall file, PA. *The Brooklyn City Directory for the Year Ending in 1871,* comp. George T. Lain (Brooklyn, N.Y.: Lain & Co., 1871).

4   Arthur Little, *Early New England Interiors* (Boston: A. Williams and Co., 1878), "Sparhawk House" staircase and banquet hall, n.p.

5   Denys Peter Myers, "The Historic Architecture of Maine," *Maine Catalog: Historic American Buildings Survey* (Augusta: Maine State Museum, 1974), 18, 176n; the pineapple carving first appears in James W. Corner and E.E. Soderholtz, *Examples of Domestic Architecture in New England* (Boston: Boston Architectural Club, 1892), pl. 2; Bellamy's hawk on spar carving first appears in the hallway in Virginia Robie, "A Colonial Pilgrimage III: Sir William Pepperell and His Staircase," *House Beautiful* 15 (Apr. 1904): 316. It is now in the PA Reading Room and illustrated in Yvonne Brault Smith, *John Haley Bellamy, Carver of Eagles* (Portsmouth, N.H.: Portsmouth Marine Society, 1982), 71.

6   "Famed Maine Mansion Sold For Dismantling," *Portsmouth Herald,* Dec. 21, 1952; "More Secrets of Sparhawk," *The Kittery Press,* Jan. 30, 1953, 1, 4; "Bellamies Active in life of Sparhawk," *The Kittery Press,* Feb. 6, 1953, 2, 3. Charles Bellamy studied civil architecture (engineering) under Jon Curtize in Boston in 1834 and was the builder of the Kittery Point bridge in 1837 before being appointed to the Ashburton Commission in 1842 to settle the Aroostook boundary war. Charles and John Bellamy lived in the Sir William Pepperrell mansion.

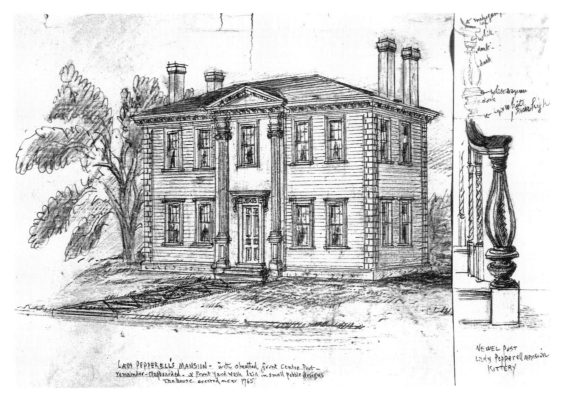

Cat. 10. William E. Barry, Lady Pepperrell's Mansion, *Kittery Point, Maine, 1760. Watercolor on paper; 12 in. x 17¹¹/₁₆ in. Courtesy, Maine Historical Society.*

The interior finish, including the Bellamy alterations, was sold to Norman Woolrich of New York and shipped to his Winthrop, Me., estate in 1953. The frame remained until 1966 when several exterior elements, including the front door and enframement with broken-scroll pediment, as well as woodwork from the front eastern chamber, were acquired by SB.

7 Moses A. Safford, "Historic Homes of Kittery," *Maine Historical Society Collections,* 2nd ser., 5 (1894): 121; Myers, *Maine Catalog,* 18. Knowledgeable observers noted in 1953 that the paneling of the front half of the large room was constructed differently than the rear; that the pilasters, chimney breastwork, and trim around the fireplace had been "put on later" as evidenced by clean bluish green paint on the underboarding; and that the shell cupboards "were made at different times." See "Many Secrets Disclosed in Sparhawk Dismantling," *The Kittery Press,* Jan. 23, 1953, 1, 4. Some confirmation of the idea of two original lower east rooms sharing a chimney in their corners can be inferred from the corner fireplaces above this room in the two upper east chambers.

8 Alice R. Parsons, insurance estimate, Dec. 31, 1934, Sparhawk Hall file, PA; clipping, "Famous Mansion at Kittery Point Destroyed by Fire," Dec. 8, 1934, Sparhawk Hall file, PA. See also the entry for Jaffrey Cottage (cat. 13) in this volume; Little, *Early New England Interiors,* "Sparhawk"; Safford, "Historic Homes," 122; Kate Sanborn, *Old Time Wall Papers: An Account of Pictorial Papers on Our Forefather's Walls* (New York: Literary Collector Press, 1905), 91–92; Richard C. Nylander et al., *Wallpaper in New England* (Boston: SPNEA, 1986), 48, 51, 54.

9 Frost, *Colonial Village,* 30; "Kittery Point Kabbelow," *York Courant,* Nov. 13, 1891, 1, and June 14, 1895, 1; Corner and Soderholtz, *Examples of Domestic Colonial Architecture,* pls. 2, 3; *Inland Architect and News Record* 27, no. 6 (July 1896): n.p.; Frederic Hutchinson Porter, "A Survey of Existing Colonial Architecture in Maine," Part III, *Architectural Review* 7 (Nov. 1918): 94–97.

10 Robie, "Colonial Pilgrimage," 315; "A Cordial Reception to Mr. Taft at the Sparhawk Mansion," *Portsmouth Times,* Oct. 23, 1912, Sparhawk Hall file, PA; Safford, "Historic Homes of Kittery," 122. An inventory of Jane S. Brown's estate confirms the absence of colonial furnishings; see Sparhawk Hall file, PA.

11 Robie, "Colonial Pilgrimage," 315–17.

10

LADY PEPPERRELL HOUSE
Kittery Point, Maine, 1760
Remodeled John Mead Howells (1868–1959), 1922

The Lady Pepperrell house is the most elaborate pre-Revolutionary Georgian-style residence in Maine. Its distinctiveness becomes particularly evident when the house is compared with the earlier Kittery home which Lady Pepperrell shared with her husband, Sir William Pepperrell. Although containing much fine Georgian woodwork, that large gambrel-roof house reflects a much simpler exterior treatment. The impressive classical facade of the Lady Pepperrell house captured the attention of architects in the colonial revival period, as is reflected in a late nineteenth-century watercolor sketch by William E. Barry (cat. 10) and a polished rendering of the 1920s by John Mead Howells.

In 1760, within a year of her husband's death, Lady Mary Pepperrell erected her refined mansion opposite the meetinghouse at Kittery Point. Her architect remains unknown. Some have speculated that the designer was Peter Harrison of Rhode Island, based on the similarity of the house to the Vassall-Craigie-Longfellow house in Cambridge, Massachusetts, which also has been attributed to Harrison. There are striking similarities between the Lady Pepperrell

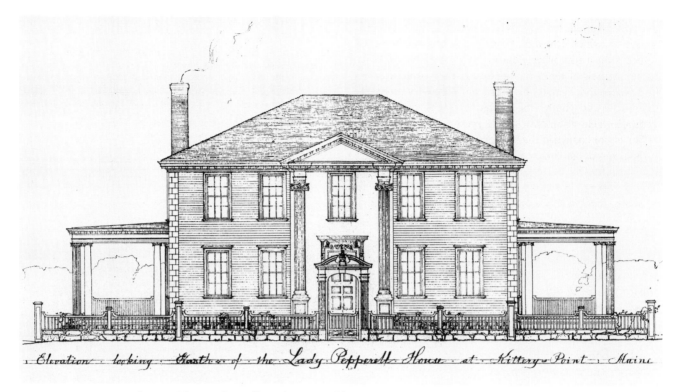

Cat. 10a. John Mead Howells, Lady Pepperrell house elevation, ca. 1923, Kittery Point, Maine.
Courtesy, Society for the Preservation of New England Antiquities.

house and the one John Vassall built a year earlier in 1759. Both houses feature a hipped roof and five-bay facade, a central pavilion with a triangular pediment, dentils and Ionic pilasters, and a doorway embellished with consoles supporting a horizontal pediment. The room arrangements, with front and rear staircases, are also similar.

Many of these features, however, were common to substantial houses of the period, making the differences equally significant. The Lady Pepperrell house has a lower pitch in its hipped roof and no balustrade or dormers. There are quoins instead of pilasters on the outside corners of the principal facade. The pavilion has flushboard siding instead of clapboards, and there are four exterior wall chimneys instead of two interior chimneys. Moreover, other differences, such as the carved twin dolphins over the doorway, can be traced to eighteenth-century English builders' guides.

Regardless of who designed the Lady Pepperrell house, it is clearly one of the finest examples of Georgian design in the Piscataqua region. As such the house has long been admired by students of American colonial architecture. These included two men who played important roles in the fate of the house, John Mead Howells and William Sumner Appleton.

The house passed through a number of owners after Lady Pepperrell's death in 1789, but only a few changes were made. By 1874 its occupant, Sally Cutts, had allowed the building to fall into disrepair. When Oliver Cutts acquired the property, he made numerous necessary repairs. It was probably at this time that the windows were replaced with

two-over-two double-hung sash, a second story was added to the ell, and the exterior received a polychromatic paint scheme. A carriage barn was also erected.[1] That was the condition of the house when purchased by William M. Wood III of Piqua, Ohio, in 1922. Mr. Wood engaged New York architect and Kittery summer resident John Mead Howells, who was "asked to undertake its rehabilitation" (cat. 10a).[2]

Howells was not an architect then generally associated with the colonial revival. Born in Cambridge, Massachusetts, he was educated at Harvard, the Massachusetts Institute of Technology, and the Ecole des Beaux-Arts in Paris. Howells had partnerships at various times with I.N. Phelps Stokes and Raymond M. Hood and also practiced on his own. Although he designed a few colonial revival buildings, such as Paine Hall at Harvard University in 1913, he was best known for office buildings such as the Chicago Tribune Tower of 1922 (with Raymond Hood).[3] Previous commissions, however, may have been less pertinent in the architect's selection than his lifelong familiarity with New England buildings and the fact that he had a summer home at Kittery Point. The house which became his retirement home was a mansard-style structure purchased in 1902 by his father, author William Dean Howells.

In 1922 John Mead Howells contacted his cousin, William Sumner Appleton, the director of the Society for the Preservation of New England Antiquities, informing him that he had been retained to renovate the Lady Pepperrell house. Appleton, who was familiar with the house, was consulted about the design for the restoration of the fence. Howells had obtained a sketch done before the Civil War which showed an arched entry to the fence capped with a pineapple. The architect inquired whether Appleton knew of any surviving examples of similar carved pineapples that could be copied in the restoration. Although never built, the design Howells prepared is recorded on elevation drawings he presented to the SPNEA.[4]

The major change to the house made by the architect was the addition of flanking porches. Howells explicitly justified this departure from the original design in comparing the Lady Pepperrell house to the Vassall-Craigie-Longfellow house. In a letter to "Cousin Bill," Howells wrote:

> I want to point out that I understand, perhaps as clearly as any possible critics, that side piazzas are not archaeologically of the moment with respect to this type of square two story Colonial house . . . [W]hile such side porches as these on the Longfellow House at Cambridge have undoubtably been added, yet I am inclined to believe that the Perez Morton House in Roxbury may have had the side piazzas in Bulfinch's original design. Anyway he discusses such piazzas in a correspondence with his friend, Copley, as being then fashionable.[5]

Thus Howells was sensitive to criticisms that his changes were not historically correct. As was common at that time, he blurred any distinction between colonial and federal-period architecture. In this sense, citing Charles Bulfinch as an authority was justified, because the porches on the Vassall-Craigie-Longfellow house were apparently added in 1793. The north porch on the Lady Pepperrell house had little practical value (there were no internal entrances), and, indeed, was later removed. Thus, its construction appears to have been largely dictated by aesthetic considerations inspired by the Vassall-Craigie-Longfellow house.

Other changes to the house were glossed over by Howells, who either did not consider them significant or open to question. The two-over-two sash were replaced with six-over-six, again following Vassall-Craigie-Longfellow. The sash in the latter, however, were probably 1793 replacements of smaller paned windows. The historical incongruity of six lights on the Lady Pepperrell house is less apparent because, unlike the Cambridge house, it retains its original casements which project well out from the plane of the walls. Other alterations include the addition of a window and a door with a classical pediment off the south porch and the remodeling of the carriage barn with federal-style arched doors and dormers.

William Sumner Appleton did not gain entry to the Lady Pepperrell house until 1935 when, under the guise of making an inquiry for a Pepperrell descendant, he contacted Virginia Hodge, then the owner. Five years later Mrs. Hodge donated the property to the SPNEA.[6]

EGS

1 *Portsmouth Journal,* June 13, 1874, 2. Richard M. Candee brought this article to my attention.

2 John Mead Howells to William Sumner Appleton, Oct. 10, 1922, Appleton Papers, SPNEA Archives.

3 *Who's Who in America 1920–21,* ed. Albert N. Marquis (Chicago, 1920), s.v. "Howells, John Mead." Jane G. Feaver, *Macmillan Encyclopedia of Architects* (New York: The Free Press, 1982), s.v. "Howells, John Mead."

4 Howells to Appleton, Oct. 10, 1922, Appleton Papers.

5 Howells to Appleton, Apr. 22, 1922, Appleton Papers.

6 Appleton to Virginia Hodge, July 8, 1835, Appleton Papers.

Cat. 11a. Childe Hassam, The Athenaeum, Portsmouth, New Hampshire, *1915. Etching; 8¼ in. x 5¾ in. Courtesy, The Historical Society of the Town of Greenwich, Connecticut.*

II

READING ROOM, PORTSMOUTH ATHENAEUM
Portsmouth, New Hampshire, 1805
Remodeled Henry B. Ball (1867–1901), 1892

Designed in 1804 as the headquarters of the New Hampshire Fire and Marine Insurance Company by architect Bradbury Johnson of Saco, Maine, the Reading Room's original interior woodwork was installed the next year by local joiner James Nutter. Since its creation, the high-ceilinged oval-ended room has been a place to gather and read newspapers, even before the building was acquired by the Proprietors of the Portsmouth Athenaeum in 1823 (cat. 11a). In 1892 the old decorative wall frescos added in 1852 were replaced by "colonial" wall colors; a new fireplace and chimneybreast became the visual centerpiece of the room, while historical artifacts reinforced a new gentility.[1]

The 1892 remodeling of the Reading Room of the Portsmouth Athenaeum is an especially well-documented example of a colonial revival redecoration for an historic public space. James Rindge Stanwood, an antiquarian and secretary for the committee supervising the remodeling, kept letters and notes on the restoration that illustrate the aesthetic choices made by the committee and their architect. Henry B. Ball, of the Boston architectural firm of Ball and Dabney (cat. 38), originally came from Portsmouth. As his late father had been a shareholder in the Athenaeum, Ball offered "his valuable services freely to the Committee" as they had hoped he might. Ball's architectural competence and stylistic bias was already known. In 1891 he had designed a new colonial revival house on Middle Street for Athenaeum proprietor Wallace Hackett, and the firm would later design the city's Cottage Hospital (1894). Stanwood sought Ball's professional help in restoring the room "as far as possible upon the architectural ideas prevalent at the time" of its 1805 construction. The architect agreed, saying "I shall take much pleasure in the interesting work of keeping the spirit of the charming old building intact in the re-decoration and other alteration."[2]

Ball arrived at the Athenaeum on September 3, 1892, and, after studying the room, "sketched in a few words an outline of how, in his opinion, the room should be decorated, giving the colors and also plans for a pair of new front doors." These main entrance doors were "sashed in the colonial pattern and glazed with plate glass . . . with side lights" from Boston suppliers, and later proclaimed "the finest in the city."[3]

After his draftsman took measurements, Ball returned to Portsmouth with "elaborate drawings showing the alterations proposed" (cat. 11). The "beautiful plans" included a design for a "head piece" to be placed over the room's rear curved door that was never executed. The old fireplace, "cherished by many former members," was to be "re-opened and enlarged, surmounted with heavy mouldings, ornamented with rich figures and carvings" which Ball claimed reproduced "the characteristic features of the room." The new fireplace, two feet wider than the original, was constructed with Philadelphia brick instead of being faced with tiles as Ball first suggested. The elaborate chimneypiece was made in Boston by W.F. Ross.[4]

But the restoration committee and Athenaeum members balked at the architect's proposed color scheme. There "was strong opposition to painting the walls in anything like a terra-cotta shade." Instead, all agreed on walls "a shade of Colonial Buff (numbered 13 in Sampson's sample-book of colors from T. Strahan & Co.)" with the woodwork and cornice of ivory-white, the latter lightly touched with Roman gold, and the ceiling a light shade of cream. According to a newspaper account, Ball's plans also originally included "a border of frieze enriched with ornaments of sculpture and deeply inlaid with gold" of which no other evidence survives.[5]

All this decorative work set off a mixture of old and new furnishings. A center table, perhaps from Ball's designs, was donated by Thomas P. Salter and made by the Davenport Company. Another member donated "a pair of ornate andirons." Iron newspaper racks were nickel-plated and "confined to the westerly side" of the room. "Mahoganized" newspaper reading desks replaced those from the early nineteenth century that were moved to the attic.[6]

Stanwood also began to refurnish the room with artifacts:

> A fine pair of Elk Horns is found in the attic of the Athenaeum . . . presented to the Athenaeum by George Jaffrey. The horns are of considerable antiquity and are in an excellent state of preservation, dating to a period anterior to the Revolution. It is decided that these shall be mounted upon a shield, which is to be painted white, and fastened over the fireplace on the chimneybreast.

Moreover, "A search in the attic results in the finding of six old fire-buckets . . . inscribed 'Fire and Marine Ins. Co.'"[7] The installation of the horns as decoration, rather than as scientific specimens in the Athenaeum's original cabinet of curiosities, invested them with new historical and distinctly domestic associations. Like firebuckets hung near the stairs, ancient antlers were still found in some of the best colonial mansions of the city, including the Warner and Moffatt-Ladd houses.

Between 1894 and 1895 several of the Athenaeum's historical artifacts were also restored and others donated or, where originals were unavailable, reproduced. The Athenaeum's John Smibert eighteenth-century portrait of Peter Warren was cleaned and repaired, and the companion portrait of Sir William Pepperrell at the Essex Institute in Salem, Massachusetts, was copied by local artist U.D. Tenney. Two small cannons captured from a British vessel at the Battle of Lake Erie and long owned by the Peirce family were "mounted, muzzle down, upon a granite base" on either side of the front door. Oval bronze tablets commemorating the founding of the Athenaeum were mounted on the brick wall above them. The redecoration thus visually linked the Athenaeum's turn-of-the-century proprietors to past heros, events, and old families.[8]

RMC

1 See James L. Garvin, "Academic Architecture and the Building Trades in the Piscataqua Region of New Hampshire and Maine, 1715–1815" (Ph.D.

Cat. 11. Henry B. Ball, Elevation of Fireplace, *1892. Ink on linen; 28 in. x 20 in. Courtesy, Portsmouth Athenaeum.*

Cat. 12. Dining room, 1905–6, Governor John Langdon Mansion, Portsmouth, New Hampshire. Photograph, 1906. Courtesy, Strawbery Banke Museum.

diss., Boston University, 1983), 379–98; "Portsmouth Athenaeum will be remodeled and improved," *New Hampshire Republican*, Sept. 14, 1892.

2 The Hackett house is documented in *New New Hampshire Homes* (Concord: James A. Wood, 1895), 85; Restoration Committee Minutes, Aug. 27, and Sept. 14, 1892, PA Records, box 9, folder 26; Ball and Dabney correspondence, [Aug. 27?]–Aug. 31, 1892, PA Records, box 9, folder 30.

3 Restoration Committee Minutes, Sept. 3–14, 21–30, 1892; Ball and Dabney correspondence, Sept. 20–22, 1892; "Athenaeum," *Portsmouth Chronicle*, Nov. 3, 1892, 2.

4 Restoration Committee Minutes, Sept. 3–17, 1892; correspondence, Stanwood to Ball, Sept. 15; Ball to Stanwood, Sept. 16–17, Oct. 1892, PA Archives.

5 Restoration Committee Minutes, Sept. 17, 1892; *New Hampshire Republican*, Sept. 14, 1892, reported the change from terra-cotta to buff three days before the meeting.

6 Restoration Committee Minutes, Sept. 16–Nov. 3, 1892; "Athenaeum," *Portsmouth Chronicle*, Nov. 3, 1892.

7 Restoration Committee Minutes, Oct. 17, 1892; correspondence, Ball to Stanwood, Oct. 17, 1892, PA Archives.

8 Restoration Committee correspondence, Ball to Stanwood, Nov. 22, 1892, PA Records, box 9, folders 31–33 (Stanwood-Salter correspondence), 34 (Pepperrell portrait), 35 (bronze tablets), 36 (cannons), 37 (ship model *Clovis* restoration), 38 (Warren portrait restoration). Two years later, the Reverend Alfred Langdon Elwyn donated a U.D. Tenney copy of John Trumbull's portrait of Gov. John Langdon; see "Local," *Portsmouth Chronicle*, Oct. 30, 1897, 2.

❋ 12 ❋

GOVERNOR JOHN LANGDON MANSION
Portsmouth, New Hampshire, 1783–85
Additions McKim, Mead and White, 1905–6

This high-style Georgian house (see fig. 1.10) was designed and built for merchant John Langdon (1741–1819) between 1783 and 1785 by two Portsmouth men: Daniel Hart and Michael Whidden III. It is a late example of a Portsmouth building tradition that began in the early eighteenth century with the Macphaedris-Warner house and continued through the construction of the Wentworth-Gardner house of 1760. Elements common to the tradition that are found in the Langdon mansion include its overall cubic mass crowned by a hipped roof with dormers, as well as ornate carving on the interior.[1] The southeast parlor contains carved detailing based on designs first published in *The British Architect* by Abraham Swan in 1745, work that has been called "some of the finest carved rococo ornament in any American interior."[2] Additions made to the Langdon mansion during the first decade of the twentieth century did not compromise the existing Georgian structure, although they added a neoclassical element to the design. Moreover, the addition of a large formal dining room with modern bedrooms, bathrooms, and servant's quarters above transformed the mansion into a genteel summer retreat.

In 1836 the mansion had passed out of the hands of the descendants of John Langdon, who served as governor of New Hampshire from 1805 to 1809, and again in 1810 and 1811. However, the house returned to Langdon ownership in 1877 when it was purchased by Woodbury Langdon, the descendant of Governor Langdon's brother who had also been named Woodbury Langdon. Langdon was a wealthy dry-goods merchant from New York and was married to Elizabeth Langdon Elwyn, herself a descendant of Governor John Langdon.[3] The marriage of Woodbury and Elizabeth Langdon Elwyn thus brought together the two Langdon lines, and the additions to the Governor John Langdon mansion that they planned served to symbolically unite the two eighteenth-century Langdon brothers in the same building.

As architects for the project, the Langdons chose the firm of McKim, Mead and White of New York City. Not only were the architects the leading producers of historicist designs in America at the time, but they had also seen the Langdon mansion as early as 1877 when a sketching tour of eighteenth-century New England architecture had taken them to Portsmouth.[4] A memorandum written by a member of the firm in August 1905 outlined the program for the addition which was to replace an existing ell. The aesthetic intentions of the client were clearly spelled out at this time: "In the finish of the dining-room, Mr. Langdon's idea is to reproduce the Colonial dining-room in the Rockingham Hotel, which was originally one of the fine Colonial Houses in Portsmouth."[5] In fact, the octagonal dining room at the Rockingham Hotel (cat. 12a) was the only part of the neoclassical house built by Woodbury Langdon in Portsmouth in 1785 to survive. By insisting that this symbol of his own Langdon ancestry be introduced into the mansion, the twentieth-century Woodbury Langdon gave the house an ancestral meaning to match the significance it already had for his wife.

Although the Woodbury Langdon dining room inspired the design for the Langdon mansion addition (cat. 12), the architects were leery enough of undertaking an exact replication that Chauncey E. Barrott, who supervised the project, was cautioned to "Take a look at this dining room [at the Rockingham], but do not, at present, give anybody the idea that we are proposing to reproduce it."[6] Barrott's correspondence with John Howard Adams, the draftsman in the New York office of McKim, Mead and White who actually produced the drawings for the project, indicates that the eighteenth-century dining room nonetheless served as a continual point of reference during the construction

Cat. 12a. Langdon Room, 1785, Rockingham Hotel, Portsmouth, New Hampshire. Photograph, ca. 1902. Courtesy, Portsmouth Athenaeum.

process. For example, with respect to a lighting fixture for the new dining room the architects were left without a model since in the Woodbury Langdon dining room "There is a central chandelier. There is a plaster centre, but one that was put in new, not in the Colonial style."[7] Although a new plaster medallion had therefore to be designed, other details were based on the historical prototype. This concern with accuracy also extended to the firm of Irving and Casson of Boston who manufactured the woodwork; in January 1906 Charles P. Casson informed the architects that his company had made drawings of details in the Woodbury Langdon dining room which he had compared with trim elements called for in the plans for the Langdon mansion addition.[8]

The design of the new dining room had an important historical precedent but its function responded to the needs of its twentieth-century owners. A modern kitchen and pantries were located to the rear of the dining room and provided for large-scale entertaining in an historical setting. In this sense, the Langdons' addition corresponds to modifications that were made by many owners of historic houses in the Piscataqua region during the colonial revival. The Langdons combined their interests in the history of the mansion with the entirely new use to which they intended to put it.

KDM

1 Barbara Ann Cleary, "The Governor John Langdon Mansion Memorial: New Perspectives in Interpretation," OTNE 69, nos. 1–2 (Summer-Fall 1978): 22–36.

2 Brock W. Jobe and Marianne Moulton, "Governor John Langdon Mansion Memorial, Portsmouth, New Hampshire," Antiques 129, no. 3 (March 1986): 639.

3 Jobe and Moulton, "Governor John Langdon Mansion Memorial," 639.

4 Leland M. Roth, McKim, Mead and White Architects (New York: Harper & Row, 1983), 46.

5 "Memorandum in regard to Langdon House," Aug. 14, 1905, McKim,

Mead and White Papers, New-York Historical Society. The New-York Historical Society documents were located by Barbara Ann Cleary; copies are in the SPNEA Archives. This document also indicates that the Rev. Alfred L. Elwyn, father of Elizabeth Langdon Elwyn, resided at The Rockingham Hotel during the years that his daughter and son-in-law were occupied with renovations to the Langdon mansion. Blueprint plans for the addition are at SPNEA.

6 "Memorandum in regard to Langdon House." According to Boston directories, Chauncey E. Barrott was a member of the architectural firm of Richardson, Barott, and Richardson between 1910 and 1930.

7 Chauncey E. Barrott to McKim, Mead and White, Oct. 17, 1905, McKim, Mead and White Papers. John Howard Adams was born in Pawtucket, R.I., in 1876 and studied architecture at the Massachusetts Institute of Technology (1895–99) and in Europe (1899–1900). Upon his return he apprenticed with the firm of Peters and Rice in Boston for a short time, and then worked for McKim, Mead and White for eight years before relocating to Providence, R.I., in 1908. Obituary for John Howard Adams, *Journal of the American Institute of Architects* 39, no. 1 (Jan. 1925): 39.

8 Charles P. Casson to McKim, Mead and White, Jan. 15, 1906, McKim, Mead and White Papers.

Cat. 13a. Jaffrey cottage. Photograph by Halliday Historic Photograph Co., 1900. Courtesy, Society for the Preservation of New England Antiquities.

13

JAFFREY COTTAGE
New Castle, New Hampshire, ca. 1780
Renovations, 1865–1905; burned, 1968

During the nineteenth century, the Jaffrey cottage in New Castle, New Hampshire, was regarded as an early colonial relic (cat. 13a). The ways that successive owners used and altered the property from 1865 to 1905 demonstrate significant differences in their architectural responses to the colonial past. The first was to preserve the quaint building entirely for its historical associations. After the turn of the century, however, the house formed the core of a much larger structure as new summer residents transformed it into a home for their retirement.

John Albee, a former Unitarian minister, philosopher, and sometimes librarian of the Portsmouth Athenaeum, acquired the so-called Jaffrey cottage in 1865. After the construction of The Wentworth Hotel (cat. 2) he supported himself and his wife by breaking up his nearby farm into house lots for summer visitors. An intellectual among the island's fishermen, Albee became the historian of the community and published *New Castle Historic and Picturesque* with drawings by Abbott F. Graves in 1884.[1]

Citing John Ruskin's statement that "a house is not fit to be lived in until [it is] three hundred years old," Albee firmly believed local tradition that his small cottage was the oldest house in New Hampshire.[2] His neighbor, Barrett Wendell, thought the Jaffrey cottage dated from "Cromwell's day" and in 1881 described it as "an unpretentious one-story farm-house, framed about a large central chimney, with a long lazy lean-to."[3]

Modern deed research shows that the cottage was actually built on land originally granted to the Waldron family,

and historic photographs of the interior suggest that the farmhouse dated to the late eighteenth century.[4] Its parlor, "a large and incongruous portion of the cottage," where Albee believed the 1682 Provincial Assembly had met, Wendell described as "a large panelled room, separately framed and big enough to be called a hall—sixteen or eighteen feet square . . . and above ten foot high." "In Albee's day," he recalled, old furniture was to be had for the asking in these parts,

> and he had instinctive taste . . . So at least the great panelled hall of his house, with its corner "beaufat" [corner cupboard], whose concave top contained a painted cherub . . . was full of such chairs as might have been there under the Crown.[5]

Albee sold the land across Wild Rose Lane in the late 1880s and early 1890s, and built himself a new house in New Castle in 1888; the old cottage was rented out, and Albee and his wife spent increasing amounts of time in the White Mountains.[6] In 1900 he sold the Jaffrey cottage and the remaining sixteen acres of land to Samuel Barrett who transferred it to Edward G. Niles of Boston the next year. The Nileses greatly enlarged Jaffrey cottage as a summer home between 1901 and 1904, when they moved permanently to the island community. In August 1905 the new house was vacated for use by the Assistant Secretary of State Herbert H.D. Peirce, President Franklin D. Roosevelt's representative to the Russo-Japanese Peace Conference. Over the next few years Niles also acquired the Stedman house, Kelp Rock cottage, and a guest cottage known as the Yellow House.[7]

Edward G. Niles (1859–1908) entered Boston's Museum School of Drawing and Painting in 1877 and after 1886 always listed himself in the city directories as an artist. Inheriting his father's Boston advertising agency wealth, he increased it as an investment banker, which enabled him to retire "while still a young man." Edward and his wife, Emily Mary Niles, began to summer in New Castle around 1895.

Cat. 13. Jaffrey cottage, built ca. 1780, renovations 1865–1905, New Castle, New Hampshire. Photograph, ca. 1905. Courtesy, Portsmouth Athenaeum.

Known locally as a generous supporter of worthy causes, Niles was said to have been "closely associated with the landscape artists, Tarbell and Benson, and his own work with the brush did not suffer by comparison to theirs."[8] At his wife's demise in 1912, the attic of the adjoining "Yellow House" was filled with "6 studies in oils," "8 oil paintings," three dozen framed watercolors and oils, and "2 lots [of] paintings by Mr. and Mrs. Niles, all unframed."[9]

To sustain their retirement in the Jaffrey cottage the Nileses enlarged the small house with a large two-story colonial revival addition facing the road (cat. 13). The small cape joined the new addition behind a columned side portico. A projecting entrance pavilion was framed by giant pilasters like those at the Lady Pepperrell house (cat. 10). Above the fan and side lights of the neoclassical front door was a Palladian window, which one commentator called "the most popular single exterior feature" of new colonial work and the "most frequently misplaced."[10]

Inside, a staircase "copied line for line" from that at Sparhawk Hall in Kittery Point (cat. 9) was somewhat smaller than its model and climbed the opposite wall of the entrance hall. But to Virginia Robie in 1904, the Niles staircase was "so faithfully reproduced" that it might deceive Sir William Pepperrell, unless he looked at the wallpaper.[11] The pillar-and-dome paper used on the Sparhawk stairhall, now known to have been added sometime after Sir William Pepperrell's death in 1759, was not commercially available to the Nileses. Instead, they used the same pillar-and-arch design recently reproduced for Emily Tyson's 1898 restoration of Hamilton house in South Berwick (cat. 16).[12] Herbert Browne of Little and Browne in Boston, Emily Tyson's architect, had arranged for the restoration of that paper and may, perhaps, have designed the Niles addition.

The couple were members of both the Boston and the Portsmouth Athenaeum, and a bookcase in the upper main hall held some three hundred volumes; a separate library contained over "350 books of fiction, standard literature . . . and a collection of French novels in paper." American antique furniture lined the front hallway (including a "grandfather's" clock on the stair landing) and oriental rugs covered most of the floors in what was commonly believed to be the authentic colonial manner. But Japanese and Chinese vases and several pieces of Japanese furniture in the hall and drawing room also attest to the impact of the aesthetic movement upon the interests of this artistic couple. Yet, except for "8 water colored pictures" that shared Mrs. Niles's bedroom wall with an oak-framed mirror, the inventory of rooms suggests walls bare of any paintings and treated with striped and floral papers.[13]

The formal "colonial" facade of the Niles addition to the Jaffrey cottage masked eight new rooms plus service rooms (and bedrooms for three servants) arranged in a U-shaped plan. A federal-style fence and new stable completed the circa 1902 additions. As a home for two genteel middle-aged artists, architectural details from the 1740s to the early 1800s were melded to create specialized room use, separation from service staff, and accommodations for modern living that the simple Albee farmhouse could not provide.

RMC

1 Kenneth E. Maxam, "New Castle, New Hampshire, circa 1630–1700: Jerry's Point and the Walfords" (typescript, PA, 1979); Rockingham Co. Registry of Deeds, Exeter, N.H., 484:331, 512:226, 566:304, 375:345.

2 John Albee, *New Castle Historic and Picturesque* (Boston: George F. Thompson, 1884), 35.

3 Barrett Wendell to Col. Robert White-Thomson, Aug. 7, 1881, Wendell Papers, PA, cited in Woodard Dorr Openo, "The Summer Colony at Little Harbor in Portsmouth, New Hampshire, and Its Relation to the Colonial Revival Movement" (Ph.D. diss., University of Michigan, 1990), 89–90.

4 Maxam, "New Castle"; photographs of the Jaffrey cottage are in the Piscataqua History Club collection, PA, and the SPNEA Archives.

5 Albee, *New Castle*, 30; Wendell to White-Thomson, 1881, cited in Openo, "Summer Colony at Little Harbor," 90.

6 The *Portsmouth Journal* reported on Jan. 11, 1888, that "Mr. Moses Yeaton is building a handsome new house at Newcastle, for John Albee, Esq."

7 Openo, "Summer Colony at Little Harbor," 50; Maxam, "New Castle," 7; Peter E. Randall, *There Are No Victors Here* (Portsmouth, N.H.: Portsmouth Marine Society, 1985); inventory of Emily Mary Niles, 1912, Rockingham Co. Probate Records, Exeter, N.H., docket 15923.

8 Obituary of Edward G. Niles, *Portsmouth Herald*, Aug. 17, 1908, 3. Boston city directories list Niles as an artist from 1886 to 1904, with a working address only from 1886 to the early 1890s. Niles lived with his parents at 392 Beacon Street until 1899 when he and his wife moved to 318 Beacon Street; from 1902 to 1904 their listing was 318 Beacon Street and New Castle, N.H. Emily Mary Niles acquired her Boston Athenaeum share in her married name in 1896.

9 Inventory of Emily Mary Niles, 1912.

10 Joseph Everett Chandler, *The Colonial House* (New York: Robert McBride & Co., 1916), 287.

11 Virginia Robie, "A Colonial Pilgrimage III: Sir William Pepperrell and His Staircase," *House Beautiful* 15 (Apr. 1904): 317. Interior photographs of the additions were taken during the later occupancy of former N.H. Gov. Floyd.

12 Richard C. Nylander et al., *Wallpaper in New England* (Boston: SPNEA, 1986), 48–49, 59–60, 268–69.

13 Inventory of Emily Mary Niles, 1912.

14

SAYWARD-WHEELER HOUSE
York, Maine, ca. 1720
Renovations Winslow and Bigelow, ca. 1902

By the late nineteenth century, the Barrell mansion, known today as the Sayward-Wheeler house (cat. 14), was recognized as a relic of York's bygone era. Published accounts of the area cited it as "among the most interesting of the many historic houses in the old and ancient town of York."[1] Although the house was privately owned until it was donated to the Society for the Preservation of New England Antiquities in 1977, its history and treasures had been shared with the community since the 1860s. Unlike many other houses in the region, its ultimate preservation was the result of strong family associations, rather than architectural importance.

The Sayward-Wheeler house remained remarkably untouched for most of the nineteenth century because of a fortuitous combination of the reversals of fortune and the longevity of its occupants. Built about 1720, the house was owned by Jonathan Sayward from 1735 until his death in 1797. Sayward, a merchant in the West Indies trade, was one of York's most prominent citizens, active in both civic and religious affairs. Before the Revolution, he had been a justice of the peace and a representative to the General Court. Even though he was a Tory, he was allowed to remain in his house during the Revolutionary War, albeit under the constant scrutiny of the townspeople. Of all his activities, however, it was his participation in the capture of Louisburg in 1745 and the booty that he had brought back to York that appealed most to the late nineteenth-century writers.

Sayward left the house and its contents to his oldest grandson and namesake, Jonathan Sayward Barrell. Sayward Barrell continued the mercantile activities of his grandfather, but "the embargo of 1807, as well as the war of 1812, were alike disastrous in its consequences to him as to many others." He never completely recovered financial stability, and by the early 1820s had to mortgage both "the ancient homestead" and the "valuable tide-mill, noted for its antiquity."[2]

After his death in 1857, the house continued to be occupied by his two unmarried daughters, Mary and Elizabeth.[3] The Barrell sisters, by then both in their fifties, did little to change the house in which they had grown up. Their frugal upbringing and their reverence for their venerable ancestor were responsible for keeping the house intact and for passing its rich traditions on to the next generation. The Barrell sisters could well have been on Sarah Orne Jewett's mind when she commented that her "head was full of dear old houses and dear old women."[4] They embodied "all the individuality and quaint personal characteristics of rural New England" that Jewett sought as models for her stories.[5] Their simple life was captured less

Cat. 14. The Barrell sisters at the Sayward-Wheeler house, York, Maine, built 1720. Photograph, 1880. Courtesy, Society for the Preservation of New England Antiquities.

eloquently by an anonymous family member in a poem, "The Old Family Mansion in York," written before 1883:

> In this old house through joy and pain,
> Have lived, now live, two sisters rare,
> Upon whom showers of blessings rain
> From those, who prosper by their care.
>
> Here live they from the world apart,
> With simple hopes and simpler ways,
> Surrounded by the works of art,
> The monuments of bye-gone days.[6]

In addition to welcoming their relatives, Mary and Elizabeth Barrell also apparently delighted in sharing their ancestral home with summer visitors to York, especially those seeking a glimpse of the past. The earliest and most complete description of these relics and curiosities was published in 1869. In it the authors note that architecturally, the house "resembles the Wentworth House at Little Harbor." After being shown the antique furniture in the sitting room, they were invited to see the parlor (cat. 14a) which

> contained numerous curiosities, which well paid for our visit. Three full-length oil paintings were hung at the end of the room . . . the family coat-of-arms hung on the mantel; and below it were old engravings of the commanders of the English Army and Navy in 1760 . . . A long damask curtain was drawn away from a recess at one corner of the room, displaying an elegant set of India China and other curiosities of the last century. Among them was a brass tea urn taken at the capture of Louisburg. This room, like the first, was filled with ancient furniture.[7]

The best parlor was obviously regarded as a relic room; all subsequent published accounts make reference to the "great number of articles worth the attention of those of historical, antiquarian taste" located there.[8] Frequently noted were the portrait of Sayward's only daughter, Sally (Mrs. Nathaniel Barrell), and the china and other items that were booty from Louisburg.[9]

The Barrell sisters remained in contact with their many cousins and a visit to the house on Barrell Lane was anticipated by family members who were passing through York or spending part of the summer there. Among these were the four daughters of their first cousin Henry Cheever of Worcester, Massachusetts. Two of them, Ellen Cheever Rockwood and Elizabeth Cheever Wheeler, developed a particular fondness for their great-great-grandfather's house and became concerned about its fate when George Octavious Barrel died in 1901.[10] After five months of negotiations with his heirs, Dr. and Mrs. Leonard Wheeler of Worcester purchased the property. From the outset, their purpose had been "to preserve the house and all of its contents intact exactly as they were . . . as an ancestral place."[11] The Wheelers hired the Boston architectural firm of Winslow and Bigelow to prepare plans for the additions and alterations necessary to turn the house into a summer residence. Plans dated 1902 proposed a small addition on the first-floor ell for a lavatory and a piazza, surrounding the parlor, whose central section was a lattice enclosure in the form of a three-part bay with a pitched roof; the lattice work of each bay was to be pierced with an arched opening. On the second floor two small chambers under the eaves were to be completely reworked to provide space

for a bathroom, a small bedroom, and attic stairs; two dormers were designed to bring light into the new rooms. All changes were labeled "new" on the plans, and to emphasize them either the architect or the client marked each one with a yellow crayon.

Apparently the architects had gone beyond what the Wheelers had envisioned. In the final plans the central portion of the piazza was greatly simplified. The bay was squared off and Doric columns were substituted to support a simple sloped roof. Comments such as "leave old partition" and "leave room unfinished and do not touch beam" reveal that the Wheelers wanted to retain as much of the original finish as possible even in the secondary spaces of the ell.

The renovations were carried out by a local contractor, E.W. Baker, for a cost of $1,400. In addition to what was called for in the plans, photographs taken after the renovations were completed show that other changes included new dormers on the river side to match the originals that faced Barrell Lane and the open ocean, and a new pair of blinds for each window. The entire house received a fresh coat of paint, including the chimneys which were finished with a black band around the top.

The Wheelers also kept interior architectural changes to a minimum and redecorated the rooms in keeping with fashionable early twentieth-century taste.[12] The woodwork was painted white, new wallpapers were applied to the

Cat. 14a. Parlor, Sayward-Wheeler house. Photograph, ca. 1890. Courtesy, Society for the Preservation of New England Antiquities.

walls, and straw matting was laid on the floors. The majority of the furnishings remained where they had always been.

Mrs. Wheeler was intent on preserving her family's heritage in a very tangible way. Her children shared her desire to keep the property intact and by donating it to the SPNEA fulfilled her wish "that the attractiveness and associations of this house and personal property as a unified whole may be preserved as long as practical."[13]

RCN

1 *Boston Journal,* quoted in Charles Sayward, *The Sayward Family* (Ipswich, Mass.: By the author, 1890), 84. For additional information on the house, see Richard C. Nylander, "The Jonathan Sayward House, York, Maine," *Antiques* 106, no. 3 (Sept. 1979): 567–77.

2 Obituary of Jonathan Sayward Barrell, May 25, 1857; clipping in SPNEA Archives.

3 Joseph Barrell had purchased the mortgage on his father's house and conveyed title to his sisters in 1841.

4 Willa Cather, preface to *The Best Stories of Sarah Orne Jewett* (1925), reprinted in *The Country of the Pointed Firs and Other Stories* (Garden City, N.Y.: Doubleday & Co., 1955), n.p.

5 Sarah Orne Jewett, *Deephaven* (1893; reprint, New Haven, Conn.: College and University Press, 1966), 33.

6 "The Old Family Mansion at York" (manuscript, SPNEA Archives, n.d.).

7 "A Visit to Cape Neddick," *Historical Magazine and Notes and Queries Concerning the Antiquities, History, and Biography of America* 6 (Aug. 1896): 101 (manuscript copy, SPNEA Archives).

8 Sayward, *Sayward Family,* 85.

9 Although Joseph Blackburn's bill for painting the portrait in 1761 survives, the picture was often attributed to John Singleton Copley. The story of the china was written down in 1841 by Jonathan Sayward's oldest grandchild, Sally Sayward Barrell Keating Wood. Madame Wood, as she was known later in life, was born in 1759 and spent much of her life at her grandfather's house.

10 George O. Barrell had inherited the house and contents from his aunt Mary Barrell in 1889.

11 Ellen Cheever Rockwood to Samuel Junkins, Apr. 30, 1901, SPNEA Archives.

12 Only one comment on the plans suggests any thought of interior "restoration." A note regarding the sitting room chamber, the only room that retains its 1720 paneling, reads: "IN THIS ROOM—SCRAPE OFF PAINT AND FINISH WOODWORK IN ITS NATURAL COLOR, WHICH IS OAK." The work, however, was never carried out.

13 See an abstract of the will of Elizabeth Cheever Wheeler, June 20, 1945, SPNEA Archives.

❋ 15 ❋

ELIZABETH PERKINS HOUSE
York, Maine, ca. 1730–50
Renovated and enlarged, 1898–1935

In 1924, Elizabeth Perkins wrote to William Sumner Appleton, "I love the hunt for the old houses and the old things, but I need much instruction."[1] Attracted to its bucolic situation on the banks of the York River and its air of gently decaying antiquity, Mary Sowles Perkins (1845–1929) and her daughter Elizabeth Bishop Perkins (1879–1952) purchased the eighteenth-century "Piggin House" (cat. 15) during a visit to relatives in York in the summer of 1898.[2] Intended as a summer retreat from their home in New York City, the purchase of the house by the Perkinses was an outgrowth of earlier family interests and activities in antique collecting and the colonial revival movement.[3] At the time, it was a somewhat socially renegade thing to do, as it clearly separated them from the wealthy summer colony at York Harbor, where they would have found a group of seasonal residents who shared similar backgrounds and interests. The Perkins house was, literally and figuratively, a backwater outpost of the summer colony at York. While most summer residents were staying at the fashionable hotels or in new shingle-style cottages near the ocean, the Perkinses made the deliberate decision to acquire and remodel an old house and capitalize upon its antiquity as a setting for social activities. In this regard, mother and daughter placed themselves squarely in the vanguard of an emerging local movement by select members of the summer elite increasingly attracted by the lingering atmosphere of colonial prosperity in the Piscataqua region. In the Perkins house, one finds a seminal regional example of a vernacular colonial house remodeled for use as a seasonal residence to retain an image of colonial gentility, while incorporating alterations and additions designed to enable the leisured way of life sought by late Victorians.

The development of the house from a simple four-room-and-ell structure that existed in 1898 to a spacious colonial revival home incorporating neo-Palladian, Georgian, and federal architectural elements did not come about through any one preconceived plan, nor, evidently, through any professionally prepared designs.[4] Rather, the house evolved as needs dictated and finances allowed. The first addition, made about 1900, was a second floor over the rear ell to provide space for a domestic servant.[5] This was followed by more sweeping changes around 1904, including a projecting entry at the front of the house (replacing an early transomed front doorway) complete with a federal-type sidelighted front door. Also added at this time were a large porch just off the dining room on the river side of the house and a one-story kitchen wing at the rear. In 1905 these new additions, especially the porch with its river view, assisted the Perkinses in making the house one of the centers of York summer society when they hosted a much-noted tea party honoring the delegations who were then meeting in Portsmouth to negotiate the treaty ending the Russo-Japanese War.[6]

It was fifteen years before any further changes to the house were made. Elizabeth Perkins spent the years from 1914 to 1919 in Europe as a member of the American Committee for a Devastated France, and on her return to York in the summer of 1920 she supervised the addition of a new second-floor bedroom for herself and the construction of a modern bathroom. The bedroom, built over the riverside porch, commanded views of the York River and the

Cat. 15. Elizabeth Perkins house, York, Maine, built ca. 1730–50. Photograph, 1899. Old York Historical Society.

eighteenth-century Sewall's Bridge that leads to the village. The bedroom appears to be the earliest documented use of salvaged colonial period woodwork in the creation of an entirely new interior space in York, the walls of the room having been made up from paneling and doors taken from the Phoebe Weare house in Cape Neddick, demolished in 1919.[7] This woodwork was stripped and finished in a natural pine to create a decorative background for antique furnishings. The fireplace and hearth in the bedroom were based on the design of the fireplace in the 1804 wing of the Old Gaol. A garage, designed to harmonize with the house, was also added in 1920. Like the modern bathroom, this addition showed that the Perkinses could make use of the latest innovations in domestic technology while choosing to vacation and entertain in a highly individualistic version of colonial life.

The final phase of change in the Perkins house spanned the years 1924 to 1935, and responded to a changing view of the house by its owners, the declining health and death of Mary Sowles Perkins, and later, a conscious effort on the part of Elizabeth to preserve the house as a memorial to her mother. There is no evidence to suggest that in the work done in the first quarter century of Perkins ownership there was any purpose beyond making a comfortable summer residence with a colonial feel, but it is evident that preservation of the house as a museum was envisioned by Elizabeth

by 1924. In that year she approached William Sumner Appleton of the Society for the Preservation of New England Antiquities as to the suitability of the Perkins house as a future SPNEA property. With great tact, Appleton informed her that in his opinion the original condition of the house had been too far altered for it to be useful as a museum, but suggested that the house might be better preserved if it were let out to private organizations or "men of letters" as a retreat or center for scholarship.[8]

Appleton's assessment of the house evidently lifted some self-imposed constraints, for Elizabeth proceeded to embark on an ambitious program of enlargement and remodeling to provide additional space and bring the house closer to her idea of early New England. Between 1926 and 1931 the kitchen wing was moved back from the house and attached to the garage and a massive two-and-a-half-story kitchen wing with servants' rooms and a large attic was constructed between it and the main house. The resultant structure created an L-shaped configuration that almost tripled the usable space within the house and added the distinctive gabled York River facade embellished with three Palladian windows. Inside, a modern kitchen and pantries brought about a formal separation of entertainment and work areas and precipitated the most notable interior "restoration" to date—the stripping and renovation of the dining room

Cat. 15a. Dining room, Elizabeth Perkins house. Photograph by Douglas Armsden, ca. 1953. Old York Historical Society.

(cat. 15a) to reflect a purported seventeenth-century building date.[9] The room was basically taken down to an early structural system. This room with exposed beams and timbers on ceilings and walls, rough white plaster, and natural finishes on woodwork and floors, accentuated with Jacobean-type furniture of dark oak, banister-back and rush-seated chairs, and pewter and Canton china, was the first local instance of a style emulated in a number of later dining rooms in the York vicinity.

Elizabeth Perkins believed that she was returning the dining room to its original appearance. In 1932, she began work on a short story entitled "The Codfish Ghost: A Biography of a House from the Seventeenth Century to the Present Day" (cat. 52) in which she recorded her beliefs concerning the restoration of what she believed to be a seventeenth-century section of the structure. In the last chapter, she appears in the character of a female "home-hunter" who works at restoring a recently purchased antique house. Her excitement in the process is evident:

The cleaner removed the dirty carpets, and scrubbed the floors, so that old broad boards of the seventeenth century were again in their glory. The cleaner tore off layer after layer of wall paper from the mid-Victorian design back through the years to the architectural design of the eighteenth century, until the rough old plaster of the early eighteenth century shone glistening white, and the overmantel stood revealed in broad panels painted in layers of as many colours as Joseph's coat.

The home-hunter stood by in excited ecstacy. "There is a piece of plaster on the south wall that is cracked and should be cut out, but be careful not to break any more, for I want to keep the old walls bumpy and rough as they are," she said.

The mason chipped at the cracked piece, and the house-owner watched him closely. Suddenly, she grabbed the tool from his hand and commenced herself to hack furiously at the wall. The astonished man exclaimed: "Look out, you'll break all the plaster!"

"I want to", she answered, as she continued her furious attack. "I want to get rid of it all; don't you see what's underneath? Sheathing! Hand-bevelled pine boards!!"...

"Now," said she, breathless with exhaustion and surprise, "Down with the ceiling! Maybe we shall uncover beams!"[10]

The last documentable change to the house was the removal of wallpaper in the parlor and the introduction of

Moses Eaton–style wall stenciling along with the creation of paneling on the fireplace wall in 1935.[11] With these changes, Elizabeth Perkins essentially "finished" the house and turned her attention to endowing it as a private museum.

TBJ

1 Elizabeth Bishop Perkins to William Sumner Appleton, June 1924, Perkins Coll., OYHS.

2 The Rev. J. Newton Perkins (1854–1915), husband of Mary and father of Elizabeth, was an Episcopal minister in New York City and remains a shadowy figure in the history of the Perkins house. He evidently chose to stay in New York during the summers while mother and daughter came to York. His name was not connected with the purchase of the house in 1898; the project was truly a mother-daughter undertaking.

3 Antique collecting and genealogical interests, leading to an interest in old houses and architecture, can be traced to J. Newton and Mary Sowles Perkins as far back as the late 1870s. See Thomas Johnson, "The Feel of the Colonial: Interiors of the Perkins House" (typescript, OYHS, 1989).

4 No floor plans or elevation drawings for alterations to the Perkins house survive in the Perkins Coll., OYHS, yet scattered references and payment receipts to local carpenters exist in the Perkins Coll., leading to the conclusion that she and her mother probably planned the changes in consultation with local workers and artisans and supervised the work themselves.

5 See Johnson, "Perkins House Chronology," in "The Feel of the Colonial."

6 "Grand Japanese Fete, Grounds of Mrs. Newton Perkins Scene of Brilliant Assemblage, Representatives from Peace Conference Present," *Portsmouth Herald*, Aug. 4, 1905.

7 I am indebted to Virginia Spiller, Librarian, OYHS, for providing this information.

8 William Sumner Appleton to Elizabeth Perkins, June 8, 1924, Perkins Coll., OYHS.

9 Helen Psarakis, "Beaming with Pride: The Restoration of the Dining Room in the Elizabeth Perkins House" (typescript, OYHS, 1989).

10 Elizabeth Perkins, "The Codfish Ghost: A Biography of a House from the Seventeenth Century to the Present Day" (typescript, OYHS, 1932).

11 Diary of Elizabeth Bishop Perkins, May 15, 1935, Perkins Coll., OYHS. When Elizabeth Perkins died in 1952, the house passed intact to the Society for the Preservation of Historic Landmarks and Buildings in York County. It is now the property of the successor to that organization, the OYHS.

❀ 16 ❀

HAMILTON HOUSE
South Berwick, Maine, ca. 1787
Renovations Herbert W. C. Browne (1860–1946), 1899

Hamilton house (see fig. c) in South Berwick, Maine, represents one of the most complete colonial revival environments in the Piscataqua region. The classically proportioned house, its prominent location on a bluff overlooking the river, and its deeply rooted local traditions provided the raw materials for transformation of the property into a romantic representation of the past beginning in 1899. The work carried out over the following thirty years represents two distinct phases that reflect

Cat. 16. Hamilton house, South Berwick, Maine, built ca. 1787. Photograph by Sarah Orne Jewett, ca. 1889. The back of the photograph is inscribed "H.D.S. to remember a summer morning ride. S.O.J." Courtesy, Society for the Preservation of New England Antiquities.

changing attitudes toward the past during the first half of the twentieth century.

When it was built about 1787, Hamilton house over-looked prosperous warehouses and bustling shipyards, but by the end of the nineteenth century the property had fallen into a state of disrepair typical of many large eighteenth-century houses in the region. The property was a favorite of Sarah Orne Jewett, who often took visitors there to see the "quiet place, that the destroying left hand of progress had failed to touch" (cat. 16).[1] In "River Driftwood," she noted that it was the last of "the stately old colonial mansions that used to stand beside the river" and was "unrivaled for the beauty of its situation, and for a certain grand air which I have found it hard to match in any house I have ever seen."[2]

Upon learning that the property was for sale, Jewett began trying to interest some of her wealthy Boston ac-quaintances to purchase it for a summer place. She finally succeeded with Mrs. George Tyson and her stepdaughter Elizabeth, who jointly purchased the house and 110 acres in 1898. Each had seen the house only once before—Emily Tyson the previous winter when it was surrounded by three feet of snow and Elise, as her stepdaughter was known, on a June day a year and a half earlier. Elise later wrote, "so strong was the charm for us that nothing more was neces-sary, and we neither of us saw it again till we owned it."[3]

The Tysons immediately embarked on a project to restore the house to its former glory and to lay out the gardens which tradition maintained had surrounded the house.[4] Mrs. Tyson hired Herbert W.C. Browne, the Boston architect who was recognized for his knowledge of colonial buildings, and with his help they turned Hamilton house into a "wondrous old place."[5] The project is listed in Little and Browne's account book as "Alterations to House at So. Berwick, Maine. 1899." Because the work was done by local contractors, no further details are given except that the total cost was $9,403.[6]

During the restoration, two wings were added to the north side of the house so that the modern improvements would intrude on the original house as little as possible. The addition toward the garden provided space for a new kitchen and china pantry, balanced on the river side by a new covered porch. Both additions were encased in lattice and topped by a balustrade in the Chinese Chippendale style. The lattice, intended to be covered with vines, served both to conceal the new additions and to provide a visual link between the house and the garden with its similarly styled pergola. The door surround on the north facade was extended to include two side lights to provide light to the rear of the central hall and to the new lavatory tucked under the front stairs. A glazed door replaced the original solid-paneled door on the south facade so that the river would al-ways be in sight from the inside; the windows which led onto the porch and balconies were extended and made into doors. For the first time, blinds were installed on every win-dow, including those of the dormers.

The interior finish had remained remarkably untouched since the house was built, but was suffering from neglect by the time the Tysons purchased the house. The large draw-ing room was being used for storage; its woodwork was "black as the inside of the chimney" from having been used as a kitchen when the house was a two-family tenement.[7] The only major interior change the Tysons made was to re-move the side stairhall on the first floor in order to create a larger dining room. The corner posts were camouflaged as fluted columns with broken entablatures and the stairs were reused for cellar stairs. Other interior work included reproducing the front parlor mantel for the back parlor and installing bathrooms on the second and third floors.

A series of photographs taken over a thirty-year period documents the changes to the interior decoration of the Hamilton house.[8] They illustrate a subtle evolution from a comfortable late nineteenth-century summer home to one where more formal arrangements of American antiques prevailed. Elise Tyson Vaughan's candid and artistic com-positions capture the rooms as they were initially dec-orated. The photographs show the rooms furnished with an informal combination of antiques, new painted furniture, and comfortable wicker. Many of the antiques were family pieces that had been brought up from Mrs. Tyson's native Pennsylvania or were acquired locally.[9] Straw matting cov-ered all the floors and dimity curtains with netted fringe hung at each window. With one notable exception, the wallpapers chosen for the rooms were fashionable patterns of the 1890s. The foliage wallpapers in the parlor and dining room and the design of roses climbing a trellis on the walls of the back parlor made more of a statement of the owner's interest in her garden than her interest in eighteenth-century decoration (cat. 16a).

The hall wallpaper, however, made a dramatic statement about the Tysons' interest in the historical nature of the house. For this space, they reproduced Jonathan Hamilton's origi-nal pillar-and-arch wallpaper, using the Boston firm of Gregory and Brown.[10] Whether the reproduction was made as a deliberate attempt to recreate the original appearance of the hall is unclear. The design of columns, arches, and swags may have appealed to Mrs. Tyson and even more to Herbert Browne purely because of its architectural nature, while the change in background color, from gray to light blue, may have been part of an overall decorative scheme to harmonize the interior colors with the garden and river. Photographs taken in 1898 show the original paper in a pile on the dining room floor, indicating that a great deal, if not all of it, had remained on the walls until that time.

The decorative themes of the garden and the past were later enhanced by the murals painted in the dining room and parlor by George Porter Fernald (cat. 17).[11] A trip to Italy in the spring of 1905 may have inspired the redecora-tion of the dining room. The views of Italian gardens did even more than the foliage paper over which they were painted to unite the room with the garden just outside. The murals in the parlor evoked the past in their depiction of

Cat. 16a. Parlor, Hamilton house. Photograph by Elise Tyson Vaughan, 1905.
Courtesy, Society for the Preservation of New England Antiquities.

Cat. 16b. Parlor, Hamilton house. Photograph by George Brayton, 1923. Courtesy, Society for the Preservation of New England Antiquities.

the area's historic houses and emphasized their relationship to the river and "the flourishing trade with the West Indies" (cat. 16b).[12]

By the time the first articles on the house appeared about 1910, the decoration of the interior was complete, the garden had matured, and the studio or garden cottage had been added. Mrs. Tyson had treated each element with "half-whimsical, half-loving sympathy" but not with complete historical accuracy.[13] Her creation, however, fulfilled a certain romantic vision of the past. Hildegarde Hawthorne stated:

> The house itself is pure colonial of the best type. Since she came into possession, Mrs. Tyson has not only succeeded in restoring all its old beauty, but she has also given it the very atmosphere of its own time— harmonious, with the free movement of a new land, yet withal exquisitely expressive of the ancient culture drawn from older and more finished countries.[14]

Five years later, Louise Shelton remarked "In isolation,

simplicity, and ripeness the atmosphere of the whole place breathes of olden days."[15]

In 1923, a year after her stepmother's death, Elise, by then Mrs. Henry G. Vaughan, wrote to her long-time friend William Sumner Appleton asking him to suggest the name of a photographer who could take "some really good photos of Hamilton House" because she was planning to put the property on the market.[16] After suggesting the name of George Brayton, Appleton warned her that she should be prepared for a "chorus of sincere lamentations" from him and his cousins that "should be enough to make you hold on to the old house forever and forever, and then bequeath it to this Society [for the Preservation of New England Antiquities] as a home for decayed antiquarians, especially such as have the misfortune to be bachelors as a result of mental paralysis at the critical moments of their lives."[17]

Appleton's letter must have been persuasive, because Mrs. Vaughan did not sell Hamilton house and by 1926 had made arrangements to bequeath it to SPNEA with a sizable endowment. Her intent, as expressed in her will, changed over time. At first she wanted the house to be "maintained and preserved for posterity as a place of historical and antiquarian interest" and to be used as a residence, open to the public but not "used as a period house, so called, or for museum purposes." Thirteen years later, after her husband's death, she changed her will and stated simply that her object was "to have said 'Hamilton House' & the Cottage in the garden pass into the hands of said Society comfortably and appropriately furnished for preservation." Her final will gave the house and furnishings to SPNEA "for the purpose of preserving and displaying to the public the antiques of New England."[18]

After making the decision to keep Hamilton house, Mrs. Vaughan redecorated at least one of the rooms and refined many of the furnishings. Some of the changes were made in the spirit of her mother's original plan. For example, the rose-trellis wallpaper of the back parlor was replaced with a pattern of ivy growing on a thin trellis to mirror the vine-covered porch that now extended the entire length of the west side of the house.[19] China trade objects were brought from Mrs. Tyson's Boston house and added to the main parlor as further evocation of trade with exotic ports.

Mrs. Vaughan's own collecting instincts were responsible for additional changes. The well-chosen and carefully placed examples of colored glass, hooked rugs, Currier and Ives prints, and children's furniture suggest that she was limiting her collecting to icons of the American past. The garden cottage witnessed a complete change from a studio furnished with objects of European origin to a large living room filled with folk art and early American furniture in pine and maple.

Mrs. Vaughan's imprint on the Hamilton house and its gardens can be seen in the photographs taken by Paul Weber that were used as illustrations for four articles on the property published in *House Beautiful* in 1929. The interiors remained essentially unchanged from that point until the house became a property of the SPNEA in 1949. In 1987, after several projects intended to give the house a more accurate eighteenth-century appearance, SPNEA restored Mrs. Vaughan's composed arrangements as a prime example of how the early twentieth century viewed the past.

RCN

1 Sarah Orne Jewett, "River Driftwood," in *Country By-Ways* (1881; reprint, South Berwick, Me.: Old Berwick Historical Society, 1981), 17.

2 Jewett, "River Driftwood," 15–16.

3 Elizabeth R. (Tyson) Vaughan, "The Story of Hamilton House" (typescript, SPNEA Archives, n.d.), 5. This paper was probably prepared for the meeting of the Garden Club of America in York, July 9–10, 1934.

4 Vaughan, "Story of Hamilton House." The house and gardens were the setting for Sarah Orne Jewett's *Tory Lover* (cat. 50). Her novel reinforced local tradition that the house was built before the American Revolution. In reality the house was not begun until about 1787. It was built for Jonathan Hamilton, a South Berwick native who made Portsmouth his mercantile base. After Hamilton's death in 1802 the property was owned briefly by his son-in-law Joshua Haven before it was purchased as an investment by Nathan Folsom in 1815. In 1839 it was sold to Alpheus Goodwin, from whose children the Tysons purchased it.

5 Elizabeth (Tyson) Vaughan to William Sumner Appleton, June 29, 1923, SPNEA Archives. Thomas Nelson Page, "Miss Godwin's Inheritance," in *The Novels, Stories, Sketches and Poems of Thomas Nelson Page* (New York: Charles Scribner's Sons, 1910), 18. In 1910 Thomas Nelson Page wrote "Miss Godwin's Inheritance," a thinly disguised short story describing the restoration. If it is correct, Mrs. Tyson had a great deal to say about what was to be done and needed an architect only "to carry out my ideas."

6 Little and Browne account book, listing under Mrs. George H. Tyson, SPNEA Archives. In a letter to William Sumner Appleton, Sept. 3, 1928, Elizabeth Vaughan states: "Mr. [Lester] Couch of Little & Browne, architects, . . . had charge of all the work here."

7 Vaughan, "Story of Hamilton House," 4.

8 The photographs were taken successively by Elise Tyson Vaughan, from 1898 to 1906 (cat. 31), George Brayton in 1923, and Paul J. Weber sometime between 1925 and 1929. All photographs are in SPNEA Archives.

9 Like her counterpart in "Miss Godwin's Inheritance," Mrs. Tyson "was rummaging around through the country picking up old furniture and articles" while the house was being worked on; see Page, "Miss Godwin's Inheritance," 23.

10 Early articles on Hamilton house state that the wallpaper was made in England. See Louise Shelton, "The Garden at Hamilton House," *American Homes and Gardens* 6, no. 5 (Nov. 1909): 422. Little and Browne account book, SPNEA Archives.

11 *House Beautiful* 65 (Jan. 1929): 62. There is no indication that Mrs. Tyson knew of Hamilton's detailed inventory and used it as a guide in furnishing the rooms.

12 *House Beautiful* 65 (Jan. 1929): 62

13 Hildegarde Hawthorne, "A Garden of Romance," *Century Magazine* 80 (Sept. 1910): 785.

14 Hawthorne, "A Garden of Romance," 779–80.

15 Louise Shelton, *Beautiful Gardens in America* (New York: Charles Scribner's Sons, 1915), 17.

16 Elizabeth R. (Tyson) Vaughan to William Sumner Appleton, June 26, 1923, SPNEA Archives.

17 William Sumner Appleton to Mrs. Henry Vaughan, June 27, 1923, SPNEA Archives.

18 Extracts from the will of Elizabeth R. (Tyson) Vaughan dated 1926, 1939, and 1948, SPNEA Archives.

19 By 1928, the open porch on the river side had been enclosed to make a first-floor guest room and a second story had been added that housed two additional bathrooms and a sun porch.

※ 17 ※

HAMILTON HOUSE MURALS
South Berwick, Maine
George Porter Fernald (1869/70–1920), 1905–6
(see plate 4)

The scenic murals at Hamilton house, commissioned by Emily Tyson and Elizabeth Tyson Vaughan from painter George Porter Fernald, link the Georgian house and its surroundings with the architecture and landscape of the Italian Renaissance. Such a comparison was made by Sarah Orne Jewett in 1881 when she described her view of Hamilton house as being "like a glimpse of sunshiny, idle Italy."[1]

By 1898, when she urged her friends the Tysons to buy Hamilton house, Jewett had made three trips to Europe, traveling in Italy, Greece, and other Mediterranean countries. It is unlikely that Mrs. Tyson, widowed in 1877, and

Cat. 17. Italian landscape mural by George Porter Fernald in the dining room at Hamilton house, 1906. Photograph probably by Elise Tyson Vaughan, 1905. Courtesy, Society for the Preservation of New England Antiquities.

her twenty-six-year-old stepdaughter Elise had as yet embarked upon a grand tour. But one hardly needed to go abroad, for in Boston in the 1890s, classical and Renaissance influences abounded in music, literature, painting, architecture, and the decorative arts.

The Tysons' social circle included writers, artists, and architects, and through the latter they no doubt knew that Palladian proportions and late Renaissance designs were the inspiration for American Georgian architecture. Through North Shore social circles, Mrs. Tyson would have visited the summer cottages of friends, many with classical "beaux-arts" influences and others paying homage to American colonial forms. Among the architects responsible for cottages in this style was Charles A. Platt, an artist-turned-designer who also published *Italian Gardens* in 1894. Platt saw the Italian villa as a useful model for American houses and gardens, writing that:

The evident harmony of arrangement between the house and the surrounding landscape is what first strikes one in Italian landscape architecture—the design as a whole, including gardens, terraces, groves, and their necessary surroundings and embellishments, it being clear that no one of these component parts was ever considered independently, the architect of the house being the architect of the garden and the rest of the villa.[2]

In 1904 Edith Wharton published her second book, *Italian Villas and Their Gardens.* Her first, *The Decoration of Houses,* coauthored with Ogden Codman, Jr., and published in 1897, had widespread influence on attitudes toward interior design. Just as certain choices made by the Tysons in renovating and restoring the interior of Hamilton house were drawn from Wharton and Codman's tenets of proportion and arrangement, *Italian Villas and Their Gardens,* the new lexicon of classical and Renaissance design principles adapted for American taste, affirmed their attitudes toward the integration of houses and gardens. Along with its text, the book contained a

Cat. 17a. Les Vues d'Italie *wallpaper in Wallingford Hall, Kennebunk, Maine, built ca. 1804. Photograph, ca. 1880. Courtesy, The Brick Store Museum.*

visual compendium of photographs, line drawings, and color illustrations.

In the spring of 1905, with images of Italy still fresh in their minds, the Tysons hired George Porter Fernald, a Boston artist, to design and paint an Italian landscape on the walls of the dining room right over the wallpaper they had selected just a few years before (cat. 17). The Tysons were undoubtedly influenced by the new interest in the Renaissance classicism of Italian frescoes and by a passion for French scenic wallpapers of the early nineteenth century which had been an imported symbol of wealth and taste; many of the latter were to be seen in Boston, Marblehead, Salem, and nearby in Portsmouth and South Berwick.[3] It is likely that the Tysons had also seen landscape murals by Rufus Porter and other New England itinerants who decorated walls with painted scenes in imitation of the more expensive papers. By the end of the nineteenth century these had become valued as part of the American folk tradition.

In 1905, a year after Wharton's *Italian Villas and Their Gardens* appeared, and just after the Tysons had returned from their grand tour, Kate Sanborn published *Old Time Wall Papers: An Account of Pictorial Papers on our Forefather's Walls.* In the introduction she recalls fondly:

> For although a native of New Hampshire, I was born at the foot of Mount Vesuvius and there was a merry dance to the music of the mandolin and tambourine round the tomb of Virgil on my natal morn. Some men were fishing, others bringing in the catch; farther on was a picnic party, sentimental youths and maidens eating comfits and dainties to the tender notes of a flute. And old Vesuvius was smoking violently. All this because the room in which I made my debut was adorned with a landscape or scenic paper.[4]

The paper described by Sanborn is the monochromatic version of *"Les vues d'Italie,"* first printed in 1822–23 by the firm of Dufour and Leroy and popularly known as "The Bay of Naples" paper (cat. 17a).[5] Although Sanborn did not know the manufacturer or precise date, she knew many examples that had survived in New England. Sanborn also describes other scenic papers with classical, European, and literary themes, giving their locations and observing that "summer tourists are looking up old walls to gaze at with admiration."[6] Sanborn also notes that:

> One of the most delightful papers of the present season is one copied from a French paper originally on the walls of a Salem house and known to have been there for over one hundred years . . . This reproduction will be seen on the walls in houses of Colonial style in Newport this summer.[7]

The Tysons could have seen any number of old walls nearby. In Portsmouth "The Bay of Naples" paper still exists, though heavily retouched, at the Moffatt-Ladd house, and in the Tysons' time there would still have been scenic papers at the Langley Boardman house and the Wendell house. Kate Sanborn had also drawn attention in her book to the painted murals at the Macpheadris-Warner house. The closest example of the "Bay of Naples" paper existed on Maine Street in South Berwick in the old tavern then owned by the Convent of the Sisters of St. Joseph. Elizabeth Perkins photographed this paper on an outing to South Berwick, which may even have been on the same day in 1898 that she visited her friends the Tysons and photographed the Hamilton house kitchen wing under construction.

Apparently painted walls were not a part of the Tysons' original decorating scheme. Photographs taken in 1899 show new papers in both the dining room and the parlor. But even in these patterns the owners demonstrated a predilection for leafy, garden-inspired patterns; an all-over blue-green foliate block-printed paper for the parlor and a repeat pattern of a landscape with pointed cypresses for the dining room.[8]

Something quite persuasive must have occurred in 1905 to convince the Tysons to hire an artist to paint a mural over the new paper. The Tysons may have conceived of the idea while traveling in Italy that winter or they may have known the paintings and murals of George Porter Fernald through clients of the firm of Little and Browne. Perhaps they had ruled out the exorbitant cost of reproduction papers. In any case during the summer of 1905, Fernald completely covered the wallpaper in the dining room with a painted mural depicting Renaissance villas, gardens, grottos, and picturesque hill towns reminiscent of Sicily and southern Italy.

George Porter Fernald knew not only Italian villas and gardens, but had a sophisticated knowledge of the architecture of the American country house. Fernald was born in New Castle, New Hampshire, in 1869 or 1870, but as a boy moved with his family to Medford, Massachusetts. His natural talent for drawing and penchant for architecture landed him a job as an office boy for the firm of Little and Browne. By 1888 his demonstrated talents had assured him

Cat. 17b. Villa d'Este, Tivoli. Photograph by Elise Tyson Vaughan, 1906. Courtesy, Society for the Preservation of New England Antiquities.

work as a draftsman and illustrator. Fernald's obituary in the *Boston Transcript* tells us that "the artist made numerous trips abroad to continue his studies."[9]

Most probably the Tysons were introduced to the artist by their architect friend Herbert Browne. Regardless of who initiated the dialogue, the resulting triumph must have been a collaboration between artist and client. While Fernald was more familiar with the medieval hill towns, Greek ruins, villas, and gardens of his beloved Sicily, the Tysons, fresh from their winter in Italy, may have insisted on references to the Villa d'Este or the gardens at Tivoli outside of Florence where they had lunched with friends (cat. 17b). One cannot help but wonder if George Fernald Vaughan and Elise Tyson Vaughan compared photographs of Italian gardens, for both were accomplished photographers, sharing similar sensibilities in subject matter and composition.[10]

One particular detail of the dining room murals must have been inspired by Sarah Orne Jewett. In describing Piscataqua River gundalows, she wrote, "I never see the great peaked sail coming round a point without a quick association with the East, with the Mediterranean or the Nile [itself . . .]."[11] No doubt with his clients' encouragement,

Fernald obligingly included several romanticized watercraft—"sailing gondolas"—on the east wall of the dining room. A blue-green palette blended the murals with the gardens and added a watery link with the river vista to the south and to Jewett's "River Driftwood."

In spite of its rich personal iconography, the mural in the dining room still owes its impulse to the many versions of *"Les vues d'Italie"* papers. Fernald's very style of painting seems in part derived from the application of opaque distemper paints used in the block printing of scenic wallpapers. His illustration style ranges from the bold and dark silhouettes of cypress trees which punctuate the sky, to a lighter, more painterly application for the architectural details. The figures of playful youths and maidens in diaphanous dress, and the sailing gondolas and swans, reveal the very lightest touch. Fernald successfully combined the bold patterning of wallpaper with a style derived from French Impressionism. He also incorporated elements of the style of Maxfield Parrish, whose illustrations appeared on the covers of popular magazines of the time and whose renderings were the choice of the publishers of Edith Wharton's *Italian Villas and Their Gardens.*

A Boston critic provides yet another source for Fernald's neoclassical style. A description of murals at the Essex Country Club in Hamilton, Massachusetts, which from photographs appear startlingly similar to the murals at Hamilton house, reads:

> In These Excellent Works by George P. Fernald, the Artist has Cleverly Bent Himself to the Particular Requirements of Mural Decoration-Taking a Leaf from the Book of [Puvis de] Chavannes, He Has Gone Back to the Classic for his Subjects and Has Handled Them in the Light and Deft Manner of the Master—The Drawing is Strong but the Artist Has Kept to the More Restrained Color Scheme Required in This Style of Art.[12]

Having accomplished a tour de force of Mediterranean classical imagery in the dining room, the Tysons seemed determined to give equal importance to an American colonial past and engaged George Porter Fernald to paint another mural in the parlor. In the Piscataqua region at the turn of the century, examples of Georgian and federal-period architecture had become as important as the temples of Greece and the ruins of Rome. Americans seeking a classical past became passionately interested in the homes of their ancestors from hardly more than a century before. Sarah Orne Jewett had called this eighteenth-century commercial and social network "the river aristocracy."

Again the artist turned to an historic wallpaper for inspiration. Dufour's "Monuments of Paris," printed first in 1815 and pictured in *Old Time Wall Papers,* proudly depicts the neoclassical, Renaissance revival buildings constructed during the Napoleonic years.[13] The cityscape extends horizontally along the Seine. By placing the viewer on the left bank, the composition provides a foreground, then a long strip of river in the middle ground, broken occasionally by large trees.

Fernald was quick to see the possibilities in this format for his mural. Taking advantage of the lush foliage provided by the block-printed paper already in place, Fernald created trees at each corner of the room and framed the doorways with classical ruins and vines. On each expanse of wall he painted the device of connecting the foreground to the background by adding a series of bridges that span the blue ribbon of water. Marching along a Seine-like Piscataqua, the houses are connected by the very river whose tidal reaches flow just beyond the windows of the room. The Wentworth-Gardner house, the Wentworth-Coolidge mansion, the first brick factory building at the Cocheco Falls in Dover, the William Pepperrell house, St. John's Chapel, the Governor John Langdon house, the Jewett house, Coventry Hall, and Fort McCleary are all included (see cat. 16b). In the foreground are scenes inspired by other scenic papers. A large seventeenth-century ship appears to have just off-loaded treasures from distant ports, notably ceramics from China and an old English chair. Farther along four ladies looking very much like courtesans

of Louis XIV are seated drinking tea at an unmistakably Piscataqua gate-leg table of about 1730.[14] All along the quay there is activity, and a gundalow, lateen sail billowing, awaits its cargo (see pl. 4).

George Porter Fernald signed his name boldly and conspicuously on this mural and also added his own note of architectural whimsy. In a corner of the mural hidden by an open door, Fernald added a depiction of Thomas Jefferson's "Monticello"—a sly tribute to the great American whose republican ideals were often manifested in the classical vocabulary of Palladian Georgian architecture. Fernald's footnote immediately enlarges the concept of Piscataqua architecture and secures it in a national context.

The author of Fernald's obituary may have had the Hamilton house murals in mind when he wrote that "the work of Mr. Fernald is found on the dining rooms, drawing rooms, music rooms and other apartments in many places where owners have desired specially executed decoration in keeping with the architectural work or in harmony with period finish or furnishings."[15] The Tysons must have considered Fernald's depictions of both classical and "colonial" monuments to be appropriately "in keeping" with the architecture of Hamilton house. Together, the powerful imagery of these interior landscapes makes visible the associations between Hamilton house and its gardens, its architectural significance, and surrounding arcadian landscape that had been described by Sarah Orne Jewett as early as 1881.

SSA

1 Sarah Orne Jewett, "River Driftwood," in *Country By-Ways* (Boston: Houghton Mifflin Company, 1881), 17.

2 Charles A. Platt, *Italian Gardens* (New York, 1894), quoted in Keith Morgan, *Charles A. Platt* (Boston: Northeastern University Press, 1988), 44.

3 For a listing of particular papers and their locations, see Nancy McClelland, *Historic Wallpapers* (Philadelphia: J.P. Lippincott Company, 1924).

4 Kate Sanborn, *Old Time Wall Papers: An Account of Pictorial Papers on Our Forefather's Walls* (New York: Literary Collector Press, 1905), 49.

5 Catherine Lynn, *Wallpaper in America* (New York: W.W. Norton, 1980), 200, pls. 9-12.

6 Sanborn, *Old Time Wall Papers,* 109.

7 Sanborn, *Old Time Wall Papers,* 109.

8 An example of the latter less costly paper which was roller printed with a tapestry-like texture survives in the hallway of Chesterwood, the home of sculptor Daniel Chester French near Stockbridge, Mass.

9 George Porter Fernald, obituary, *Boston Transcript,* July 27, 1920.

10 "Sicily, its Architecture as seen by Mr. George Porter Fernald" (photographs), *The Year Book of the Boston Architectural Club* (1919).

11 Jewett, "River Driftwood," 9–10.

12 Microfilm, Appleton clipping file (before 1916), SPNEA Archives. Other mural commissions by Fernald include: house at Bar Harbor, Me., ca. 1911; house at Sherborn, Mass., Little and Brown, ca. 1916; Essex Country Club, Little and Browne, Hamilton, Mass., date unknown. Other possible commissions include the Ole Bull house, Little and Browne, Cambridge, Mass., and the Lars Anderson house, Brookline, Mass.

13 Sanborn, *Old Time Wall Papers,* pls. LVI, LVII.

14 A large gate-leg table known to have descended through the Pepperrell and Gerrish families of Kittery is now in the collection of OYHS.

15 Obituary, *The Boston Transcript.*

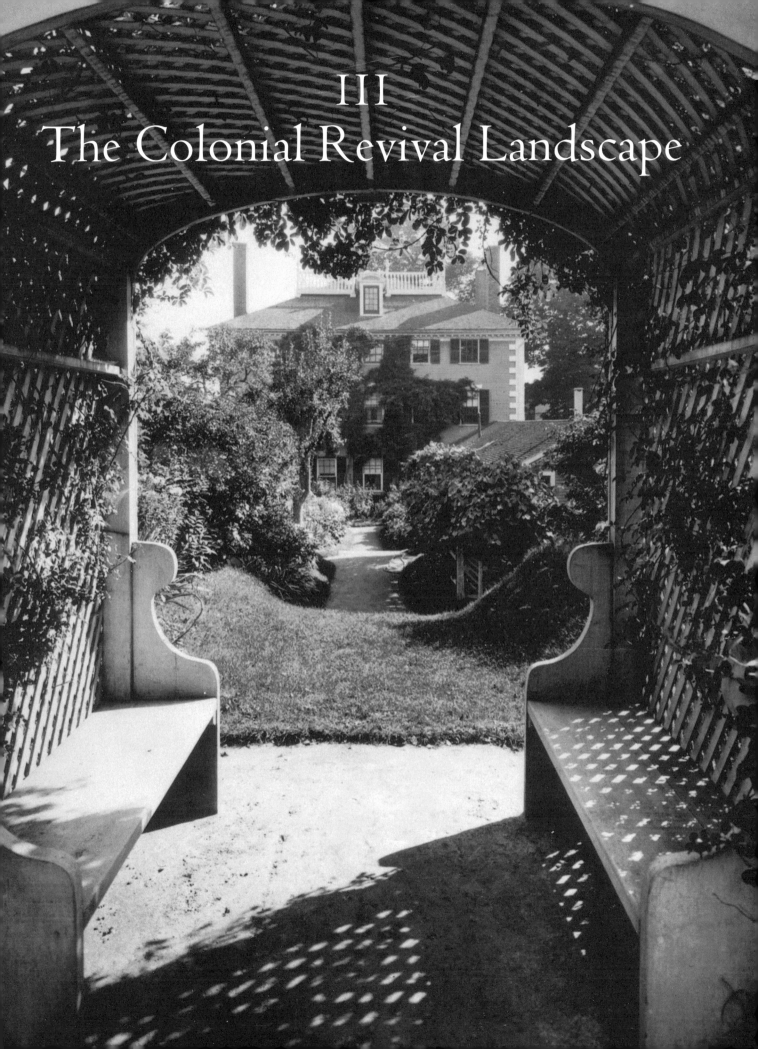

III
The Colonial Revival Landscape

Fig. 3.1. The Southwest Prospect of the Seat of Colonel George Boyd at Portsmouth, New Hampshire, New England, 1774. *Oil on canvas; 17 in. x 32 in. Courtesy, The Lamont Gallery, Phillips Exeter Academy, gift of Thomas W. Lamont, Class of 1888.*

Preceding page: *Garden, Moffatt-Ladd house, Portsmouth, New Hampshire. Photograph, 1924. Courtesy, The National Society of The Colonial Dames of America in the State of New Hampshire.*

"Tempus Fugit":
Capturing the Past in the Landscape of the Piscataqua

LUCINDA A. BROCKWAY

SINCE THE seventeenth century, the landscape of the Piscataqua River Basin has been ordered and shaped by men and women according to their economic, political, and social needs. Indeed, it was the landscape that first drew those interested in mercantile activities in the eighteenth century, who then shaped the land for those retreating from the city more than one hundred years later. In the seventeenth and early eighteenth centuries, the plentiful fishing, ample and accessible timber, and protected harbors provided incentive to develop successful ports throughout the Piscataqua region. To accommodate commercial and residential needs, large tracts of common land and privately held land were subdivided into narrow lots averaging forty to eighty feet. These lots included small kitchen gardens and other spaces for domestic work, as well as craft-related activity spaces. Land closest to the Piscataqua River and its accompanying inlets was particularly attractive because of its waterfront shipping access and was often developed for combined residential and commercial structures.[1]

The mercantile economy of the region produced an upper class in the eighteenth century who established fashionable residences complete with designed pleasure yards and classically inspired gardens. In comparison with the grand formal landscapes of Mount Vernon and Monticello in the southern colonies, Piscataqua gardens were of a more modest scale. While perfect symmetry was not necessarily employed, eighteenth-century Piscataqua garden plans were geometrical and linear, and showed little evidence of the current picturesque landscape designs of Britain. Although a few Piscataqua residents employed foreign gardeners, none are known to have visited British gardens.[2] The developing nursery trade along the eastern seaboard and personal trading provided plants, both American and European, for the area's gardens.[3] Long cold winters and a short growing season prohibited the planting of some English species, requiring these northern inhabitants to adopt native alternatives.

One landscape painting of a Portsmouth garden exists from the eighteenth century. *The South West Prospect of the Seat of Colonel George Boyd at Portsmouth, New Hampshire, New England, 1774* (fig. 3.1) depicts an estate once located on the south shore of the North Mill Pond, just outside of Portsmouth proper. The Boyd garden was rectangular and was divided at irregular intervals by paths radiating out

from a central hub, which was perhaps a small pool. One central axial path ran from the door of the house to a garden gate. Bilateral symmetry was not present in the rest of the garden design: placement of the other garden paths seems to have been purposely directed at outbuildings or access gates. Trees of various sizes were scattered randomly among the angular tracts of grass. According to a nineteenth-century historian, Boyd found an Irish gardener, Johnny Cunningham, in England, "and sent him here before the Revolution to be his gardener—for which business he had been educated."[4]

James Grant's map of 1774, entitled "A Plan of Piscataqua Harbor, Town of Portsmouth, Ec." (fig. 3.2), illustrates a large garden, orchard, and open farm land at the Benning Wentworth estate in Little Harbor. The estate had a garden plan similar to that of the Boyd estate with straight paths leading from a central point to the sides and corners of the rectangle. An advertisement leasing the property for three years describes the site as having 113 acres and including a house, gardens, and farm. The gardens consisted of kitchen, fruit, and flower gardens, "in the latter a profusion of rose bushes making from 20 to 30 bottles of rose water [annually]." The advertisement boasted that the kitchen garden contained a variety of fruit trees, thirty large beds of asparagus, and alone would produce yearly from two to three hundred dollars. Additional features of the property included a nine-acre rocky pasture for sheep and two wells near the house.[5]

John Stilgoe defines landscape as "shaped land, land modified for permanent human occupation, for dwelling, agriculture, manufacturing, government, worship, and for pleasure."[6] Stilgoe suggests that vestiges of the past landscape become virtual icons that inform judgments about cities, factories, and other products of the Industrial Revolution. In the Piscataqua region, the residences of the eighteenth-century elite and their accompanying pleasure grounds and gardens drew a new group of settlers in the late nineteenth century. Paradoxically, these homes and gardens of the elite evoked images of simpler, humbler times in the minds of late nineteenth-century viewers. The decaying vestiges of the eighteenth-century landscape, including cemeteries, fences, commons, and farmsteads, constituted part of the region's charm by the end of the following century, as a 1893 article from the *Lewiston Journal* on the town of York suggests:

Close by the sounding sea lies the old First Parish cemetery of York. Lulled by the whispering waves, its peaceful dead calmly slumber, awaiting the final summers. Covered with moss and bowed by the flight of centuries, are its crumbling tombstones with their quaint, half erased inscriptions. Here is the antiquarian's paradise. With the ancient jail, its old cemetery and weatherbeaten, decaying garrison houses, its antique mansions and Indian relics, York is a historical treasure trove unexcelled in New England.[7]

As Frederick Law Olmsted, H.W.S. Cleveland, Charles Eliot, and others worked to create urban parks that kept a small portion of the country within reach of city residents, many urbanites left the city to experience the "antiquarian's paradise" and the natural beauty of the New Hampshire and Maine coast. However, they also brought with them a desire to own their own piece of the country and to make private the once public, unfertile ocean-front property. Charles Eliot, writing in 1889, described how the summer tourists were rendering the wild beauty of the coast inaccessible:

the impartial observer can find but two points about which are in any considerable degree discouraging or dangerous: . . . the small amount of thought and attention given to considerations of appropriateness and beauty by the builders and inhabitants of the summer colonies of the coast. The squalid aspect of the public parts of these settlements, the shabby plank walks, and the unkempt roadways are other causes of reproach. The houses themselves, if cheap, are too often vulgarly ornamented, and if costly, are generally absurdly pretentious.

Eliot went on to complain that the smooth lawns, made of imported soil, kept green only by continual watering, did not blend well with the rough ledges and scrubby woods of the coast. Similarly incongruous were flower beds scattered over rocky and uneven ground (fig. 3.3). He wrote of the summer visitors that "this annual flood of humanity, with its permanent structures for shelter, may so completely overflow and occupy the limited stretch of coast which it invades as to rob it of that flavor of wildness and remoteness which hitherto has hung about it, and which in great measure constitutes its refreshing charm."[8] Eliot went on to encourage the State of Maine to enact legislation promoting the formation of a coastal preservation association.

While Eliot felt that the gardens and cottages of the summer residents were destroying the landscape, many city residents concluded that the rural landscape fell short of their expectations. The Piscataqua region's towns lacked city amenities such as running water, electricity, hospitals, paved roads, and trees. The idea of preservation went hand in hand with beautification and improvement. Throughout the region, village improvement societies, such as the Old York Historical and Improvement Society (cat. 18), founded in 1900, were formed to create parks and walking paths, to beautify railroad stations, railroad tressels, and other unsightly spots, and to preserve burying grounds and historic buildings.

Fig. 3.2. Detail of James Grant, "A Plan of Piscataqua Harbor, Town of Portsmouth, Ec.," 1774. Watercolor and ink on paper; 21¼ in. x 18 in. Courtesy, New Hampshire Historical Society.

Fig. 3.3. Garden, William Dean Howells house, Kittery Point, Maine. Photograph by Marvin Breckinridge Patterson, 1933. Courtesy, Piscataqua Garden Club.

In addition to their creation of a town green for York, the Old York Historical and Improvement Society cared for the cemetery, restored the jail, and created a system of picturesque walking paths throughout the village and harbor. The paths were built and maintained by the society which believed itself to be enhancing the naturalistic feeling of the town. Although the society was originally organized by men, women played an increasingly important role in actually carrying out the society's projects. Because York had a flourishing summer community, there were many women in the area with the leisure and the organizational abilities to execute a wide variety of civic improvements.

Dr. Birdsley Northrup, an advocate for village improvement who promoted the movement throughout New England, suggested that women be involved in improvement work. He felt that many efficient associations had been formed by women, and that nearly all or at least some of the officers of the organizations he advocated should be female. Northrup suggested that executive committees have fifteen members, eight of whom should be women considered to be superior fund-raisers. Other authors agreed that village improvement was especially suited for women. One commentator suggested that improvement required the sort of systematic attention to detail, especially in the constantly recurring duty of "cleaning up, that grows naturally out of the habit of good housekeeping."[9]

The Old York Historical and Improvement Society officers, eight of whom were women, hoped that by providing an example of attractive design, other residents would apply the techniques to their own homes. Earlier, in 1881, Sarah Orne Jewett had lamented over the state of yards (fig. 3.4) in New England, attributing their decline to the new status of women:

> Whether the house was a fine one and the enclosure spacious, or whether it was a small house with only a narrow bit of ground in front, the [eighteenth-century] yard was kept with care, and was different from the rest of the land altogether. People do not know what they lose when they make way with the reserve, the separateness, the sanctity, of the front yard of their grandmothers.[10]

Jewett attributed the loss of front yards to the "altered position of women" stating that "the whole world is their front yard nowadays."[11] Alice Morse Earle, a popular garden writer, also mourned the disappearance or lack of upkeep of front yards. She believed that in the past they had been emblematic of woman's life "of that day: it was restricted and narrowed to a small outlook and monotonous likeness to her neighbor's; but it was a life easily satisfied with small pleasures."[12]

Door yards, filled with ornamental herb gardens and

Fig. 3.4. Job Wells house, York Harbor, Maine. Lantern slide by Elizabeth B. Perkins, ca. 1900. Old York Historical Society.

colorful flowers such as phlox, day lilies, lilacs, and peonies, became popular in the colonial revival (fig. 3.5). Where once serving as functional, sheltered areas for growing foodstuffs in the colonial period, the colonial revival door yard served an aesthetic function. Perhaps because they were seen as the woman's domain, door yards at the turn of the century once again became important parts of the residential landscape.[13]

Celia Thaxter's garden at the Isles of Shoals (cat. 25) is representative of a woman's approach to viewing her door yard aesthetically. She extended her door yard with trellises and framed her garden with flowers, such as phlox and peonies, from her grandmother's time. While Thaxter did pay attention to her door yard, it is significant that it looked outward toward the ocean, rather than inward. The whole world was her front yard and she made her home accessible to numerous artists and writers.

Jewett's suggestion that the position of women was changing could be seen throughout the region as upper-middle-class women began stepping out of the home and into the public sphere. Women's clubs, garden clubs, improvement societies, and other philanthropic organizations were founded in the region in response to the "altered position of women." The preservation of historic houses was also seen as an appropriate activity for women. The ideology of separate spheres in the nineteenth century rested on the assumption that women's true place was in the home and that when out of the home, they were best suited to doing work, whether philanthropic or for wages, that replicated housework. The Old York Historical and Improvement Society's main preservation effort was the restoration of the Old Gaol (cat. 53), a project seen as a way to improve the town's morals. The editor of the *Old York Transcript,* in describing the Gaol, stated that "In the dawn of the twentieth century it stands, a part of the seventeenth century, a living testimonial as it were, to prove the worth, dignity, the strength, and endurance of our forefathers." The establishment of the Old Gaol Museum created for

women a public role within the Improvement Society, allowing them a more appropriate role than "cleaning up the streets."[14]

Of the numerous gardens that were designed or owned by women between 1900 and 1930, perhaps the most elaborate and best preserved are those appended to colonial properties that opened as museum houses at the turn of the century. Members of The National Society of The Colonial Dames of America in the State of New Hampshire renovated the gardens at the Moffatt-Ladd house (cat. 19) shortly after the turn of the century, and Thomas Bailey Aldrich's widow repurchased her husband's boyhood home and created a poet's memorial garden (cat. 23) in 1908 which incorporated the latest theories in "colonial" garden design. When the all-male Portsmouth Historical Society restored the John Paul Jones house in 1919, they did not restore the garden; it was not until 1923 that members of the Piscataqua Garden Club established a colonial revival garden around the house.

The profusion of books, magazine articles, lectures, and garden club activities provided ample opportunity to learn the design and contents of the colonial garden. Instead of adhering to exact duplication of the early American garden, the new garden plans were romantic allusions to the past. The revival versions of colonial gardens were gardens of pleasure, not of necessity. Designers therefore had artistic license to mass hollyhocks, phlox, and mignonettes around a sundial, or use larkspur, poppies, and lavender as a backdrop to a classically inspired garden seat. The flowers were often revivals of what had been in the garden from only two generations earlier. Although supposedly old-fashioned, the flowers were actually the latest hybrids. Alice Morse Earle suggested that it was not slavish historical re-creation that counted, but rather the capacity of particular flowers to invoke an image of the past:

> There is a quality of some minds which may be termed historical imagination. It is the power of shaping from a few simple words or details of the far-away past, an ample picture, full of light and life, of which these meagre details are but a framework.[15]

Historical designs and flowers were thus often freely adapted to modern requirements. As landscape architect Arthur Shurcliff advised in 1932, it was the spirit of the colonial design that could be incorporated into gardens. Often elements from a variety of periods and countries were included in a supposedly "colonial" garden. At the Elizabeth Perkins house (fig. 3.6; see also cat. 20), a combination of eighteenth-century geometric elements and curvilinear picturesque components existed side by side. The plantings were massed in a planned, but informal, manner in geometric beds, while nearby ran a curving tree-lined drive planted earlier in the nineteenth century. The rural, pastoral setting of the eighteenth-century farmhouse also provided inspiration for the Perkinses. Embedded millstones for steps and a birch tree shading a cigar-store

Indian spoke of difficult times in York's past. The inclusion in the Perkins garden of lilacs, peonies, and roses also created an air of antiquity. Plants reminiscent of industriousness and a temperate home life in colonial days were selected for their romantic and aesthetic beauty.[16] Elizabeth Perkins used orchard trees to line her drive, and Lilian Aldrich planted hops over her back-door arbor.

Similarly, the eighteenth-century landscape around the Moffatt-Ladd house provided a "framework" for the Colonial Dames' garden restoration (cat. 19). Originally the terraced, eighteenth-century gardens may have been used, for the most part, for subsistence. As at the Benning Wentworth estate, kitchen, fruit, and garden plots may have been separated into functional units. This prototype of functional plants, used for subsistence and medicinal purposes, and geometrical garden beds was adapted by the Colonial Dames to create a garden based on aesthetic considerations.

Although designed and shaped by products of the Industrial Revolution and by women with newfound leisure, the colonial revival garden was often viewed philosophically as a retreat from both the present and from industrialized city life. As Louise Shelton wrote in 1915:

If only we could live in the world more as we live in the garden, what joy and contentment would be

Fig. 3.6. Garden, Elizabeth Perkins house, York, Maine. Photograph by Elizabeth B. Perkins, July 1906. Old York Historical Society.

brought into the daily life! In the garden hurry and noise are needless, for perfect system can prevail where each plant, each labor has its own especial time, and where haste is a stranger, quiet reigns.[17]

In the Piscataqua region, the majority of colonial revival gardens flourished in the summer retreats and house museums created by city residents. The gardens often incorporated transitional elements between indoor and outdoor spaces such as patios, terraces, outdoor seating

Fig. 3.5. Job Wells house. Photograph, 1932. Courtesy, Society for the Preservation of New England Antiquities.

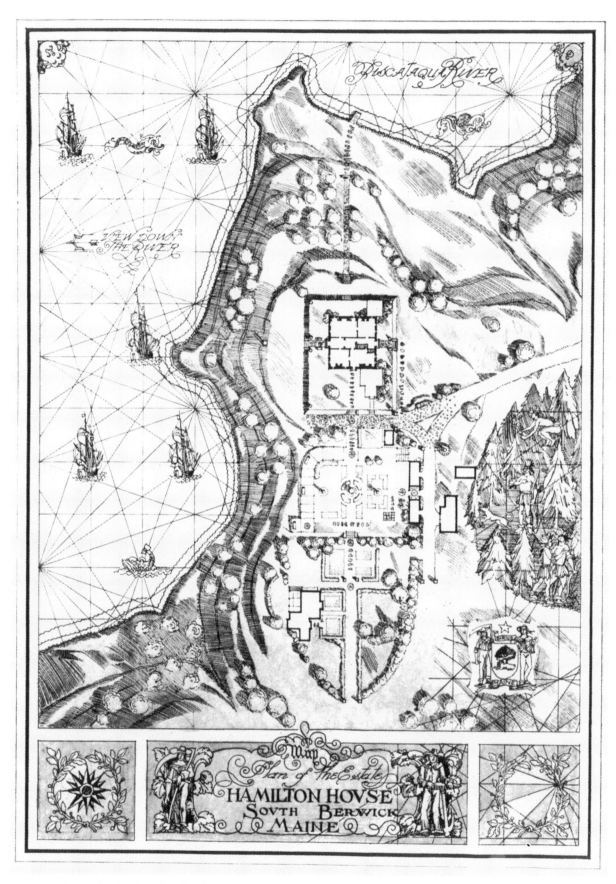

Fig. 3.7. Garden plan, Hamilton house, South Berwick, Maine. From Great Georgian Houses of America *(1937). Courtesy, Society for the Preservation of New England Antiquities.*

areas, and arbors, that facilitated entertaining and dining. The Moffatt-Ladd house was even changed architecturally so that garden and parlor might be melded together. The Tysons also made architectural changes to their dining room at Hamilton house in order to allow access to the garden.

Elements of Italianate gardens, rediscovered by landscape architects in the late nineteenth century, were also mixed with the colonial in Piscataqua gardens. Just as the American architecture and gardening movement had been inspired by the classical in the eighteenth century, so were the colonial revival gardens of the early twentieth century. Alice Morse Earle commented:

I have the same love, the same sense of perfect satisfaction, in the old formal garden that I have in the sonnet in poetry, in the Greek drama as contrasted with the modern drama; something within me is ever drawn toward that which is restrained and classic.[18]

It was the sense of order and classic restraint that made the Italianate so attractive when creating retreats from hectic city life. The Hamilton house garden plan (fig. 3.7) incorporated classically inspired architectural elements with a colonial revival flower garden. Pergolas enclosed a garden that was divided into four equal parts by a cross-axial path. Rectangular beds were filled with perennials.

This large-scale classical revival garden was designed as a series of garden "rooms," walled by box hedges, lines of trees, and architectural features. Arbors, a garden cottage, pergolas, and trellises framed the doors of the garden. Like the interior parlor, the garden was often used as an outdoor living space. Picnics, teas, and other social activities were centered around the garden in good weather. As Hildegarde Hawthorne wrote of her afternoon in the Hamilton house garden:

I recall a summer afternoon in a Maine garden overlooking the shining reaches of a river. The great Colonial house merged through green arbors into the beds gay with flowers, separated each from each by grassy paths edged with box and given seclusion by rose-hung wall and pergola. The small group sat idly enough among the fragrant smells and gentle sounds . . . tea was over and the west was smoldering with intense color . . . And altogether delightful as were the days and the amusements of that hospitable week, it is the garden hour that lingers in the memory . . . Such gardens and such hours are multiplying with us, and are a valuable indication of our increasing sanity of life, our developing taste and realization of what it is that is truly worth while, and that leisure and peace and seclusion are assets for which we should be willing to make some sacrifices.[19]

The social rituals that took place in the highly aestheticized spaces of colonial revival gardens frequently became the subjects of works of art in many media. In their leisure, women such as Elizabeth Perkins and Elise Tyson Vaughan also began new hobbies including garden photography. One observer noted:

Gardening has been called one of the most sensitive of the fine arts, and the making of a garden as near as a man may get to the exercise of divine powers. If art be an expression of beauty, then gardenmaking should be ranked among the fine arts . . . These great gardens have performed another valuable service to the arts; they have helped to turn photographers into artists, have lifted the mechanical science to the plane of the arts.[20]

Photography and colonial revival gardens seemed destined for one another. The room-like qualities of the garden designs, the views and vistas into and out of the garden, the architectural features and alleys which framed the garden helped the photographer to capture these qualities in the frame of his photographs.

Professional and amateur photographers were plentiful in the Piscataqua region. Elise Tyson Vaughan (cat. 31) used the gardens at Hamilton house as the subject for much of her photography. Emma Coleman (cat. 41) used the agricultural and rural scenes of the region in her work. Elizabeth Perkins documented the preservation work of the Old York Historical and Improvement Society, work on her own home, and the pastoral scenes of the region. In 1884, Mary Devens photographed the region in its early years as a summer resort. Frederick B. Quimby, a Massachusetts professional photographer, used the York region as a subject for his work while summering at Ground Nut Hill, his family farm (fig. 3.8). Albert Gregory, the Davis Brothers, Carl Meinerth, Lafayette Newell, Caleb Stevens Gurney, and Walter Chesley Staples recorded sites throughout the greater Portsmouth area, including streetscapes and private residences.

Through writers such as Alice Morse Earle, Louise Shelton, and Hildegarde Hawthorne, and amateur and professional photographers such as Elise Tyson Vaughan, Elizabeth Perkins, and others, the gardens of the Piscataqua region became known as design prototypes outside of the region. The Hamilton house gardens were featured in five magazine articles and photographed for Louise Shelton's *Beautiful Gardens in America*. As Shelton writes: "In isolation, simplicity, and ripeness the atmosphere of the whole place breathes of olden days, and might well be taken as a model for a perfect American garden."[21] The Chinese puzzle garden and its surrounding arbors and trellises at the Wendell house (see cat. 24) were recorded by Fletcher Steele and used as design inspiration for his work at the Stockbridge Mission House. Celia Thaxter's garden at the Isles of Shoals was the subject of numerous paintings by Childe Hassam and John Singer Sargent; Thaxter's book on the garden was widely read. Lilian Aldrich published a volume highlighting the flowers featured in her husband's poetry.

While these published gardens inspired many amateur

gardeners, they also influenced professionally trained landscape gardeners. Individuals trained in civil engineering, horticulture, botany, floriculture, and architecture had formed the bulk of professionals, known as "landscape gardeners," who were hired to conceptualize and install designed landscapes in the nineteenth century. Most of these early landscape architects had a combination of scholastic training in engineering and practical, apprentice-based training in the profession. The first university curriculum of professional training in landscape architecture was established at Harvard University under the direction of Frederick Law Olmsted, Jr. The Society of Landscape Architects was begun in 1899. Although the field was dominated by men, several important female landscape architects had a strong influence on the future of landscape architecture as a profession, including Beatrix Jones Farrand (the only female founding member of the American Society of Landscape Architects), Ellen Shipman, Martha Brooks Hutchinson, Marion Coffin, and Florence Yoch. In the early twentieth century, the Cambridge School of Architecture and Landscape Architecture for Women and the Lowthorpe School of Landscape Architecture, Gardening, and Horticulture for Women produced some of the finest female landscape architects of the period.

These women were socially connected to summer communities such as Cornish, New Hampshire, and Boston's North Shore.[22]

Several landscape architects were commissioned to develop plans for parks, subdivisions, and private residential landscapes in the Piscataqua region—all for summer residents. The Olmsted Brothers (1898–1957), the successor firm to Frederick Law Olmsted, Sr.'s practice, were the most active in the region, listing nine commissions in the region between 1894 and 1958.[23] Although the Olmsted Brothers were asked to develop plans for a park system in Dover in 1903–4, these plans were never fully realized. The Olmsted Brothers consulted on the development of two summer cottage subdivisions: the James C. Sawyer subdivision, Durham (1922), and the F.A. Whiting subdivision, Ogunquit (1922–58). The firm was sent plans for the Fogg Memorial and the Berwick Academy in South Berwick in 1894, but they never developed plans for either site. Olmsted Brothers, however, did develop the grading, siting, and final planting recommendations for the Francis L. Stetson house (1901–2) and the Harold C. Richard house (1929) in York Harbor, and the James Earle residence in Cape Neddick (1910–26). These designs enhanced the rocky terrain and wind-swept conditions of each site and did not

Fig. 3.8. Garden, Cape Neddick, Maine. Photograph by Frederick Quimby, ca. 1894. Old York Historical Society.

reflect the formal, symmetrical designs more typical of the colonial revival.

The thirty-seven plans developed for the gardens at the Alvan Fuller residence and Union Chapel in North Hampton, New Hampshire (1938–41), more closely reflect the interest in colonial and classical garden designs typical of the period. Plans for these gardens included the design and layout of the "garden room" shaped by hedges and fencing, filled with beds of roses and perennials, and decorated with trellises, gates, arbors, and pools whose details were specified by the Olmsted Brothers.

Ellen Biddle Shipman (1870–1950), whose work ranged from Texas to Michigan, and from North Carolina to Maine, is best known for her gardens and estate designs. Shipman lists two clients in the Piscataqua region: the oval garden and grounds for Mrs. Russell Alger, York Harbor (1937, fig. 3.9), and the flower garden for H.W. Lewis, York Village (1944–45).[24] Shipman was asked to design the Alger gardens at the same time she was commissioned to develop the grounds of the Algers' Grosse Point, Michigan, estate. Her designs for both gardens reflect the interest in cottage gardens and "Grandmother's cutting gardens" popular during the colonial revival period.

Arthur Shurcliff (1870–1957) and his son, Sidney, were very active in the region. Although the exact nature of their involvement in the projects they undertook here is as yet unknown, they list as clients Mrs. Henry Chalfant (York Harbor), Mrs. William Nichols, Jr. (York Harbor, 1940–43), the Dover Park Commission, Leverett Saltonstall (Dover), Lucius Varney (Dover, 1928), and Ross W. Wittier (Dover), in addition to the Old York Historical and Improvement Society/First Parish Church (York Village, 1950). The Shurcliffs list Mrs. John C. Breckenridge (York Village, 1942, fig. 3.10) as a client; Guy Lowell includes this same family in his list of clients for the early twentieth century.[25]

With a strong background in plants developed from working in his father's Reading, Massachusetts, nursery, Warren Manning (1860–1938) was placed in charge of most of the Olmsted Brother's planting plans while he was apprenticing with that office. While with the Olmsted Brothers, Manning completed planting plans for 125 projects in twenty-two states including the designs for the World's Columbian Exposition of 1893 and Biltmore (1888–95) in Asheville, North Carolina. Manning opened his own landscape architecture office in 1896 in Cambridge, Massachusetts, and was a founding member of the American Society of Landscape Architects in 1899. Manning's client list includes five properties in the Piscataqua region, most of them summer estates whose owners had enlisted Manning's help in landscaping their permanent residences in other parts of the country. His work in the Piscataqua region includes the residential landscape designs for Bryan Lathrop (York Harbor, 1898), Hamilton Smith (Durham, 1903), Mrs. A.H. Gross, "Yorkholme" (York, 1916), Charles E. Pits (Rye Beach, 1918), Alvan Fuller (North Hampton, 1918), Louis L. Green

Fig. 3.9. Alger garden, York Harbor, Maine. Photograph by Marvin Breckinridge Patterson, 1933. Courtesy, Piscataqua Garden Club.

Fig. 3.10. Garden, River House, York, Maine. Photograph by Marvin Breckinridge Patterson, 1933. Courtesy, Piscataqua Garden Club.

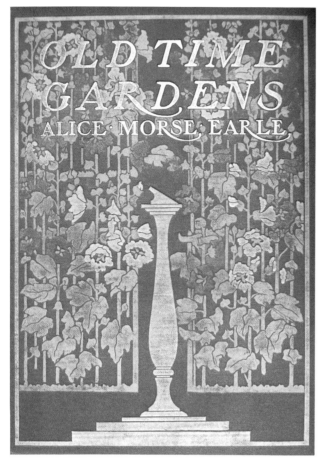

Fig. 3.11. Alice Morse Earle, Old Time Gardens *(1901). Old York Historical Society.*

(New Castle, 1926), New Hampshire State College (University of New Hampshire, Durham, 1913), Exeter Cemetery (Exeter, 1914), Ambrose Swasey / Swasey Parkway (Exeter, 1915–26), and Alfred Gross/Long Beach Boardwalk (York, 1926).[26]

The pastoral ideal has always dominated the American psyche. In the late nineteenth century, when men and women turned from the cities toward the country, it was toward those areas that seemed most ancient, scenic, healthful, and accessible to them. Yet they could never leave the city completely behind. Summer visitors brought with them distinct ideas of ways to preserve and improve the landscape. They brought gardening tools, ideas of landscape design, new forms of technology, and landscape designers to adapt the land to their own requirements. They also brought the opportunities for year-round residents to capitalize on the beauty of their surroundings. It was the Industrial Revolution that sparked changes to both the cityscape and the countryside. Trains and profitable businesses gave visitors the opportunities to escape the cities. New technologies gave them the leisure time to improve the streets and create elaborate gardens. Permanent residents in the Piscataqua region found a market for their raw materials in the cities and their

scenic surroundings at home. For both groups, their expanded world only made them more aware of a way of life rapidly disappearing. The motto inscribed on the sundials common to the colonial revival garden—"tempus fugit"—suggests this worry. Yet the garden also became a space in which change was resisted through the free interpretation of past landscapes.

1 For the eighteenth-century history of the Piscataqua region, see Charles Edward Banks, *History of York, Maine,* 3 vols. (1931, 1935; reprint, York, Me.: OYHS, 1990) and John Durel, "From Strawbery Banke to Puddle Dock: The Evolution of a Neighborhood, 1630–1850" (Ph.D. diss., University of New Hampshire, 1984).

2 Little research has been completed on the professional gardeners of Portsmouth for any period.

3 See plant lists and archaeological data in unpublished manuscripts, Landscape Department, SB.

4 Charles W. Brewster, *Rambles About Portsmouth,* first series (1859; reprint, Somersworth, N.H.: New Hampshire Publishing Co., 1971), 295.

5 *New Hampshire Gazette,* June 18, 1816.

6 John Stilgoe, *Common Landscape of America* (New Haven, Conn.: Yale University Press, 1982), 3.

7 Quoted in "Old Burying Ground at York," *Biddeford Record,* May 23, 1898, 1.

8 Charles Eliot in 1889, quoted in *Charles Eliot, Landscape Architect* (Boston: Houghton Mifflin, 1902), 312–15.

9 Warren Manning, "History of Village Improvement in the United States," *Craftsman* 5 (Feb. 1904): 98; and Mary Caroline Robbins, "Village Improvement Societies," *Atlantic Monthly* 79 (Feb. 1897): 212.

10 Sarah Orne Jewett, *Country By-Ways* (1881; reprint, South Berwick, Me.: Old Berwick Historical Society, 1981), 58.

11 Jewett, *Country By-Ways,* 63.

12 Alice Morse Earle, *Old Time Gardens* (New York: The Macmillan Company, 1901), 49.

13 In addition to door yards, gardens at the turn of the century included numerous themes, such as the "grand tour" of Italian, French, Moorish, Japanese, and English cottage gardens.

14 Linda Kerber, "Separate Spheres, Female Worlds, Woman's Place: The Rhetoric of Women's History," *Journal of American History* 75, no. 1 (June 1988): 9–39. *Old York Transcript,* June 8, 1899, 2.

15 Earle, *Old Time Gardens,* 34.

16 Earle, *Old Time Gardens,* 214.

17 Louise Shelton, *Beautiful Gardens in America* (New York: Charles Scribner's Sons, 1915), 2–3.

18 Earle, *Old Time Gardens,* 78.

19 Hildegarde Hawthorne, *The Lure of the Garden* (New York: The Century Company, 1911), 101–2.

20 *Touchstone Magazine* 2 (Dec. 1917): 278.

21 Shelton, *Beautiful Gardens in America,* 17.

22 See Norman T. Newton, *Design on the Land* (Cambridge, Mass.: Belknap Press, Harvard University Press, 1971).

23 For complete details on these commissions, see the Olmsted Archives, Frederick Law Olmsted National Historic Site, Brookline, Mass., and the Library of Congress, Washington, D.C.

24 For complete details on these commissions, see Ellen Shipman Archives, Cornell University, Ithaca, N.Y. A 1933 photo (fig. 3.9) suggests that Shipman's work for Alger may have begun before 1937.

25 Arthur Shurcliff client list, Shurcliff Collection, Frances Loeb Library, Harvard University, Cambridge, Mass. A 1933 photo (fig. 3.10) suggests that Shurcliff may have worked for Breckinridge before 1942.

26 For Manning's commissions, see Olmsted Archives.

Cat. 18. York Village Center from the southwest. Photograph by Angie Gowen, ca. 1900. Old York Historical Society.

18

OLD YORK HISTORICAL AND IMPROVEMENT SOCIETY
York, Maine
Founded 1899

In 1898 C. Alice Baker, an antiquarian from Deerfield, Massachusetts, visited York and later reported on her visit at an annual meeting of the Pocumtuck Valley Memorial Association. She complained that "Old York is now New York. Many of its old-time houses have been drummed out by the so-called march of improvement. The straggling cottages of the fishermen have disappeared from the landscape . . . the rugged face of the cliff over which the woodbine and beach pea used to scramble, is now disfigured by the unsightly waste pipes of modern improvement that wriggle like so many foul serpents to bury themselves beneath the ocean."[1]

Most of York's active summer residents saw the town's development very differently than did Baker and her several York friends. On June 22, 1899, an article appeared in the *Old York Transcript* stating: "The ringing in of the new has not, as is often the case, caused the breaking up and dissolution of the old, but the two are being welded together in a manner which brings not only industrial development alone, but human progress as well."[2] This integration of the natural and modern landscape was similar to the welding of historicism and modernity that was seldom expressed as a problem in York. In fact, development

and preservation were seen as compatible, and preservation articles often appeared in the newspaper next to discussions of development.

York, like similar resort towns, was seen as a pure, unspoiled village for retreat and spiritual rejuvenation among morally upright villagers. Nowhere were the "Old York" and the "New York" more knit together than in the Old York Historical and Improvement Society. Founded in 1899 largely by summer residents, the organization had two purposes: to beautify the village and to preserve York's past. Perhaps this group had been motivated by Baker: members immediately set to work recreating the village green, restoring the Old Gaol (cat. 53), planting trees, covering up unsightly spots of modernity—such as the railroad station—with shrubs, and planning for the town's Tercentenary celebrations (1902). In short, they saw themselves as rejuvenating a declining village.

The restoration of the village green was a major part of the Improvement Society's activities. Reformers knew exactly what they had in mind for the new common. In 1899 the editor of the *York Courant* wrote that "it is hoped that another season may see the village green handsomely graded into a neat triangular park with the cannon mounted in form of a monument and a curb placed around. Clean sidewalks and well mown roadsides, with the magnificent elms, unsurpassed in beauty by any New England Village, will make York only more and more attractive." The author of this article warned that "whatever is done should be done in rural style and not in imitation of the city. The country and the country village have charms of their own and they make a great mistake who suffer the rare beauty of a village street and corner to fall into neglect while they strive to substitute something more pretentious but sure to be only disappointing in the end."[3]

Despite this warning, city planning, particularly as then practiced in Chicago, had a direct influence on the development of York's center. Henry Lathrop, a Chicago real estate magnate and chairman of the Improvement Society's Street Improvement Committee, was familiar with plans to improve Chicago which were first stimulated by the "White City" of the 1893 World's Columbian Exposition. Lathrop's brother-in-law, Owen Aldis, was a director of the Columbian Exposition, as well as a summer resident of York. Several other Improvement Society members are also known to have attended the Exposition.[4] Numerous articles on the Columbian Exposition were featured prominently in local newspapers with descriptions of its architecture, a plan for Jackson Park, and the improvements to Chicago's city plan which called for wide tree-lined boulevards that were to provide vistas of important buildings and the incorporation of parks designed in an informal picturesque fashion. It seems safe to assume that the ideas put forth at the Columbian Exposition had a direct effect on the image Improvement Society members created for the village green.

The village green, as we know it today, is often a construct of turn-of-the-twentieth-century reformers. And indeed, York's was just such a product of the colonial revival. The earliest record of York's center referred to as a "town green" occurred in 1882, when the First Parish Church was rededicated after extensive renovations that included turning the church to face the road. At this time, the concept of the Village Green came to York. The church dominated the landscape and presided over York Street, the burying ground, and Lindsay Road, the main thoroughfare from the village to the York river (cat. 18).

The reports at the first annual meeting of the Improvement Society in 1901 reveal a certain amount of frustration with initial attempts at beautification. Mrs. James T. Davidson reported that the group had successfully planted shrubs and trees at the corner by the church, but that a grass plot in the center of York Street had been destroyed

Cat. 18a. Trees planted by Improvement Society, York, Maine. Photograph, ca. 1901. Old York Historical Society.

by the water company. Vandals had also destroyed some of the society's work by pulling up newly planted trees on Long Beach Avenue. Members concluded that "the year's work was very unsatisfactory."[5] Henry Lathrop, chairman of the committee on planting trees, suggested at the same meeting that the grass of the village green should be cut every few days and that the trees should be weeded and cultivated. He stated that "the Green belongs to the people of the town of York and if well cared for they will take great pleasure and pride in it."[6] Lathrop then hired his York Harbor neighbor—Thomas Nelson Page's garden designer, O.C. Simonds from Chicago—to provide a plan for York's green.

By 1904 the village green was greatly "improved" and photographs reveal the results of the Improvement Society's plantings (cat. 18a). Bushes appeared around the church and the town hall, which had recently been painted white. The vacant lot at the corner of Lindsay Road and York Street, where Jefferds Tavern now stands, was planted with "a large bed of flowering shrubs, lilacs, Japanese lilacs and elder, a few little pine trees and the Mountain Ash."[7] Opposite the First Parish Church were set out four elms, two Japanese lilacs, a mountain ash, some honeysuckles and seven or eight laurel-leaved willows. By 1908 the society had achieved its goal: "the Village Green of York is surpassed by few, if any, in New England. In the midst of grounds laid out by expert landscape artists arises the First Parish Church crowned by one of the most beautiful spires in existence."[8]

Perhaps in the face of indifference, or even opposition from "natives," the need of the summer residents of York to construct a village green reveals a desire to create an important icon they felt was missing from the town's landscape. The colonist's center, the village green attended by the spired church, was believed to be a constant in New England villages.[9] The idea of common land, going back to the seventeenth century, took on an added dimension in the nineteenth century. No longer simply the physical and symbolic center of the community, the common now seemed necessary to counteract emerging forms of urban life. The common symbolized a landscape where people could collectively benefit from the land. Thus parks were created in cities, and village greens were added or improved in rural villages.

The conscious improvement of the Village Green coincided with real estate development and activities designed to bring to York such city amenities as town water and electricity. The idea of preservation for the future was at the heart of the Improvement Society. The Old York Historical and Improvement Society, like many other improvement societies, was intimately tied to the social and cultural transformations at the turn of the century, and the historicism found within improvement societies coexisted with an enthusiasm for progress.

SLG

1 C. Alice Baker, "A Trip to Old York," *History and Proceedings* (Pocumtuck Valley Memorial Association, Deerfield, Mass.) 3 (1901): 335.

2 "The Chimney Corner," *Old York Transcript*, June 22, 1899, 2.

3 *York Courant*, June 29, 1899, 3.

4 *Old York Transcript*, Aug. 11, 1893, 1.

5 "Improvement Society," *York Transcript*, Aug. 31, 1900, 3.

6 Old York Historical and Improvement Society Minutes, OYHS Ms. Coll., 65.

7 Patricia Todisco, "Old York Historical Society Site Analysis and Historic Landscape Plan" (typescript, OYHS, 1983), 31.

8 Quoted in John D. Bardwell, *The Diary of the Portsmouth, Kittery, and York Electric Railroad* (Portsmouth, N.H.: Portsmouth Marine Society, 1986), 75.

9 See Ronald Lee Fleming and Lauri A. Halderman, *On Common Ground* (Harvard, Mass.: Harvard Common Press, 1982), xv.

⇒ 19 ⇔

MOFFATT-LADD HOUSE GARDENS
Portsmouth, New Hampshire, 1763
Restored 1900

"A house and a garden are inseparable," wrote Philip Dana Orcutt in 1935 in reference to the Moffatt-Ladd house in Portsmouth, New Hampshire.[1] This notion of the "inseparability" of the architecture and its grounds, discussed in terms of historic significance and design elements, suggests the importance of the "garden room" in the colonial revival home. The National Society of The Colonial Dames of America in the State of New Hampshire restored the Moffatt-Ladd house for its architecture, its original owner's lineage and patriotism, and for the elements of the colonial period that formed a "cluster [of] historic memories"; however, the Dames also found the garden (cat. 19) to be "as individualistic as the house, although much later in date."[2]

The garden was added to the Moffatt-Ladd house sometime between 1820 and 1840 and was designed in keeping with the original colonial forms. Although an urban dwelling, the Moffatt-Ladd house is situated on a large piece of property stretching backward from the house for several hundred yards. All that is known about the original land use is that it housed an orchard, roses, a horse-chestnut tree, several outbuildings, and a wall to mark its boundaries and, perhaps, to contain small livestock. What is significant about this early garden was that it was modified as the needs of the household changed. As Portsmouth (a mercantile community) and the Moffatt family (merchants and shipowners) prospered, the Moffatt-Ladd grounds were transformed from a plot used for subsistence, to a plot used to make an aesthetic statement. This shift was due, for the most part, to the availability of services, goods, and leisure time as merchants of the new nation increased their capital.

Cat. 19. Garden, Moffatt-Ladd house, Portsmouth, New Hampshire. Photograph, 1924. Courtesy, The National Society of The Colonial Dames of America in the State of New Hampshire.

The family's decision to transform a large portion of the land into a garden did not, however, preclude the land use and elements of the colonial landscape; in fact, most of the older elements were incorporated into the new garden design. This sensitivity, or perhaps sentimentality, on the part of the Ladd family then formed the backbone for the Colonial Dames' interpretation of this historic site. When the Moffatt-Ladd house was transformed from a private dwelling to a house museum, these elements of the landscape imbued the interpreter's presentation of local colonial history.

The garden was a haven in Portsmouth, then a growing urban environment, and to preservationists the garden illustrated their forebears interest in natural, but cultivated, beauty: an idea that the Colonial Dames continue to foster. Orcutt describes the garden as a room, making the parallel to the house's drawing room both in terms of its privacy and comfort. The variety of fruits, flowers, shrubs, and trees "make this a paradise of colour and of shade." Further, the garden is adorned with rose trellises, grape arbors, and carefully designed walking paths giving this outdoor room a feeling of civilized natural beauty. The garden also offered sustenance and thus provided an element of the colonial need for self-sufficiency: fruit and herbs were plentiful.

Even before the Colonial Dames began the organized efforts to preserve the house and garden, the Moffatt family, friends, and early revivalists were fostering a sense of "plant lineage" in the Moffatt-Ladd garden. Today, there exists cherished lore around two plants, the grandmother's rose bush and the grandfather's horse-chestnut tree (cat. 19a), whose age, fertility, and rank make their new spring shoots collectors' items of sorts. Situated at the heart of the garden, the Damask rose bush is said to have been "planted by the family's first tragic little bride," and many generations of brides "have taken slips from it to their new homes. 'As if in response to the romance and sentiment which cluster around it, it blossoms as freely and beautifully now as in its youth, a living witness to the eternity of love and life.'" The imbuement of the rosebush is one of few examples where merit is placed on the lineage of women and their roles as wives and mothers.

The horse-chestnut tree embodies an equally important history but one that mirrors the masculine colonial experience. The tree was planted by General William Whipple, the son-in-law of Captain John Moffatt, and a brigadier general in command of the first New Hampshire Brigade during the Revolution. Considered the oldest tree in Portsmouth, it is associated with the general's fight for liberty, with his "strength of character and [with] the beauty of [his] relationship with the life of their period." The nuts of this tree, like the new spring sprigs of the rose bush, were "carried away by admirers" for many years.

It is important to place this garden in the larger landscape of Portsmouth. The Moffatt-Ladd house is situated on the edge of a steep bluff facing Portsmouth harbor, the

Cat. 19a. Horse-chestnut tree, Moffatt-Ladd house. Photograph, ca. 1912. Courtesy, The National Society of The Colonial Dames of America in the State of New Hampshire.

Moffatt-owned wharf, and the Atlantic Ocean. These elements of the landscape were thus easily kept under the watchful eye of Captain Moffatt, and, in turn, show the architecture's intrinsic link to the out-of-doors and to the public sphere. The garden is situated in the back of the house, and its privatized design suggests that access is allowed only to the house's occupants and the family's guests. The dichotomy of the Moffatt-Ladd house's front facing toward business and toward the wildness of the sea and its back opening upon the leisure-oriented "garden room" epitomizes the early American search for balance; balance between work and leisure, natural and cultivated landscape, public and private space, as well as male and female spheres.

AWH

1   Philip Dana Orcutt, *The Moffatt-Ladd House: Its Garden and Its Period, 1763, Portsmouth, New Hampshire* (Norwood, Mass.: Plimpton Press for the New Hampshire Society of Colonial Dames of America, 1935), 48. Unless otherwise noted, all quotations in this entry are from this source.

2   *Boston Journal*, Dec. 8, 1911.

❖ 20 ❖

ELIZABETH PERKINS HOUSE GARDENS
York, Maine, 1900–1940

Situated on the edge of the York River and surrounded by expansive lawns with pristine river views, the Elizabeth Perkins house, restored to a summer residence, epitomizes the culmination of preservation and improvement at the turn of the twentieth century in York. As the founder of the Old York Historical and Improvement Society, the Society for the Preservation of Historic Landmarks in York County, and the Piscataqua Garden Club, Elizabeth Perkins was an advocate for restoration and beautification projects in York beginning as early as 1900. Her own property was as much a part of these projects as were the more public restorations of the Old Gaol Museum, Jefferds Tavern, the Old Schoolhouse, and the John Hancock Warehouse.

Perkins considered the grounds around her house representative of the colonial past and thus included them in her restoration efforts. The site is indicative of a revivalist's use of the landscape showing a sensitivity to original plant material and land use while simultaneously enhancing the land with objects and plant material reminiscent of the past.

Elizabeth Perkins's treatment of the landscape was an amateur effort in that no landscape designers were employed to render her garden plans. Rather, she drew from the writing of Alice Morse Earle, her visits to gardens, and information which was circulated through the Garden Club of America and the Piscataqua Garden Club. The literature, coupled with sightseeing and lectures, formed a foundation from which Perkins chose her garden patterns. Included in her personal papers are the published reports of the Garden Club of America's annual meetings. Along the margins, in between paragraphs, and inside the book covers are animated notes about plant material, gardening techniques, conservation committee reports, and lists of people with whom she met while attending the conferences. It is clear from these notes that Perkins was very interested in historic plant material and planting techniques. For instance, Perkins underlines "unsowed flowerbeds," stars "Dolly Madison roses," and lists, in great detail, the herbs that are appropriate for an "old tyme herb garden."[1]

Most of the garden was removed by Historic Landmarks in the 1950s due to the expense of maintaining the site. However, elements of Perkins's original garden and landscape plan still exist. Some of the most obvious "colonial" elements of the Elizabeth Perkins landscape, thought to be original and thus preserved by Perkins, were the birch tree north of the front entrance, some of the old elms and maples that line both the road and the riverbank, and the apple trees (the originals had died, but new trees were replanted by Perkins in the same places). All other plant material on the site results from plantings by the Perkinses between 1900 and 1940.

Cat. 20. Garden, Elizabeth Perkins house, York, Maine. Photograph, 1906. Courtesy, Garden Club of America.

Photographs taken by Elizabeth Perkins of her garden and the surrounding landscape reveal that the first alterations of the property were the stone walls that defined its boundaries. Located along the road and riverbank, and terracing parts of the lawn, the stone walls, an historic marking technique, are one of the most prominent colonial revival landscape treatments surviving on the property. Notable, too, is the use of old gristmill stones, objects often used to symbolize the colonial past, as steps.

The most formal plantings consisted of two raised beds, edged with cedar planks and running parallel for about seventy-five feet on each side of a walkway lined by roses and rose arbors. Planted in the beds that lined the arbors was a clustered mixture of hollyhocks, phlox, lilies, and an assortment of native wildflowers. These plantings were located on the south side of the property and led to an old well, adorned with a well sweep and bucket. The plantings and arbored walkway created a vista to the well, imbuing the garden with a rough sense of history and old colonial folkways. Lining the raised beds are fruit trees: apple, pear, and peach. The fruit trees remind the visitor of the colonial orchard; further, they allude to the function of the garden being more than just an aesthetic experience.

Early photographs show the garden arbors as made of twigs and sticks, while later the arbors were constructed from metal piping. The rose and the arbor are other symbols of the colonial revival, for the rose was thought to be the first flower cultivated by the colonists (cat. 20).

The Perkins house was hedged with peonies, and up many of its eastern walls climbed wisteria. On an outer wall, just outside the dining room, is mounted a large sundial. Sundials, classic and honored, spoke of a period when time was measured by the elements; its presence, in the words of Alice Morse Earle, "echoed antiquity."

On the banks of the York River, Perkins placed a life-sized cigar-store Indian (see cat. 52). Perched on a small outcropping of land along the York River's edge, the Indian served as an icon of the colonial struggle for survival in the early 1700s and as a reference to the Candlemas Massacre, as well as to the landscape's first inhabitants. Ironically, when removed from its function as a gimmick for merchandisers and placed at the edge of the York River, the Indian becomes the "noble savage" rather than the savage red. The carved wooden form was statuesque and perhaps represented Perkins's interest in the folk art tradition more than an alignment with Indian experience.

Elizabeth Perkins did not decorate her landscape with objects and plant material alone. Folk tales and myths were as prevalent as the flowers. These tales, such as the one about the secret tunnel which ran from the river's edge into the house and whose purpose was for the smuggling of goods so as to avoid taxation, functioned to give historic importance to Perkins's property. She dug holes in the yard seeking archaeological evidence of shell heaps and thus of Indian presence. Furthermore, she told of a colonial dump site on the right side of the property where one could find old pottery and glass.[2] In this way she decorated the landscape of her garden with history and fiction, adding ambiance to the property.

AWH

1 Perkins Coll., OYHS, box 6, folders 11–17.
2 Perkins Coll., OYHS, box 3, folder 23.

❧ 21 ❧

Hamilton House Gardens
South Berwick, Maine, 1901

Since the construction of the Hamilton house in 1783 on a broad point of land overlooking the Salmon Falls River, the property has served as a merchant house/business site, a farm, a summer home, and a historic house museum. Encapsulated in this one site are layers of more than two hundred years of landscape use and change that reflect broader patterns of the Piscataqua region's landscape history.

On January 13, 1783, Colonel Jonathan Hamilton purchased thirty acres at Pipe Stave Point, South Berwick, complete with barns, warehouses, wharves, and outhouses. Hamilton, a local merchant, transferred the bulk of his shipping and retail trade to this newly purchased site, and by 1787–88 had erected a fine Georgian mansion on the top of the bluff overlooking the river.[1] Hamilton's landscape efforts around the new mansion included terraced lawns

and gardens overlooking the river to the south and west. To the north lay a long entrance drive which terminated east of the house in a service court with additional stables and outbuildings. Rolling green fields opened the view from the Hamilton site to "Old Fields," the estate of General Ichabod Goodwin which sat east of the Hamilton property.

In April 1839, Alpheus and Betsey Goodwin purchased the house and the "stores, barn, woodhouse and other outhouses belonging thereto, and also a wharf contiguous to said mansion" from Folsom.[2] Goodwin tore down the neglected warehouses and storage buildings, and began farming the surrounding fields. Though the farm produced a variety of goods, sheep farming was its most prosperous aspect. According to tradition, "the formal garden became his apple orchard, but he moved old-fashioned perennials and Scotch roses up near the kitchen door where Betsey could step out to tend them when the cares of the household were at their ebb."[3] Photographs taken about 1880 show the house set amidst the apple orchard, with farm pasture and forage land separated from the house by a dirt entrance road, a large barn, and a series of three-board fences.

It was this combination of a stately home situated in a rural, farm landscape that made the property so attractive to the Tysons. In the summer of 1898 the Tysons bought Hamilton house and its surrounding 110 acres. Over the next few years Emily Tyson and her stepdaughter proceeded to turn the farmstead into a true expression of the colonial revival. Despite extensive documentation for the project, no one designer can be credited with the design and contents of the Hamilton house gardens. It seems that the landscape changes begun in 1901 and constantly evolving throughout the Tysons' ownership were the result of the collaborative influences of Emily Tyson, Elise Tyson Vaughan, architect Herbert Browne, artist George Porter Fernald, and visitors to the garden (cat. 21).

George Fernald was intimately familiar with Sicilian gardens and may have influenced the Hamilton house landscape designs (cat. 17). The Tysons traveled to Europe and toured Italian gardens shortly after the garden construction was under way. Emily Tyson may have been influenced by her parent's garden at Hill Top, just outside of Philadelphia. Her photograph albums (cat. 31) include numerous photographs of the William Morris and Elizabeth Jacobs Davis garden at Hill Top. Some individual features of this garden are similar to portions of the Hamilton house garden.

No doubt the Tysons were responsible for the selection of plant material in the garden. Published articles concerning the garden describe the two women and their preferences for specific plants and planting effects. Elise Tyson Vaughan was very active in the Garden Club of America during the 1920s and 1930s, planning a national annual meeting in York Harbor in 1934 and attending ten national meetings throughout the country between 1925 and 1941. During these events, Elise Tyson Vaughan would have toured the residential gardens of club members and undoubtedly returned to South Berwick inspired with new garden design and horticultural ideas. She was known to have tried the latest hybrids and unusual varieties in her South Berwick garden.[4]

The fencing which surrounded the house during the Goodwin period was removed by 1900, and the barn which sat east of the house was moved in its entirety up the entrance driveway to its present location at the end of Vaughan's Lane. In its place, a formal garden was added east of the house. A wide stone path led from the east door of the house, across a flagged courtyard area, through a latticed garden gate into a rectangular perennial garden, enclosed by a vine-covered pergola on three sides. The pergola terminated its northern side in a series of small outbuildings imperceptibly constructed within the framework of the pergola. To the south, the pergola made a wide turn and ran along the crest of the south river bank, terminating in a small garden seating area. The eastern edge of the garden was defined by a raised grass bank and spirea hedge. The garden's main axis walk extended through an arbor in this hedge into a smaller garden room filled with cut flowers, and terminated between two columned posts topped with pineapple finials. Beyond these posts the view opened up the hillside through rolling fields to a hilltop orchard.

The pergola-enclosed garden was divided into four equal parts by a cross-axis path which ran north to a gate opening to the service yard and south to a small bench and opening through the pergola to a view of the river (cat. 21a). A sundial marked the garden's central intersection. Rectangular beds were scattered throughout the garden, defining path edges and accentuating the angularity and formal symmetry of the garden plan. These beds were filled with perennials of all types and varied from year to year. Small trees and various shrubs added height and some informality to the overall garden design. Garden seats, benches, fountains, various potted plants, and garden statuary provided additional accent and spots of interest as one roamed the garden.

In 1909 the first published article appeared on the Hamilton house gardens. The author, Louise Shelton, observed: "There are larger gardens, and gardens of more elaborate design, but Hamilton House garden is the dream fulfilled of a nature-lover and artist, who, while living in the atmosphere of an old mansion under the shade of ancient elms by the river, wove into the scheme a garden fashioned after the spirit of the place."[5]

In 1910, Hildegarde Hawthorne described a walk through the pinewood at Hamilton house along "narrow paths which leap sudden chasms or small brooks on bridges so fashioned of the material at hand as hardly to seem made by man." She wrote of the pergola garden:

Most romantic is the outlook over the inclosed garden, from which rises a perfume of flowers and the low splash and rustle of a fountain . . . Narrower grass paths separate the long beds crowded with flowers,

the brilliant colors of which seem unstudied, and the arrangement so easy and withal so sure that only the finest art could have succeeded in being at once so manifest and yet so hidden . . . [T]he garden belongs to the heart of the summer—planned mostly for the month of July, with iris, rose, delphinium, country pinks, Canterbury bells, spotted lilies, heliotrope, sweet alyssum, pansies, tall hollyhocks.

Hawthorne also described the garden cottage and surrounding plantings:

Arches lead out of the garden and over a little hill to a little house fit for a Hans Anderson story before which, enclosed by a low fence, is the quaintest and most charming of cottage gardens. Small paths, laid in uneven brick, divide it into oblong beds, bordered with tiny box-hedges, and crowded with old-fashioned flowers: phlox, sweet-william, rose geranium, wall-flower, and stock, forget-me-not, fragrant mignonette, and golden marigolds. In one corner cluster dahlias . . . foxgloves stand by the cottage wall . . . and off against the fence a clump of sunflowers . . . then one may see five-o'clocks open, their perfume mingling with that of lemon verbena . . . gilly-flower, love-lies-bleeding, rue, columbine, cinnamon pink.[6]

Elise Tyson Vaughan continued the care and upkeep of her mother's gardens after her mother's death in 1922 until 1949. Though the bones of the garden plan remained as her stepmother had intended, the overall planting philosophy became more refined. Beds of lower-growing annuals mixed with the older perennial species, creating a more controlled look to the overall garden plan, as well as masses and accents of color.

In 1929, Edith Kingsbury described the site: "The grass-covered slopes of the bluff have been left untouched, with no attempt made to restore the terraced [Hamilton period] gardens and their steps, but very recently rows of crab apples have been planted to border the pathway to the old pier."[7] The former commercial part of the property was thus domesticated as an element of a landscape suited to leisure.

Elise Tyson Vaughan grew frail after her husband's death in 1938; during her last years she was bedridden. Undoubtedly few landscape changes were made between 1938 and her death in 1949, as the garden's structural features aged and the trees and shrubs matured. In 1949, the Society for the Preservation of New England Antiquities was bequeathed the house, gardens, and ninety-one acres. The "pinewood" described in early articles was given to the State of Maine for public use and is now known as Vaughan's Woods.

When SPNEA acquired the site, many of the structural features had deteriorated and many of the plantings had overgrown their intended spaces. A concern for the cost of

Cat. 21. Garden, Hamilton house, South Berwick, Maine. Photograph by Paul J. Weber, before 1929. Courtesy, Society for the Preservation of New England Antiquities.

Cat. 21a. Pergola, Hamilton house garden. Photograph by Paul J. Weber, published in House Beautiful (1929). Courtesy, Society for the Preservation of New England Antiquities.

upkeep and repair to the twentieth-century garden features at a time when the society was particularly interested in the earliest history of the house, meant the removal of many of the garden elements. However, in 1980 a group of interested and knowledgbale volunteers began a concerted effort at rejuvenating the gardens in conformity with their appearance during the colonial revival.

LAB

1 Burton W.F. Trafton, Jr., "Hamilton House, South Berwick, Maine," OTNE 48, no. 3 (Jan.–Mar. 1958): 57–58.

2. YCRD, 165:81.

3 YCRD, 165:81.

4 Alan Emmet, "Hamilton House and Its Gardens" (typescript, SPNEA Archives, 1981), 16–17.

5 Louise Shelton, "The Gardens at Hamilton House, South Berwick, Maine," American Homes and Gardens 6 (Nov. 1909): 422–25.

6 Hildegarde Hawthorne, "A Garden of Romance: Mrs. Tyson's, at Hamilton House, South Berwick, Maine," Century Magazine 80 (Sept. 1910): 778–90.

7 Edith Kingsbury, "Hamilton House, A Historic Landmark in South Berwick, Maine," House Beautiful 65 (June 1929): 782–89, 874–75.

HAMILTON HOUSE GARDEN COTTAGE
South Berwick, Maine, ca. 1907

"Mrs. Tyson is at Miss Beaux—& dines Sunday at Beauport," wrote Henry Davis Sleeper (1878–1934) to his friend and neighbor A. Piatt Andrew (1873–1936) when Emily Tyson visited Gloucester, Massachusetts, in the summer of 1908.[1] Sleeper, who had just completed his own summer cottage, Beauport, was especially anxious for the mistress of Hamilton house (cat. 16) to see his creation. "It was going to her house, you remember, that you discovered the possibilities of the Cogswell house—therefore she is much interested."[2]

These two serendipitous events—Sleeper's visit to Hamilton house in South Berwick and his accidental discovery of the disintegrating Cogswell house (ca. 1740) along the road in Essex, Massachusetts, the same day—provided the catalyst for Sleeper's famous architectural and decorative fantasy on Eastern Point. Crammed with salvaged woodwork from eighteenth-century dwellings and furnished with spectacular displays of European and American decorative arts, Beauport's reputation as a "colonial" creation grew.[3] Later, as one of the nation's leading interior designers in the English and American taste, Sleeper's influence reached thousands through the popular press, decorating books, and commissions, helping to shape and disseminate his special vision of the colonial revival.[4] Winterthur, Sleeper's most famous commission for Henry Francis du Pont (1880–1969), continues to influence the colonial revival movement in America.[5]

Hamilton house left less of an impression on Sleeper during his initial visit to South Berwick in 1907 than the Tysons' newest building project. When Sleeper first visited on August 6, together with Cecilia Beaux, A. Piatt Andrew, John Templeman Coolidge, and his daughter "Molly" (cat. 29), Emily and her stepdaughter Elise had just completed a one-room cottage in the garden, using paneling and materials salvaged from several nearby dwellings (cat. 22). As Elise recounted many years later:

> We were told of an old house in Newmarket [sic], crumbling on its foundations and about to be demolished. Of course we investigated, and the result was a couple of big wagon-loads (it was the day before trucks) of decrepit looking material, and the weeks of construction that followed were the most delightful imaginable. In these days of more careful correctness in detail, especially in early American affairs, it, probably, would have been planned differently. But that was the year 1907 before the early American had fully come into his kingdom![6]

The materials for the new cottage studio probably came from the remains of the Sally Hart house (ca. 1740), a

Cat. 22. Garden cottage, built ca. 1907, Hamilton house, South Berwick, Maine. Photograph by Paul J. Weber, before 1929. Courtesy, Society for the Preservation of New England Antiquities.

deteriorated building actually located in Newington, New Hampshire, about four miles out of Portsmouth on the Dover Road.[7] The lower story had virtually disintegrated by 1907 allowing for salvage only of material from the chambers and roof. A paneled fireplace wall, stripped of paint, determined the width of the western wall in the new building and became its chief focal point. The old front door served as a facing for a new chimney stack that reached preposterously through the open ceiling to the ridgepole, and salvaged stair balusters were used to create tiny balconies on either side of the chimney. Much of the framing, including the chamfered joists and roofing system, was resurrected and left exposed.[8] On the wall opposite the fireplace, old window shutters and paneled doors were rehung to conceal new cabinets and to help create the illusion of a fully paneled interior (cat. 22a). The oversized studio window on the north wall and the three smaller French doors along the southern elevation were inspired references to the arched window on the stair landing of Hamilton house. All four admitted ample sunlight while the doors opened onto

a terraced lawn overlooking the Salmon Falls River. The balance of woodwork, doors, moldings, and planking were salvaged from a jumble of material from the Hart house and two other dwellings, including the Columbia Warren house in South Berwick that was pulled down around the same time.[9]

The result was a romantic retreat paneled in pumpkin-colored pine and comfortably furnished with the trophies of European travel.[10] This was the building as Sleeper found it immediately following his discovery of the Cogswell house and while the plans for his own home revolved in his head; the results were electrifying.

Sleeper subsequently purchased the woodwork from the Cogswell house and with the help of Gloucester architect Halfdan M. Hanson (1884–1952) set about creating Beauport. The salvaged paneling was used in several downstairs rooms. Old window shutters created the wainscoting in the stair hall. A fireplace endwall with a door leading nowhere added visual interest in the master bedroom, and scattered about, Sleeper carefully arranged his burgeoning

Cat. 22a. Interior of garden cottage, Hamilton house. Photograph by Paul J. Weber, published in House Beautiful *(1929). Courtesy, Society for the Preservation of New England Antiquities.*

collection of decorative arts objects and furnishings in cluttered, yet balanced, configurations. So when Mrs. Tyson visited Beauport in 1908, she came expectantly as a fellow restorer and progenitor; what she found resembled her own work on a grander scale.

Both Tyson and Sleeper knew of earlier efforts to reuse old woodwork. Mrs. Tyson originally summered at Eagles Rock in Prides Crossing, Massachusetts, and spent time at Sharksmouth, the Jacobean revival mansion in Manchester-by-the-Sea, Massachusetts, where Greely Curtis installed the main staircase from the historic John Hancock house (demolished 1863) in 1868.[11] The Essex Institute in Salem opened its set of period rooms the very year that Sleeper visited South Berwick, and both Tyson and Sleeper were friendly with Isabella Stewart Gardner (1840–1924), whose Fenway Court in the Back Bay of Boston included architectural elements salvaged from numerous European buildings.

For Sleeper and his contemporaries, old paneling possessed historic and romantic qualities thought to be inherent in eighteenth-century design, whether of European or American colonial origin. Some, like Sleeper, whose resources were not inexhaustible, reused salvaged woodwork for simple economy to achieve the desired effect; others, like the Tysons, favored its romantic associations or quaint beauty. Their cottage garden, built for "the fascination there is in old pine paneling," provided an instant relic of olden times.[12]

Neither Sleeper nor Tyson worked in a vacuum. Both personally knew architects who favored the colonial revival style. Herbert W.C. Browne (1860–1949) of Boston, who may have helped with the additions to the Hamilton house, might also have had a hand in the garden cottage as well.[13] Browne, his partner Arthur Little (1852–1925), and another Boston architect, Ogden Codman, Jr. (1883–1951), dubbed themselves the "colonial trinity" for their mutual admiration of eighteenth-century design.[14] Given the close-knit nature of Boston society, Emily Tyson udoubtedly knew these men.

Sleeper certainly did. He moved in Boston's social and artistic circles, knew Codman through professional organizations, and spent childhood summers in the rambling shingle-style house Arthur Little designed for the family on Marblehead Neck.[15] This house, like many of Little's projects, included numerous eighteenth-century details culled in part from sketching forays into old houses, including a number in the Portsmouth area.[16] The spirit of the Marblehead house permeated Beauport, so when Little first saw it, he enthusiastically encouraged Sleeper to work professionally, "offering me the services of his draftsmen, superintendents, contractors, etc. if I should want to build a house for anyone else!"[17]

Yet neither the Marblehead house, the garden studio, nor Beauport were accurate historical creations. Each combined design elements drawn from a variety of sources. The Marblehead house used architectural conceits never seen in eighteenth-century America. The cottage contained European furnishings. The Beauport rooms, with thematic titles like the Byron Room, the Shelley Room, and the Strawbery Hill Room, named for the home of the antiquarian Horace Walpole (1717–97), made historical allusions to English antecedents. The old paneling served merely as a backdrop for a series of domestic settings that blurred distinctions between Europe and colonial America.

As Sleeper continued to draw on Europe for inspiration, articles in newspapers and the design press began to laud Beauport's antiquarian feel and praise Sleeper as a designer in the colonial style. He dabbled in patriotic American activities briefly during World War I, when he helped raise funds for the American Ambulance Field Service, but by 1921 he was again referring to Beauport as an "old English house."[18] In the 1920s he opened a design office in Boston specializing in English and French interiors and seventeenth- and eighteenth-century American paneling, but Sleeper's clients increasingly preferred his services as an expert in solely the colonial taste, and this frustrated and constrained him. By 1928 the national craze for anything colonial had completely redefined Sleeper's work in the public eye; that year he began his work at Winterthur.

The Hamilton house garden cottage underwent a similar transformation, and Sleeper may have had a hand in it. The cottage gradually shed its European furnishings for early American things, largely at the behest of Elise Tyson Vaughan after she inherited the property in 1922. By 1929, the transformation was complete. Pine and maple furniture, Windsor chairs, and folk art, accented with apricot chintzes and blue net window hangings, suggest Sleeper's strong influence. Moreover, he and Vaughan periodically exchanged objects, including a small weathervane that is still at Beauport.[19] Sleeper even used the garden cottage as a model for the master bedroom in a commission he executed for Mr. and Mrs. Frederick Luther Morrill of Gloucester around 1920.

Henry Sleeper's visit to Hamilton house in 1907 was perhaps the single most important catalyst behind the creation of Beauport, and through Beauport, Sleeper's ideas reached a national audience. It demonstrated to others the broad possibilities of reused woodwork arranged to suit modern needs, but it also emphasized a special brand of colonial revival architecture with its origins firmly rooted in the Old World: architecture that was quickly given a "colonial" label by outside observers, critics, and the press, helping to create new, popular images of the American past.

PAH

1 Henry Sleeper to A. Piatt Andrew, Aug. 28, 1908, quoted in E. Parker Hayden, Jr., and Andrew L. Gray, eds., *Beauport Chronicle: The Intimate Letters of Henry Davis Sleeper to Abram Piatt Andrew, Jr., 1906–1915* (Boston: SPNEA, 1991), no. 23. "Beaux" is Cecilia Beaux (1855–1942) the portrait painter, who summered at Green Alley four doors south of Beauport.

2 Sleeper's first recorded visit to Hamilton house occurred on Tuesday, Aug. 6, 1907, with Cecilia Beaux, A. Piatt Andrew, John Templeman

Coolidge, and Mary Coolidge (Perkins), spending a *"wonderful 2 hours"* (Cecilia Beaux diary, 1907, AAA). Both Emily Tyson and Beaux were from Philadelphia; she most certainly introduced Sleeper to Tyson on this visit.

3 See David Bohl et al., *Beauport: the Sleeper-McCann House* (Boston: David R. Godine and SPNEA, 1990); Philip Hayden, "Beauport, Gloucester, Massachusetts" *Antiques* 129, no. 3 (March 1986): 622–25.

4 For example, A.M.B., "The New Old House," *House Beautiful* 40 (Aug. 1916): 129–33, 164; [Reginald T. Townsend], "An Adventure in Americana," *Country Life* 55 (Feb. 1929): 35–42; Russell H. Kettell, *The Pine Furniture of Early New England* (New York: Doubleday, Doran & Co., Inc., 1929), 65, 115, 142; Nancy McClelland, *Furnishing the Colonial and Federal House* (Philadelphia: J.B. Lippincott Company, 1936), 163–67; Nancy McClelland, *Historic Wall-Papers* (Philadelphia: J.B. Lippincott Company, 1924), 96–99; Nancy McClelland, *The Practical Book of Decorative Wall Treatments* (Philadelphia: J.B. Lippincott Company, 1926), 187. For a list of Sleeper's commissions, see Appendix in Bohl, *Beauport*, 108–9.

5 See Jay Cantor, *Winterthur* (New York: Harry N. Abrams, 1985).

6 [Elise Tyson Vaughan], "The Story of Hamilton House," Paper delivered to the Garden Club of America, South Berwick, Maine (typescript, SPNEA, ca. 1934), 5.

7 Newmarket, Newington, and Newfields are often confused. John Mead Howells, in *The Architectural Heritage of the Piscataqua* (New York: Architectural Book Publishing Co., 1937), fig. 57, identifies the source of the woodwork as the Sally Hart house in Newington. A house marked "S. Hart" appears on the *Plan of Newington, Greenland, and Portsmouth* by Alfred M. Hoyt, 1851. This location is approximately four miles from Portsmouth on the Dover Road. I am indebted to Jane Porter of the PA and Barbara Myers of the Newington Historical Society for identifying this building.

8 [Vaughan], "Hamilton House," 5; Edith Kingsbury, "The Cottage at Hamilton House in South Berwick, Maine," *House Beautiful* 66 (Dec. 1929): 691–95. Additional information is written on the back of several photographs of the cottage now in the SPNEA Archives.

9 Handwritten note on the back of a photograph of the Columbia Warren house, South Berwick, Me., SPNEA Archives.

10 Kingsbury, "Cottage at Hamilton House," 691.

11 Christopher Monkhouse, "The Making of a Colonial Revival Architect," in Pauline Metcalf, ed., *Ogden Codman and the Decoration of Houses* (Boston: David R. Godine and the Boston Athenaeum, 1988), 49. Greely purchased the stair from John Russell Sturgis (1834–88) for that purpose.

12 [Vaughan], "Hamilton House," 5.

13 George Porter Fernald, who painted the scenic wallpaper in the living room and dining room of Hamilton house, worked for Little and Browne.

14 Ogden Codman to Arthur Little, Aug. 17, 1891, quoted in Metcalf, *Ogden Codman*, 7.

15 Walter Knight Sturgis, "Arthur Little and the Colonial Revival," *Journal of the Society of Architectural Historians* 32, no. 2 (May 1983): 147–63.

16 Arthur Little, *Early American Interiors* (Boston: A. Williams and Co., 1878), introduction.

17 Henry Davis Sleeper to A. Piatt Andrew, Sept. 3, 1908, in Hayden and Gray, *Beauport Chronicle*; Beauport guestbook, 1908–21, Cape Ann Historical Association, Gloucester, Mass.; Andrew diary and Red Roof guestbook, A. Piatt Andrew Archive; and Cecilia Beaux diary, AAA.

18 Henry Davis Sleeper to Isabella Stewart Gardner, Mar. 6, 1919, Gardner Papers, Gardner Museum, Boston; Sleeper to Halfdan M. Hanson, Sept. 13, 1921, Hanson Papers, SPNEA Archives.

19 William Sumner Appleton to Elizabeth Tyson Vaughan, Oct. 22, 1945, Papers of the Corresponding Secretary, SPNEA Archives.

❖ 23 ❖

THOMAS BAILEY ALDRICH HOUSE GARDENS
Portsmouth, New Hampshire, 1908

Restored in 1908 by the Thomas Bailey Aldrich Association, the Aldrich Memorial represents life as it was for the poet in his youthful years of the 1840s in the home of his grandfather on Court Street in Portsmouth. A reference to the garden and yard layout is made by Aldrich himself in *The Story of a Bad Boy,* published in 1869: "My grandfather's house stood a little back from the main street, in the shadow of two handsome elms, whose overgrown boughs would dash themselves against the gables whenever the wind blew hard." At the rear of the house Aldrich described a garden, covering a quarter of an acre, with purple plum trees and gooseberry bushes. In the northwestern corner of the garden were the stables and the carriage house, opening upon a narrow lane.[1]

The restored garden was laid out under the direct supervision of association member Mrs. George Tyson.[2] Volunteering for the job, Mrs. Tyson intended to include the old-fashioned flowers it once had, and she turned to the poet's wife for a list. Mrs. Aldrich later wrote:

> I knew my husband had mentioned all of them at one time or another in his poems. One day I sat down with a volume intending to go through it and merely mention the flowers named. In making the list, I found the lines enclosing the flower in nearly every case so much a part of the flower itself that I copied them out as in gathering the actual flowers of the garden. I would have surrounded each with leaves belonging to it.[3]

In 1912 Lilian Aldrich published the excerpts in *The Shadow of the Flowers.*[4]

Photographs from 1908 (cat. 23), a description from a 1909 newspaper, and an informal sketch from 1910 describe the results of Mrs. Tyson's efforts.[5] Directly south of the house one entered the garden through an arched arbor attached to the house and underlaid with flagstones. Hopvines trained on poles flanked the entrance to a central walkway paved with cobbles which terminated at an arched summer house. Radiating from the central path were four symmetrical garden beds, with shrubs at each corner. Along the western edge of the garden was a grape arbor with colonial urns capping the posts. An eight-foot-high solid board fence surrounded most of the garden, enclosing the space from the unseemly sites on Jefferson Street. A 1909 article in Boston's *Sunday Herald* stated: "In this secluded enclosure are the old, old flowers cared for clearly by someone who loves them. There are hollyhocks, heliotrope, pansies, striped grass, hop vines and various other shrubs and flowers."[6]

The Thomas Bailey Aldrich Association continued to

Cat. 23. Garden, Thomas Bailey Aldrich house, Portsmouth, New Hampshire. Photograph by Talbot Aldrich, 1908. Courtesy, Historic Photograph Collection, Strawbery Banke Museum.

develop the property through the 1920s and 1930s. By 1919 the cobblestone walks had been replaced with brick, a practical move still in keeping with the desire for a "colonial look." The addition of a hemlock grove followed the extension of the eastern property line in 1920. By 1940 the garden was described as "a charming old-time garden with quaint summer house, sundial and attractive brick walks. It was a sweet-scented and secluded garden."

The garden was indeed a complete "restoration"; little remained in the garden from Aldrich's youth. The gooseberrys and plum trees were never replaced, the two elms were removed, and the stable and carriage house taken down. One description of the garden stated: "No more old-time garden could be imagined—and yet, before the house was reclaimed as a memorial, this garden had become nothing but a place of bare, trodden earth."[7] The words of his poetry bring to life those years, drawing life from the

garden into their lines and creating a remembrance for all who visit the "old, old garden."

AMM

1 Thomas Bailey Aldrich, *The Story of a Bad Boy* (Boston: Houghton Mifflin Co., 1908), 35–36.

2 "Thomas Bailey Aldrich Memorial Dedicated," *Portsmouth Herald*, June 30, 1908, 2.

3 "Vivid with his Memory," clipping from an untitled Boston newspaper, ca. 1913, Aldrich Collection, SB.

4 Lilian Aldrich, *The Shadow of the Flowers* (Boston: Houghton Mifflin Co., 1912), 1.

5 The 1908 photograph of Aldrich garden is at SB; the 1910 sketch is at Houghton Library, Harvard University, Cambridge, Mass.

6 "Portsmouth: The Old Town by the Sea, and Its Attraction to the Visitor," *Sunday Herald* (Boston), Aug. 15, 1909.

7 "The Spectator," *Outlook* 103 (Mar. 8, 1913): 551.

❧ 24 ❧

JACOB WENDELL HOUSE GARDENS
Portsmouth, New Hampshire, 1815–1988

The landscape at the Jacob Wendell house was created, developed, and preserved by a single family for more than 170 years. From the purchase of the property by Jacob Wendell in 1815 to the end of family occupancy in 1988, the site was shaped by the Wendells' desire to preserve and maintain the historical significance of the house and surrounding property. However, it is in the Barrett Wendell period of ownership during the early twentieth century that the garden most reflected the colonial revival.

In 1815, Jacob Wendell hired Benjamin Akerman to survey his new lot and make a landscape plan.[1] Receipts and bills for labor on Wendell's house, barn, woodhouse, and fences document the existence of outbuildings on this relatively small lot. The deed of sale states that the property ran only one hundred feet down Edward Street and was about the width of the house fronting on Pleasant Street. The stable and attached barn lay at the rear of the property. Wendell's handwritten notes, apparently written in 1832 but inserted among the pages of an 1829 almanac, list the following:

Feb. 23 purchased hay for my cow. April 21 made my garden. May 2 planted a few radish and parsely seed in garden. May 6 sowed radish seed and pepper seed and bush beans under the currant buses . . . May 19 Planted beans, double parsely and sage seed. May 22 planted one bed beans and peppers. May 26 Planted pole beans, red beans large and white, planted cranberry.[2]

Cat. 24. Garden, Jacob Wendell house, Portsmouth, New Hampshire. Photograph, ca. 1920. Courtesy, Portsmouth Athenaeum.

By 1855, the Wendell garden was evolving from a functional to an ornamental space. The garden must have been very small with vegetables, flowering shrubs, and flowers coexisting but possibly divided into designated areas as in Akerman's plan of the Elisha Crane house. The first reference in Wendell's business receipts to ornamental plant material appears in 1835. "Paid James F. Shores: For 1 Honeysuckle, mostly variegated, very fragrant."[3] Additional reference to ornamental plantings is made in a letter dated 1855 from Jacob to his daughter Caroline mentioning dahlias and gladiolas.[4]

Jacob Wendell died in 1865, leaving the property to his unmarried daughter who resided there with her nephew, James Rindge Stanwood, until her death in 1890. Receipts from both florists and nurseries document roses, tulips, and palm plants being purchased for the gardens and house. An order to a rose company reveals some of the existing plants in the garden:

> Please send one hardy and vigorous variety of Climbing rose, selection to be at your discretion and in favor of a plant as well advanced in growth as will insure its ready advancement. Soil of garden: a loam with clay bottom. Excluding these varieties which are already in the garden: Gen'l Jacqueninot, Mme. Plantier, Duchess of Brabrant, Regent of York and a double damask.[5]

Upon Stanwood's death in 1910, the house became a summer home occupied by Harvard professor Barrett Wendell and his wife Edith. From the beginning, they strove to make the property, in Edith's words, "the tangible expression of an early New England." In an article written in 1925 for *Garden Magazine,* she described her feelings toward the garden, stating that it was:

> Not a great garden, surely, nor an elaborate one; merely a few square feet of cultivated soil, yielding such posies as they did a century ago; changing annually and yet fundamentally unchanged; the same today, yesterday, and let us hope, tomorrow.[6]

The Wendells proceeded to plant "only such simple flowers as might have always bloomed there." They planted digitalis, hollyhocks, pansies, heartease, and fuchsia. Vines created garden rooms and included a honeysuckle on the trellis flanked by clumps of spirea and dahlias, a trumpet vine over the porch, and grapevines on the pergola. Ferns were planted in the shade of the pergola, and at the entrance of the pergola there was "the fast bleaching vertebræ of a whale washed ashore one daren't guess how many years ago."[7]

Located in the same space once cultivated by Jacob Wendell in the early nineteenth century and later by his daughter Caroline and her nephew James Stanwood, was a garden that, according to family history, was laid out after a Chinese puzzle that had been brought home in the 1860s from an Asiatic voyage by George Blunt Wendell, one of the sons of Jacob, Sr. (cat. 24). The tangram consisted of seven pieces, each piece representing a garden bed, the overall design forming a square.[8] In the center of the formal gardens, to complement the oriental theme, Edith and Barrett Wendell planted a small box tree, trained on the wire frame of a Chinese man whose "living body topped by a terra cotta head and hands was adequately symbolic of times inanimately past and ever living present."

Shortly after Barrett Wendell's death in 1921, Edith began to develop the property further. In 1926 she contracted to have the barn on the site turned into living space and hired the Boston landscape architect Fletcher Steele to draw up a plan of the property. Steele's plan for the back garden included areas for flower beds, a Chinese pagoda, and a sundial. In addition to the landscape plan, Steele also made detailed drawings of the grape arbor and covered walk in the puzzle garden. These drawings, along with the measured plot plan of the Wendell property, were sent to Steele's client Mabel Choate for her restoration project at the Mission House in Stockbridge, Massachusetts.[9] In 1937, as chairman of the Warner House Association, Edith Wendell engaged Steele to draw up plans for the grounds of the Warner house including details for a well house.[10]

Edith Wendell died in 1938, and after that time her son William Greenough Wendell took up summer residence. Further changes to the landscape were few. Today, the puzzle garden remains "fundamentally unchanged" along with the surrounding pergola and arbors, "the same today, yesterday, and let us hope, tomorrow."

AM

1 Akerman produced other Portsmouth landscape plans during the first half of the nineteenth century; his 1841 plan for the Elisha Crane property on Middle Street illustrates a simple landscape with areas designated for flowers, vegetables, and yard. *New England Farmer's Almanack* (1829) (handwritten pages inserted), Jacob Wendell Papers, PA.

2 *New England Farmer's Almanack* (1829), Jacob Wendell Papers, PA.

3 Business receipts, Wendell Papers, Baker Library, Harvard University, Cambridge, Mass., case 13.

4 Jacob Wendell to Caroline Wendell, Nov. 22, 1855, Caroline Wendell Papers, Houghton Library, Harvard University, Cambridge, Mass.

5 Jacob Wendell to Caroline Wendell, Nov. 22, 1855, Caroline Wendell Papers, Houghton Library.

6 Edith Greenough Wendell, "Jacob Wendell Garden" (typescript, Jacob Wendell Papers, PA, 1925), 3 (written for publication in *Garden Magazine*).

7 Edith Greenough Wendell, "Jacob Wendell Garden."

8 Edith Greenough Wendell, "Jacob Wendell Garden."

9 Fletcher Steele to Edith Wendell, July 29, 1937, and Sept. 28, 1937, Fletcher Steele Papers, Collections of the Manuscript Division, Library of Congress, Washington, D.C., containers 75–80, client cards 256–4, 256–4A, 256–109.

10 Papers of the Warner House Association, Portsmouth, N.H.

25

CELIA THAXTER'S GARDENS
Appledore Island, New Hampshire, begun ca. 1880

On a small plot of land on Appledore Island, poet Celia Thaxter planted the garden that was preserved in both her book, *An Island Garden,* and in the works of the American Impressionist painter Childe Hassam (cat. 25). Flourishing in the 1880s and early 1890s, Thaxter's garden was representative of an aesthetic approach to organizing the landscape in order to create a controlled space that served as both a setting and a subject for artistic production. Thaxter aligned the passions of the gardener with those of all artists, writing, "Like the musician, the painter, the poet, and the rest, the true lover of flowers is born, not made."[1] Thaxter's garden became a subject for the artistic and literary circles of the Piscataqua who summered at her family's resort at the Isles of Shoals.

The island garden was a plot of land fifty feet long and fifteen feet wide that ran behind the parlor of Thaxter's house. Thaxter counted as many as fifty-seven different varieties of flowers in her garden. Even in her choice of plant material, she followed the trend of the colonial revival to stress both aesthetic interest and historic precedent. On the one hand, Thaxter planted series of poppies and roses, using various colors and varieties of the same species to create an artistic effect in her garden: "I think for wondrous variety, for certain picturesque qualities, for color and form and a subtle mystery of character, Poppies seem, on the whole, the most satisfactory flowers among the annuals." On the other, she was drawn to such favorites of the period as phlox and peonies. She wrote of her planting choices, "They are mostly the old-fashioned flowers our grandmothers loved." Thaxter's fellow garden writer Alice Morse Earle described phlox as "the only native American plant" and lauded the planting of peonies as a New England tradition.[2]

Thaxter melded her outdoor and indoor spaces through the use of her garden, creating a surrounding typical of the colonial revival period and, specifically, of shingle-style architecture. A small flight of stairs provided entry from the house into the garden, and two gates allowed access to the shore. The garden was a mediating space between her parlor and the rocky coastline of the islands (cat. 25a). Trellises, fencing, paths, and flower beds defined the space, dividing the plot into three distinct square areas. Though this design at first seems typical of the colonial revival "garden room," Thaxter's garden did not include central open spaces for seating and viewing the garden as an enclosed space. Thaxter's garden was unique in that it focused outward to encompass the larger views of the ocean. She wrote:

> From the flower beds I look over the island slopes to the sea, and realize it all,—the rapture of growth, the

delicious shades of green that clothe the ground, Wild Rose, Bayberry, Spirea, Shadbush, Elder, and many more. How beautiful they are, these grassy, rocky slopes shelving gradually to the sea, with here and there a mass of tall, blossoming grass softly swaying in the warm wind against the peaceful, pale blue water!

In her own writings, she told little of the social uses that the "garden rooms" usually served; similarly, of Hassam's many images of the garden, few include people enjoying the garden. Known for her gatherings of artists, writers, and musicians, Thaxter entertained primarily in her parlor, using her garden to frame vistas toward the ocean.

Thaxter further created a sense of continuity between her outdoor and indoor properties by literally bringing into her house the products of her garden. She wrote:

> Altogether lovely [the flowers] are out of doors, but I plant and tend them always with the thought of the joy they will be within the house also . . . to bring a few indoors for purposes of study and fuller appreciation is another and desirable thing . . . And in the garden they are planted especially to feast the souls that hunger for beauty, and within doors as well as without they "delight the spirit of man."

Thaxter appears to have considered the picking and arranging of her flowers for the house an integral part of her gardening duties. She wrote of getting up early in the morning to create the arrangements that enlivened her salon. The arrangement of flowers gave Thaxter the opportunity for a more formal approach to natural beauty, while in her outdoor garden she chose to respect the almost random aspect of nature. David Park Curry, in *An Island Garden Revisited,* writes, "Thaxter favored a naturalistic, amorphous explosion of softer tints and tones, planted in irregular drifts and masses that intertwined and overlapped."[3]

Curry suggests that in her indoor displays Thaxter was influenced by the writings of James McNeill Whistler on color harmonies in interior decoration, indicating the links between the colonial revival and the aesthetic movements.[4] Thaxter, in fact, quoted extensively in *An Island Garden* from the writings of John Ruskin, one of the proponents of the aesthetic movement in Britain. Both Ruskin and his contemporary William Morris advocated careful attention to home decoration and garden design as a form of moral education, and specifically championed the role of women in this task. In the 1870s and 1880s, the theories of Ruskin and Morris, as well as the more specific interior schemes designed by Whistler, were popularized in American periodicals such as *Scribner's Monthly Magazine* and *House Beautiful.*[5] Thaxter's garden and indoor flower arrangements represented the intersection of the aesthetic and colonial revival movements in the late nineteenth century.

Although her garden was planted with an eye to aesthetics, and was designed to the extent that she could draw a

Cat. 25. Childe Hassam, The Garden in Its Glory, *1892. Watercolor on paper; 19¹⁵⁄₁₆ in. x 13⅞ in. Courtesy, National Museum of American Art, Smithsonian Institution, gift of John Gellatly.*

Cat. 25a. *View from Celia Thaxter's piazza through the garden. Photograph by Karl Thaxter, ca. 1892. Courtesy, University of New Hampshire.*

Cat. 26. *Roadside clean-up sponsored by the Piscataqua Garden Club. Photograph by Marvin Breckinridge Patterson, 1933. Courtesy, Piscataqua Garden Club.*

detailed garden plan for it, Thaxter wrote of having no extensive decorative devices. She stated, "I have not room to experiment with rockworks and ribbon-borders and the like, nor should I do it even if I had all the room in the world." Rather, she relied on the natural qualities of her flowers to dictate their planting arrangement: "For instance, in most cases tall plants should be put back against walls and fences and so forth, with the lower-growing varieties in the foreground." Indoors, however, the flowers were used as decorative props, as in her "altar" of poppies, displayed in order of hue from the white "bride" poppy to the deepest red, following the teachings of Whistler.[6]

Despite the aesthetic appeal of flowers in the garden or the parlor, Thaxter, in her own writing, stressed the process of gardening over its end results. She wrote her book in response to friends' requests: "Tell us how you do it." Thaxter detailed the implements she used, glorifying the seeming simplicity of agrarian labor: "So deeply is the gardener's instinct implanted in my soul, I really love the tools with which I work,—the iron fork, the spade, the hoe, the rake, the trowel, and the watering-pot are pleasant objects in my eyes." From the preparation of seeds in egg shells, to the actual planting, to her constant war with weeds and snails, Thaxter reveled in the work of her garden, recalling an earlier ethic of labor and the pride in its results.

Thaxter's remembrance of her garden on Appledore Island detailed one year in the life of her garden. *An Island Garden* begins with a discussion of the necessary preparations to be taken in the fall and winter months, then describes the planting in spring, the watering and weeding in summer, and ends with the early fall chill that marks the end of her garden's growth season. By following the planting cycle in her prose, Thaxter revealed the extent to which her garden followed the seasonal patterns of nature. Though Thaxter never truly lived in an industrialized

environment in which agrarian patterns were replaced with those of industry, she did watch the seasons become defined less by the fishing and planting schedules than by the tourist communities that were the by-product of increasing industry. Her garden was a reminder of the agrarian and fishing communities that had existed at the Isles of Shoals.

MM

1 Celia Thaxter, *An Island Garden* (Boston: Houghton Mifflin, and Co., 1894), 5. All quotations from Thaxter in this entry are from this source.

2 Alice Morse Earle, "Front Dooryards," in *American Garden Writing*, ed. Bonnie Marranca (New York: Penguin Books, 1988), 6–7; originally published in Alice Morse Earle, *Old Time Gardens* (New York: Macmillan, 1901.)

3 David Park Curry, *Childe Hassam: An Island Garden Revisited* (Denver: Denver Art Museum in association with W.W. Norton, 1990), 70.

4 Curry, *An Island Garden Revisited*, 49.

5 Eileen Boris, *Art and Labor: Ruskin, Morris, and the Craftsman Ideal in America* (Philadelphia: Temple University Press, 1986), 53–56.

6 See also the visual record of this arrangement in Childe Hassam's *The Altar and the Shrine*, in Thaxter, *An Island Garden*, between 94 and 95.

26

THE PISCATAQUA GARDEN CLUB
Founded 1926

The Piscataqua Garden Club, founded in 1926 as a women's group, is representative of the organized efforts to preserve and beautify the Piscataqua region's landscape. The club's six founding members first met at the home of Elizabeth Perkins; there they drafted the club's by-laws which read:

Cat. 26a. Garden, Governor John Langdon mansion, Portsmouth, New Hampshire. Photograph by Marvin Breckinridge Patterson, 1933. Courtesy, Piscataqua Garden Club.

"To arouse interest in gardens, to stimulate interest in plants, to preserve the wildflowers, to protect the trees on the highways, to preserve all ornamental shrubbery, to eliminate disfiguring signboards, to enforce the forest fire laws, to cultivate the habit of destroying refuse at picnics, and to teach children to avoid throwing paper" (cat. 26).[1] Many of the club's projects fostered an appreciation for that which was pastoral, natural, and historic.

The club met once every two weeks for a formal program by an outside guest and an exchange of ideas among the members. Lectures ranged from "How to Fight Dutch Elm Disease" to "New Innovations in Garden Design." The speakers often brought photographs of other gardens and in a question-and-answer session would offer suggestions on the preservation of early American plant material and the restoration of colonial gardens.

The Piscataqua Garden Club perceived the past as picturesque. Although the club had members from the region as a whole, many of its projects concentrated on the beautification of York and its immediate surroundings. This emphasis was due in part to the limited economic growth in the town in the nineteenth century, which left its landscape relatively unchanged from the colonial era. In 1934–35, the club drafted a petition which proposed that all businesses and houses along York Street be painted white with green trim "to restore its character as an old time New England village."[2] Endorsed by the Women's League and the Village Improvement Society, this petition encouraged York residents to reconsider the appearance of their town center. Although never acted upon, this request was evidence of the attempt during the colonial revival period to recreate what was perceived to be a unified community. The Piscataqua Garden Club was interested in creating a "purer" and "more natural" environment using York Village as the setting.[3] At the first annual flower show in 1927, Helen Coggill, chairman of the Conservation Committee, set up a booth informing guests how they could "tidy up" their buildings and grounds. Many townspeople asked for assistance and thus started the planting of trees, shrubs, and flowers around York businesses.

In 1935, the club's campaign to eliminate billboards from the roadsides of Maine was met with government support. Since its founding in 1926, the club had been actively working on this initiative. During the first year of the club's existence, Helen Coggill addressed the state legislature on behalf of the effort; such speeches were made each year by members of the Garden Club, the Improvement Society, and the Women's League. From 1930 to 1935, the club sponsored letter-writing campaigns to both the legislature and the companies whose billboards lined the major roads. Members also sought the impressions and literary expertise of authors such as Kenneth Roberts who encouraged the club members in these campaigns. In 1931, the club hired Judge Deering of Saco, Maine, to represent their case legally. Finally, in 1935, Henry Vaughan, a husband of a club member, introduced a bill to the state legislature which,

while it did not remove billboards, strictly controlled their size and placement: billboards had to be one hundred feet from the side of the road, could be no larger than forty-two by twelve feet, and had to be painted green. As a result, thousands of "illegal" billboards were removed from Maine roads. This project reveals the tension that arose when the tourist economy that relied on a pastoral landscape began, in fact, to change that landscape.

Many of the Piscataqua Garden Club's members owned restored colonial houses. These included Indian Hill (owned by Mrs. Moseley of Newburyport and Boston), Langdon house (cat. 26a) in Portsmouth (Mrs. Kremer of New York City), the Emerson Wilcox house in York (Mrs. Hungerford of Boston), the Elizabeth Perkins house (Miss Perkins of New York City), Sayward-Wheeler house (Mrs. Wheeler of Worcester, Massachusetts), and the Hamilton house (Mrs. Vaughn of Sherburne, Massachusetts). Often the landscape was as important to the original owners and later preservationists as the architecture. After restoring their own homes and beautifying them with gardens, club members extended their interests in preserving the past to other sites. For instance, the Garden Club was involved in the preservation of the original design of Sewall's Bridge in York. Furthermore, the club solicited donations for the preservation of Jefferds Tavern in which they had a meeting space. The club also offered support in the preservation of the Warner house in Portsmouth in the 1930s and the Sarah Orne Jewett house in South Berwick in the 1940s. The preservation of these historic sites was one aspect of the Piscataqua Garden Club's larger goal to preserve a pastoral and community-oriented landscape that its members believed was threatened by the tourist industry.

AWH & MM

1 Minutes, Piscataqua Garden Club, June 25, 1926, Piscataqua Garden Club Coll., OYHS.

2 Piscataqua Garden Club notebook (1933–35), general notes, Piscataqua Garden Club Coll.

3 Piscataqua Garden Club notebook (1933–35), general notes, Piscataqua Garden Club Coll.

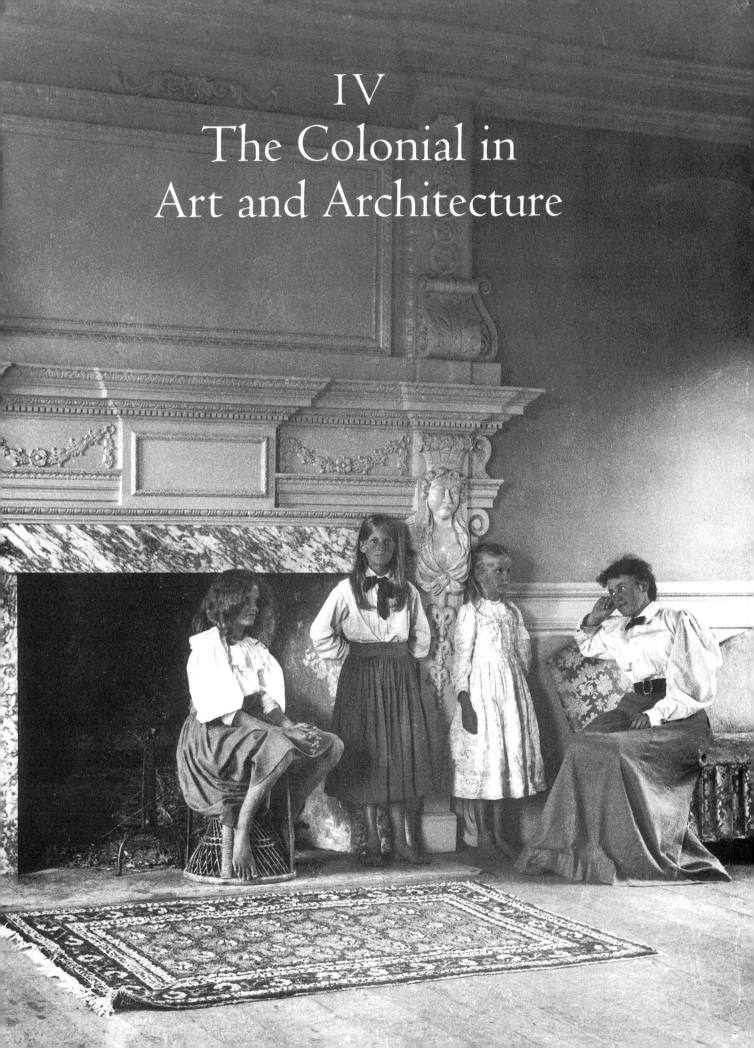

IV
The Colonial in
Art and Architecture

Fig. 4.1. Wentworth Mansion, Little Harbor, New Hampshire, 1895. Courtesy, Historic Photograph Collection, Strawbery Banke Museum.

Preceding page: *Molly Coolidge Perkins,* Children at Wentworth-Coolidge House, *1896. Photograph; 9½ in. x 7½ in. Courtesy, Molly Coolidge Perkins Collection, Strawbery Banke Museum.*

Artistic Circles and Summer Colonies

Woodard D. Openo

For artists and architects living in Boston during the last two decades of the nineteenth century, Paris was the artistic capital of the West, although the writings of British art critic and theorist John Ruskin enjoyed a special popularity.[1] Beginning in the 1870s, the paintings of the French Barbizon school were commercially and critically successful in Boston, and the artistic training offered in Paris was considered indispensable for ambitious artists. American painters who arrived in Paris during the last quarter of the nineteenth century were influenced by the French academic painters, and by the mid-1890s, by the Impressionists. By that time they also could have had knowledge of the post-Impressionists such as Paul Gauguin and Georges Seurat, as well as of emerging modernists like Paul Cézanne. Significant formal differences existed between the works produced by each of these painters, but there was an element of consistency in their practices: central to all of these camps was the idea of retreat from urban life. From the Barbizon painters who went to paint in the Fontainebleau forest during the 1830s, through Cézanne who retreated to the south of France in the mid-1880s, withdrawal from the city became almost a prerequisite for professional practice.[2]

Americans who found themselves in Paris during the 1880s and 1890s saw suburban and rural scenes promoted as subjects appropriate to serious art, and executed in a variety of techniques.[3] Boston artists combined an interest in nonurban motifs with the historical perspective of Ruskin when they returned to the United States and searched out rural enclaves in which to work. The result of such an amalgam of continental and British influences was the migration of artists to rural areas along the Eastern seaboard that boasted not only unspoiled landscapes, but also visible histories. Among the New England towns possessing these characteristics were Old Lyme, Connecticut; Cornish and Dublin, New Hampshire; Gloucester, Massachusetts; and the communities bordering the Piscataqua River in Maine and New Hampshire. In such spots, painters produced works that celebrated leisure activities and that frequently derived their formal characteristics from French Impressionism. But even after that style had lost its dominance in the early twentieth century, the concept of retreat remained as an example from the earlier generation. Where Boston painters of the 1880s and 1890s had fled the cities for rural New England, later generations of East Coast artists would set up colonies in such remote and "primitive" locales as the American Southwest.

Of the resort areas popularized by artists between the 1880s and the First World War, the Piscataqua region was unique for its blend of unspoiled seacoast and historically interesting communities dotted with fine examples of eighteenth- and nineteenth-century architecture. The particular characteristics—topographical and historical—of each of the Piscataqua-region communities drew artists who had special sensitivities to these qualities.

Summer colonists—artists and architects among them—were attracted to particular New England resorts by word of mouth and by published accounts. Of the latter, among the most important were a series of articles on historic seacoast towns published in *Harper's New Monthly Magazine* in the 1870s and Samuel Adams Drake's *Nooks and Corners of the New England Coast* (1875).[4] Many other popular publications of the 1870s and 1880s likewise publicized the nascent resorts surrounding the Piscataqua River: Ogunquit, York, and Kittery Point, Maine; the Isles of Shoals; and Little Harbor (comprised of parts of New Castle, Rye, and Portsmouth), New Hampshire. The *Harper's* articles on the Piscataqua towns and Drake's *Nooks and Corners* appealed to an educated audience, mixing ample amounts of history and description with personal anecdotes, humor, interesting engravings, and comparatively slight reference to purely resort activities. Although certain monuments and natural features had long been famous, these publications identified many colonial revival icons for the artists and summer colonists who would follow.

By the date of these writings in the mid-1870s, the eighteenth-century mansion built by Governor Benning Wentworth at Little Harbor was long the subject of local legends (fig. 4.1). During that decade it also became well known regionally and nationally through Henry Wadsworth Longfellow's poem "Lady Wentworth" in his *Tales of a Wayside Inn* (second series, 1872) and through a novel entitled *Student-Days at Harvard,* published in 1876 by alumnus George Henry Tripp.[5] The poem took as its subject the romantic historical incident of the marriage of the aging governor to his servant, Martha Hilton, at the mansion, while the novel described the fictional adventures of Harvard student Samuel Wentworth, scion of the family at Little Harbor.[6]

Fig. 4.2. "Colonial" Figures, Little Harbor, New Hampshire. Photograph by Gregory Wiggins, ca. 1900. Courtesy, Henry Parsons Coolidge.

Longfellow's poem and Tripp's novel promoted both the natural advantages and historical interest of Little Harbor. The two literary works would have had particular significance for a group of students who became acquainted at Harvard, many of whom worked on early issues of the *Harvard Lampoon* and who remained friends throughout their lives. A number of them took courses in history from Henry Adams, and in art history from Charles Eliot Norton. The friendship of this group and the interests in history and art that developed among them led them to Little Harbor.

Among the circle that was established in the coastal village were Barrett Wendell, John Templeman Coolidge III, Arthur Astor Carey, Edmund March Wheelwright, and Alexander Wadsworth Longfellow, Jr. Shortly after graduation, Wendell was hired to teach English at Harvard at the instigation of professor Adams Sherman Hill; the Hills later purchased the eighteenth-century Sheafe farmhouse at Little Harbor. Arthur Astor Carey built a house on Fayerweather Street in Cambridge (next to the Hills' new winter home) in 1882; this early colonial revival house was designed by John Hubbard Sturgis, the Boston architect whose nephew (and professional successor) R. Clipston Sturgis purchased the eighteenth-century Martine cottage at Little Harbor from Carey in 1889.[7]

John Templeman Coolidge III provided a center for the Little Harbor group when he purchased the Wentworth

mansion in 1886. Coolidge is known principally for his portraits, most of which depict members of his family, done in the early 1880s. The way in which he combined an interest in European culture and a fascination with local history is represented by two sculptures of colonial figures (fig. 4.2) carved in wood by J. Gregory Wiggins to stand in the garden at the Wentworth mansion. These works were modeled after two small French baroque bronzes which Coolidge had brought back from Paris but were transformed by eighteenth-century garb in Wiggins's interpretations of them to become appropriate guardians for the Wentworth mansion.

The eighteeth-century Hamilton house (cat. 16) in nearby South Berwick was presided over by sculptures that likewise proclaimed their owners' knowledge of both European and American culture. Purchasing the house in 1898, the mother-and-daughter team of Emily Tyson and Elise Tyson Vaughan transformed the country seat into an artistic enclave surrounded by gardens (cat. 21). Forming focal points around the property were sculptures of Greek goddesses, as well as mass-produced figures of George and Martha Washington that dated from the mid nineteenth century. These sculptures suggest that the Tysons saw in the rural life of the Piscataqua a modern parallel to classical culture, in which their role was to provide a setting where art and nature could be brought together. Their renovation of Hamilton house provided an opportunity to gather

Fig. 4.3. Charles Woodbury, Perkins Cove, Ogunquit, Maine, 1901. *Oil on canvas; 10 in. x 14 in. Courtesy, Nancy Flentje.*

writers, artists, and architects around them. When the work was complete, they used the building and gardens as a backdrop for the production of classically inspired photographs (cat. 31). The establishment of an artistic community in South Berwick (largely in the form of the Tysons and their visitors) depended upon the personal introduction of native Sarah Orne Jewett. A small community without the advantage of coastline, South Berwick did not appeal to the large numbers of summer colonists drawn to other towns in the Piscataqua region.

Samuel Adams Drake called Ogunquit "a little fishing village spliced to the outskirts of Wells." Charles H. Woodbury (cat. 36), a Boston painter and art teacher, was attracted to the village in 1888 by its pastoral setting and maritime activities, not coincidentally the very qualities emphasized by Drake (fig. 4.3). Woodbury conducted a popular summer art school there beginning in 1898. In the early twentieth century, Hamilton Easter Field opened a rival school of art in Ogunquit which was oriented toward New York (fig. 4.4). The more modernist-inspired

(right) *Fig. 4.4. Hamilton Easter Field,* Hamilton Easter Field, Self Portrait, *n.d. Oil on wood panel; 23½ in. x 17½ in. Courtesy, Portland Museum of Art, Portland, Maine, Hamilton Easter Field Art Foundation Collection, gift of Barn Gallery Associates, Inc., Ogunquit, Maine, 1979.*

Fig. 4.5. Emma Coleman, Haying, *York, Maine, 1883–84. Photograph; 7½ in. x 4⅝ in. Old York Historical Society.*

of Hamilton Easter Field filled their shacks with folk art collected in the area (cat. 33), and created a mythology around these objects that depicted their producers as autonomous artists unconstrained by academic tradition and training, thus justifying their own modernist practice. More than the other Piscataqua region towns, and in its own rustic way, Ogunquit became an artist's colony.

The *Harper's* article on York provides a good indication of the qualities which attracted artists and others to that town. The author, Sarah D. Clark, describes York's center "with the usual adjuncts of a country village," a group of "three little old-fashioned houses about two hundred years old" at York Harbor, the house where the author stayed, apple trees and the ocean, Mount Agamenticus, Brave Boat Harbor, the river, and the sunset. Drake, too, describes natural features such as Nubble Rock and Mount Agamenticus, but also buildings, including the First Parish Church, the jail, the old burying-ground, and the McIntire and Junkins garrison houses. His emphasis is heavily on the colonial era of the settlement, which he suggests is "one of those places toward which the history of a country or a section converges." It was this association with colonial history, and the buildings that represented the period, that made York different from Ogunquit. Tellingly, Charles Woodbury chose to settle in Ogunquit—which had a landscape and history more consistent with his aesthetic outlook—but came to York to paint the *Old Gaol* (cat. 36; see also pl. 6) during the time when he was completing a series of works depicting historic buildings.[9]

The interest in vernacular culture that drew Woodbury to Ogunquit was shared by photographer Emma Coleman (cat. 41). However, she was able to find vestiges of ancient agricultural traditions and craft techniques in York. Between 1883 and 1886 she staged photographs of such obsolete occupations, and captured instances of their actual survival (fig. 4.5). These images were produced under the direction of Sarah Orne Jewett and were used to illustrate an edition of her novel *Deephaven* (cat. 47).[10] If popular publications made each of the towns of the Piscataqua seem different, there were, however, continuities among all of their histories.

Drake's approach to York is similar to his treatment of Kittery Point (fig. 4.6). He describes the church, built in 1714, with "its secluded cemetery, and fine old elms" and the Lady Pepperrell house across the road (cat. 10), Fort McClary and its block-house, the tomb of the Pepperrells and the "very ancient dwelling of Bray," the latter an eighteenth-century house that was well known locally. Like York, Kittery Point provided examples of colonial architecture for study by architects, and opportunities to design new dwellings to accommodate summer visitors in a style that fitted in with the town's historic structures (fig. 4.7). As was the case with many of the summer colonists, these architects had studied and traveled in Europe, so they drew on English and French sources as well as American precedents when it came to the design of new cottages.[11]

sculpture and painting produced under his tutelage contrasted with the impressionistic work of Woodbury's students.[8]

Both schools, however, emphasized landscape painting, and in different ways made use of Ogunquit's special history. Unlike Little Harbor, Ogunquit had no grand eighteenth-century houses or well-known colonial historical events associated with it. Instead, the village preserved a vernacular culture based on fishing and agriculture. Many artists who came to Ogunquit were attracted to the rugged landscape and the crude fishing shacks they appropriated to serve as studios. For Woodbury's students, Ogunquit was equivalent to the places of recreation depicted in French Impressionist paintings. In capturing the effects of atmospheric conditions on the natural topography, as well as the customs of the vacationers around them, they followed the example of Claude Monet or Renoir. The students

Fig. 4.6. Kittery Point, Maine. Photograph by Luther Dame, ca. 1902. Old York Historical Society.

In dealing with the Isles of Shoals, both Drake and the writer for *Harper's* were attracted by the isolated, windblown setting of the islands and the way in which this geography determined the history of the area. The rise and decline of the fishing colony, shipwrecks, the White Island lighthouse (fig. 4.8), the stone meetinghouse on Star Island, and the story of Thomas Laighton and his daughter, the poet Celia Thaxter, are all described.[12] Some of these motifs became subjects for the painter Childe Hassam. Such subjects perpetuated the interests of the French Impressionists in rural places and sunny interiors. As David Park Curry has argued, the colony which gathered each summer in Celia Thaxter's parlor on Appledore Island, one of the Isles of Shoals, was a cosmopolitan one that had assimilated the theory of John Ruskin.[13] Ruskin's emphasis on the close observation of nature would have complemented the lessons of Monet and his contemporaries whose paintings recorded fleeting atmospheric effects. Ruskin also advocated a return to preindustrial craft techniques. Hassam and Thaxter shared an interest in the decorative arts and cooperated on the book *An Island Garden* (1894), while Thaxter herself decorated and sold pottery.[14]

Ruskin's writings must also have significantly stimulated the interests of the Appledore circle in historical subjects. In *The Seven Lamps of Architecture* (1849) Ruskin, who was critical of the over-restoration of old buildings, wrote

that "I cannot but think it an evil sign of a people when their houses are built to last one generation only."[15] Correspondingly, Hassam sought out venerable buildings in nearby Portsmouth which he depicted in etchings, including the federal-period Athenaeum (cat. 11) and a group of old houses bordering the South Mill Pond. Hassam's work thus illustrates the draw of not only the area's untamed topography, but of its historic buildings as well. That the artist knew of these attractions from popular publications is evidenced by the fact that his 1883 gouache painting entitled *Church Point, Portsmouth, New Hampshire* duplicates the subject and vantage point of an engraving (fig. 4.9) that illustrated Thomas Bailey Aldrich's article, "An Old Town by the Sea," published in *Harper's* in 1874.[16]

In the small village of New Castle, just outside of Portsmouth, the Paris-trained artist Edmund C. Tarbell, co-chair of the School of the Museum of Fine Arts in Boston, created a family retreat which became the setting for many of his paintings (cat. 30). An enthusiastic collector of architectural fragments, Tarbell transformed the summer house he purchased in New Castle in 1905 by incorporating into it fragments of old buildings.[17] The resulting environment combined unspoiled landscape with local history; a photograph of the Tarbell children (fig. 4.10) playing on a federal-period doorway set up in the yard at New Castle encapsulates the values of rural life, history, and

Fig. 4.7. Russell Cheney, Pepperrell Cove, *Kittery Point, Maine, ca. 1929. Oil on canvas; 24 in. x 30 in. Private collection.*

family (not to mention the sense of humor) that prevailed in this setting. The painted representations of family life that Tarbell produced at New Castle were only part of the work that went on there; the real "art" of New Castle was a sensibility that permeated every aspect of the Tarbells' life and that tended to set itself in opposition to the contemporary urban world. This kind of quiet artistic retreat was not without precedent. In the 1880s, Monet established a similar enclave in Giverney, outside of Paris, where he concentrated his artistic energies on his home and garden, and created a backdrop for paintings that depicted nature and family within its confines.

There were numerous personal connections among the various summer colonies, although each one claimed to be unique. While each resort had its own character, all were tied together in a larger cosmopolitan society based in Boston, New York, and other urban centers. Architects followed their friends and clients to the resorts, as is demonstrated by the summer home designs of the Boston architect William Ralph Emerson, scattered along the Maine coast from Bar Harbor to Kennebunkport, York Harbor, and Kittery.[18] Emerson, who had many Boston social connections, designed a number of cottages for clients with artistic interests, such as the Thaxter family (cat. 39), and provided them with suitable rural retreats. His designs featured natural materials that helped his houses fit in with their natural sites, while they also displayed forms seen in the traditional architecture of the area.

European influences were combined with local colonial sources by various architects and artists (most of them from Boston, but some from Portsmouth, Portland, and Kennebunk) who were friends or colleagues and aquainted with one another's work. Summer colonists along the coasts of southern Maine and New Hampshire thought in terms of building groups and not just isolated structures, and at the same time recognized the need to adapt new

(above) *Fig. 4.8. Childe Hassam,* White Island Light, Isles of Shoals, New Hampshire, 1899. *Oil on canvas; 27 in. x 27 in. Courtesy, The Smith College Museum of Art.*

(right) *Fig. 4.9. Portsmouth, New Hampshire. From* Harper's New Monthly Magazine *(1874). Courtesy, Strawbery Banke Museum.*

Fig. 4.10. Tarbell family, New Castle, New Hampshire. Photograph, ca. 1934. Courtesy, Mrs. John B. Staley.

buildings to their historical settings. During the 1880s, architects in the Piscataqua region were among the earliest to study American colonial (or, more specifically, Georgian and federal) architecture *in situ* and design new buildings which would fit into their built environments. Thus, by 1890, the Wentworth mansion at Little Harbor could fit in comfortably with its recently acquired neighbors to form a rustic village. Materials and motifs were borrowed from earlier architecture to unite new and old. An example of such a form was the gambrel roof. Among the earliest examples of the use of the gambrel roof as part of a revival aesthetic was the cottage built by Celia and Levi Thaxter after 1880, the design of which is attributed to Emerson.

In addition to being mentioned specifically by influential Boston architect Robert Peabody in an 1877 essay in the *American Architect and Building News,* the gambrel roof was frequently painted by artists, including Charles

Woodbury, who featured the form in his painting of the Old Gaol at York, and Sarah Haven Foster of Portsmouth, who depicted the gambrel roof of the Bos'n Allen House in New Castle (fig. 4.11).[19] The form was continued in John Thaxter's 1887 additions to his house at Cutts Island at Kittery Point, and in the house built to the north on the Thaxter property by his brother Roland (also attributed to Emerson). Colonial features such as diamond-shaped window panes in Roland Thaxter's house and the gambrel roofs in both houses, combined with "shingled" features like the arch under the added rear ells in both houses, suggest the difficulty of trying to separate the colonial revival from the shingle style.

Several other Boston-trained architects were working in the Piscataqua region during the 1880s as well. Edmund March Wheelwright embodied the artistic eclecticism and fascination with history of the local colonial revival. He had a keen interest in genealogy, was an accomplished art historian, and had studied in Europe at the beginning of his career.[20] Employed in the architectural office of E.P. Treadwell of Albany, New York, Wheelwright's first two independent commissions were the Jacob Wendell and Edmund Clarence Stedman summer houses (fig. 4.12) in New Castle, built between 1882 and 1883.[21] These buildings show the diverse sources of his inspiration and demonstrate his stylistic freedom.

The Jacob Wendell home in New Castle, called "Frostfields" (cat. 27), was located in what is now Great Island Common. The sea could be seen from three sides of the long, shingled house. Its balanced asymmetry and simple trim suggest a knowledge of the nearby eighteenth-century Wentworth mansion. Specific features from the mansion, such as the two cross gables, were incorporated here and in other "colonial" houses by other Boston-based architects including Arthur Little.

Fig. 4.11. Sarah Haven Foster, Bos'n Allen House, New Castle, New Hampshire, *ca. 1885. Watercolor on paper; 2¾ in. x 5 in. Courtesy, Portsmouth Public Library.*

Fig. 4.12. Clarence Stedman house, New Castle, New Hampshire. Photograph, ca. 1883. Courtesy, Society for the Preservation of New England Antiquities.

In comparison with summer homes in Newport, Rhode Island, or Long Island, New York, those in the Piscataqua region were, almost without exception, modest in size and decoration. These were houses of the upper-middle class, not of the very rich. Moreover, many were built by the so-called Boston Brahmins, a group notable for its lack of display. Others were built by New Yorkers with Boston or Portsmouth connections. In speaking of the summer residents of Newport, one author said:

> The leading elements are Boston and New York, and the tone of the former, candor compels me to say, is rather the better on the whole. Boston does not dress so well as New York; is not so round, so graceful, so mellow; has nothing like the style. But it regards more the furniture of the mind and the spiritual aspects of life; its vanities are the vanities of culture, Bunker Hill, and the Mayflower, rather than of Worth gowns, first-water diamonds, and high-stoop mansions—whether you can read the title clear to them or not.[22]

Newport was known for its high fashion. For that reason, quiet Bostonians with an interest in history often chose to vacation elsewhere. Professor Charles Eliot Norton chose to settle in rural Ashfield, Massachusetts, while a number of his art history students at Harvard (in the classes of the later 1870s) went to Little Harbor. Barrett Wendell was among these; his father had grown up in Portsmouth, so he had visited the area since he was a child.

Both family associations and national publications drew summer colonists to the Piscataqua region, but writers based in the area also promoted its natural and historical landmarks. The production of guidebooks for visitors to Portsmouth and other nearby communities has not ceased since Sarah Haven Foster first published her *Portsmouth Guide Book* (cat. 1) in 1876. However, something happened over the years which changed the significance of these guidebooks, particularly those with architectural pretensions. Colonial architecture as a source of new design became disconnected from place. Houses like the Wentworth mansion at Little Harbor, the William Pepperrell house, and Sparhawk Hall at Kittery Point were avidly studied in the 1870s and 1880s by architects who, in turn, incorporated their knowledge into new designs in the same region. By the 1920s, however, publications such as the *White Pine Series of Monographs* were distributing photographs and drawings of attractive houses all over the country. This meant that a Dutch colonial house, with no historical connection with the Piscataqua area, could be built in Portsmouth using a national publication for inspiration.

This development was the result of an increasingly widespread knowledge of New England's historic buildings from the 1890s. The Commonwealth of Massachusetts, repenting the 1863 demolition of the Hancock mansion in Boston (fig. 4.13), built a reproduction of the building to serve as its headquarters at the Columbian Exposition in Chicago in 1893. By that time, the original had become the regional equivalent of Mount Vernon in the popular mind. Despite differences, the Hancock mansion may well have been the model for Dr. Francis Langdon's 1884 rebuilding of the ca. 1840 Frink farmhouse in Newington, New Hampshire (fig. 4.14). Likewise, in 1906, the Governor John Langdon mansion in Portsmouth received an elegant addition (cat. 12). The ensuing statewide publicity for the house resulted in a movement to reproduce the original block as the New Hampshire building at the Jamestown Exhibit of 1907.[23] Although not actually carried out, the incident suggests how widely known certain key colonial monuments were by the early twentieth century.

The project to reproduce the Langdon mansion might be considered stylistically intermediate between the shingled summer homes of the 1880s and the national colonial revival aesthetic of the 1930s. The latter is illustrated by the 1930 alteration of the Edmund Clarence Stedman house in New Castle (fig. 4.15). Originally built in 1883 (see fig. 4.12), it was redesigned by the architect William L. White of Exeter, New Hampshire. This transformation from what had been called an "old French lanterne" suggests a desire to eliminate the oddities of a half-century-old design which architect and client probably regarded as gloomily Victorian. The tower (the most important feature of the original house) was removed, while the roof and dormers were regularized, leaving little of the original exterior besides the stone

Fig. 4.13. Hancock house, Boston, Massachusetts, built 1737, demolished 1863. Photograph, ca. 1862. Courtesy, Society for the Preservation of New England Antiquities.

Fig. 4.14. Woodbury Langdon II farmhouse, Newington, New Hampshire, built ca. 1840, rebuilt 1884. Photograph, 1922. Courtesy, Mrs. John B. Staley.

Fig. 4.15. Clarence Stedman house, New Castle, New Hampshire, built 1883, altered 1930. Photograph, 1991. Courtesy, Woodard Openo.

arches of the porch. All the ruggedness of the house, which fit in so well with the rocky shoreline, was concealed.[24]

The Stedman house reconstruction announced the demise of the wonderfully productive artistic relationship between the summer colonists, artists and architects (often one and the same), and the natural, historical, and architectural resources provided by the Piscataqua region. Later still, as the area became increasingly commercialized for summer visitors, some of the distinctions between the various towns were lost beneath the sprawl of motels, restaurants, and shops. An example of this phenomenon is found in Perkins Cove in Ogunquit, where the meandering Josias River (fig. 4.16) was transformed during the 1950s (fig. 4.17) into a basin for commercial and pleasure craft, and many of the fishing shacks that once provided studio space became shops catering to the tourist trade.[25] At the same time, the closing of Woodbury's and Field's art schools diminished the importance of Perkins Cove as an artistic center. Nonetheless, the works of art produced by summer colonists between the late nineteenth century and the first decades of the twentieth remain as testimonies to the importance of the Piscataqua region in American culture.

1 The painter William Morris Hunt helped make Ruskin known in Boston, and was also responsible for bringing the work of the Barbizon School to the city.

2 The significance to modernism of the concept of retreat is addressed in a dissertation currently being completed by Laurie Milner at Northwestern University, entitled "Modernism's Absent Father: Constructing Cézanne and His Art in Paris, 1886–1901."

3 The relationship between the Impressionists and their nonurban subjects is discussed in T.J. Clark, *The Painting of Modern Life: Paris in the Art of Manet and His Followers* (London: Thames & Hudson, 1984).

4 Samuel Adams Drake, *Nooks and Corners of the New England Coast* (New York: Harper & Brothers, 1875).

5 George Henry Tripp, *Student-Days at Harvard* (Boston: Lockwood, Brooks & Co., 1876).

6 The "mammoth hotel for summer guests" across the harbor from the Wentworth Mansion described by Tripp undoubtedly corresponds to

The Wentworth Hotel (cat. 2) built just two years before the publication of the novel.

7 Information on Cambridge, Mass., houses from Cambridge Historical Commission files, and Margaret Henderson Floyd, "Measured Drawings of the Hancock House by John Hubbard Sturgis: A Legacy to the Colonial Revival" in *Architecture in Colonial Massachusetts,* ed. Abbott Lowell Cummings (Boston: Colonial Society of Massachusetts, 1979) 87, 111.

8 Drake, *Nooks and Corners,* 114; Patricia E. Hart et al., *A Century of Color, 1886–1986* (Ogunquit, Me.: Barn Gallery Associates, 1987), 37.

9 Sarah D. Clark, "A Summer at York," *Harper's New Monthly Magazine* 65 (Sept. 1882): 487–98. Drake, *Nooks and Corners,* 118–39.

10 This information was drawn from the text of a photographic exhibition organized by Amy Hufnagel and Marina Moskowitz at OYHS in 1990.

11 Drake, *Nooks and Corners,* 140–52.

12 Drake, *Nooks and Corners,* 153–95, and John W. Chadwick, "The Isles of Shoals," *Harper's New Monthly Magazine* 49 (Oct. 1874): 663–76.

13 David Park Curry, *Childe Hassam: An Island Garden Revisited* (New York: Denver Museum of Art in association with W.W. Norton, 1990), 14.

14 See Beverly Kay Brandt, "Mutually Helpful Relations: Architects, Craftsmen, and the Society of Arts and Crafts, Boston, 1897–1917" (Ph.D. diss., Boston University, 1985).

15 John Ruskin, *The Seven Lamps of Architecture* (1849; reprint, New York: Noonday Press, 1971), 170.

16 Thomas Bailey Aldrich, "An Old Town by the Sea," *Harper's New Monthly Magazine* 49 (Oct. 1874): 633; Curry, *An Island Garden Revisited,* fig. 1.12; Joseph S. Czestochowski, ed., *94 Prints by Childe Hassam* (New York: Dover Publications, 1980), figs. 1, 2, 24; fig. 24 shows Church Point from another viewpoint.

17 Family tradition maintains that Tarbell hired Frank L. Wells of Dorchester, Mass., to design the additions he made to his house. Wells was related to Mrs. Tarbell and later appears in the Boston directories as an architect. However, it is likely that his role here was simply that of a draftsman; practically nothing else is known of the man.

18 For Emerson's work in Maine, see Roger G. Reed, *A Delight to All Who Know It: The Maine Summer Architecture of William R. Emerson* (Augusta: Maine Historic Preservation Commission, 1990).

19 A collection of watercolor paintings by Sarah Haven Foster is in the Portsmouth Public Library.

20 On Wheelwright's art historical knowledge, see his letters in Houghton Library, Harvard University, Cambridge, Mass.

21 Carole A. Jensen, "Edmund M. Wheelwright, 1854–1912," in *A Biographical Dictionary of Architects in Maine* 4, no. 13 (1987), published by the Maine Historic Preservation Commission.

Fig. 4.16. Joseph Davol, The Josias River, *ca. 1919. Oil on canvas; 34 in. x 40 in. Courtesy, The Museum of Art of Ogunquit.*

22 Junius Henri Browne, "The Queen of Aquidneck," *Harper's New Monthly Magazine* 49 (Aug. 1874): 318.

23 An article in the Mar. 12, 1907, edition of the *Portsmouth Herald* proclaimed that the Langdon mansion duplicate would be finished in thirty days, that only the original building was to be reproduced, and that plans had been completed by "Architect Whitcher" of Manchester, N.H.: "The exposition building will be open for the convenience of all visitors from New Hampshire and there will be colonial exhibits, as well as exhibits emphasizing New Hampshire's attractions as a Summer resort state." I am indebted to Jane Porter of the PA for calling my attention to this article.

24 *Architecture Near the Piscataqua* (Portsmouth, N.H.: Strawbery Banke, Inc., 1964), 49–50.

25 Carrie Boyd, Kathryn Ryan, Betty Wills, and William Wills, *The Cove: Perkins Cove at Ogunquit, Maine* (Ogunquit, Me.: By the authors, 1976), 77.

Fig. 4.17. Perkins Cove. Photograph, ca. 1950. Courtesy, The Historical Society of Wells and Ogunquit.

Cat. 27. Frostfields, New Castle, New Hampshire, built 1882. Photograph, ca. 1885. Courtesy, Portsmouth Athenaeum.

❋ 27 ❋

"FROSTFIELDS," JACOB WENDELL RESIDENCE
Little Harbor, New Hampshire, 1882; burned, ca. 1946
Edmund March Wheelwright (1854–1912), architect

Jacob Wendell II (1826–1898) grew up in the family home in Portsmouth (cat. 4), and later settled in New York where he became successful in the textile business. Although Jacob was not a writer or historian like his son Barrett Wendell (1855–1921), his reverence for family history brought him back to Portsmouth. As Barrett wrote:

> By mere chance, I think, my mother decided to pass the whole summer of 1876 at Appledore [one of the Isles of Shoals]. She liked it so much that she went back there for six successive season[s] . . . My father's weekend visits during these summers tended to grow longer . . . Thus the summer vagrancy of the family came to an end. One reason for this new fixity of domestic habit, though hardly conscious, I can now see to have been profound. For my father, and through him for us all, this resort to the region where he had been born was something like a return of natives . . . Portsmouth, after all, was where he really belonged . . . he used to speak of his trips there as going down home . . . His love for the old town never wavered; and the old town was content with him. Our pleasant personal relations there . . . were really his, and those of his father and his grandfather before him. His roots there were in the heart of the soil; through his mother and his grandmother he descended from some of the earliest and worthiest stocks which had made the place, in its more prosperous days, a royal capital.[1]

In 1882, Jacob Wendell decided to build a summer home. He purchased land from George Bartlett, assistant professor of German at Harvard, through the poet John Albee (who lived nearby). The land had originally belonged to the Frost family and was known as "Frost Fields." As Barrett relates in his recollections of his father, Jacob's experience with a New York architect and business acquaintance who produced a disastrous design ("disastrous" because it was an eclectic urban house, unsuitable to the site) led to Barrett's recommending his Harvard friend Edmund March Wheelwright, then working for the architect E.P. Treadwell in Albany, New York. "Frostfields" (cat. 27) was Wheelwright's first independent design.[2]

Located on what is now called Great Island Common, the house was a long, shingled structure designed to maximize its scenic peninsular location overlooking the Isles of Shoals and the entrance to Portsmouth harbor. It extended east to west, with the east end, close to the shore, containing the family quarters. As was the case with several other houses at Little Harbor, the servants' quarters formed the other end of the house; here, they were deemphasized by being set back from the main (south) facade of the house. In a letter to Jacob Wendell (received July 18, 1882), Wheelwright described the development of the plans:

> I have covered the outside cistern with a roof and show on the elevations, for your approval, a yard off the laundry surrounded by a shingled wall that the clothes may be hung out to dry without being unsightly. This adds to the long effect I have tried to get and is an improvement to the building from an artistic as well as a practical point of view.[3]

An undated letter (from July 1882, judging from its context) from Wheelwright to Wendell states that revision of the plans has increased the cubic footage of the house from 36,000 to 74,000. This was primarily due to the addition of two more servants' bedrooms, bringing the total to three—a large number for this type of house—as Wheelwright noted. At the same time, Wendell was apparently urging economy, leading the architect to say:

I shall make the interior detail no more expensive than in 10¢ a cubic foot houses. The exterior detail I also shall keep extrem[e]ly simple, relying principally for my effect on the texture of the shingles and the outline of the building.[4]

By the following spring, decisions were being made concerning the finishing of the house. Wheelwright wrote Mrs. Wendell on April 2, 1883, saying that he intended to paint the shingles "raw sienna. A brownish yellow. Like the tones in iron rust," and added:

As to the coloring. The woodwork is to be stained throughout a color between that of cherry and mahogany. I will send you a sample of the color. You can select your stuffs to harmonize with that and the color of the walls we will base on the color of the woodwork and your selections. Don't you like the Wakefield rattan arm chairs? I think them very pretty and suitable.[5]

One can see in Frostfields three features which appear in other Little Harbor houses: enclosing the work yard at one end of the house, differentiating the servants' end of the house architecturally, and giving the whole a low profile. These features were common solutions to practical problems, but also grew out of the interaction between the major architects working at Little Harbor. The 1882 Frostfields, with its completely shingled exterior, multiplicity of windows, and long horizontal main elevations, shows how quickly the shingled colonial aesthetic had taken over in the country house architecture produced in Boston.

There is little information about the interior, so that the plan must be inferred from exterior photographs. Barrett's comment about one oversight by the architect shows how interior utility was sacrificed to exterior appearance:

In some practical aspects . . . the plans ultimately revealed Ned's inexperience; for one thing, which my father never happened to notice, and which the family carefully kept from his attention, the bedrooms—faultless so far as the relation of windows to views went—had no convenient places for the beds . . . On the whole, though, the house was a success . . . its elevations were so subtly adapted to the site that it looked as if it had grown there.

The sea views and "local conditions" were, however, important to Jacob Wendell—enough so, that they determined the style of the house, which Barrett termed "nowise colonial in character"; this judgment seems to have been due to the fact that the house was not a regularly massed rectangle.[6]

Frostfields was the center of Wendell family gatherings for many years. More so than for many of the other summer colonists, family ties were important to the Wendells and were perpetuated in numerous family gatherings, frequently marking important occasions, including the anniversary of Jacob Wendell's leaving Portsmouth to seek his fortune. Barrett Wendell did much of his historical writing during the summer in the tiny studio near the shore at Frostfields, and thereby made the house a place to contemplate both personal and public history.

WDO

1 Barrett Wendell, "Recollections of my Father, Jacob Wendell, 1826–1898" (typescript, Wendell Papers, PA, 1918), 107.

2 Wendell, "Recollections of my Father," 127–35. Barrett Wendell to Col. Robert White-Thomson, May 12, 1914, in "Letters of Barrett Wendell to Col. Robert White-Thomson," 1879–1917, vol. 3, Wendell Papers, PA.

3 Edmund March Wheelwright to Barrett Wendell, [July 1882], Wendell Papers.

4 Edmund March Wheelwright to Barrett Wendell, [July 1882], Wendell Papers.

5 Edmund March Wheelwright to Mrs. Jacob Wendell, April 2, 1883, Wendell Papers.

6 Barrett Wendell, "Recollections of my Father," 134ff.

Cat. 28. Creek Farm, Little Harbor, New Hampshire, built 1897. Photograph, ca. 1890. Private collection.

※ 28 ※

"CREEK FARM," ARTHUR ASTOR CAREY RESIDENCE
Little Harbor, New Hampshire, 1897
Alexander Wadsworth Longfellow, Jr. (1854–1934), architect

Arthur Astor Carey (1857–1923) was the son of John Carey and Alida Astor Carey. John was a prominent English botanist, while Alida was a descendant of John Jacob Astor. Arthur inherited an active mind, along with ample financial resources. After graduating from Harvard College in 1879, he found an outlet in building a colonial revival house in Cambridge, Massachusetts (in 1882, designed by John Hubbard Sturgis with his nephew R. Clipston Sturgis, recently graduated from Harvard, assisting).

In the summer of 1887, Carey followed his friend John Templeman Coolidge III from Cambridge to Little Harbor, purchasing land adjacent to Coolidge's Wentworth mansion grounds. Soon thereafter, Carey hired another Harvard classmate, Alexander Wadsworth Longfellow, Jr., to design a large summer cottage in the shingled colonial style, overlooking Sagamore Creek (cat. 28).

The gregarious Longfellow, who had worked for about four years in the architectural office of the late H.H. Richardson, was concurrently designing a summer home for Miss E.F. Mason in Dublin, New Hampshire. Both were published in the leading architectural periodical of the day, the *American Architect and Building News*.[1] Although they show Richardsonian influence, particularly in the stonework of the Mason house's first story, they also demonstrate that Longfellow had firm ideas of his own about domestic architecture—ideas rooted in the colonial and the classical. As a result, the Carey house presents a gambrel roof (a favorite feature of Longfellow's) with dormers, along with classical trim and a balanced asymmetry in its main elevations. It is a country version of several houses which he would design in and around Cambridge in the same period. The plan was a very open one, with the dining and living rooms both running through from the front to the back of the house, and a porch on the water side extending around to the main entrance on the driveway.

In 1889, Carey married Agnes Whiteside, an English-woman who was then serving as companion and governess for the Empress Eugénie, widow of Napoleon III of France. Although the marriage was not a happy one, Agnes loved Little Harbor, which she considered her home; unlike the other summer colonists, she lived there from the early spring to the late fall. Based on European gardens with which she was familiar, she created an "Italian Garden" to the west of the house, decorated with box hedges, symmetrical gravel paths, a central stone font, and two Venetian stone lions. Contemporary photographs suggest that the garden provided a green, shady contrast to the very open (and relatively informal) surroundings of the house.[2]

At least three additions to the Creek Farm house (which overlooks Sagamore Creek to the south) followed within a few years: a lower eastern extension, a large ell running north from that, and, balancing the eastern ell, one to the west. The eastern ell contains a paneled music room on the first floor, while the western one contains additional bedrooms and an archway for the drive. As is the case with a number of Little Harbor "cottages," the Carey house was originally divided into family and servants' quarters; the latter occupied the east end of the house. The architect of the additions is unknown, but the classical details and the wrought iron clockface (akin to objects in the Boston Arts and Crafts exhibition of 1897) in the added tower suggest that it was Longfellow. Other buildings on the estate included an elaborate shingled stable, a barn (into which was built an apartment for Mrs. Carey's sister about 1900), and an existing early nineteeth-century house which was moved back from the creek to make way for the new house. This became "The Red Elephant"; there was another small house built, "The Elephant's Child," and other constructions included a tidal swimming pool and a shingled playhouse on tiny Goose Island, which was part of the property. In 1902, a chapel was built, designed by Richard Arnold Fisher of Boston.

The largest of several houses at Little Harbor which are known, or believed, to have been designed by Longfellow, Creek Farm's architectural connections with Cambridge are typical of the Little Harbor summer colony. A good comparison with the Carey house is Longfellow's house for Mary Longfellow at 115 Brattle Street in Cambridge, which is slightly more formal, but otherwise similar in exterior appearance.

In the early 1880s, Arthur Carey had studied painting in Paris with his friend John Templeman Coolidge III. In 1896, they joined other Little Harbor settlers as well as Boston friends and relatives to rescue the failing Chelsea (Massachusetts) Keramic Arts Works, move it, and rename it the Dedham Pottery. Carey provided the financial backing for the company, which became a noted arts and crafts pottery. A brochure published at that time lists the directors as Arthur A. Carey, A. Wadsworth Longfellow, Jr., J. Templeman Coolidge, Jr., R. Clipston Sturgis, Joseph Linden [*sic*] Smith, Sarah W. Whitman, and William Sturgis Bigelow. The superintendent (and chief potter) was Hugh C. Robertson.[3]

Many of the same people were involved the following year in the First Exhibition of Arts and Crafts, an exhibition of industrial arts held in Boston from April, and in the founding of the Society of Arts and Crafts in Boston (SACB) on June 28, 1897. The society was the first one in America modeled on the Arts and Crafts Exhibition Society in England (founded 1888). The first president of the SACB was the aging Charles Eliot Norton, professor of fine arts at Harvard, and the second was Arthur Astor Carey. Among the charter members were Carey, Alexander Wadsworth Longfellow, Jr., and John Templeman Coolidge III. They were soon joined by R. Clipston Sturgis and Edmund March Wheelwright. In fact, as Beverly Brandt points out, many architects were prominent in the society. Their interests, as revealed in the First Exhibition, covered the spectrum of furnishings and architectural decoration. Longfellow exhibited fireplace equipment, revealing an interest in metalwork which may also have come out in the unattributed 1890s exterior clock at Creek Farm.[4] Longfellow and Sturgis (and probably most of the architects in the society) had long been interested in design; Sturgis revealed this in two notebooks of foreign travels (dating from 1884–86), preserved at the Boston Architectural Center. In these, along with the architectural sketches which one would expect, are sketches of objects labeled "SK" for the South Kensington (now the Victoria and Albert) Museum in London, famous for its collection of decorative arts.

Despite a break with the society in 1903, over philosophical differences, Arthur Astor Carey remained interested in art and architecture, and kept in touch with SACB member Mary Ware Dennett and her husband, the architect Hartley Dennett.[5] Hartley would design a house for Arthur at 48 Fayerweather Street in Cambridge and buildings for the New Church School (Swedenborgian) at Waltham, Massachusetts, a project endowed by him.

Arthur Astor Carey's diverse artistic interests were typical of the Little Harbor summer colonists. Creek Farm included a shingled colonial house, an Italian garden, a Georgian revival chapel, and an iron tower clockface which clearly suggests that its designer had studied French Renaissance examples. Carey, Coolidge, Longfellow, Sturgis, and Wheelwright were all equally well versed in European medieval and Renaissance art, Georgian and federal architecture, American folk art, and the arts and crafts movement.

WDO

1 The Carey house was published in *American Architect and Building News* 23, no. 646 (May 12, 1888); the Mason house in the same journal (26, no. 727 [Nov. 30, 1889]).

2 Telephone interview with Joan Carey Cunningham, Feb. 21, 1991, and various interviews, 1989.

3 *Dedham Pottery: Formerly known to the Trade and to the Public as Chelsea Pottery, U.S.* (Dedham, Mass.: Dedham Pottery, 1896). *Dedham Pottery: Catalogue,* historical background by J. Milton Robertson (Dedham, Mass.: Dedham Pottery, 1938).

4 Beverly Kay Brandt, "Mutually Helpful Relations: Architects, Craftsmen, and the Society of Arts and Crafts, Boston, 1897–1917" (Ph.D. diss., Boston University, 1985), 69–103, app. A–D, and *passim;* and Beverly Kay Brandt, "The Essential Link: Boston Architects and the Society of Arts and Crafts," *Tiller* 2, no. 1 (Sept.-Oct. 1983): 7–32.

5 The Dennetts were summer residents of Saco, Me. A collection of Dennett family photographs and correspondence is in the York Institute Museum, Saco.

⚬ 29 ⚬

MOLLY COOLIDGE PERKINS (1881–1962), PHOTOGRAPHER
Little Harbor, New Hampshire, ca. 1900

The photographs of Molly Coolidge Perkins reveal the extent to which the ideologies of the colonial revival affected youths of the period; Perkins began her endeavors in photography at the age of fourteen and was most prolific in the early years of her life. Perkins was not of a generation to

Cat. 29. *Molly Coolidge Perkins,* Jack, Eliza, and Louise Coolidge, 1896. Photograph; 7½ in. x 9½ in. Courtesy, Molly Coolidge Perkins Collection, Strawbery Banke Museum.

recognize the increase in industrialization, immigration, and urbanization that spawned many proponents of the colonial revival movement. Rather, she was a member of a second generation, raised to value the natural environment and the simplicity of rural life, but without as strong a sense of escape from urban life as their parents had. Perkins's photographs, as well as her writings, celebrated the freedom that she felt in the pastoral landscape of her summer home in the Piscataqua River region, but in a much more personal sense. Perkins reacted against the urban society that she knew in Boston only to the degree that it dictated confining rules of propriety for young women like herself.

The summer life in the Piscataqua region was apparently that which suited Perkins best; she referred to her time in the Little Harbor area of Portsmouth as "normal living."[1] She clearly saw the difference in the tenor of her home life in the two varied settings; for many families of the colonial revival period, urban dwellings were decorated in the high-style fashions of the Victorian period, often sparked by European influence, while country summer homes were decorated with pieces of Americana. Perkins wrote of this difference in her uncle's country home and how much she preferred the rural approach: "we hurried down to the living room. I was relieved to see that this did not in any way resemble the red one in Boston, but was early American, filled with the most lovely old furniture that can be imagined."[2]

Perkins's photographs reflected the seasonal activities commonly found in the Piscataqua summer communities, emphasizing an idealized vision of rural life (cat. 29). Perkins took this summer situation to heart; she described herself and some friends dressed as wandering minstrels as "justified in feeling that we looked like very poor country children."[3] In their Wentworth-Coolidge mansion, the Coolidge family created a simple rural life within a historic homestead, which had originally belonged to the royal

Cat. 29a. Molly Coolidge Perkins, Wood Sprites, 1896. *Photograph; 9½ in. x 7½ in. Courtesy, Molly Coolidge Perkins Collection, Strawbery Banke Museum.*

governor, Benning Wentworth. Perkins recounted that this association had always attracted local historic lore: "As the Mansion had been open to the public before Papa bought it, sightseers still came occasionally, and our friends loved to make up stories for them."[4] Perkins used these two characteristics of her summer home, the pastoral setting and the historic aura, as backgrounds for images of her family in both exterior and interior settings.

At an early age, Molly Coolidge Perkins learned the idea of staging photographs, as a subject, however, rather than as a photographer. She recalled that at the age of six, "I rowed as far as the end of the island till Papa called through the megaphone for me to turn slowly and pass close to the float as Mr. Deland had a camera."[5] This notion of carefully crafting the positions of her subjects was one that Perkins adopted for her own photographs. Her compositions were often quaint farm scenes, taken in or near the family estate in Little Harbor, with her sisters and brother posed with animals or simple agrarian equipment such as wagons or carts. Perkins also staged more elaborate scenes, such as a series of photographs taken in a forest with her siblings dressed as imaginary figures (cat. 29a). She wrote:

As it was not easy to get everyone up in the woods I had brought my camera, in hopes of getting a few

photographs of fairies and wood sprites. We had a way of making garments, or wreaths that sufficed as such, out of oak leaves strung together with their own stems. Katherine and I made a few of these and I suggested that as we had lots of time before going home I would like to get a few pictures.[6]

The staged photographs taken by Perkins were closely linked to the wide variety of pageants and plays that were produced by the children of the summer communities in the Piscataqua region. The Coolidge children were involved in numerous projects, including one play written by Molly Coolidge Perkins, inspired by her grandfather Francis Parkman's writings on the history of the American West. Perkins documented this production with photographs, obviously in a similar vein as the crafted images of her siblings that she had created.[7]

Such amateur dramatic events became gathering places for the summer community of both children and adults. Usually produced outdoors, the plays symbolized both the interest in pastoral settings and the leisure time available to members of the summer colonies. In the early twentieth century, pageantry was a popular form of affirming community identity and cohesion, through both work prior to the production and the actual performance.[8] Perkins described her tribute to Western Americana: "The day for the final show was bright and fair and the train had had directions to stop at the gates on the road to let out the audience from Boston, while others drove from Weston, Lincoln and Concord; more than we could have hoped for."[9] In another instance, Perkins recounted that "Mrs. Jack Gardner was coming on the train from Boston to see the play and was spending the night at our house."[10] Clearly the same events that served as inspiration for Perkins's photography provided social occasions in the summer communities at large.

In style, as well as in spirit, Perkins's work was tied closely to that of an upper-class Boston artistic community, many of whom sought similar retreats in the Piscataqua region as the Coolidge family. Perkins's father was J. Templeman Coolidge III, an amateur painter and a trustee of the Boston Museum of Fine Arts; her grandfather, Francis Parkman, was the first president of the St. Botolph Club, an elite arts club in Boston that sponsored exhibitions and lectures.[11] Perkins herself, upon graduation from the Winsor School, began sculpture classes at the School of the Museum of Fine Arts in 1899 under the tutelage of Bela Pratt, as well as academic classes at Radcliffe.[12] Perkins pursued not only sculpture and photography, but also painting and a variety of crafts, including wood carving and ceramics. Through these associations, Perkins was acquainted with many of the central figures of the Boston school of American painting. Perkins wrote in her memoirs of a childhood meeting with Frank Benson and Edmund Tarbell, two of the leading painters of the circle and directors of the Department of Painting and Drawing at the Museum School in Boston from 1890 to 1912; when she

Plate 1. Charles Woodbury, The Junkins House, York, Maine, ca. 1888. Oil on canvas; 9 in. x 13½ in. Old York Historical Society. (See cat. 5.)

Plate 2. Russell Cheney, Interior at Sparhawk Hall, Kittery Point, Maine, ca. 1930. Oil on canvas; 24 in. x 36 in. Courtesy, The Mitchell Family. (See cat. 9.)

Plate 3. Edmund C. Tarbell, My Family, 1914. Oil on canvas; 30 in. x 38 in. Private collection. (See cat. 30.)

Plate 4. George Porter Fernald, parlor mural, Hamilton house, South Berwick, Maine, 1906. Tempera on wallpaper, 83 in. x 74 in. Courtesy, Society for the Preservation of New England Antiquities. (See cat. 17.)

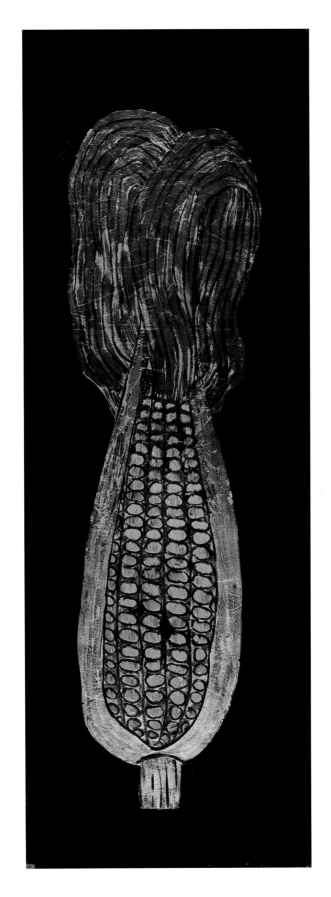

Plate 5. Marsden Hartley, Ear of Corn, *1917.*
Reverse painting on glass; 19 in. x 6½ in. Courtesy, Nancy Flentje. (See cat. 33.)

Plate 6. Charles Woodbury, The Old Gaol, York, Maine, ca. 1888. Oil on canvas; 8¼ in. x 12¼ in. Old York Historical Society. (See cat. 36.)

Plate 7. John J. Enneking, The Gaol Kitchen, York, Maine, 1888. Oil on canvas; 21¼ in. x 29½ in. Old York Historical Society. (See cat. 37.)

Plate 8. Childe Hassam, The Room with Flowers, 1894. Oil on canvas; 34 in. x 34 in. Collection of Mr. and Mrs. Arthur G. Altschul. (See cat. 42.)

recounted the event to her father, he replied, "I'm glad they knew you . . . I think they are the best artists painting today."[13] Many of the pastoral images and ideologies of the colonial revival movement were incorporated into the paintings of Benson and Tarbell, becoming a strong influence for amateur photographers such as Perkins.

In her interior images and family portraits, Perkins appears to have been particularly influenced by the work of John Singer Sargent and Cecilia Beaux, both of whom were family friends of the Coolidges. Sargent and J. Templeman Coolidge met when each was studying under Carolus Duran in Paris; their contact was maintained in Boston, especially through such mutual friends as Isabella Stewart Gardner, the patroness of the arts whose collection was eventually opened as a museum. Coolidge, in fact, wrote the introduction for the catalogue to a retrospective of Sargent's paintings held by the Museum of Fine Arts in 1925.[14] One of Perkins's photographs of her sisters and mother by a fireplace in the Wentworth-Coolidge mansion, in particular, is similar to Sargent's group portraits of prominent Boston families, such as *Daughters of Edward D. Boit* of 1882 (Museum of Fine Arts, Boston). Like Sargent, Perkins placed her subjects in a formal domestic context, highlighting not only the family bonds but the importance of the home setting. In the case of Perkins's photograph, the home is again the historic Wentworth-Coolidge mansion (see illustration on p. 113), revealing the colonial revival reverence for the past.

MM

1 Molly Coolidge Perkins, *Once When I Was Very Young* (Milton, Mass., 1960), 8.

2 Molly Coolidge Perkins and John Forbes Perkins, *Stories* (Milton, Mass., 1963), 18.

3 Perkins, *Once When I Was Very Young*, 20.

4 Perkins, *Once When I Was Very Young*, 70.

5 Perkins, *Once When I Was Very Young*, 4.

6 Perkins, *Once When I Was Very Young*, 50–51.

7 Perkins, *Once When I Was Very Young*, 55.

8 David Glassberg, *American Historical Pageantry: The Uses of Tradition in the Early Twentieth Century* (Chapel Hill: University of North Carolina Press, 1990), 137.

9 Perkins, *Once When I Was Very Young*, 54–57.

10 Perkins, *Once When I Was Very Young*, 16.

11 Woodard Dorr Openo, "The Summer Colony at Little Harbor in Portsmouth, New Hampshire, and Its Relation to the Colonial Revival Movement" (Ph.D. diss., University of Michigan, 1989), 41–43; Trevor J. Fairbrother, "Painting in Boston, 1870–1930," *The Bostonians: Painters of an Elegant Age, 1870–1930* (Boston: Museum of Fine Arts, 1986), 41.

12 Perkins and Perkins, *Stories*, 9; enrollment records, Art School of the Museum of Fine Arts, Boston; Cynthia Fleming, "Instructors and Courses in the Museum School, 1876–1935," in Fairbrother, *The Bostonians*, 234.

13 Perkins, *Once When I Was Very Young*, 22–23.

14 Openo, "Summer Colony at Little Harbor," 41–43.

30

EDMUND C. TARBELL (1862–1938)
My Family
New Castle, New Hampshire, 1914
Oil on canvas; 30 in. x 38 in.
Private collection
(see plate 3)

Edmund C. Tarbell's *My Family* encapsulates the colonial revival aesthetic in turn-of-the-century New England. Begun in 1912 and completed in 1914, the painting depicts the artist's wife, Emeline, their three daughters, Josephine, Mercie, and Mary, and their son, Edmund Arnold. The group is engaged in leisure activities in the sunlit living room of their renovated summer home in New Castle, New Hampshire.[1] Not only is the painting a celebration of the family's bountiful surroundings, it also serves to domesticate the past by stressing the old New England values of commitment to family and home.[2]

Tarbell was born in 1862 in West Groton, Massachusetts, into a family with an extensive New England lineage.[3] He received academic training at the Académie Julian in Paris during the early 1880s and by 1886 returned to Boston, exhibiting there and in New York. In 1889 Tarbell began to teach painting at the School of the Museum of Fine Arts, Boston, a position he held until his resignation in 1912. During these years, Tarbell achieved the acme of his success and was hailed the leader of the "Boston School," also dubbed "The Tarbellites," which included such artists as Frank W. Benson, Joseph De Camp, and Philip Leslie Hale.[4] His works of the 1890s reflect experimentation with the Impressionist aesthetic, resulting in brightly colored and sunny plein-air landscapes and genre scenes such as *In the Orchard* (1891, private collection). By 1904, with the completion of the pivotal *Girl Crocheting* (Canajoharie Library and Art Gallery, Canajoharie, New York), the mood of Tarbell's work changed to reflect a more subdued palette and conservative brushstroke. Subjects of sparsely furnished interiors with nostalgic overtones now dominated his oeuvre and were often remarked upon for the direct inspiration of the seventeenth-century Dutch Little Masters, especially Vermeer.[5] Tarbell's ties to the Piscataqua region were well established by the time he completed *My Family* and other historically oriented paintings. In 1905 Tarbell adapted a nineteenth-century house, "a charming home with copper beaches bordering the Portsmouth Harbor," as a summer residence for his family (cat. 30a).[6] Tarbell continued to maintain his home in New Castle where he had summered since the 1880s, after he left Boston in 1918 to become the principal of the Corcoran School of Art in Washington, D.C. He retired to New Castle in 1926, where he died in 1938.[7]

Tarbell's New England heritage is evoked in the many works in which his family is his primary subject matter. The interior of the living room shown in *My Family* reflects the curious juxtaposition of "old" and "new" elements, a com-

Cat. 30a. Edmund C. Tarbell, Morning, New Castle Harbor, *ca. 1928. Oil on canvas; 26¼ in. x 20¼ in. Private collection.*

mon trait in the colonial revival interior.[8] Though Dutch masters may have served to a moderate degree as a formal and technical inspiration in this painting, one writer noted perceptively:

It is not Holland but New England that speaks in these pleasant rooms with their large wall spaces, their polished mahogany, their shining silver, and their Chinese porcelains. It is New England also that finds expression in the reticence of types and the definite precision of the gestures. The young girls who bend their extremely graceful heads over their books or their needle, who pour tea, of a perfect strength and temperature one is certain, who have long clever fingers, small feet and simple gowns, are as characteristically American as Pieter de Hooch's housemother is Dutch.[9]

Renovated with elements of colonial "woodwork" such as the mantelpiece, Tarbell's living room exemplifies the late nineteenth-century "early American" interior that was less a product of historical accuracy than of a nostalgic perception of the past.[10] The ceiling displays elements of nineteenth-century balloon-frame construction in its machine-finished joists. Instead of plastering the ceiling as would have been done in the colonial period, and thereby covering the modern structure, Tarbell chose to leave the painted joists exposed. Furthermore, with disregard for colonial building practices, the crudeness of the exposed ceiling is juxtaposed with more formal paneling on the walls and above the fireplace. The inglenook, on which one of the artist's daughters sits, was added by Tarbell around 1907.[11] The diamond-paned casement windows are a standard colonial revival feature, as are the French doors. Indeed the light-colored interior and generous windows are

far more indicative of contemporary taste and practicality than of the colonial past.

Tarbell's interest in things "antique" is evident in the disparate furnishings shown in *My Family.* The painting is indicative of contemporary collecting habits, though certainly a record of the artist's personal taste. Although speaking of *Girls Reading* (1907, private collection, Massachusetts), Francis Hamilton's comments in his 1925 article "Artists' Homes as They Paint Them," could well be applied to *My Family.* The author describes

a decidedly pleasing room . . . [with] the precisely right yet unconventional placing of the Chinese covered jar, the conjunction of the early American mahogany settee with wall and window, the gate-leg table and ladderback chair. Here is an American interior, simple, yet finely harmonious, that may well serve as an inspiration to the professional or amateur decorator.[12]

Aside from the more modern rattan wicker chair and stool, the objects shown in *My Family* suggest the grand old days of New England with which Tarbell associated himself. The maple gate-leg table depicted in *My Family* dates to about 1700 and was owned by the artist. It appears in many of his twentieth-century works, and recalls the Puritan heritage of New England. The federal-period circular card table, dating from the 1790s, has veneered mahogany panels with surrounding crossbanding of satinwood. The straight-legged Chippendale-style side chair, like the card table, celebrates the prosperity of Boston, Salem, and Portsmouth.[13] The most obvious manifestations of this wealth are the two Oriental blue-and-white porcelain jars, products of the China trade.[14]

Tarbell completed a number of paintings with colonial revival overtones. These most often depicted leisure-time vignettes featuring the Tarbell family and friends. In many instances, the artist's New Castle home provides the setting for these affectionately rendered works.[15] The element of stillness in canvases such as *Mother and Mary* (1922) may be linked to a colonial revival ethos that quietude bred permanence. *Mother and Mary* is situated in the same living area as *My Family.* The rearrangement of the furnishings evidenced in this later painting suggests not only Tarbell's ongoing interest in collecting, but also his desire to create an aesthetic interior.

Tarbell's *Going to Ride* (cat. 30b), like *My Family,* provides a fascinating synthesis of old and new elements. The artist depicts three of his children outside their white-painted New Castle home. The seemingly omnipresent gate-leg table and Chinese jar now occupy a prominent spot on the porch. Although these motifs lend a historic flavor to the painting, the scene is disrupted by the invasive telephone pole in the near distance. The idealistic setting, replete with a white-painted fence, is thus not immune to the progress and technological advances of twentieth-century culture.

Tarbell's production of historically inspired subjects was part of a larger cultural angst in Boston which affected the "genteel" society of the upper-middle class.[16] Tarbell, like many of his artist confreres, responded to contemporary

Cat. 30b. Edmund C. Tarbell, Going to Ride, *1912. Oil on canvas; 38 in. x 42½ in. Courtesy, Mr. and Mrs. Thomas Rosse; photograph courtesy of Vose Galleries.*

socioeconomic malaise by escaping to rural, and supposedly more harmonious, locales. These areas, seen as untouched by the trials of modern life, were a route back to the nobler, simpler days of the past. In addition to summering in New Castle, Tarbell also produced paintings that celebrated early America through the inclusion of furniture, architectural motifs, and other elements of the past for their aesthetic beauty, as well as historic and moral significance. Already, in 1905, Charles Caffin observed Tarbell's retreat from modernity, questioning:

> Where in his pictures shall we find an echo of the spiritual and mental conflict that is seething around him? He has retired into a quiet backwater, far from the real stream of thought and conduct, to paint little glimpses of his own home and surroundings.[17]

For Tarbell, the Piscataqua region was fertile with motifs from the past, motifs that also offered inspiration to an entire generation of artists, writers, photographers, and architects. Likewise, Tarbell's withdrawal from urban life is hardly an isolated case among artists. For example, William Merritt Chase spent many summers at Shinnecock, Long Island, Childe Hassam vacationed on the Isles of Shoals, and Winslow Homer eventually withdrew to Prout's Neck, Maine, on a year-round basis. American Impressionist artists, in particular, eschewed subjects which were reflective of the changing times, focusing instead on leisure-time vignettes and landscape subjects. *My Family* is a model example of Tarbell's successful embrace of this current aesthetic with overtones from the past.

TTM

1   Tarbell married Emeline Arnold Souther in 1888.

2   For a thought-provoking discussion of the role of paintings in the colonial revival period, see Celia Betsky, "Inside the Past: The Interior and the Colonial Revival in American Art and Literature, 1860–1914," in Axelrod, *Colonial Revival,* 241–77. Many of the concepts introduced in the Betsky essay have served as a basis for ideas elaborated on in this entry.

3   Tarbell's family had a long New England lineage, coming from the west of England and Wales in 1638, and settling in Watertown, Mass., where they remained until 1663. They then moved to Groton, near where Tarbell was later born. See *Dictionary of American Biography,* s.v. "Tarbell, Edmund Charles."

4   The term "The Tarbellites" was coined by Sadakichi Hartmann in "The Tarbellites," *Art News* 1 (March 1897): 3–4.

5   A Vermeer rediscovery had begun in France in the late 1860s with the writings of Thoré-Burger. Artists were inspired by Vermeer's sparse yet elegant furnishings, quiet mood, and subdued light and tonality. Although Tarbell was surely aware of this trend, the influence of Vermeer is most directly manifested in the publication on the artist in *Master of Art: A Series of Illustrated Monographs* 5 (Boston: Bates & Guild Co., 1904) by Tarbell's friend and colleague Philip Leslie Hale. Hale later published a second monograph on the artist, *Jan Vermeer of Delft* (Boston: Small, Maynard, & Co., 1913).

6   *Dictionary of American Biography,* s.v. "Tarbell, Edmund Charles."

7   For the most thorough and accurate biography of Tarbell, see Trevor J. Fairbrother et al., *The Bostonians: Painters of an Elegant Age, 1870–1930* (Boston: Museum of Fine Arts, 1986), 226–27.

8   For a detailed formal analysis of *My Family,* see Bernice Kramer Leader, "The Boston Lady as a Work of Art: Paintings by the Boston School at the Turn of the Century" (Ph.D. diss., Columbia University, 1980), 207–10.

9   "Important Painting by E.C. Tarbell Sold," *New York Times Magazine* (Sept. 16, 1917), 12, c. 1.

10 I am most grateful to Morrison Heckscher, Curator of American Decorative Arts, Metropolitan Museum of Art, New York, for his useful comments on the architectural elements and furnishings in this painting.

11 I would like to thank Woodard D. Openo for information regarding the renovation of the Tarbell house.

12 Francis Hamilton, "Artists' Homes as They Paint Them," *International Studio* 81, no. 340 (Sept. 1925): 417–18. The use and collecting of antique furnishings was first made popular by Clarence Cook in *The House Beautiful* (New York, 1878). In this volume, and in previously published articles in *Scribner's Monthly,* Cook stressed both the aesthetic appeal and durable craftsmanship of these pieces.

13 In "Inside the Past," Betsky supports the notion that "the prevalent Chippendale style was a form of shorthand in fiction for a durable Patrician personality" (294).

14 By far the most useful scholarship on Tarbell's interiors has been conducted by Trevor J. Fairbrother. See his "Edmund Tarbell's Paintings of Interiors," *Antiques* 131, no. 1 (Jan. 1987): 224–35, esp. 232 for photographic reproductions of Tarbell's often-depicted gate-leg table and Chinese jar.

15 Among the paintings depicting Tarbell's friends and family in and around their New Castle home are: *Breakfast on the Piazza* (1902, private collection); *A Rehearsal in the Studio* (1903, Worcester Art Museum, Worcester, Mass.); *Going for a Ride* (1912, private collection, Concord, Mass.); *Nell and Elinor* (1916, private collection); *Mother and Mary* (1922, National Gallery of Art, Washington, D.C.); *Solitaire* (1927, private collection, New Hampshire); *Mother, Mercie, and Mary* (present location unknown); and *Morning, New Castle Harbor* (cat. 30a).

16 For additional cultural background information, see Gilbert Vincent Tapley, "American Artists and Their Changing Perceptions of American History" (Ph.D. diss., University of Delaware, 1982), 725ff., and William L. Vance, "Redefining Bostonian," in Fairbrother, *The Bostonians,* 9–30.

17 Charles H. Caffin, "The Art of Edmund C. Tarbell," *Harper's New Monthly Magazine* 117 (June 1908): 65. Though Caffin discusses Tarbell's depictions of his family, he perceived their nostalgic, sentimental overtones with skepticism.

Cat. 31. Elise Tyson Vaughan, Looking East from House, *1902. Photograph; 5 in. x 7 in. Courtesy, Society for the Preservation of New England Antiquities.*

❀ 31 ❀

E LISE T YSON V AUGHAN (1871–1949)
Photograph Albums
South Berwick, Maine, 1901–5
Society for the Preservation of New England Antiquities

The photographs of Elise Tyson Vaughan are similar in style to those of other amateur women photographers who used this form of expression in the Piscataqua River region between 1880 and 1910. Vaughan pursued photography as a leisure activity, as a way of documenting both her personal and public life, and as a form of artistic expression.

The largest collection of her work exists in four large leather-bound albums (now in the collection of the Society for the Preservation of New England Antiquities) containing photographs, mostly of Hamilton house, taken between 1901 and 1905. The albums form a visual diary that records the passage of personal time and lifestyle, as well as the landscape of the South Berwick area through the seasons.

Vaughan framed the spring apple blossoms, the fall harvest, and the winter's snow each year. This attention to the natural world and its continuity is typical of colonial revival imagery.

Vaughan's organization of her photographs into albums is indicative of her need to document and validate her existence as a woman of leisure. In discussing albums of collected photographs assembled by European women, Anne Higonnet has stated that "albums group images into structured units. Domestic journals recorded scenes of everyday life, of places and people so familiar to their original audiences that they require only the briefest captions"; furthermore, "albums commemorate a more chronologically specific experience such as a trip," while simultaneously creating an enduring memory of daily activities.[1] This characterization might also apply to Elise Tyson Vaughan's albums of her own photographs. Women had very few options for the display of their image making. Photography was a hobby, and photographs were rarely framed and even more rarely exhibited in public. In using the book form, Vaughan created a context for her photographs and a place where they could be viewed in relation to one another. This format was imperative for women seeking to use the photograph as a form of documentation and self-preservation. Each photograph was dated; some are accompanied by short handwritten accounts or descriptions. All reveal carefully deliberated compositions illustrating Vaughan's precise exposure and development technique.

Within the albums, images central to the colonial revival abound. There is the hearth, the spinning wheel, the old rundown country homestead, the horse-drawn hay wagon, chickens in the barnyard, fallen stone walls, and the dilapidated old fence. By recording such images, Vaughan added to her visual diary an ode to elements of the past that survived at the turn of the century.

However, Elise Tyson Vaughan dedicated most of her photographic efforts to documenting the Hamilton house gardens. The photographs show that in the "garden room" the women were at play as well as at work documenting its progress. There are images of afternoon tea, young women on the garden steps, and other such social gatherings.

Vaughan's most didactic work is the result of the juxtaposition of the controlled garden landscape and the more natural landscape visible just on the other side of its wall (cat. 31). Here, the tension between the photographer's urban upbringing and the simplicity of the local agrarian way of life seems almost overstated: Vaughan makes visible the conflicts between new and old, tamed and wild, rural and urban, simplicity and modernity. These tensions were not perceived by Vaughan alone, but were shared within a larger artistic and literary circle in the Piscataqua River region.

AWH

1 Anne Higonnet, "Secluded Vision: Images of Feminine Experience in Nineteenth-Century Europe," *Radical History Review* 38 (April 1987): 21.

❖ 32 ❖

MARCIA OAKES WOODBURY (1865–1914)
The Sunday Dinner
South Berwick, Maine, 1893
Sepia watercolor on paper; 11 in. x 16¼ in.
Society for the Preservation of New England Antiquities

The 1893 edition of Sarah Orne Jewett's *Deephaven* featured halftone engravings after drawings by artists Marcia Oakes Woodbury and her husband, Charles (1864–1940).[1] *The Sunday Dinner* (cat. 32), a watercolor by Marcia Woodbury, served as the preliminary inspiration for one of these illustrations. Its setting was the dining room of Sarah Orne Jewett's eighteenth-century house in South Berwick, Maine.[2] Built by John Haggins in 1774, the large house, which fronts

the village square, long afterwards passed into the hands of Captain Theodore Jewett, Sarah Orne Jewett's grandfather.

Born in 1865, Marcia Oakes grew up in South Berwick, the daughter of a traveling probate judge. She received a public school education, and then graduated from Berwick Academy in 1882. Her son David recalled, "all her life, and during her school years in this little Maine town, and into marriage, my mother had wanted to be an artist, but had not the making, nor the cooperation at home that would make so great a change possible."[3] Determined to receive artistic training, Oakes moved to Boston where she studied with Tommaso Juglaris (b. 1845), an Italian artist.[4] By 1887, Oakes and an older sister enrolled in art classes taught by Charles Woodbury, a recent graduate of the Massachusetts Institute of Technology. Oakes and Woodbury had met previously while he was a student at M.I.T., and by the summer of 1888, they were engaged. The couple was married on June 20, 1890, in the Congregational Church in South Berwick.

The Woodburys' honeymoon in Europe heralded the establishment of Marcia's artistic identity. In the winter of 1890–91, while Charles studied at the Académie Julian in Paris, she pursued course work at Lazar's School.[5] The couple spent June through October in Holland, where Marcia was fascinated by the Dutch culture and became well-versed in its history and artistic heritage. Sketchbooks from her trips to Holland, as well as drawings and paintings, focus on renderings of peasant children and other sentimental genre scenes with native Dutch characteristics (cat. 32a).[6] For several years, the Woodburys alternated between summers in Holland and winters in Boston, culminating in a year and a half abroad in the rural Dutch towns of Volendam and Laren.[7]

Presumably during one of the Woodburys' return trips to Boston and South Berwick, most likely the winter and spring of 1893, they completed the series of illustrations for *Deephaven*. Although *Deephaven* was originally published in 1877, the 1893 edition was the first with accompanying illustrations (cat. 43). Most certainly, Marcia's friendship with Sarah Orne Jewett gained the Woodburys this commission. Of the approximately fifty halftone engravings after drawings, the majority were completed by Charles and were primarily landscapes, reflecting his area of greatest artistic interest. Marcia completed at least a dozen genre scenes including *The Sunday Dinner*.[8]

As did many other artists at the turn of the century, Marcia Oakes Woodbury translated her expertise in the rendering of Dutch-inspired themes into works with colonial American overtones. Similar in spirit to the Dutch subjects, the painting for *Deephaven* represents a conflation of past and present. The couple depicted in *The Sunday Dinner* is surrounded by federal-style furnishings, devoid of any references to the late nineteenth century. As with Jewett's story, Woodbury's illustrations stress the slow movement of time in a preindustrial rural New England town modeled on South Berwick.

Cat. 32. Marcia Oakes Woodbury, The Sunday Dinner, *1893. Sepia watercolor on paper; 11 in. x 16¼ in. Courtesy, Society for the Preservation of New England Antiquities.*

The Sunday Dinner is illustrated in the chapter "Deephaven Society" which chronicles day-to-day activities in the small village. Jewett's nostalgic description of the town elders is captured in Woodbury's drawing: "these faces were not modern faces, but belonged rather to the days of the early settlement of the country, the old colonial times."[9] The furnishings—the sideboard, Chippendale-style chairs, and the glassware—also belonged to the colonial past. Even the multipaned windows and wide floorboards eschew any references to modernity. The watercolor is labeled on the rear as a picture of the Reverend and Mrs. David B. Sewall, who were Woodbury's modern-day models, yet *The Sunday Dinner* corresponds in the text of *Deephaven* to the scene when the town minister, Mr. Lorimer, and his sister, Miss Lorimer, dine together after Sunday church service:

the old Lorimer House not far beyond was occupied by Miss Rebecca Lorimer. Some stranger might ask the question why the minister and his sister did not live together, but you would have understood it at once after you had lived for awhile in town. They were very fond of each other, and the minister dined with Miss Rebecca on Sundays, and she passed the day with him on Wednesdays, and they ruled their separate household with decision and dignity. I think Mr. Lorimer's house showed no signs of being without a mistress any more than his sister's betrayed a master's care and authority.[10]

Contemporary critical reaction to the 1893 edition of *Deephaven* stresses that the text and the illustrations together embodied life in a rural village. One reviewer noted

it was the first in a series of charming volumes describing with absolute fidelity, abounding sympathy, the most delicious humor, and the most engaging literary skill, certain phases of New England life and character never so fitly portrayed. "Deephaven" offers many a salient situation to tempt an artist's pencil, and now Mr. and Mrs. Woodbury have designed for a Holiday edition of the favorite book about fifty illustrations that harmonize admirably with the sketches—they not only illustrate its scenes and incidents, they indicate its tone and atmosphere.[11]

The author went on to praise Marcia Oakes Woodbury for her exquisite reproductions of New England interiors and commented "the artists know intimately the scenes, the types of characters, the very atmosphere of Miss Jewett's stories, and this knowledge is supplemented by the power to depict them fitly."[12]

Unquestionably Marcia Oakes Woodbury's childhood years in South Berwick gave her a perspective on rural New England life, perhaps not intuitively shared by other artists who pursued colonial revival subjects. She also translated this insight into the design and construction of the Woodburys' Ogunquit home which overlooks Perkins Cove. Built in 1898, the shingle-style house features large verandas and open porches on several stories. Son David described the eccentricities of the house, which consisted of "three full stories, nine rooms and an attic, innumerable dormer windows and piazzas, jogs and jags, hip roofs, stairs corkscrewing hither and yon. It cost, I've heard, just $2500, including a half-ton kitchen stove."[13] The Woodbury house continued to be renovated over the years as necessary, and it melded easily with the centuries-old vernacular architecture of the coastal town. Later, a separate studio was constructed for Marcia.

Woodbury's success as an artist was cut short in 1914 when she died in Ogunquit at age forty-eight. Charles Woodbury organized a memorial exhibition of her work at the Museum of Fine Arts, Boston, in the year of her death. An obituary noted that "the illustrating of books interested her for awhile. The late Sarah Orne Jewett gave her the pleasure of illustrating in part, her "Deephaven," and she also did considerable other work in that direction."[14] *The Sunday Dinner* is not only representative of Woodbury's artistic skill, but also of her ability to put Sarah Orne Jewett's perceptions of the colonial era into visual form.

TTM

Cat. 32a. Marcia Oakes Woodbury, *Katwijka, 1891. Oil on canvas; 16 in. x 11¾ in. Estate of David O. Woodbury.*

1 Sarah Orne Jewett, *Deephaven* (Boston and New York: Houghton, Mifflin and Company, 1893), with illustrations by Charles and Marcia Woodbury.

2 A label on the reverse of the work states "Picture of Rev. and Mrs. David B. Sewall entitled 'The Sunday Dinner', painted by Marcia Oakes Woodbury, to be used as an illus- / tration in the 1893 edition of 'Deep / Haven,' by Sarah Orne Jewett. / The setting was the dining room of / The Jewett House. / Presented by Miss Marion Soule." I am grateful to Richard C. Nylander, Curator of Collections, SPNEA, for generously sharing this material with me.

3 David O. Woodbury in *Charles H. Woodbury, N.A., Marcia Oakes Woodbury* (Boston: Vose Galleries, 1980), n.p.

4 Obituary of Mrs. Marcia Oakes Woodbury, clipping from unidentified newspaper, Nov. 13, 1913, Marcia Oakes Woodbury Papers, AAA, microfilm roll 4281, frame 977.

5 William Howe Downes, "Charles Herbert Woodbury and His Work," *Brush and Pencil* 6, no. 1 (April 1900): 7.

6 Sketchbooks are located in the Marcia Oakes Woodbury Papers, AAA.

7 Downes, "Charles Herbert Woodbury and His Work," 7–8. The Woodburys continued to return to Holland repeatedly in subsequent years.

8 The breakdown in illustrations in *Deephaven* is thirty-three by Charles and thirteen by Marcia with another four not possible to attribute to either artist because they are not signed or particularly characteristic of either hand. The drawings which can be attributed with certainty to Marcia Oakes Woodbury are "Mrs. Kew," "Mrs. Patton (The Widow Jim)," "Miss Brandon at Her Piano," "Mrs. Dockim," "Widow Tully," "The Sunday Dinner," "Mr. Dick & Mr. Lorimer," "The Old Captains," "Captain Sands," "My Sakes, Ain't He Big!," "The Lecture Notice," "Mrs. Bonny at Home" (fig. 5.5), and "Miss Sally Chauncy" (cat. 47a).

9 Jewett, *Deephaven*, 93.

10 Jewett, *Deephaven*, 95.

11 Untitled review or advertisement for *Deephaven*, Charles Herbert Woodbury Papers, AAA, microfilm roll 1255, frame 1158.

12 Untitled review or advertisement for *Deephaven*.

13 David O. Woodbury, "Granpa was an Inventor, Or How to Increase Your Capacity for Surprise" (typescript, Woodbury family, n.d.), 4–42. The *York Courant* reported on July 14, 1899, that "Artist Charles Woodbury, with his family and several guests, is occupying his new summer home near his studio at the [Perkins] Cove."

14 Obituary of Mrs. Marcia Oakes Woodbury.

33

Marsden Hartley (1877–1943)
Ear of Corn
Ogunquit, Maine, 1917
Reverse painting on glass; 19 in. x 6½ in.
Private collection
(*see plate 5*)

"A gorgeous array of brilliant colors" was the description applied in 1860 to the genre of painting that inspired Marsden Hartley's *Ear of Corn* (pl. 5), executed in Ogunquit in 1917.[1] The brilliant colors—yellow, magenta, and green—of the kernels, tassels, and husks shimmer against the opaque black background, subtly intensified by the gleam of foil backing. A re-creation of "tinsel" painting, a popular nineteenth-century form of reverse painting on glass, *Ear of Corn* represents the most directly expressed influence of folk art painting on the modern artists working in Ogunquit early in the twentieth century.

Ear of Corn is a convincing example of Hartley's mastery of tinsel painting, known in the mid nineteenth century as "pearl" or "oriental" painting. Like Hartley's later re-creations, it incorporated a sheet of crinkled tinfoil applied as a backing against the glass on which the design, surrounded by opaque black paint, was thinly painted in transparent colors. Flowers and birds were especially favorite and suitable subjects for this technique, for it allowed the brilliant glint of petals or plumage to shine through the transparent paint.[2]

The folk art collected and displayed by members of the Ogunquit School of Painting and Sculpture, founded by Hamilton Easter Field and his protégé, the sculptor, Robert Laurent, provided inspiration for many of the young modern artists at the Perkins Cove school who were seeking an American rationale for their work (cat. 33a). The "simplicity," "honesty," and "strong compositional aspect" of the work of the young modernists reflects the indirect influence of folk art, as the artist John Laurent, the son of Robert Laurent, recalls.[3] The modern artists sought to emulate the directness and individuality of form and expression of the folk artists rather than copy their specific techniques or subject matter. Thus the Ogunquit artists interpreted nineteenth-century art in ways that validated their own modernist works.

Marsden Hartley, who spent the summer of 1917 at Perkins Cove, however, proves an exception. So intrigued was he with the reverse paintings on glass in Robert Laurent's collection of nineteenth-century looking glasses and folk art paintings that he determined to reproduce both their technique and subject matter. "What I most wanted to do," he wrote to a friend, "was to paint some scenes in black and gold that one sees in early mirrors."[4] By summer's end he had executed at least ten oil or tempera paintings on glass, some incorporating tinsel backgrounds, which were exhibited in a one-man show at Perkins Cove in late August and September.[5] The "scenes in black and gold" on the "early mirrors" that Hartley emulated would have been landscape scenes or, occasionally, floral compositions. They were a common decoration on the two-paneled, gilt-framed, mirrors affordable, and thus popular, among middle-class consumers in the nineteenth century.

The "academic" technique of reverse painting which nineteenth-century folk artists emulated had originated in England in the preceding century; its success depended on the artist's skill in transferring a design from a mezzotint engraving onto glass. The artist next filled in the "print" by painting first the highlights and light colors and then the darker shades; that is, by applying the colors in the reverse order of traditional painting on canvas. By the end of the century, artists' manuals advanced a "freehand" method of drawing the design, which encouraged the proliferation of this technique by amateur as well as professional artists. Such paintings adorned the panels framed above mirrors and the glass doors of "banjo" clocks, as well as countless "fancy pieces" of household art. They testify to the popularity of this art form in the nineteenth century.[6]

Despite Hartley's exposure to examples of this folk art technique in Bavaria, he indicated to Robert Laurent it was the examples of reverse painting on glass in the latter's collection that triggered his interest in the medium.[7] Duplicating the symmetrical composition of their folk art counterparts and, occasionally, their distorted perspective, most of Hartley's paintings depict single flowers or floral bouquets, usually in a vase or basket, centered on a small pedestal table. Although only the top of the stylized stands and the upper turnings of the pedestals appear, they are suggestive of nineteenth-century vernacular candlestands. As in the folk art examples, the unrelieved dark, opaque background of Hartley's paintings emphasizes the brilliant hues of the flowers. Overall, they are remarkably similar to their models. Whether the effect lay more in Hartley's intention or execution is the subject of debate. Gail Scott cites the "deliberately naive" manner of paintings, while Barbara Haskell attributes their "formal simplicity" and "occasionally crude execution" to the difficulty of the technique of painting on glass.[8]

Hartley's paintings that portray shocks of wheat or ears of corn may have had their genesis in his fascination with early American saloon windows. Barbara Haskell surmises as much from Hartley's reference to saloon windows with "glorious weavings of wheat and malt blossoms" in his 1917 correspondence with fellow artist Carl Springchorn.[9] Yet, such saloon window painting may have had its origins in individual reverse paintings of agricultural subjects—evidence of the interaction of commercial art and decorative art in the nineteenth century and the appeal of both to twentieth-century modern artists such as Hartley.[10]

Despite his initial fascination with reverse painting on glass, Hartley continued his venture in this genre for only several years after discovering it in Ogunquit. The fragility

Cat. 33a. Hamilton Easter Field, Washington Andirons, *undated. Oil on canvas; 42 in. x 35 in. The Brooklyn Museum, John B. Woodward Memorial Fund.*

of the medium prompted his explanation that "it nearly killed me and I never had the courage to take it up again."[11] Fortunately, a few of Hartley's works survive in a "gorgeous array of brilliant colors"—reminders of Hartley's particular debt to folk art and of the modern artists' appropriation of its "American" character to confirm their own art.

FHL

1 *Art Recreations* (Boston, 1869), quoted in Nina Fletcher Little, *The Abby Aldrich Rockefeller Folk Art Collection: A Descriptive Catalogue* (Williamsburg, Va.: Colonial Williamsburg Foundation, 1957), 258.

2 Little, *Abby Aldrich Rockefeller Folk Art Collection,* 259.

3 Personal interview with John Laurent, Oct. 12, 1990.

4 Hartley to Carl Sprinchorn, summer 1917, AAA, quoted in Barbara Haskell, *Marsden Hartley* (New York: Whitney Museum of American Art in association with New York University Press, 1980), 141.

5 Haskell, *Marsden Hartley,* 196.

6 Little, *Abby Aldrich Rockefeller Folk Art Collection,* 259.

7 Remarks made by Laurent to Thomas N. Armstrong III, Aug. 20, 1968, quoted in Haskell, *Marsden Hartley,* 57. Haskell credits Hartley's use of "solid paint areas and blocky background divisions" to German folk art traditions.

8 Gail M. Scott, *Marsden Hartley* (New York: Abbeville Press, 1988), 64; Haskell, *Marsden Hartley,* 57.

9 AAA, quoted in Haskell, *Marsden Hartley,* 141.

10 See, for instance, the reverse painting on glass entitled *Wheat Stack* (ca. 1825–50), in Little, *Abby Aldrich Rockefeller Folk Art Collection,* 261, pl. 128.

11 Hartley to Rebecca Strand, Jan. 1929, AAA, quoted in Haskell, *Marsden Hartley,* 57.

34

"DUNELAWN," GEORGE F. SMITH RESIDENCE
Ogunquit, Maine, 1921
James Purdon, architect

"Dunelawn," one of the most elaborate estates constructed as a summer residence in the Piscataqua area, was designed in 1921 by architect James Purdon for manufacturer George Ferguson Smith (1868–1942) of Brookline, Massachusetts (cat. 34). The main house bears a closer relationship to colonial revival residences built in suburban areas of the Northeast than it does to the contemporary cottages of Ogunquit and other nearby summer watering places. Built on an expanded Georgian plan, Dunelawn resembles more closely a Southern plantation house than a Maine summer residence. Finished in smooth stucco, the expansive house presents an impressive facade to Ogunquit Beach with a two-story columned portico and center entrance with fanlight. Originally, formal gardens and outbuildings were located to the rear of the main house.[1]

James Purdon apprenticed as a draftsman in a Boston architectural firm between 1899 and 1901, and he was first listed in the *Boston Directory* as an independent practitioner in 1902. Shortly thereafter he was associated with J. Lovell Little for a short time about 1905; both partners eventually

Cat. 34. Dunelawn, Ogunquit, Maine, built 1921. Postcard, ca. 1930. Courtesy, The Historical Society of Wells and Ogunquit.

went on to design colonial revival houses in Ogunquit (see cat. 35). Purdon was the architect for many large residences in the suburbs around Boston, including a number in Brookline where he undoubtedly met George Smith. The fact that Purdon's practice, which ended around 1942, was based in Boston explains why the architect is only known to have carried out one other commission in the Piscataqua area: the second of the two projects was executed in 1909 for the York Harbor Reading Room.[2]

George Smith had already spent time in Ogunquit before building Dunelawn. During the summer of 1918 the Smith family stayed at Walnut Hill, in the southern part of the town near the York line. Smith's initial connection with Ogunquit may have come through his wife Anne Lawton Crandon, whom he married in Ogunquit in 1913. At the time of his marriage, Smith was president of the Smith and Dove Manufacturing Company, which had been founded by his father in western Massachusetts to make flax yarns for carpets, sail twines, and other uses. The extensive funds required for the construction of Dunelawn were probably amassed by Smith during the First World War when his company held the license from the War Industries Board for all sales and shipments of linen thread.[3]

Although the early summer residents of Ogunquit did not share the same passion for historical projects as did their counterparts in York, they nonetheless made reference to the past in some of the pageants staged in the community. One such event of the 1920s was a mock "Indian raid" on colonial settlers enacted on rafts floated down the Ogunquit River in front of Dunelawn. The animator of this and other lavish spectacles was Merry Delle Hoyt, whose Tudor revival summer house named "Fieldstone" adjoined that of George F. Smith and family.[4]

KDM

1 Mrs. Harriet Smith kindly provided information concerning the history of Dunelawn. During the 1980s the original house was converted to condominiums and additional units built on the grounds.

2 Boston Architects Card File, Fine Arts Reference Library, Boston Public Library. A number of houses in the Boston suburbs designed by Purdon are illustrated in Frank Chouteau Brown, "Boston Suburban Architecture," *Architectural Record* 21 (Apr. 1907): 245–80.

3 *The National Cyclopaedia of American Biography* (1897; reprint, Ann Arbor, Mich.: University Microfilms, 1967), 32:147–48.

4 Patricia E. Hart, ed., *A Century of Color, 1886–1986* (Ogunquit, Me.: Barn Gallery Associates, 1987), 38–40.

35

"STONECROP," GRACE MORRILL COTTAGE AND STUDIO
Ogunquit, Maine, 1924
Little and Russell, architects

This residence and studio (cat. 35) was built for Grace Morrill, a painter and student of Charles Woodbury's, in 1924 using the frame of an eighteenth- or nineteenth-century barn, as well as other materials salvaged from historic buildings throughout York County. The design combines weathered box-board siding and a fieldstone chimney and foundation to create an impression of age and a sympathetic relationship with the visual qualities and textures of the site which is characterized by granite ledge and wild scrub vegetation. Although her account of the construction of "Stonecrop" makes it clear that Grace Morrill was responsible for the basic concept that the building be pieced together out of the fragments of old structures, she nonetheless sought a professional architect to assist her in combining the salvaged materials into a new house. Morrill described the evolution of the building in an article published in the July 1929 issue of *House Beautiful*:

> When I bought a strip of rocky ledge, hoping some day to build a studio on it, I named it at once

Cat. 35. Stonecrop, Ogunquit, Maine, built 1924. From House Beautiful *(1929). Private collection.*

Cat. 35a. Stonecrop, Ogunquit, Maine, built 1924. From House Beautiful *(1929). Private collection.*

Cat. 35b. Studio of Stonecrop. From House Beautiful *(1929). Private collection.*

'Stonecrop,' knowing that no other crop would ever be forthcoming. For 'stonecrop,' as gardeners know, is one of the Sedums which clothes the rocks with starlike yellow bloom.

I confess I had some stationery marked, on which to write a doubting family, and probably this precipitated matters, since soon after I found a weather-beaten barn and an architect who approved of using this old material in carrying out his plan.[1]

The architects selected by Morrill were the firm of Little and Russell from Boston, Massachusetts. Their association had begun in 1915 when J. Lovell Little, Jr., and Benjamin F.W. Russell became partners and specialized in residential building. Little had been previously associated for a short time about 1905 with Boston architect James Purdon who was also responsible for a colonial revival house in Ogunquit built in the 1920s (see cat. 34).[2] Approximately five years prior to the Morrill commission, Little and Russell had planned a group of public buildings in Peterborough, New Hampshire, including the Town House based on the design of Boston's Faneuil Hall.[3]

The earlier commissions carried out by the architects may have recommended them to Morrill. However, in an article on "Modern English Plaster Houses" published in 1919, Little lamented the popularity of the colonial style among potential clients since he believed its forms to be inappropriate for modern living, concluding that:

Colonial house architecture to-day lacks significance, except in special cases. That is the truth of the matter. It is the architecture of a more aristocratic time, the architecture of men and women who lived more formally and with less of American independence than we do to-day. It isn't democratic, as we are democratic and as even the average Englishman is democratic.[4]

Little's characterization of the colonial style as undemocratic stands in contrast to contemporary discussions that interpreted early American architecture as evidence of a period in which individualism and freedom prevailed. Despite his overall negative assessment of the colonial revival in architecture, Little nonetheless conceded that in some circumstances the style achieved "significance." This quality he took to be "the successful harmonizing of the needs of the client with the natural setting of the house."[5] Little and Russell's house for Grace Morrill could be said to possess both of these characteristics, since the design effectively responds to the site as well as to its dual function as a residence and studio.

Photographs of the interior of the Morrill house published in 1929 (cat. 35b) show that the historical and rustic character of the architecture itself was complemented by early American furniture, iron implements such as a fireplace crane, and hooked rugs. These collections paralleled the interests of other Ogunquit artists in acquiring exam-

Cat. 35c. Davol cottage, Ogunquit, Maine, built 1912. Photograph, 1912. Courtesy, Paul S. Stevens.

ples of handcrafts that evidenced preindustrial production methods. Hooked rugs were almost indispensable to the colonial revival interior by the 1920s and large collections were amassed in the Piscataqua region by Elizabeth Perkins, Elise Tyson Vaughan, and others. Stonecrop thus attests to the historical interests of its original owner, as well as those of the circle of artists around Charles Woodbury.

While Grace Morrill chose to incorporate fragments of earlier buildings into her studio and house, other of Woodbury's students had new colonial revival summer cottages designed for them. An important example of this latter type of residence is the cottage and studio commissioned from Portland architect John Calvin Stevens by Woodbury's student Joseph B. Davol in 1912 (cat. 35c).[6] Stevens was well known for resort houses that blended the open floor plans and organic shingled masses typical of the shingle style with details based on early American precedents.

KDM

1 Grace Morrill, "'Stonecrop,'" *House Beautiful* 65 (July 1929): 61.

2 Henry F. and Elsie Rathburn Withey, *Biographical Dictionary of Architects (Deceased)* (Los Angeles: Hennessey & Ingalls, Inc., 1970), 375–76.

3 Bryant F. Tolles, Jr., with Carolyn K. Tolles, *New Hampshire Architecture, An Illustrated Guide* (Hanover, N.H.: University Press of New England for the New Hampshire Historical Society, 1979), 111.

4 J. Lovell Little, Jr., "Modern English Plaster Houses," in *Architectural Styles for Country Houses*, ed. Henry H. Saylor (New York: Robert M. McBride & Company, 1919), 27–28.

5 Little, "Modern English Plaster Houses," 26.

6 John Calvin Stevens II and Earle G. Shettleworth, Jr., *John Calvin Stevens, Domestic Architecture, 1890–1930* (Scarborough, Me.: Harp Publications, 1990), 78–81.

36

CHARLES H. WOODBURY (1864–1940)
The Old Gaol
York, Maine, 1888
Oil on canvas; 8¼ in. x 12¼ in.
Old York Historical Society
(*see plate 6*)

Cat. 36a. Charles Woodbury, The Island House, *before 1912. Oil on canvas; 19½ in. x 29½ in. Courtesy, Estate of David O. Woodbury.*

Charles Herbert Woodbury is most often recognized for his marine paintings, particularly those that celebrate the beauty of the southern Maine coastline.[1] The artist is also known as the founder of a summer art colony in Ogunquit, Maine, in 1898, where his teaching and writings profoundly influenced a generation of early modern artists. Woodbury's depictions of architectural subjects such as *The Old Gaol* (pl. 6) are less well known than his seascapes, and they are less characteristic of his oeuvre. Nonetheless, *The Old Gaol* is a seminal painting because it foreshadows colonial revival interest in the building and sheds light on the mystique generated by old abandoned structures.

Woodbury graduated with honors from the Massachusetts Institute of Technology's mechanical engineering program in 1886, yet, even as a student, he pursued a strong interest in painting and drawing. After graduation, he began to paint and teach professionally, and in 1887, to exhibit his works at the J. Eastman Chase Gallery in Boston.[2] In the summer of 1888, Woodbury traveled to Ogunquit for the first time while visiting the family of his fiancée Marcia Oakes who lived in nearby South Berwick and summered at York Beach. Woodbury later became one of the first artists to settle in this unspoiled region where the natural surroundings offered inspiring artistic possibilities. Later in the summer, he rented a room at Captain Charles Littlefield's Ogunquit House so that he could draw and paint these environs.[3]

Completed in 1888, *First Sketch of Ogunquit* offers a glimpse of schooners on the Ogunquit River where local goods such as fish and lumber are being loaded for trade, as had been done since the eighteenth century. Ogunquit's removed, rural locale, as well as its economic dependence on its natural resources—from both land and sea—are captured in this painting, and unquestionably affected Woodbury.

Woodbury's *Old Gaol* also suggests the artist's interest in historic elements in the region, an interest demonstrated through the painting's formal qualities and cultural associations. Woodbury rendered the barn-like Gaol from the rear at a low perspective, increasing the prominence of its hilltop location. Although the Gaol is located in the center of York Village, he edited out surrounding structures, choosing instead a seemingly isolated setting. The impressionistic brushstrokes, typical of Woodbury's style, add to the sense of an overgrown, unkempt landscape surrounding the Gaol. Later, in 1900, William Howe Downes

commented on Woodbury's plein-air paintings of similar subject and date:

> The distinctive characteristics of the place were grasped; strong light and dark contrasts were brought out, the coloring was brilliant and gay, and the work might have been set down as good, clear, candid prose-painting, chiefly enjoyable for the freshness of the first impression.[4]

Howe's critique captures Woodbury's lifelong emphasis on interpretation and examination over stylistic issues, seen in *The Old Gaol* and later codified in his writings.[5]

Woodbury's choice of the Old Gaol as his subject is unusual since he rarely depicted well-known buildings with specific historical associations. Whether or not Woodbury subscribed to the lure of the Gaol's morbid past, his painting does not evoke any reminders of its celebrated status. It simply reflects the artist's interest in describing the physical qualities of an early American building and the nostalgic values associated with an unchanged colonial structure.

Woodbury, like many late nineteenth-century artists, began to show an interest in colonial architecture by depicting old buildings in his work.[6] Not only is *The Old Gaol* an accurate rendering of the structure, but it carries associations of historic and nostalgic value. During the late 1880s, Woodbury completed many renditions in several media of historic houses with picturesque qualities that he encountered on sketching trips to southern Maine, Cape Ann, and Nova Scotia (cat. 36a).[7] Vernacular buildings such as the Gaol represented the preindustrial past rather than the encroaching urbanization of the present. Woodbury's exhibition at Chase's Gallery in 1888 featured paintings and sketches with titles such as *An Old Salem House, A Swampscott Shanty, A Nova Scotian Homestead,* and *An Old Fence in Nova Scotia.*[8] Two critics for the *Art Interchange* praised Woodbury's success in capturing the essence of these buildings:

Cat. 36b. Charles Woodbury, Agamenticus River, York, Maine, *1889. Etching, 5⅜ in. x 10¼ in. Courtesy, The MIT Museum.*

the construction and arrangement of these drawings are masterly. His houses have been lived in; they are scenes and stages of events; they have played their part in the drama of life, and that is what makes them so interesting. Combined with an exceptionally fine workmanship, these black-and-white pictures exhibit an imaginative quality which plunges us into the eighteenth century until we are steeped in the spirit of those sleepy old times.[9]

By 1889, Woodbury was commissioned to do illustrations of old houses for *Century Illustrated Monthly Magazine, New England Magazine,* and *Harper's Weekly.* One of these engravings, *Agamenticus River* (cat. 36b), illustrated in a contemporary article by Frank T. Robinson, further supports Woodbury's historical interest in the Piscataqua region. Robinson commented, "he [Woodbury] is particularly fascinated with old buildings."[10] Similar in composition to *The Old Gaol, Agamenticus River* is rendered from a distant viewpoint. Not only was Woodbury praised for the technical proficiency of his paintings and drawings, he was commended for his ability to bring life to his quaint subjects: "Old buildings like old people, have souls; they have lived, formed a character, and exist for a purpose; they tell of the past and suggest the future of all things."[11]

TTM

1 For recent scholarship on Woodbury, see Joan Loria and Warren Seamans, *Earth, Sea and Sky: Charles H. Woodbury, Artist and Teacher, 1864–1940* (Cambridge, Mass.: The MIT Museum, 1988), and Patricia E. Hart, ed., *A Century of Color, 1886–1986* (Ogunquit, Me.: Barn Gallery Associates, 1987). Trevor J. Fairbrother et al., *The Bostonians: Painters of an Elegant Age, 1870–1930* (Boston: Museum of Fine Arts, 1986) also contains concise biographical information on the artist.

2 In 1887, Woodbury exhibited thirty paintings and sketches at the Chase Gallery; in 1888, he showed forty-five. For a complete listing of Woodbury's one-man exhibitions, see *Charles Woodbury, N. A., 1864–1940* (Boston: Vose Galleries, 1978).

3 Hart, *A Century of Color,* 3.

4 William Howe Downes, "Charles Herbert Woodbury and His Work," *Brush and Pencil* 6, no. 1 (April 1900): 6.

5 Woodbury published three books on his teaching principles: *Painting and the Personal Equation* (1919), *The Art of Seeing* (1925), and, with Elizabeth Perkins Ward, *Observation: Visual Training Through Drawing* (1922).

6 See Gilbert Tapley Vincent, "American Artists and Their Changing Perceptions of History, 1770–1940" (Ph.D. diss., University of Delaware, 1982), 106.

7 Woodbury also traveled to Halifax in the summer of 1888. The "Island" or "Adams" house at Perkins Cove (cat. 36a) was later remodeled by Hamilton Easter Field as his residence.

8 "Paintings by Charles Herbert Woodbury, From February 10 to February 24, 1888" (Boston: Chase's Gallery, 1888), Charles Woodbury Papers, AAA, microfilm roll 1255, frame 1138.

9 "Some Living American Painters. Critical Conversations of Howe and Torrey. Nineteenth Paper. Charles Herbert Woodbury," *Art Interchange,* ca. 1892, undated clipping in Charles Woodbury Papers, microfilm roll 1255, frame 1141.

10 Frank T. Robinson, "Among the Artists: A Painter and Etcher of New England Scenery," clipping in Charles Woodbury Papers, microfilm roll 1255, frame 1180.

11 Robinson, "Among the Artists."

37

JOHN J. ENNEKING (1841–1916)
The Gaol Kitchen
York, Maine, 1888
Oil on canvas; 21¼ in. x 29½ in.
Old York Historical Society
(see plate 7)

Completed in 1888, *The Gaol Kitchen* (pl. 7) is representative of a small group of John Enneking's paintings of interiors which have colonial revival overtones. Primarily known as a landscape artist, Enneking undertook this series of works in the 1880s and early 1890s. In 1895, one critic, Frederick Roy Miller, perceptively observed that

> the march of modern progress disturbs Mr. Enneking in more ways than one. He mourns the migration of the country people to the cities, and has traveled through all parts of the country in search of the old interiors, which are so rapidly disappearing.[1]

Enneking and other late nineteenth-century American artists who lamented the rush of urbanization responded in measure by producing paintings that promoted the morality of the colonial era. Foremost amongst those with effective old-fashioned symbolism were paintings that depicted colonial kitchens with large open hearths, such as *The Gaol Kitchen*.

The display of the New England Farmer's Home and Modern Kitchen at the Philadelphia Centennial Exhibition in 1876 was the catalyst for artistic interest in the colonial interior as a metaphor for solid upright values.[2] The purpose of the exhibition was to contrast a 1776 kitchen with a contemporary one, in order to observe the progress of the past century as well as to celebrate and reinforce the values of colonial life. Many artists, particularly in the 1870s and 1880s, responded by producing paintings with subject matter revolving around America's past. They strove for accuracy in their renderings of early American buildings, documenting their physical and aesthetic qualities, and often imbuing them with symbolic resonances—the spinning wheel and the open hearth being the two most nostalgic motifs of the supposedly simpler colonial days.[3]

The architectural elements and the rustic furnishings of *The Gaol Kitchen* domesticate its historical setting and idealize values associated with the colonial past. Unlike Edmund Tarbell's *My Family* (cat. 30), Enneking's work includes no references to contemporary society and is intended entirely as a comment on life in early America. The wide wooden floorboards, irregularly placed wallboards, and multipane window suggest the lack of modern technology available to the colonial settlers. In addition, the plaster-covered ceiling and peeling gray-green paint also add to the kitchen's aura of old age. Not surprising, the open hearth is the focus of *The Gaol Kitchen*, which would

be seen by viewers in marked contrast to the modern cook-stove or furnace. The fireplace has all its usual accoutrements including the hanging cauldron, andirons, bread oven, and copper bedwarmer. Various tin vessels and glass bottles are placed on a rough-hewn wooden mantel above the hearth. To the right of the door, the table, draped with a red cloth, is set with a tea service and food. Like the mantel, the table is simple, suggesting the provincial location of the kitchen. The woven basket filled with yarns symbolizes the arch-colonial handicrafts of knitting and weaving, and indicates that this space is a feminine domain.

Unlike many contemporary paintings of kitchens, there are no people depicted in *The Gaol Kitchen*. Rather, Enneking has successfully arranged the composition in order to infer a human presence. The doorway to the entrance hall is ajar, allowing the viewer a glimpse of the outside door beyond. A broom leaning in the hallway corner, the food on the table, and the blaze of the fire suggest that the kitchen's occupant is not far removed from the scene. Enneking may have chosen not to include figures in order to document the room's historical character, rather than focus on sentimental genre. In his 1895 article on Enneking, Miller also observed:

> New England subjects, pure and simple, have always interested him . . . There is a quaint picturesqueness about the low-studded rooms, the blazing logs, the old English window panes, the powder horns, the old clocks, and the other once-familiar adjuncts of the early houses of this country that the artist has tried to preserve.[4]

Another rendering of the Gaol kitchen, *The Old Kitchen,* is remarkably similar in composition, and its colonial revival resonances are even more striking. In this work Enneking has depicted all the archetypal symbols of the early American kitchen, including an old clock, herbs, fruits suspended from the ceiling, and a gun and powderhorn hung between the hearth and the door. The inclusion of people—an older woman leaning over her sewing and two children playing—makes this painting more anecdotal than *The Gaol Kitchen.*

As in Charles Woodbury's *The Old Gaol,* Enneking does not associate his painting with the notorious legends surrounding the Gaol's history. The Vermeeresque flow of light through the door and window removes any somber overtones that might be associated with hard labor in a colonial kitchen, especially one that served a jail. When Enneking completed his painting, the building was being used as a warehouse; hence the quarters formerly occupied by the Gaol keeper and his family were vacant. Drawn to the old building for its artistic and historic potential, Enneking was free to return to the past in the empty kitchen, blissfully void of any references to the present day.

Enneking's interest in colonial subject matter may have stemmed, in part, from his artistic training. In 1872, he traveled to Europe, visiting Germany, Switzerland, and Italy, and then studying under Parisian master Léon Bonnat for three years. Bonnat, best known for his portraits and genre subjects, taught Enneking the rudiments of figure painting.[5] Enneking also was influenced by Charles François Daubigny and Eugène Boudin in his conception of landscape, ultimately leading Enneking to his greatest artistic success. Many American artists returning from study in Europe applied American subject matter to formal practices they assimilated abroad. In 1878, Enneking spent six months in Amsterdam, Rotterdam, and The Hague where he studied the works of the Dutch Little Masters.[6] Consequently, Enneking's interest in Vermeer's use of light and composition format is directly manifested in *The Gaol Kitchen*.

Upon his return to the United States in 1876, Enneking settled in Hyde Park, a suburb of Boston, where he had earlier built a house. Enneking and his wife, Mary, a native of Maine, also had a summer home in North Newry, Maine, near Bethel. This remote region offered vast potential for the artist's landscape subjects. Enneking's interest in depicting old interiors first appears in the early 1880s after he returned from his second trip to Europe, and continued until at least 1895. His treatment of the colonial interior ranged from sentimental to documentary. Though Enneking is best remembered for his Barbizon-inspired landscapes with distinctly regional features, he also captured the essence of the colonial American kitchen, as it was understood nostalgically in the late nineteenth century. Ralph Davol, in the introduction to Enneking's memorial catalogue, not surprisingly referred to the artist as "the interpreter *par excellence* of New England in painting . . . Emotion, freedom, idealism flooding his personality were the impulses of his artistic self-expression."[7]

TTM

1 Frederick Roy Miller, "Boston Artists: John J. Enneking, the Noted Landscape Painter," *Boston Journal*, Feb. 10, 1895), 18, John J. Enneking Papers, AAA, microfilm roll 877, frame 649. Among the works discussed and illustrated were *The New England Smithy*, *Pulling the Splinter*, and *The Old Interior* which is remarkably similar to *The Gaol Kitchen* in its furnishings and formal qualities. According to the article, *The Old Interior* was painted in the Peasely House at Rock's Village in New Hampshire, and "the Peaselys were ancestors of the poet Whittier as well as of the Elliotts, the old family from which Mr. Enneking picked his wife, whose grandfather was born in this quaint home. The artist has also made studies from other rooms in this old house."

2 For further background, see Rodris Roth, "The New England, or 'Olde Tyme,' Kitchen Exhibit at Nineteenth-Century Fairs," and Celia Betsky, "Inside the Past: The Interior and the Colonial Revival in American Art and Literature, 1860–1914," in Axelrod, *Colonial Revival*, 159–83, 241–77.

3 See Gilbert Tapley Vincent, "American Artists and Their Changing Perceptions of History, 1770–1940" (Ph.D. diss., University of Delaware, 1982), 89ff.

4 Miller, *Boston Journal*, 18.

5 H. Barbara Weinberg, *The Lure of Paris: Nineteenth-Century American Painters and Their French Teachers* (New York: Abbeville Press, 1991), 178.

6 Patricia Jobe Pierce and Rolf H. Kristiansen, *John Joseph Enneking, American Impressionist Painter* (North Abingdon, Mass.: Pierce Galleries, 1972), 76–77.

7 Ralph Davol, in *Memorial Exhibition of Paintings by John J. Enneking* (Boston: Boston Art Club, March 2–17, 1917), n.p.

WILLIAM H. DABNEY, JR. (1855–97), ARCHITECT
York Harbor, Maine, ca. 1885–94

The development of watering places along the Maine coast during the last quarter of the nineteenth century provided opportunities for architects who specialized in designs for cottages and small-scale commercial buildings. The colonial revival and shingle styles—or, as was often the case, an amalgam of the two—were both favored for resort architecture since they complemented visually the natural and built environments of seacoast areas. William H. Dabney, Jr., produced a number of such designs for buildings in York Harbor during the 1880s and 1890s; his collaboration with Dr. Frederick D. Stackpole, an important real estate developer in the area and likely the architect's cousin, illustrates how an architectural practice could be established in a budding resort town.

Dabney was born in the Azores, received his architectural education at the Massachusetts Institute of Technology, and entered into a partnership with Henry B. Ball (b. 1866), a Portsmouth native, by 1890 (cat. 11). The first of Dabney's York Harbor commissions—which he carried out independently even while in partnership with Ball—came in 1882 when he designed the small cottage called "Redcote" (cat. 38) for a site on the York River. Probably built for a member of Dabney's family, Redcote constitutes an early incorporation into new designs of forms drawn from American vernacular architecture of an earlier period, with its shingle and clapboard exterior, irregular fenestration, and modest scale.[1]

Frederick Dabney Stackpole (ca. 1849–99) was a physician from Roxbury, Massachusetts, who provided Dabney with a group of significant commissions. Among "the earliest residents of York Harbor's summer colony and . . . a prominent figure in its development," Stackpole was said at the time of his death to have had sufficient funds that he practiced his profession in order to help the lower classes, rather than for "the purpose of realizing pecuniary remuneration."[2] Stackpole also made use of his professional standing to promote "York as a Health Resort" and claimed of York in 1895 that "in my fifteen years of experience and practice here I have never known a case of serious illness to originate here."[3]

Stackpole's contribution to the development of York Harbor went beyond the construction of cottages; he provided buildings to house a number of institutions that fostered the social life of the summer community. Among these structures was the Union Chapel and Library built in 1887 to contain a place of religious worship and a reading room. Aesthetically, the building incorporated the wide roof profile and variety of exterior sheathing materials that were thought to have been characteristic of vernacular architecture of the colonial period. At the same time, the

Cat. 38. Redcote, York, Maine, built 1882. From American Architect and Building News (1882). Courtesy, Society for the Preservation of New England Antiquities.

design drew references from a more high-style Palladian idiom, as seen in its windows and cupola.[4]

About eight years following the completion of the Union Chapel and Library, Frederick Stackpole erected a large commercial building on an adjacent site in York Harbor, the design of which has been attributed to Dabney. Known as the Stackpole Block and subsequently as the Lancaster Building (cat. 38a), the structure housed shops and later a movie theatre. The Lancaster Building is unique among Dabney's York Harbor commissions by virtue of its allusions to high-style Georgian architecture in the form of

elaborate window detailing, carved brackets below balconies, and corner pilasters with Corinthian capitals. York Harbor's most prominent commercial building from the colonial revival period thus outstripped surviving examples of eighteenth-century architecture in York in terms of its sophistication of details as well as its sheer size. The Lancaster Building is more urban in scale and bespeaks an optimism on the part of its builder and architect toward the future development of York Harbor as a summer resort. Such expansion could have been expected to provide numerous opportunities for an architect who was well connected with those who had the means to build cottages.

KDM

1 See my entry on "William H. Dabney, Jr., 1855–1897" in A Biographical Dictionary of Architects in Maine 6 (1991), published by the Maine Historic Preservation Commission. The design for Redcote was published in the American Architect and Building News 12 (Sept. 1, 1882).

2 "Death of Dr. F.D. Stackpole," Old York Transcript, Dec. 28, 1899, 1; and "York Mourns its Loss," Old York Transcript, Jan. 4, 1900, 2. The latter quotes in full Stackpole's obituary from the Boston Herald.

3 Frederick D. Stackpole, "York as a Health Resort" in Health Resorts of the South and Summer Resorts of New England (Boston: George H. Chapin Co., 1895), 335.

4 The Union Chapel and Library design was published in Building 7 (Nov. 5, 1897). Now St. George's Episcopal Church, the building was moved to its present location on York Street in York Harbor in 1982, at which time substantial changes were made. See the "York Harbor Intensive Architectural Survey" (typescript, OYHS, 1987).

Cat. 38a. Lancaster Building, York, Maine, built ca. 1895. Photograph, 1896. Old York Historical Society.

CHAMPERNOWNE FARM, JOHN THAXTER RESIDENCE
Kittery Point, Maine, 1880; addition, 1887
William Ralph Emerson (1833–1917), architect

ROLAND THAXTER HOUSE
Kittery Point, Maine, 1887; addition, 1892
William Ralph Emerson (1833–1917), architect

Cat. 39. Champernowne Farm, Kittery Point, Maine, built 1880. Photograph, 1887. Courtesy, Maine Historic Preservation Commission.

After several months of searching the New England coastline for a suitable family homestead, Celia and Levi Thaxter purchased the Cutts Farm in Kittery Point, Maine, in May 1880. The property included an eighteenth-century farmhouse and 136 acres of land bordered by the Atlantic Ocean.[1] The land was intended to serve as both a home for the Thaxter family as well as a place for Celia and Levi's three sons, Karl, John, and Roland, to pursue their individual interests. John, aged twenty-six, had recently returned from a farming apprenticeship in West Virginia and was anxious to set up a similar operation of his own. Roland, twenty-two-years old, was studying botany at Harvard, and Karl, twenty-eight-years old, wanted to set up a workshop.[2] In addition to serving the needs of the young men, the location was convenient to the Isles of Shoals where Celia Thaxter spent her summers.

By the time of its purchase by the Thaxters, the existing farmhouse had fallen into disrepair. John and Levi decided it would be more economical to tear it down and build a new house rather than repair the old building. The construction of the new Thaxter homestead was underway by the summer of 1880; the design has been attributed to Boston architect William Ralph Emerson (cat. 39).[3] He was a member of the Boston Society of Architects and in 1869 had given a lecture to the group on the destruction of New England houses which he considered "the only true American Architecture."[4] Emerson was among the first architects to take an interest in American colonial architecture, and the Thaxter house is one of the earliest examples of colonial revival architecture in the Piscataqua region.

The foundation of the original house, built by Captain Francis Champernowne in 1665, was reused by Emerson.[5] In addition, the architect also made use of "many of the old materials, including the great old chimneys."[6] Emerson's incorporation of salvaged materials into the new building, as well as his employment of forms drawn from historic architecture, clearly indicate colonial revival attitudes on the architect's part. The few decorative elements on the house include a balcony on the north end and a ram's-head carving above the initials "L.L.T." (for Levi Lincoln Thaxter) on the south and are attributed to Kittery sculptor, John Haley Bellamy.[7]

John Thaxter promptly set up a farm and dairy on the property while Celia began some work on the interior of the house. In a letter to Annie Fields dated November 15, 1881, she wrote, "I have got some carpets on the floor, hung some pictures, painted the fire bricks and hearth red, made the brass andirons like gold . . . Over in Portsmouth, the other day, I got such a lovely wide old armchair."[8] Levi Thaxter only enjoyed his new home for a few years; he died in 1884. The land had been purchased in John's and Roland's names; just prior to their marriages in 1887, the Thaxter sons decided to divide the property equally.[9] John retained the house and Roland acquired the land to the north.

Soon after his marriage, John Thaxter made several additions to his house; their style suggests that they also may have been the work of William Ralph Emerson. The additions transformed the simple house into a more elaborate home, thus providing a suitable setting in which to begin married life. A porte cochère was added on the land side. The rooms above, resting on stone piers, provided extra bedrooms for servants. A two-story addition with a gambrel roof was erected along the seaward side. The 1880 parlor and Celia Thaxter's former bedroom were combined to create a new sitting room with a bay window overlooking the sea. The ocean view was further enhanced by the addition of a porch which ran the length of the east facade.[10]

Cutts Island witnessed much construction in 1887. In addition to the work being done on John Thaxter's house, Roland Thaxter decided to erect a summer residence on his portion of the family land (cat. 39a). The architectural affinity between Roland's house and the additions to John's house leads one to surmise that the two were the work of the same architect. The assumption that William Ralph Emerson was again commissioned by the Thaxters seems plausible considering that he designed a house for Roland Thaxter in Cambridge, Massachusetts, in 1891.[11]

The Roland Thaxter house at Kittery Point exemplifies elements of both colonial revival and shingle-style architecture. The main entry of this house consists of stone piers supporting wooden arches. The stylistic similarity of this entry to John's porte cochère is evident. Patterned shingles, typical of the shingle style, were utilized on all

Cat. 39a. Roland Thaxter house, Kittery Point, Maine, built 1887. Photograph by Richard Cheek, 1990. Courtesy, Maine Historic Preservation Commission.

four sides of the house. In John's 1887 addition, shingles were employed on the gambrel of the porte cochère and patterned shingles were incorporated above the windows. Notable colonial revival elements in Roland's home include a steep gambrel roof, dormer windows, and an eyebrow window with diamond-shaped panes above the front door.

A rear ell was added in 1892 to house Roland's laboratories as well as to provide extra bedrooms. An inscription in the woodwork reads, "we pushed her through in '92." Since Emerson designed Roland's new Cambridge house in 1891 it is possible that he was involved in planning this addition as well.[12]

The Thaxter houses exhibit design elements common to the colonial revival style in the Piscataqua region. Through the use of traditional design elements inspired by the colonial period, the houses evoke a sense of the region's architectural heritage. As family homestead, farm, and summer retreat, the Thaxter estate also epitomizes the fundamental colonial revival ideal of living a simpler life in a pastoral landscape.

RM

1 YCRD, 376:115.

2 Rosamond Thaxter, *Sandpiper: The Life of Celia Thaxter* (Sanbornville, N.H.: Wake-Brook House, 1962), 199.

3 Rosamond Thaxter, *Aunt Rozzie Remembers* (1981), 5.

4 Cynthia Zaitzevsky, *William Ralph Emerson, 1833–1917* (Cambridge, Mass.: Fogg Art Museum, Harvard University, 1969), 3.

5 Thaxter, *Aunt Rozzie Remembers*, 5.

6 Thaxter, *Aunt Rozzie Remembers*, 6.

7 Thaxter, *Aunt Rozzie Remembers*, 6.

8 Thaxter, *Sandpiper*, 280.

9 YCRD, 415:384.

10 The porch and bay window have since been removed.

11 Roger G. Reed, *A Delight to All Who Know It: The Maine Summer Architecture of William R. Emerson* (Augusta: Maine Historic Preservation Commission, 1990), 141.

12 This house remains relatively unchanged since 1892, although it passed out of the family in 1939. John Thaxter's house remains in the family.

Cat. 40. "Sea Hill," Kittery Point, Maine, built 1907.
Photograph by Kevin D. Murphy, 1991.

Cat. 40a. Usher cottage, Kittery Point, Maine, built ca. 1900.
Photograph by Kevin D. Murphy, 1991.

❋ 40 ❋

"Sea Hill," C. Alice Baker Cottage
Kittery Point, Maine, 1907
Clarence Piper Hoyt (1868–1938), architect

Leila Usher Cottage
Kittery Point, Maine, ca. 1900

About 1900, John and Gertrude Thaxter decided to sell some portions of their property on Cutts Island in Kittery Point, Maine. However, the only transaction that actually took place was a sale made to C. Alice Baker of Cambridge, Massachusetts, in 1907. The lot she purchased on which to build a summer home was located between the two Thaxter houses (cat. 39) and fronted on the Atlantic Ocean.[1]

C. Alice Baker was born in Springfield, Massachusetts, and attended Deerfield Academy. She was an historian and a teacher and is also well known for her early work as a preservationist. She was active in the movement to save Boston's Old South Church (ca. 1876) and in the restoration of Deerfield's Frary house in 1890, which incorporated historic architectural fragments from the Piscataqua region. This house was the first to be restored in Deerfield, and Baker was one of the first women in New England to be involved in such projects.[2]

Baker only enjoyed her summer retreat for a short time; she died in 1909, leaving the house to her companion of many years, Emma Lewis Coleman. Like Baker, Coleman had strong associations with the colonial revival movement, which is seen in her photographs depicting early colonial life. She and Baker had made numerous trips to York, Maine, in the 1880s and 1890s, the years in which Coleman took most of her photographs. During one of their trips they must have discovered the peaceful environment of Cutts Island which eventually led to Baker's decision to build a summer residence there.

Baker employed architect Clarence Piper Hoyt to design her Kittery Point house (cat. 40). Hoyt was a native of Deerfield and both he and his father, Horatio Hoyt, had taken an interest in the restoration of the Frary house. Clarence had worked as a carpenter while his father had acquired panels, moldings, and doors for the house.[3] Clarence Hoyt and C. Alice Baker apparently developed their passion for bits of antiquated architecture and the reuse of old materials during this early restoration. This supposition is supported by the fact that Hoyt utilized at least one room in the Frary house as a point of departure in designing the summer residence on Cutts Island. In her paper, "Restoring Frary House," Emma Coleman wrote of the Deerfield room that inspired Hoyt, describing "a good panelled wainscoting and a mantelpiece which Miss Baker copied in her Kittery Point dining room."[4]

"Sea Hill" was the name given to the new house, appropriately so, as the house sits on top of a rise overlooking the Atlantic Ocean. The house designed for this tranquil setting is modest in scale. It is one-and-one-half stories with a shingled exterior and a row of dormer windows which face the ocean. The view is further incorporated into the design of the house through an attached, wrap-around porch, a feature common to shingle-style cottages in the Piscataqua region and other seaside locations. It has come to symbolize the idea of a summer retreat, a place to relax and enjoy an idyllic setting while escaping the hurried pace of the city and workplace.

Emma Coleman owned the property from 1909 until her death in 1942.[5] Her presence on Cutts Island was perhaps significant in drawing a number of artists to the area. Among this group was Leila Usher, who occupied a house at the end of Thaxter Lane from 1912 to 1918. Born in 1859 in Onalaska, Wisconsin, Usher was a sculptor who studied with H.H. Kitson in Boston. It is reasonable to assume that she made the acquaintance of Emma Coleman and C. Alice Baker while in the Boston area. Rosamond Thaxter, daughter of John Thaxter, referred to the artist's house (cat. 40a) as the "Hut of Usher" and described her as a sculptress of no mean talent.[6]

The house Leila Usher occupied was built by the Raynes family in the early twentieth century and was willed to her mother in 1912.[7] It was constructed, in part, out of fragments of an antiquated barn. The exterior of the house is shingled while the gables employ detailing reminiscent of the Tudor style. Although the architect of this house is unknown, it is apparent that the designer was influenced by both American colonial and English cottage-style architecture. Usher had her studio in the smaller room which was added to the south end of the house soon after it was built. This room had large windows and allowed for abundant light, an important consideration in an artist's studio. The house is also set back from the road, nestled among tall trees, offering a quiet place to work.

The designs of both the Coleman and Usher cottages combine with the shingle style, elements of the colonial revival aesthetic that represent the associations of their occupants with the movement. The two women participated in the popular practice of escaping from the city during the summer to a pastoral setting where artistic and historical interests could be pursued. C. Alice Baker, the only person to buy a retreat from the Thaxters, perhaps not coincidentally, was a person of like mind: a woman with similar sentiment about the growth of industrialization. Cutts Island provided its summer colonists with the perfect setting in which to pursue their interests in art and history.

RM

1 YCRD, 564:206.

2 This information was kindly provided by David Proper, Librarian, Memorial Library, Historic Deerfield, Inc., Deerfield, Mass.

3 Emma Lewis Coleman, "Concerning Frary House" (manuscript, Historic Deerfield, ca. 1940), 37, 40.

4 Coleman, "Concerning Frary House," 45.

5 YCRD, 567:89.

6 Rosamond Thaxter, *Aunt Rozzie Remembers* (1881), 45. Usher's work consisted primarily of busts; examples are in the collections of Bowdoin College, John's Hopkins University, the Fogg Museum, and the New York State Museum.

7 YCRD, 661:463.

❊ 41 ❊

EMMA LEWIS COLEMAN (1853–1942), PHOTOGRAPHER
York, Maine, 1883–86

The photographs of Emma Lewis Coleman are primary visual documents of the colonial revival movement in the Piscataqua River region. As elegant as the works by the French Barbizon School painters, Coleman's photographs echo their influential aesthetic. Simultaneously, Coleman's choice of subject matter layers a notable historical reference onto each image; these photographs are comparable with the work of the historians and preservationists. Emma Coleman's photographs paradoxically combine a well-trained and refined aesthetic treatment with subjects whose romanticism is born from their rural, simple, and traditional forms of work and craft.

To see this mix of technique and subject, one must start with Coleman's photographic illustrations for an 1893 limited edition of Sarah Orne Jewett's *Deephaven* (cat. 47). This edition was the product of the collaboration of Jewett the writer, painter Susan Minot Lane, historian C. Alice Baker, and photographer Coleman. Between 1883 and 1886 and under Jewett's personal direction, Coleman staged reenactments of colonial crafts and work using Lane and Baker and other "kindly farmers and fisherfolk" of York, Maine, as subjects; all were dressed in colonial costume.[1]

In the *Basketmaker* (cat. 41), one sees an unidentified York woman dressed in colonial fashion acting out the craft of basket weaving. Evidence of this image as reenactment is the circular basket-strapping at the woman's feet; these strappings imply that a basket was literally taken apart to create the prop since the strappings would not be circular until woven into place. The *Basketmaker* is one of many illustrations that accompany Jewett's tale of two young women from Boston who spend the summer in an undeveloped coastal town. The women discover traditions and a continuity that link them to New England's colonial past, much as Coleman, Lane, and Baker hoped to do with their summers in the Piscataqua. Themes such as this seem to serve as constant inspiration for Coleman's image-making. In *The Woman with Faggots* (cat. 41a), Coleman casts the notable preservationist C. Alice Baker as a rural peasant-like woman carrying sticks along a winding country road. There is a romantic simplicity to the image, one that celebrates this traditional work and the local color of the Maine culture where these forms of work still remained, but there is also a quality of foolery: C. Alice Baker is a respectable city woman who plays the part of the Maine peasant.

These photographs have often been presented to the public as documentary sources, but it is important to note the photographer's role as an interpreter of motifs. In Coleman's, Lane's, and Baker's intent to preserve there was often a temptation to "romanticize" the past, and as a result we see photographs in which the composition appears theatrical rather than realistic.

Coleman studied briefly in Paris in the 1860s, and in the 1870s she traveled extensively in Europe. Her European experience came at a time when the French Barbizon School of painting was gaining widespread recognition. Coleman's interest in this school, which focused on pastoral landscapes and the French peasantry, was further promoted by her close friendship with Boston painter Susan Minot Lane. Lane was a highly acclaimed student of William Morris Hunt, who had been trained in the Barbizon tradition by Jean François Millet, and who in turn instructed Lane.

Cat. 41. Emma Coleman, The Basketmaker, *ca. 1883–86. Photograph; 7½ in. x 4⅝ in. Old York Historical Society.*

Cat. 41a. Emma Coleman, The Woman with Faggots, *ca. 1883–86. Photograph; 4⅝ in. x 7½ in. Old York Historical Society.*

Coleman writes, "Whatever success I have had [as a photographer] is due largely to Miss Lane of Mr. Hunt's class. She taught me to see a picture."[2] Here Coleman asserts that her photographs were produced with the intent of "making a picture," and supports her belief that photography was an art form (an issue debated at the time).

The symbiotic relationship between Coleman's photography and Lane's painting is best uncovered in a photograph by Coleman of a Boston exhibition of Lane's work in the 1870s; the photograph reveals that many of Lane's paintings possessed exactly the same compositions as many of Coleman's photographs. Lane may have painted from Coleman's photographs, but may also have directed Coleman's photography when in the field.

Coleman, Lane, and C. Alice Baker vacationed together annually, and it is likely that the correspondence between Lane and William Morris Hunt, in the 1870s, inspired the women to vacation in the Piscataqua River region. Of York, Hunt writes, "There are fields full of hay and onions, or corn and stubble . . . [the fields] are fatter with suggestions of past and future than even with their overwhelming crops," and "sea and cliffs, and pasture and the grove again and the cattle scattered about so becomingly."[3] In the 1880s, Coleman writes of packing up her "clumsy tripod camera" along with the paintbox belonging to Miss Lane, and off they would go "being driven with bravado by

C. Alice Baker." She continues, "We jogged along the shore or country road until some picture held us"; it has been suggested that this path was the same as that mapped out by Hunt a few years earlier.[4] In any event, the subjects and landscape described in detail by Hunt can certainly be seen in Coleman's photographs.

Susan Minot Lane was not the only influence on Coleman's photography. C. Alice Baker, who became Coleman's companion for most of her adult life, also had a certain part in the works of Coleman. C. Alice Baker was a schoolteacher, a private tutor, a writer, and an avid preservationist. Originally from Deerfield, Massachusetts, Baker met Coleman in Boston where they worked as teachers in a small private school.[5] Later, Coleman taught with Baker in the private home of former German Consul Barthold Schlesinger. It was at Schlesinger's estate, known as "Southwood," in Brookline, Massachusetts, that Coleman is thought to have received her first experience with the collodion wet-plate process in 1882.[6] It was at this point that Coleman began collaborating with Baker on many projects.

By the 1890s Baker and Coleman were living together in one of their three residences in either Boston, Deerfield, or Kittery Point, Maine (cat. 40). Baker and Coleman researched, wrote, and illustrated the two-volume *New England Captives Carried to Canada* (Portland, Me.:

Southworth Press, 1925), and a *Historic and Present Day Guide to Old Deerfield* (Boston, 1912), as well as various papers which were presented at the Pocumtuck Valley Memorial Association's annual meetings in Deerfield (see fig. 5.1). These proceedings were later published; the volumes contain an extensive account of much of the local scholarship as well as the philanthropic activities and preservation projects of the association. Baker's death was cited in the proceedings in the form of a poignant obituary written by Coleman who continued to work on many of their unfinished projects until her own death.

Writing and research were not the only venues through which Coleman and Baker promoted preservation and colonial revival ideas. Coleman and Baker also joined with Mary and Frances Allen (both noted photographers and preservationists) and George Sheldon in the movement to preserve the historic landmarks and arts and crafts indigenous to Deerfield. As part of this larger effort in the late 1890s Coleman completed her most noteworthy series of photographs on colonial architecture. Taken both in Deerfield and in the Piscataqua River region, the images reveal many of the themes inherent to the work of colonial revivalists, as well as an aesthetic consideration similar to the architectural paintings done by Lane in the 1870s. In each case, the structures were in jeopardy of being "forgotten," and in many cases the sites were shot from the rear to enhance their "olden time" appearance.

In reference to the Deerfield preservation efforts, Fredrick C. Nims, a summer resident of the town, wrote, "Deerfield is vastly indebted to you three [meaning Coleman, Baker, and Lane] for exhuming and perpetrating its romantic and its tragic history." The same can be said for their efforts in the Piscataqua region. Nims included, in this letter to Baker, an interesting passage on photography: "I am sending you . . . a package of ten photographs, some of which I hope may be of interest to you. Although the films were developed soon after our return, the prints were but recently made, for want of time. Like most amateur efforts, they are an indifferent lot, and not much like Miss Coleman's beautiful work on that line."[7] One must note that the exchange of photographs was often the most effective means of communication for tourists and preservationists; the images established an aesthetic criteria of what was worthy of collecting and preserving, and what was not.

Emma Coleman's photography and writings earn her a prominent place in the Piscataqua's artistic and literary circles during the colonial revival. She and Baker summered in the little cottage owned by Baker, and later inherited by Coleman, on Cutt's Island in Kittery. Coleman was friend to writer Sarah Orne Jewett, associated with Emily Tyson and Elise Tyson Vaughan in South Berwick, and similarly associated with many of the Boston school painters who summered in the Portsmouth area. In 1901 Coleman photographed *The Wentworth-Coolidge Mansion*.[8] This representation of the architecture follows a tradition set

by Lane's paintings and preservationist photographers alike, as it is photographed from the rear.

Coleman's photography tells of a pastoral interest and a simplicity of composition typical of the Boston School painters. It also speaks of a romanticism inherent to the colonial revival movement in its portrayal of past ways of life, and it documents a social consciousness for historic preservation. Coleman captures old wooden schooners at a dock along the York River, the local harvest of sea hay, and the lobstering efforts of a local York fisherman. She pays tribute to historic landmarks by photographing the Junkins garrison, the Old Gaol, and the tree-lined country lane.

When in the Piscataqua region, Coleman sought escape from both the urban sprawl of Boston and the pressures of a hectic social calendar. She is not listed in any of the region's social organizations or local preservation efforts; instead, her photographs and writings speak of her contribution to the colonial revival in the Piscataqua.[9]

AWH

1 Emma Lewis Coleman, "Letters Between Two School Teachers" (manuscript, Pocumtuck Valley Memorial Association, Deerfield, Mass., n.d.). Coleman's negatives and photographs are in the collections of the SPNEA and OYHS.

2 Emma Lewis Coleman personal papers and manuscript materials, SPNEA. Quoted in Ellie Reichlin, "Emma Lewis Coleman: Photographer in the Barbizon Mood, 1880–1940" (typescript, SPNEA, 1982).

3 William Morris Hunt to Susan Minot Lane, n.d., archive of Susan Minot Lane letters, Pocumtuck Valley Memorial Association, Deerfield, Mass.

4 "From the Letters of Two New England Teachers: In the East and in the West," Deerfield Families Collection, Pocumtuck Valley Memorial Association, box 14, book 1, 97.

5 Ellie Reichlin, "Emma Lewis Coleman, 1853–1942: A Brief Biography" (unpublished manuscript, SPNEA, 1981), 1.

6 Reichlin, "Emma Lewis Coleman: Photographer," 1.

7 Frederick C. Nims to C. Alice Baker, 1909. Emma Lewis Coleman, personal papers, Pocumtuck Valley Memorial Association.

8 Coleman Papers, SPNEA.

9 Coleman gave 250 glass-plate negatives to SPNEA in 1925. Her work, for the most part, remains unknown. She exhibited occasionally in Deerfield's Memorial Hall and submitted at least two images to the Photographic Society (later known as the Royal Photographic Society) in Great Britain in 1894, but received no recognition. Since her death, her work has been published occasionally in OTNE and in Susan Mahnke, *Looking Back: Images of New England, 1860–1930* (Dublin, N.H.: Yankee Publishing, 1982).

CHILDE HASSAM (1859–1935)
The Room of Flowers
Isles of Shoals, 1894
Oil on canvas; 34 in. x 34 in.
Mr. and Mrs. Arthur G. Altschul
(*see plate 8*)

Childe Hassam, America's foremost Impressionist painter, was a significant participant in the colonial revival movement in the Piscataqua region. Despite his European-oriented style and prolific oeuvre, much of his subject matter has a specifically national bias. *The Room of Flowers* (pl. 8), which depicts the parlor of the summer cottage belonging to poet and amateur artist Celia Thaxter, is Hassam's summary statement about the revival aesthetics he encountered during the many summers he spent on Appledore Island, from as early as 1884 until 1916.

Undoubtedly Hassam felt solace and repose during his visits to the Isles of Shoals, for these "working vacations" proved among the most productive of his long career.[1] Many years later, in 1929, Hassam recalled, "Before the day of the automobile [it was] a famous summer resort. Celia Thaxter made the islands known to a great many—in the far-off days I painted there . . . many pleasant summers."[2] Nearly 10 percent (approximately four hundred) of his works, including paintings, watercolors, and pastels, depict scenes of Appledore Island and its coastline. Art historian David Park Curry has noted recently that Hassam's subjects completed at Appledore can be divided into three distinct phases: lighthouse images in watercolor from 1886, prior to his three-year tenure in Europe; scenes of Celia Thaxter's seaside garden with lavish light and color effects done between 1890 and 1894; and powerful depictions of the rocky coastline from the turn of the century to 1916.[3]

The Room of Flowers, completed in the year of Celia Thaxter's death, is Hassam's tribute to his mentor, to her parlor, and to her garden of unsurpassed natural beauty. Even the artist admitted it was among his finer works, referring to it as "wholly characteristic of her remarkable love for flowers. It was painted just before her death and I think it one of my best things."[4] The painting, a stunning rendering of Thaxter's parlor, is enhanced by its slashing brushstrokes and the compositional emphasis on bathing light and brilliant color. A contemporary visitor's description of the room's actual color attests to the vibrancy of Hassam's palette:

I have never seen anywhere such realized possibilities of color! The fine harmonic sense of the woman and artist and poet thrilled through these long chords of color, and filled the room with an atmosphere which made it seem like living in a rainbow.[5]

At first glance, Hassam's aesthetic, rather than narrative,

concerns dominate the painting, yet further examination reveals the painting as a record of late nineteenth-century collecting interests, particularly in relation to the aesthetic and colonial revival movements. Despite the casual arrangement of the room's furnishings, its contents are wide-ranging in source and style, aptly representing the eclectic tastes of Thaxter and her numerous guests. According to one visitor, the parlor was "filled with flowers and most everything else, from a Grand Rapids rocking chair to the most exquisite Venetian glass vases and period pieces of colonial furniture."[6] Thaxter gave an even more illuminating description of the magical room the year the painting was completed:

Opening out onto the long piazza over the flowerbeds, and extending almost its whole length, runs the large, light, airy room where a group of happy people gather to pass the swiftly flying summers here at the Isles of Shoals. This room is made first for music; on the polished floor there is no carpet to muffle sound, only a few rugs here and there, like patches of warm green moss on the pine-needle color given by the polish to the natural hue of the wood. There are no heavy draperies to muffle the windows, nothing to absorb the sound. The piano stands midway at one side; there are couches, sofas with pillows of many shades of dull, rich color, but mostly of warm shades of green. There are low bookcases 'round the walls, the books screened by short curtains of pleasant olive-green; the high walls to the ceiling are covered with pictures, and flowers are everywhere.[7]

Contemporary photographs reveal that Hassam's transcription of the parlor's decor into his *Room of Flowers* is only partial (cat. 42a). Nonetheless, the effect of aesthetic clutter evident in literary descriptions of the room is still prevalent in the painting; stacks of books, numerous framed pictures, vases of flowers, a wicker rocker, and a faux-bamboo table are among the elements which Hassam has assimilated with lavish detail. Yet, as Curry has perceptively noted, "the artist edited the space for pictorial purposes, slightly compressing its soaring Victorian scale and deleting some of the artworks visible in the photograph[s]."[8] Among the notable omissions is a Hassam rendering of the White Island light as well as all other references to his own work.

Hassam's painting also is a concise metaphor for many of the complex aesthetic and cultural ideals held in esteem by Celia Thaxter's guests. Among her more noted visitors were artists J. Appleton Brown (1844–1902), Ignaz Marcel Gaugengigl, Arthur Quartley (1839–1886), and Ross Turner; writer Richard Watson Gilder (1844–1909); and musicians William Mason (1829–1908) and John Knowles Paine (1839–1906). Thaxter's guests, who found inspiration in their natural surroundings, celebrated their progressive aesthetic beliefs in the parlor, which took on a "salon" atmosphere.[9] One visitor to the parlor wrote appreciatively of

Cat. 42a. Celia Thaxter's parlor, Appledore, Isles of Shoals, New Hampshire. Photograph, ca. 1890.
Courtesy, University of New Hampshire, Isles of Shoals Collection.

the refined surroundings which guests frequented mornings and evenings:

> For many years the group of musicians, artists, literary people and their friends have made a famous circle at Appledore. Although many features are similar to a winter drawing room, the surroundings give a peculiar charm to the place, and the hostess makes the needed force to hold and attract the different visitors. Since practical America has not too many salons for the cultivation of higher things, it is pleasant to think of the long time appreciation of poetry and art of Appledore.[10]

The parlor's heavenly music, pungent aroma of flowers, and visual bath of color must have had an effect approaching synesthesia on its guests. Writing of her visits to the room, Maud Appleton McDowell declared enthusiastically "such an atmosphere of beauty! Something to appeal to the eye and ear and even the sense of smell."[11]

As an integral component of the American aesthetic movement, colonial revival values found expression in Celia Thaxter's parlor, her garden, and Hassam's *Room of Flowers* as well. Both Thaxter and Hassam professed an interest in the supposedly simpler colonial past. According to one astute writer, Thaxter's selection of flowers for her island garden was hardly au courant: "all very common flowers [were] quite old-fashioned and out of date in greenhouses and gardens of good society."[12] But Thaxter intentionally opted for this outmoded selection, claiming, "they are mostly the old-fashioned flowers our grandmothers loved."[13] This old-time atmosphere was transferred to the parlor each day through Thaxter's artful arrangement of hundreds of flowers, and subsequently translated into Hassam's painting. And despite Hassam's proclivity for a European-oriented avant-garde style, much of his subject matter throughout his career was wholly characteristic of colonial revival paintings. Like many turn-of-the-century artists concerned with establishing a visual record of their nation's past, Hassam was attracted to picturesque old buildings, especially houses and churches removed from an urban setting:

I can look back and very truly say that probably and all unconsciously I as a very young boy looked at this New England church and without knowing it appreciated partly its great beauty as it stood there then against our radiant North American clear blue skies.[14]

Hassam's most obvious manifestations of interest in his American heritage are his numerous paintings, watercolors, and etchings of houses and churches which document examples of past architecture. Undoubtedly the several watercolor renderings of Portsmouth, New Hampshire, buildings, such as *Street in Portsmouth* of 1916 (Metropolitan Museum of Art, New York) were completed in conjunction with his visits to the Isles of Shoals.

TTM

1   This discussion of Hassam and the Isles of Shoals is indebted to the extremely thorough and lucid scholarship of David Park Curry; see his *Childe Hassam: An Island Garden Revisited* (New York: Denver Art Museum in association with W.W. Norton, 1990).

2   Childe Hassam to Mrs. McClellan, 1929, facsimile letter, curatorial file, *Morning Calm, Appledore,* Addison Gallery of American Art, Phillips Academy, Andover, Mass., quoted in Curry, *An Island Garden Revisited,* 13.

3   Curry, *Island Garden Revisited,* 13–14.

4   Childe Hassam to John W. Beatty, Sept. 31 [*sic*], 1895, Carnegie Institute Papers, AAA, quoted in Gail Stavitsky, "Childe Hassam and the Carnegie Institute: A Correspondence," *Archives of American Art Journal* 22, no. 3 (1982): 3.

5   Candice Wheeler, *Content in a Garden* (Boston and New York, 1901), 56–57, quoted in William H. Gerdts, *American Impressionism* (New York: Abbeville, 1984), 83.

6   Quoted in Adeline Adams, *Childe Hassam* (New York: American Academy of Arts and Letters, 1938), 83.

7   Celia Thaxter, *An Island Garden* (Boston and New York: Houghton Mifflin, 1894), 93–94.

8   Curry, *An Island Garden Revisited,* 45.

9   Richard Watson Gilder and his wife Helena de Kay, who visited Thaxter, were also noted as hosts of a Friday evening "salon," attracting the New York cultural intelligentsia during the 1870s and 1880s. The Gilder circle naturally held similar advanced aesthetic beliefs. See Thayer Coolidge Tolles, "Helena de Kay Gilder: Her Role in the New Movement" (master's thesis, University of Delaware, 1990), 12–14. Furthermore, as Curry notes, Gilder's volume of poetry *The New Day* (1876), which was illustrated by Helena de Kay, most certainly was an inspiration to the creation and design of *An Island Garden* written by Thaxter and included twenty-two charming watercolors by Hassam. See Curry, *An Island Garden Revisited,* 50–52.

10 Visitor to the Blessed Isles, "Domesticana, Life at a Summer's Salon at Appledore," in Celia Thaxter et al., *The Heavenly Guests, with other unpublished writings,* ed. Oscar Laighton (Andover, Mass., 1935), 133.

11 Maud Appleton McDowell, in *Heavenly Guests,* 127–28.

12 [*Chicago Tribune*], "Celia Thaxter, The Genius of the Isles of Shoals," in *Heavenly Guests,* 137–38.

13 Thaxter, *Island Garden,* 44.

14 Autobiographical statement, n.d., Childe Hassam Papers, American Academy of Arts and Letters, AAA, microfilm NAA-1. Hassam is referring to the white church on Meeting House Hill in his native Dorchester (see Doreen Bolger Burke, *American Paintings in the Metropolitan Museum of Art,* ed. Kathleen Luhrs [New York: Metropolitan Museum of Art in association with Princeton University Press, 1980], 362–63).

❀ 43 ❀

WHITE MOUNTAIN PAPER COMPANY OFFICE
Portsmouth, New Hampshire, 1902–3; demolished, 1984

In October 1901 the *Portsmouth Herald* reported that Frank Jones (cat. 2), the city's brewing and railroad magnate, had attracted New York capitalists who would spend five million dollars to build the world's largest paper mill along the Piscataqua River. Jones hoped to attract new industry to diversify the region's economy by selling some the land at Freeman's Point which he had acquired while serving as president of the Boston and Maine Railroad.[1]

By April 1902 the new corporation had signed building contracts for a pulp and paper mill designed by company engineers. Whether the office, one of the first buildings erected, was also designed by in-house engineers or was the product of architects from New York or Boston is unknown. The rectangular two-story brick box had a balustrade above the cornice surrounding the low hipped roof, as well as projecting front and rear pavilions. Red brick with white marble and wood detailing borrowed from both Georgian and federal styles, the building demonstrated the firm grounding in classical detailing taught in the nation's technical and professional schools at the turn of the century (cat. 43).

Unfortunately, the paper company went bankrupt in April 1903, and when the Maine-based corporation, Publisher's Paper Company, acquired the plant in 1905, their investigator found only two buildings completed. One was "the office (which looks like a Carnegie gift) and is said to have cost $50,000." The new corporate owner decided to convert "the beautiful office building . . . into a dwelling" for one of its "resident officials" by finishing the second story as an apartment. The plant was finished but never turned out any product; the office remained unfinished, without its planned portico and front steps. Once more the banks foreclosed, and yet another paper company failed to bring the mill into operation.[2]

As America entered World War I the unused paper mill attracted the interest of capitalists looking to take advantage of the nation's shortage of merchant vessels for the war effort. In 1918 the Atlantic Ship Building Corporation acquired all the buildings and land for a shipyard to construct ten 8,800-ton steel ships under a large contract from the United States Emergency Fleet Corporation. As part of this conversion, the new corporation actually moved the office from its original site to permit the construction of two ship's ways and an outfitting pier. The huge masonry pile was slowly moved by horses and a winch, set on a raised foundation to accommodate a basement restaurant, and fitted out with a new one-story entry portico and staircase. The more than two-month project was accomplished without dislocating the office staff who continued to work inside.[3]

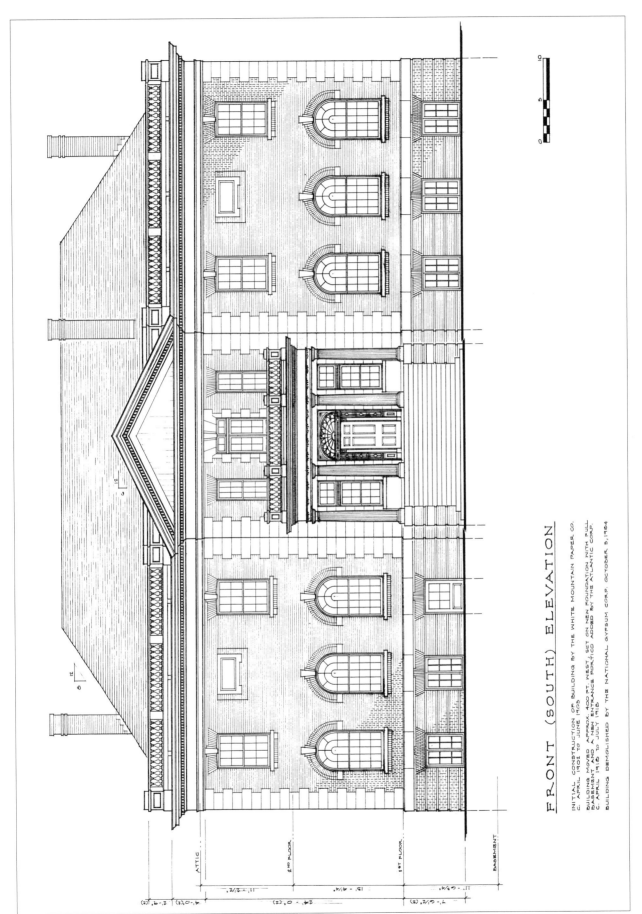

FRONT (SOUTH) ELEVATION

INITIAL CONSTRUCTION OF BUILDING BY THE WHITE MOUNTAIN PAPER CO.
C. APRIL 1902 TO JUNE 1903

BUILDING MOVED APPROX. 400 FT. WEST, SET ON NEW FOUNDATION WITH FULL
BASEMENT AND A NEW ENTRANCE PORTICO ADDED BY THE ATLANTIC CORP.
C. APRIL 1918 TO JULY 1918.

BUILDING DEMOLISHED BY THE NATIONAL GYPSUM CORP. OCTOBER 5, 1984.

Cat. 43. White Mountain Paper Company Office, Portsmouth, New Hampshire, built 1902–3. Drawing by Philip H. Kendrick, 1991.

Cat. 44a. Kilham and Hopkins, Architect's Rendering, *1918. Courtesy, Portsmouth Athenaeum.*

Called "one of the finest administration buildings in New England," the office under the Atlantic shipyard, like the earlier companies it headquartered, ultimately became a symbol of financial excess and unachievable corporate stability.[4] It later served the Atlantic Gypsum Company (1921–36) and National Gypsum Company (since 1936). In 1984, just as the office became a well-known and increasingly admired visual landmark for motorists crossing nearby bridges over the Piscataqua, it was demolished by National Gypsum for plant expansion.

RMC

1 "Five Million: That is what the Proposed Pulp and Paper Mill to be Erected here will cost," *Portsmouth Herald,* Oct. 14, 1901, 1; "World's Largest Paper Mill," *Portsmouth Herald,* Oct. 28, 1901, 1. For a detailed account of the companies building and altering the office, see Richard M. Candee, *Atlantic Heights, A World War I Shipbuilders' Community* (Portsmouth, N.H.: Portsmouth Marine Society, 1985), 13–50.

2 "Changes at Paper Mill," *Portsmouth Herald,* Aug. 10, 1910, 2; "Local," *Portsmouth Herald,* Sept. 26 and Nov. 14, 1914; *The City by the Sea* (Portsmouth, N.H.: City Board of Trade and Merchant Exchange, [1912]) shows the unfinished entrance.

3 Candee, *Atlantic Heights,* 25–61, 111–47; *Portsmouth Herald,* Apr. 8 and 17, May 1, June 1 and 25, and July 16, 1918.

4 *Portsmouth Herald,* June 14, 1919, cited in Candee, *Atlantic Heights,* s35, 152n.

 44

ATLANTIC HEIGHTS
Portsmouth, New Hampshire, 1918
Kilham and Hopkins, architects and planners

The design of Atlantic Heights (cat. 44), a garden suburb built during World War I for workers at the adjoining Atlantic Corporation shipyard in Portsmouth, demonstrates the mature relationship between architectural training, progressive ideology, nationalism, and the colonial revival. The key figure in the unified design for 278 family houses in 150 permanent individual structures, eight dormitories, a store, cafeteria, and school was Walter H. Kilham (1868–1948) of Boston. Forming a partnership with James C. Hopkins in 1901, the firm of Kilham and Hopkins became well known for the design of schools, town halls, suburban homes, and workers' housing. In this work the firm was engaged in what one scholar has called the "culture of recall," a colonial revival ideology that sought to restructure the landscape with architectural symbols of community and civic values.[1]

A Boston architect who graduated from the Massachusetts Institute of Technology in 1889, Walter Kilham became as deeply involved with the study of historic

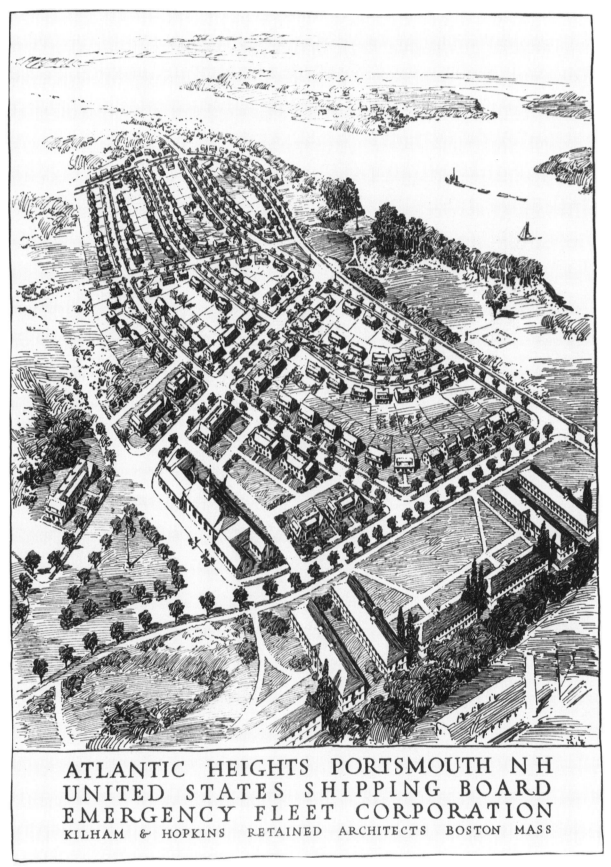

ATLANTIC HEIGHTS PORTSMOUTH N H
UNITED STATES SHIPPING BOARD
EMERGENCY FLEET CORPORATION
KILHAM & HOPKINS RETAINED ARCHITECTS BOSTON MASS

Cat. 44. Emergency Fleet Corporation, bird's-eye drawing of Atlantic Heights, Portsmouth, New Hampshire, based on original plans by Kilham and Hopkins, architects. From U.S. Shipping Board, Emergency Fleet Corporation, Types of Housing for Shipbuilders . . . *(1917). Courtesy, Portsmouth Athenaeum.*

architecture as he was with reforming the design and planning of housing for working people.[2] When the United States entered the First World War the federal government created the Emergency Fleet Corporation, a quasipublic agency to fund a massive shipbuilding program and emergency housing to sustain those shipyards. Kilham was invited by this government agency in April 1918, on the basis of his prior involvement in reform housing efforts in Massachusetts, to design and plan a million-dollar residential development for the Atlantic shipyard in Portsmouth. In ten days a village plan was developed for the site and several house designs submitted for approval. Construction began that May and, despite the need for design approval from Washington for all stages and shortages of building materials due to the war, the project was substantially completed within a year.[3]

The design process that led to the selection of the colonial revival style for the mostly brick homes and other buildings at Atlantic Heights illustrates the working methods of well-trained colonial revival architects at the turn of the century and suggests the multiple symbolic uses of the style. Kilham had sketched Portsmouth's historic buildings as a student architect and had written about the city's important colonial and federal-period brick homes as early as 1902.[4] His first step in planning this new addition to Portsmouth was to photograph those old buildings whose forms or details might be adapted to the house plans his firm had already built elsewhere. Gambrel roofs, simple federal-style fanlights set in brick arches, and triangular Georgian pediments over doorways of the city's old homes in particular provided models. A newspaper reporter concluded that the architects had followed as far as possible the colonial lines of the city, "many of the houses having reproduction[s] on a smaller scale of some of the best of the colonial doorways" (cat. 44a).[5] Using these different ornamental doorway details, brick bonding patterns, or occasional clapboard walls on seven different basic house plans not only provided variety but evoked symbolic association with local and regional building traditions.

Located along the Piscataqua, a mile beyond the city core, Atlantic Heights was laid out as a self-contained "village" according to reform ideals promoted by the English Garden City movement. Streets conformed to topography, winding around trees and rocks, while homes were clustered informally to recreate a sense of community. Public buildings, set around a New England town common at the head of the only road into the project, included a proposed village recreational hall with connected shops "of old-fashioned type" to be built in "colonial red brick with white trimming" to look not unlike a miniature Independence Hall.[6] Such architectural symbols were designed, literally, to instill civic pride and community harmony through its colonial style.

Kilham and Hopkins had not previously adapted colonial imagery for their earlier reform housing for Massachusetts workers. Its use here, during World War I, reveals several levels of symbolic cultural meaning. This was

the first use of federal funds for the construction of houses in an era and a region suspicious of government intervention in the private market. Reformers like Kilham sought to win public acceptance of this radical idea by wrapping many of the two dozen American war-housing projects in colonial garb as a patriotic gesture. Moreover, it was expected that well-built permanent homes for workers constructed under the government's war emergency programs would continue as productive industrial communities after the war. The architects and planners wanted to demonstrate that improved housing could be cost competitive with speculative forms of worker housing. They argued that such projects might also improve the nation's social order and that such stylistic associations could help avoid labor strife by inculcating American values among ethnic workers. Congress immediately canceled the program at the war's end, and the government sold all of the housing it had helped build during the war.

However, designs such as those at Atlantic Heights, widely publicized during and after the war, did have a wide impact. Colonial revival architecture had previously been exclusively an elite style for summer cottages of the rich and upper-middle-class suburban homes. War-time projects like Atlantic Heights helped democratize this modern "colonial style" as appropriate to small houses built for private industry and speculative suburban development during the 1920s and 1930s. The professional architectural press, popular plan books, and even mail-order homes all developed affordable small house designs that offered the colonial style to a growing middle class.[7]

RMC

1 Greer Hardwicke, "Town Houses and the Culture of Recall: Public Buildings and Civic Values and the Architectural Firm of Kilham, Hopkins & Greeley, 1900–1930" (Ph.D. diss., Boston College, 1986).

2 Kilham became the historian of the Boston Society of Architects and wrote *Boston After Bulfinch, An Account of its Architecture 1800–1900* (Cambridge, Mass.: Harvard University Press, 1946). For the firm's workers' housing projects, see Richard M. Candee and Greer Hardwicke, "Early Twentieth-Century Reform Housing by Kilham and Hopkins, Architects of Boston," *Winterthur Portfolio* 22, no. 1 (Spring 1987): 47–80.

3 For a more detailed account, see Richard M. Candee, *Atlantic Heights, A World War I Shipbuilders' Community* (Portsmouth, N.H.: Portsmouth Marine Society, 1985).

4 Walter H. Kilham sketchbook, 1889, in the collection of Walter H. Kilham, Jr.; Walter H. Kilham, "Colonial Brickwork of New England, II: Portsmouth, N.H.," *The Brickbuilder* 11 (Jan. 1902): 3–6.

5 "Atlantic Heights will be an Ideal Village" *Portsmouth Daily Chronicle*, Aug. 15, 1918, 1.

6 William Roger Greeley, "Erecting Memorials to Our Soldiers and Sailors," *House Beautiful* 45 (Jan. 1919): 19.

7 For industrial examples, see Candee and Hardwicke, "Early Twentieth-Century Reform Housing," 79–80; William P. Comstock, comp., *The Housing Book* (New York: William T. Comstock Co., 1919). For small suburban houses, see Robert Schweitzer and Michael W.R. Davis, *America's Favorite Homes: Mail Order Catalogs as a Guide to Popular Early 20th-Century Houses* (Detroit: Wayne State University Press, 1990); Robert T. Jones, ed., *Authentic Small Houses of the Twenties* (New York: Dover Publications, 1987); *Colonial Homes Designed by The Architects Small House Service Bureau* (St. Louis: South Central Division, 1930); *American Builder Year Book, Modern Homes* (Chicago: American Builder, 1930); *The Boston Post Book of Homes, 1936* (Boston: Model Homes, Inc., 1936).

V
The Literature
of the
Colonial Revival

Fig. 5.1. Susan Minot Lane, The Junkins Garrison, *1875. Oil on canvas; 7½ in. x 14 in. Published in Emma Coleman,* New England Captives Carried to Canada *(1926). Old York Historical Society.*

Preceding page: Elizabeth Perkins. Photograph, ca. 1905. Old York Historical Society.

"Colossal in Sheet-Lead":
The Native American and Piscataqua-Region Writers

Karen Oakes

"IT SEEMED AS IF all the clocks in Deephaven, and all the people with them, had stopped years ago."[1] At the center of Sarah Orne Jewett's *Deephaven,* this observation encapsulates much of the Piscataqua region literature during the colonial revival. Jewett gestures toward a space apart, an Edenic realm of memory that erases—or willfully forgets—the changes convulsing America in the latter half of the nineteenth century, among them, the end of the abolitionist movement and the Civil War, the suffrage movement and what feminists now call the "first wave" of feminism, the Industrial Revolution and the birth of the labor movement, and the Indian wars. A response to these changes, the colonial revival movement hearkened to earlier and ostensibly simpler times in which people lived in harmony with nature.

This proximity to nature, however, was never unproblematic. As Annette Kolodny demonstrates in *The Lay of the Land,* nature has been contested territory in the United States since the colonists landed; she argues that male colonists feminized nature, imagining it, alternatively, as a virgin/mother to be lauded (and plundered) and a whore to be conquered (and feared).[2] Furthermore, traditional American literature has from its beginnings with John Smith and Roger Williams often depicted nature by proxy in the image of the "savage," the Native American, a depiction that echoed the colonists' clashes with local tribes while it conveniently forgot the essential role of those tribes in assuring Euro-American survival in a hostile and unknown climate. Roy Harvey Pearce argues that Euro-Americans' self-definition as "civilized" depended at first upon the Indians' "savagism." Later, many writers came to invoke the idea of the "noble savage" as an antidote to the excesses of "civilization"; Thoreau's last word was reputed to be "Indians." At midcentury the affiliation between Indians, nature, and women—all potentially "savage"— was encoded by Nathaniel Hawthorne's *Scarlet Letter* in the figure of Hester Prynne, at home in the forest.[3]

The colonial revival meant for many Americans not only the celebration of traditional values and nostalgia for so-called "simpler times," but also an opportunity for reexamination of colonialism in general and Indian-white relations in particular.[4] The national preoccupation with Native Americans extended emphatically to New Englanders, who rehearsed their encounters with local tribes again and again. In 1902, for example, Thomas Nelson Page delivered an ora-tion recounting the accomplishments of Euro-American settlers to "the native-born people of York" whose ancestors were "exposed to rovers of the sea on one side" and "to the fierce savages of the forest on the other."[5]

The region's fascination with these tensions continued well into the twentieth century, for in 1926 Emma Lewis Coleman published *New England Captives Carried to Canada between 1677 and 1760 during the French and Indian Wars* (fig. 5.1).[6] Even more strikingly, chapter 25 of the *History of York,* first published in 1931, dramatized the "Massacre of Candlemas Day":

> Sunday, January 24, 1691–2 was . . . Candlemas, and on that day the pastor of the church of York, Maine, preached to his little flock, unaware that by nightfall of that Sabbath a horde of savages would reach the outskirts of the town, in the silence of night, bent upon murder.

The writer depicts the (godless) Native Americans as wild beasts waiting to pounce on innocent victims; and he delights in a most gruesome account of ensuing events, which he deplores as "astounding butchery."[7]

The Piscataqua writers' work took shape in this atmosphere of historical recollection in which the "savage," both as individual Native American and as symbol, figured prominently. Although they explore other concerns, their collective uneasiness with the tension between nature and culture, the "wild" and the "civilized," reverberates throughout their work, if only as a muted subtext. In "Confessions of a Summer Colonist," "Staccato Notes of a Vanished Summer," and *The Story of a Bad Boy,* for example, William Dean Howells (cat. 51) and Thomas Bailey Aldrich (cat. 45; see also cat. 49) figure nature alternatively as the noble savage or the murderous savage; that is, like the Native Americans whom the colonists encountered, "the wild" appears at once attractive and frightening, benevolent and hostile. For these men, regardless of its temper, it remains irrevocably other. And as we will see ultimately, for Aldrich, as for his male predecessors, nature and the "savage" are connected, however inconspicuously, to the feminine.

For Sarah Orne Jewett (cats. 47–48, 50) and Celia Thaxter (cat. 46) these connections and tensions are more complicated. Early in her career, Jewett shows a marked ambivalence about women's relationship to nature. Later,

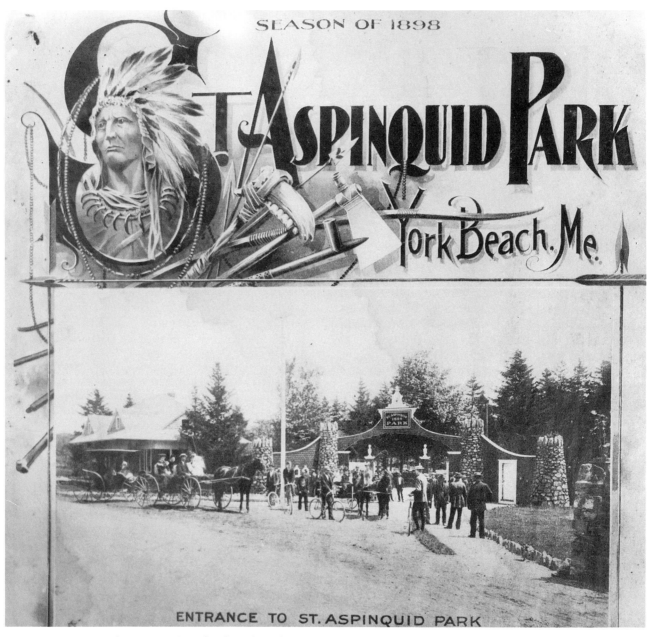

SEASON OF 1898

ST. ASPINQUID PARK

York Beach, Me.

ENTRANCE TO ST. ASPINQUID PARK

Fig. 5.2. St. Aspinquid Park, York Beach, Maine. Advertisement, 1898. Old York Historical Society.

however, she attempts to mediate an affirmative, even symbiotic connection between women and nature. Thaxter's work shows us that Jewett is able to imagine this connection in part because of her privileged class position, which to a degree insulated her from the problems of life in nature. In Thaxter, nature is awe-full in the richest sense. Its destructive power palls, however, before two problems of Euro-American culture, alcoholism and gender relations. In each of these four writers, however, the Native American is an important vehicle for ruminations on the "savage."[8]

In May 1875, *The Atlantic Monthly* included work by Thomas Bailey Aldrich, Sarah Orne Jewett, Celia Thaxter, and its editor, William Dean Howells, whose aesthetic and influence shaped the others' careers. Unlike his friends,

Howells writes of the Piscataqua region (cat. 51) from the perspective of an outsider, a summer visitor, and he combines a descriptive (if sunny) realism and nostalgic romanticism that we sometimes find in their work. Of the Piscataqua he observes, "If there is anything lovelier than the scenery of this gentle river I do not know it; and I doubt if the sky is purer and bluer in paradise."[9]

Significantly, his country Eden contains the literal figure of the savage, safely idealized, ennobled, and immobilized:

Beyond the cottage settlements [of "the Port"] is a struggling little park [fig. 5.2], dedicated to the only Indian saint I ever heard of, though there may be others. His statue, colossal in sheet-lead, and painted the copper color of his race, offers any heathen comer the choice between a Bible in one of his hands and a tomahawk in the other, at the entrance of the park [fig. 5.3].

Nature—and the potential wildness of human nature—is (barely) civilized in the image of the "struggling little" park and in the statue of St. Aspinquid, a well-known local figure in the latter half of the seventeenth century. Reputed in his youth among the Pawtuckets to be "trained to be as great and terrible a warrior as any who had gone before him," St. Aspinquid was converted to Christianity at the age of forty-three by John Eliot, after which time he became famous among both Indians and settlers for his proselytizing. In 1682 his funeral pyre attracted a huge assembly of mourners among his people; according to one account, it provided the means of salvation for four men stranded on an island off the coast who, seeing the smoke, began their own fire and were rescued by the friendly Indians—a rescue that echoed many rescues of desperate settlers by Native Americans.[10]

Howells's description of the statue itself fairly vibrates with Euro-Americans' ambivalence during the colonial revival era about their relation to Native Americans. Larger ("colossal") and more massive ("sheet-lead") than life, the statue is appropriate for a "saint," but its distorted scale also suggests the psychological weight of the Native American on the Euro-American consciousness and conscience. Equally significant is the gesture the figure makes, namely, offering a "choice" between a "tomahawk" and a "Bible." This duality suggests Euro-American fear of the tenuous nature of the civility achieved by the Native American; it is no accident that St. Aspinquid's figure offers this choice to "any heathen comer." But perhaps even more threatening for Howells is the ambiguity of the latter term, for "any heathen comer" could incorporate whites as well as Native Americans. Howells unwittingly encodes the anxiety that, after all, savage and civilized may not be polar opposites, but in fact interchangeable. Finally, the only safe location in which he can situate the Indian in a white man's paradise is cast in sheet-lead, an immobile figure in the drama of nature versus culture.

Embodied in Howells's work as the noble savage, St. Aspinquid figures the tension between nature and culture that we see elaborated also in Aldrich. What Roy Harvey Pearce observes in another context applies to Aldrich's *Story of a Bad Boy* (cat. 45):

> The Indian's nobility was something . . . not for white men to aspire to, but rather something for white men to outgrow. Thinking about it, one was thinking about his childhood; and one could afford to sentimentalize, even to celebrate, childhood.[11]

It is but a short step from viewing the Indian as a child to representing the child as an "Indian." John Crowley observes that in the boy-book the transition from boy to

Fig. 5.3. Statue of St. Aspinquid, York Beach, Maine. From St. Aspinquid Park *(1898). Old York Historical Society.*

adult "is treated as a threshold experience. The boy passes abruptly and irreversibly from the precivilized world of 'natural savagery' into the world of adult civilization, which valorizes self-knowledge, hard work, and moral responsibility." Aldrich portrays in idealistic and nostalgic terms the "natural savagery" of the boy-child, in contrast to the "real" savagery of the Native American, who becomes a proxy for nature. Hence, Tom tells us that before he moved back to Rivermouth, "I supposed the inhabitants were divided into two classes—Indians and white people; that the Indians occasionally dashed down on New York, and scalped any woman or child . . . whom they caught lingering in the outskirts after nightfall." In their murderous capacity Indians are allied indirectly with the savagery of the knowledge that comes after "nightfall" and the danger that lies "in the outskirts." We obtain a hint here of the connection between the savage and the feminine, for another kind of knowledge that comes after "nightfall" is sexual knowledge, acquired on—and beneath—the "outskirts" of daily life.[12]

In imagining "two classes—Indians and white people," Tom recognizes that the two groups have been set in opposition to one another. The psychological fear that this fantasy evinces has its roots in real events of Aldrich's boyhood: "in the wilds of the Southwest the red men were still a source of terror to the border settlers. 'Trouble with the Indians' was the staple news from Florida published in the New Orleans newspapers," where Osceola and his Seminoles had held forth valiantly against the invasion of whites.[13] News of war from the Indian territories became commonplace in the years after the Civil War; in conjunction with the region's recollection of such events as the Candlemas Day Massacre, such news dramatized for Aldrich's white contemporaries the continuing problems of defining the civilized and containing the savage. While for many, the Indians' resistance undoubtedly justified the colonizers' violence and the Indians' dispossession, for others, such resistance surely raised questions about white violence and colonialism.

Aldrich's depiction of the boys' pastimes, from the explosive Fourth of July celebration, to the battle between Tom and Conway, to the larger battle between the South End and North End boys, becomes in this context a rumination on the civilized and the savage. An indirect allusion to relations between Native Americans and Euro-Americans, the Fourth of July celebrates colonialist supremacy and ostensibly the triumph of civilized values, yet its own violence echoes the savagery over which the colonists supposedly triumphed. The battles between the South End and North End boys rehearse this conflict on another front. We find here a coded version of the Civil War and hence, the concern of colonialism with "territory." The boys, as the "natural savages" that Crowley describes, band together against the adults.[14] Yet this rehearsal of war not only parallels the psychic changes in moving from boyhood to manhood, but also echoes the determination of Euro-Americans to conceive of Native Americans as precivilized children. The Civil War was not only a literal event concerned with the freedom of African-Americans and Southern secession from the Union; it was and continues to be enacted on both figurative and literal levels as a centuries-long conflict between Euro- and Native Americans.

If racial conflict with Native Americans represents one version of civil war, gender conflict represents another, adjacent one, for an inescapable part of the transition from childhood to adulthood is a sexual awakening. As I have suggested, Aldrich's view of gender relations is at best ambivalent. At first glance, women figure peripherally in the story because it concerns itself only with preadolescence. Miss Abigail is a stereotypical "old maid," chiefly concerned with the beneficial qualities of "hot-drops" and with preventing her brother from smoking in the house; Miss Kitty is another comic figure who swoons at the reappearance of her long-lost husband in the person of Sailor Bill; Tom's mother seems sweetly invisible. These images of femininity show older women, acculturated, civilized, and most importantly, desexualized, enforcing norms of Victorian civility—in Crowley's words, "self-knowledge, hard work, and moral responsibility"—and colonialism.

From one stance, then, women represent for Aldrich another kind of adversary, a hostile civilizing force that requires the abandonment of the savage in the boy. At the same time, however, women parallel the wildness of nature—both threatening and seductive, violent and pacific. Mother nature seduces Tom and his friends in their voyage up the river for an island picnic, arraying herself in paradisiacal garb, and then betrays her children by allowing Binny Wallace to die at sea. Sailor Bill makes this connection between women and nature explicit for us in his naming the ocean as "a sort of stepmother." Stepmothers are notoriously fickle and violent in Western children's literature, and here is no exception.[15]

The affiliation between women, Indians, and nature as savage emerges most explicitly late in the story:

> On the extreme end of the peninsula was an old disused graveyard [fig. 5.4], tenanted principally by the early settlers who had been scalped by the Indians. In a remote corner of the cemetery, set apart from the other mounds, was the grave of a woman who had been hanged in the old colonial times for the murder of her infant.[16]

As the narrator's mind wanders from one savage act to another, he depicts women and Indians as similarly violent. Significantly, the graveyard is located on "Grave Point—the place where Binny Wallace's body came ashore." Mother Nature gone awry joins a mother gone awry, as Aldrich suggests that both women and Indians are savage and Other.

The context for this description is also important. Tom wanders to Grave Point as "a Blighted Being," one who has been defeated in the potentially violent contest between the sexes.[17] If older women in the story are both civilized and civilizers, younger women have only a veneer of such civility, and relations between the sexes echo those of war. An older friend who gives Tom advice about a girl urges, "'Laura is an old veteran, and carries too many *guns* for a youngster.'"[18] Sexuality represents another kind of danger facing him, and the adult writer's method of attack is humor; we must wonder how seriously we are to take his early assertion that, "By the way, speaking of the Pilgrim Fathers, I often used to wonder why there was no mention made of the Pilgrim Mothers."[19]

As Crowley observes, "The cost of becoming a man is the irrecoverable loss of the boy-world, and the sense of this loss accounts for the frequently elegiac tone of the boy book."[20] But the elegiac tone in *The Story of a Bad Boy* represents nostalgia not only for Tom's childhood, but also for America's childhood, an "Edenic" time of precivilized "natural savagery," of the idealized and racist "freedom" of colonial America in which, to use Crowley's terms, "adult" consciousness of "moral responsibility" toward native Americans had not yet formed.

Early white women's relation to the wilderness differed from that of their male counterparts. Annette Kolodny explains that their response was mediated by a number of

Fig. 5.4. Point of Graves, Portsmouth, New Hampshire. Photograph, ca. 1890. Courtesy, Patch Collection, Strawbery Banke Museum.

factors, including white patriarchal engendering of nature as female, their own disinclination to idealize the natural, and their restricted ability to own land. Their response was to engender, either in reality or in fantasy, a garden that inscribed their space in the wilderness—a space of family and community.[21] Kolodny indicates that this creation became especially important for the women who westered. I would argue that this strategy was also important, though differently, for the women who remained rooted in New England.

White women's relations, both literal and figurative, to Indians, plays an important role in the formulation of these women's spaces. Jewett's and Thaxter's work emerges from one of the earliest forms of written literature by women in this country, the captivity narrative, of which Mary Rowlandson's is prototypical. Published in 1682, it details her capture and forced march during King Philip's War, focusing on the hardships she endured and on the Providential hand of God in delivering her out of "the vast and howling Wilderness." A subtext of this narrative was the implied threat of rape; as Phyllis Rogers observes, Puritan society viewed the Indian as "a defiler of women" in spite of the fact that "all of the returning captives reported, contrary to the general consensus, that captive women were never sexually molested."[22] Rowlandson's story and subsequent captivity narratives by women suggest the affiliation between women and nature: it is left to God, the patriarch, to redeem women from nature—and from the Indians. For white women, then, nature was potentially masculine as well as feminine. By representing nature as feminine on the one hand, white patriarchy engendered women as silent object; but by encouraging its depiction by women as sometimes masculine (and Indian), it gave women a specious and victimized, yet culturally resonant, voice.

Rowlandson's story has a muted twin that subverts these connections: the tale of a woman who was captured by the Indians and chose to remain with her captors. As Phyllis Rogers points out, among the Iroquois at least women enjoyed not only close bonds with family and tribe but also an unusual degree of "authority and power." *A Narrative of the Life of Mrs. Mary Jemison,* published in 1824, testifies to these attractions. Jemison voices what we might call an anticaptivity narrative, for she undermines at every turn the attempts of her white transcriber to depict the Iroquois as merely savage, and she inserts many examples of their civility, kindness, and love. Captured at about thirteen, the only member of her family to be spared, she was adopted by two Seneca women, and by the time she was fifteen or sixteen, she chose—as she did again and again later—to retain her Seneca identity.[23]

While the popularity of Rowlandson's and other captivity narratives attests to Euro-Americans' frightened fascination with savage life, Mary Jemison's affirms on a literal level the attractiveness of life in nature with actual Indians. White women writers may have rewritten their men's violent appropriation of nature and of its Indian proxies because they did not wish to exploit a nature represented to them as analogous to their own bodies. But they may also have acquired this different attitude because of the respect accorded women by many Eastern Woodland tribes.[24] Mary Jemison's narrative represents a cultural metaphor for this difference; it prefigures Euro-American women's rejection of patriarchal silencing and their increasing involvement in, among other causes, Indian rights during the nineteenth century. As the United States government and its men pursued a course of wars, both military and cultural, against the Indians, culminating in 1890 in the Wounded Knee massacre, these women, fresh

Fig. 5.5. Marcia Oakes Woodbury, Mrs. Bonny at Home, *ca. 1893. From Sarah Orne Jewett,* Deephaven *(1893). Private collection.*

from campaigns for abolition and energized by those for women's rights, became champions—if sometimes misguided—for Indian causes.[25]

In this context of national self-examination and upheaval, Jewett published her first book, *Deephaven* (cat. 47); it was Howells who encouraged her to develop her initial sketches into a full-length book. As editor of *The Atlantic Monthly* following the resignation of Howells, Aldrich too was important to Jewett both personally and professionally. We find in *Deephaven* variations on many of the themes that he touches upon in *Bad Boy,* but we discover here a more complex attitude toward the relationship between women, Indians, and nature.[26] Because of the problematic situation of women in white patriarchy as both the enforcers of culture and embodiments of nature, Jewett finds it difficult to mediate this relationship.

Aldrich's child returns in the perspective of *Deephaven*'s protagonists, Helen Denis and Kate Brandon; by recapturing their childhoods, Helen and Kate can forget both the nation's unrest and their own impending adult responsibilities. In exploring the possibilities for their adult lives, however, Jewett studies the convergence of nature, Indians, and the feminine. The Indians that Aldrich's Tom fears become

domesticated in *Deephaven* in Mrs. Bonny, a poor old woman: "There was something so wild and unconventional about Mrs. Bonny that it was like taking an afternoon walk with a good-natured Indian." Significantly, Mrs. Bonny lives alone in the woods, and the narrator describes the passage to her home in idyllic and reverent terms: nature becomes "a great church." Incorporated into nature's timelessness and beauty, Mrs. Bonny is a powerful figure.[27]

But her closeness to nature is not simply positive. Kolodny observes that one fear of Euro-American culture was that white women in the wilderness would become masculinized and coarse, losing their domestic abilities. Mrs. Bonny's clothes confirm this fear; "she wore a man's coat, cut off so that it made an odd short jacket, and a pair of men's boots much the worse for wear." Furthermore, Mr. Lorimer amuses the protagonists by describing their hostess's reputation for marginal household skills, a reputation that is confirmed when Kate wants a drink and Mrs. Bonny produces a distressingly filthy glass (fig. 5.5).[28]

In a more affirmative vein that suggests her figurative connection with Indians, their hostess "knew all the herbs and tress and the harmless wild creatures who lived among them, by heart; and she had an amazing store of tradition and superstition." Even more tellingly, after Helen describes her as "a good-natured Indian," she adds that "we used to carry her offerings of tobacco, for she was a great smoker"; Maine Indians, like their counterparts throughout the country, used tobacco for ceremonial and spiritual occasions.[29] Here, of course, although Helen and Kate see their gift as ceremonial—"offerings"—Mrs. Bonny uses the tobacco for "'narves.'" Mrs. Bonny (Mrs. Fair?) seems to represent a confirmation of civilized fears, but Jewett's homely and comic portrait of her effectually tames the wildness around the margins of society.[30] Mrs. Bonny's story is a "captivity narrative" with the Indians deleted.

The story of Miss Chauncey—"the last survivor of one of the most aristocratic old colonial families"—parallels and contrasts with Mrs. Bonny's. As a member of the colonial aristocracy, she represents an ostensible counterpoint to the Indian nature that white settlers attempted to civilize. Yet her family members suggest how provisional such distinctions are: her father dies after becoming "partially insane"; one brother kills himself; another, mad, "became so violent that he was chained for years in one of the upper chambers, a dangerous prisoner." Miss Chauncey is herself insane, living in a home empty of its former grandeur and literally falling in around her.[31]

Miss Chauncey is another kind of captive, held by the past, by imagination, by habit, by class privilege, and by gender. Yet Helen describes her affirmatively, as a lady: "I have seen few more elegant women than Miss Chauncey. Thoroughly at her ease, she had the manner of a lady of the olden times, using the quaint fashion of speech which she had been taught in her girlhood."[32] In her nostalgia for Miss Chauncey's aristocratic past, Helen (and Jewett) elevates and longs for that past, even though her "captivity" in

THE long hill slope, the river's course,
  The high tide sleeping there—
I see them all in sunshine soft;
  September days are fair.

The wild birds sing in Britham woods,
  Far off the sea waves call;
In Scotland garrison but one
  Keeps watch and ward for all.

One woman at her spinning stands
  There in the lookout high,
Now glances at the woodland's edge,
  And now spins busily.

She bends to touch the whirling wheel,
  Or mend the thread that flies,
Then wakes from sweet day-dreams of home
  And seeks with eager eyes

Her own and only little child,
  Lest she should stray too far
From where the captain and his men
  Out in the clearing are.

There steadily the brave men work,
  Nor sigh for what they miss;
A memory of English farms
  Would shame a wild like this,

Fig. 5.6. Illustration by W.L. Taylor for Sarah Orne Jewett, "York Garrison, 1640." From Wide Awake *(1886). Courtesy, University of New Hampshire.*

a dead culture seems to make Mrs. Bonny's life as "a good-natured Indian" a far better model for emulation by the younger women.

In *Deephaven* Jewett finds problematic and simplistic Aldrich's alliance between Indians, the feminine, and nature; in her search for a more acceptable synthesis, she went on to write a ballad that encodes the sexual politics of white-Indian relations. "York Garrison, 1640" was published in 1886 in *Wide Awake*, a children's magazine (fig. 5.6). Although it purports to be for that audience, it addresses as clearly the anxieties of white middle-class parents about Indian-white relations. Jewett sets the poem before the bloody racial wars that concluded the seventeenth century, and in so doing she attempts to rewrite the course of that history. We hear the story of little Polly Masterson playing outside of York garrison. Polly's mother, inside spinning, and her father, farming with the men, forget both "the Indian fights" in this "wild" place, and Polly, who, we are told, is "unafraid of Indian foes." Lured by flowers described as "scarlet splendors" "by the brook," Polly too forgets the Indians. But when the "watcher cries," in their haste the Englishmen run into the garrison, leaving Polly behind.[33]

The phallic scarlet flowers that Jewett depicts again and

again figure the seductiveness of the Indian men and, as the captivity narratives fear, of the wilderness itself: "by the brook [are] the scarlet flowers / That tempted Polly out!" Jewett's description of temptation echoes the Genesis myth:

She hurries by the scarlet flowers,
She holds her dolly fast,
She sees the crested, snake-like heads—
The danger knows at last.

The Indians! oh the woods are full
Of dreadful shapes of men!

Although Polly clings to her doll, a symbol of childhood, the flowers and their proxies the Indians "tempt" her out of Edenic innocence. Jewett's exclamations underscore how the flowers and the "snake-like heads" encode Indian sexuality, as nature seduces but threatens to overwhelm in its "dreadful" masculinity. The woods seem not just inhabited by men, but to take on their shape, animated by them. If nature is male and Indian, women's relation to both here seems to be one of potential sexual victim, confirming and conforming to patriarchal ideology.

The narrator's fear of Polly's violation emerges indirectly, but she names her other fears: murder and captivity. No one in the garrison dares go out, in spite of Polly's cries, "Father! Father!" Here Jewett gestures toward the captivity stories' motif of the providential hand of God in the captives' salvation, yet she provides a twist to this paradigm. *Polly* redeems not only herself but also the entire garrison by requiring a feminized response to the perceived threat. For a moment the "they" in the poem blurs, as the men's difference converges into similarity; almost Christ-like, Polly captivates both the civilized English farmers and the wild men of the woods. Among the English, "no one fires a gun." The Indians laugh, perhaps because they see "her apron piled / With posies," an image that suggests her embrace of their sexual presence; and they too refrain from violence: "Perhaps it touched their savage hearts— / That frightened little face!" Jewett emphasizes Polly's peacemaking role in her self-conscious penultimate stanza:

The story seems for those dark days
A gleam of sunshine bright.
I hope they called the Indians friend,
And gave them food that night.

In "York Garrison, 1640," Jewett gestures toward elements of the traditional captivity narrative apparently to revise both historical and literary Indian-white (and nature-culture) relations by inserting a mediating feminine presence into the wilderness; and she seems to acknowledge and even embrace the seductiveness of Indian male sexuality represented in nature as a means of achieving peace.

Two observations, however, undercut my (and Jewett's) story of an idyllic ending. First, this embrace of sexuality and nature is performed by a young girl, a pre-sexual female. More problematically, Jewett writes from a perspective that is clearly allied with the transplanted English farmers, for she uses the stereotypical language of "wild" and "savage" over and over again to describe the Indians. In the stanza last cited, this sympathy emerges in the depiction of the colonists as the ones in command, able to name the Indians "friend" and to feed them, when historically such relations were often inverted. Although the poem was ostensibly written for children, it speaks vividly to the dominant culture's exploration—and confirmation—of power relations between Indians and whites, while it points toward the transformative power of the feminine.

In *The Country of the Pointed Firs* Jewett again attempts to arrive at an affirmative meeting of Indians, the feminine, and nature. At first Indians seem to signify a mysterious feminine wisdom that weaves women together in community. Hence, we see Mrs. Todd's affinity with herbs—and nature—"both wild and tame"; the world is her garden. Among the cures she distills is "the Indian remedy." Surrounded by mystery and "stealth," this "remedy" was probably an abortifacient; Mrs. Todd's favorite herb, pennyroyal, has been esteemed for that purpose for centuries.[34] Hence, this image of the Indian suggests a subversion of patriarchal control of women's bodies.

The blending of women's culture and nature reemerges in the story of Joanna's life on Shell-Heap Island. Mrs. Todd's friend Mrs. Fosdick tells the narrator that the island was "'counted a great place in old Indian times.'" Although the island seems benevolent, Mrs. Fosdick remembers a more threatening aspect:

> "Yes, I remember when they used to tell queer stories about Shell-Heap Island. Some said 'twas an old bangeing-place for the Indians, and an old chief resided there once that ruled the winds, and others said they'd always heard that once the Indians come down from up country an' left a captive there without any bo't, an' 'twas too far to swim across to Black Island, an' he lived there till he perished."[35]

Mrs. Todd enlarges on the captivity story, adding she has heard that the captive "walked the island after that" like a ghost.

Jewett undermines the fearfulness of the story, however, in Mrs. Todd's next remarks:

> "Anyway, there was Indians—you can see their shell-heap that named the island; and I've heard myself that 'twas one o' their cannibal places, but I never could believe it. There never was no cannibals on the coast o' Maine. All the Indians o' these regions are tame looking folks."[36]

Discounting the stories of the past, Mrs. Todd domesticates the wild in the concluding image of the passage, and Mrs. Fosdick's next remark locates it half a world away: "'Sakes alive, yes!' exclaimed Mrs. Fosdick. 'Ought to see them painted savages I've seen when I was young out in the South Sea Islands!'"[37]

As in Aldrich (and differently, in Howells), here the savage remains irrevocably other. Elizabeth Ammons observes, "Although the announced reading is meant to be friendly—Indians Mrs. Todd knows of are 'tame-looking'—the racism and ethnocentrism of this quick sketch are inescapable." Ammons goes on to point out the use of "totally familiar white stereotypes of Indians" in the passage: "They are lazy ('bangeing'), cruel (the abandoned captive), slippery (the comparison to Captain Littlepage's disappearing wraiths), and uncivilized (the cannibal theory)."[38]

In lieu of Indians, the island's inhabitant is a woman alone who makes, as Kolodny indicates, a garden in the wilderness. Joanna represents a distinctly different vision than that of most nineteenth-century pioneer women, however, for she is alone, apart from men, while she is connected spiritually to other women like a nun. She seems to become part of the wilderness herself, inviting the visiting minister to inspect the "old Indian remains" and wearing, as Mrs. Todd tells us, "some kind o' sandal-shoes out o' the fine rushes to wear on her feet; she stepped light an' nice in 'em as shoes."[39] Nevertheless, what happens here and in the book as a whole is not simply that women are associated with Indians: these white women in fact *replace* the Indians that seem so threatening, incorporating their herbal lore and displacing them in nature. As in *Deephaven,* Jewett's vision of racial mixing ultimately fails—there, because she privileges class, female aristocracy over "natural woman"; and here, because she hierarchizes race, domesticating and even colonizing nature to create a white woman's Eden.

In *Literary Friends and Acquaintance* William Dean Howells observes "how closely [Celia Thaxter] kept to her native field," adding, "Something strangely full and bright came to her verse from the mystical environment of the ocean, like the luxury of leaf and tint that it gave the narrower flower-plots of her native isles."[40] Although Howells characteristically emphasizes the sunny, "bright" aspects of Thaxter's poetry, we find that while she echoes her friend Jewett's relative idealism about nature, she balances it with moments of searing realism that critique the paradises of her more affluent friends.[41] While Indians are not an obvious text in her work—she makes only two explicit references to them in *Among the Isles of Shoals* (cat. 46)—the tension between civilized and savage, culture and nature, animates the book. In contrast to Kolodny, whose pioneer women seek to civilize a wild nature—or Jewett, whose female characters finally accomplish an appropriation of that nature—Thaxter accepts nature's wildness and seems to locate a more brutal savagery in Euro-American gender relations.

Thaxter spent much of her life literally in a space apart, an island, and her depiction of this life fleshes out in more detail than either Aldrich or Jewett the shadows of the real experience of being an islander, and in particular, a working woman. Her first book, *Among the Isles of Shoals,* envisions a problematic Eden patterned on her own sometimes

Fig. 5.7. *Isles of Shoals, New Hampshire. Photograph, 1900. Courtesy, Portsmouth Public Library.*

Fig. 5.8. *Haley cottage, Smuttynose, Isles of Shoals, New Hampshire. Photograph, 1875. Courtesy, Portsmouth Public Library.*

stormy life. Purity and wonder accompany Thaxter's childhood, but perhaps because she gives us an autobiography, in contrast to Aldrich's and Jewett's fictional or metaphorical "childhoods," she also speaks of nature's wildness: "In December the colors seem to fade out of the world . . . The great, cool, whispering, delicious sea, that encircled us with a thousand caresses the beautiful summer through, turns slowly our sullen and inveterate enemy"(fig. 5.7).[42] We shall see that Thaxter has a more complex view of the relationship between women and nature; but here her choice of "encircled" and "caresses" suggests maternal gestures; the summer sea rocks her as if in amniotic fluid. In the same passage, however, as an ungendered "enemy," often "raging with senseless fury," nature has its terrors.[43]

In the story of the shipwrecked sailors and cannibalism, Thaxter imagines these terrors through an indirect image for the Indian, as nature transforms white men into "fierce and reckless" savages. As Ammons notes about Jewett, cannibalism was a Euro-American stereotype for Native Americans. Equally devastating to civilized life is a cultural invention, alcohol. Alcohol and poverty combine with the hardships of nature to render the Isles' residents mad: "The misuse of strong drink still proves a whirlpool more awful than the worst terrors of the pitiless ocean that hems the islanders in." Alcohol renders the ostensibly civilized savage, and in the Isles' early history a missionary of the "Society for Propagating the Gospel among the Indians and Others in North America" attempts to convert the residents to temperance. In Thaxter's flawed Eden, nature, embodied in "the pitiless ocean," appears less malevolent than culture's "whirlpool," "strong drink," that afflicts white and Indian alike. Nevertheless, Thaxter imagines an alcoholic whom she reads about in racist and colonial terms: "an old man who lived alone and drank forty gallons of rum in twelve months,—some horrible old Caliban, no doubt." Shakespeare's Caliban embodied an aboriginal inhabitant of a remote island, a twisted and dark figure whose mother

was the witch Sycorax. Recalling Mrs. Fosdick's exclamation about the "painted savages" of the "South Sea Islands," Thaxter encodes the alcoholic as the "Indian."[44]

Thaxter erases here the fact that the disease of alchoholism was imported from Europe. Mary Jemison's narrative reverberates with anger and dismay at the destruction of her people due to alcohol; she remarks, "No people can live more happy than the Indians did in times of peace, before the introduction of spirituous liquors amongst them . . . The moral character of the Indian was . . . uncontaminated." Alcohol ultimately costs her the lives of her three sons, and she describes one of them in terms that repudiate the stereotype of the drunken Indian: "In his fits of drunkenness, Thomas seemed to lose all his natural reason, and to conduct like a wild or crazy man, without regard to relatives, decency, or propriety." Naturally peaceful and civilized, from Jemison's perspective Thomas and the tribe are contaminated by white culture.[45]

Uncritical about racial stereotypes, Thaxter is alert to Euro-American gender norms that as much as nature make women appear like savages. Describing the Isles' men in idealistic terms, she observes:

> It is strange that the sun and wind, which give such fine tints to the complexions of the lords of creation, should leave such hideous traces on the faces of women. When they are exposed to the same salt wind and clear sunshine they take the hue of dried fish, and become objects for men and angels to weep over.[46]

The difference in the sexes' appearances reflects not only nature's effects but the differences of their culturally defined labors; Thaxter ironically compares "the women, many of whom have grown old before their time with hard work and bitter cares, with hewing of wood and drawing of water, turning of fish on the flakes to dry in the sun, endless household work and the cares of maternity," with their "lords," who "lounged about the rocks in their scarlet shirts in the

Fig. 5.9. Childe Hassam, In the Garden, *1892. Oil on canvas; 22⅛ in. x 18⅛ in. Courtesy, National Museum of American Art, Smithsonian Institution, gift of John Gellatly.*

sun, or 'held up the walls of the meeting-house' . . . with their brawny shoulders." The former are "wrecks of humanity" of whom she catches "glimpses"—painful glimpses of the hard work in store for Thaxter herself as a woman. She concludes of them, "despoiled and hopeless visions, it seemed as if youth and joy could never have been theirs" (fig. 5.8).[47]

Thaxter's account is rendered more vivid and more poignant by a personal life in which she forever struggled to balance the requirements of her roles as a late nineteenth-century woman, wife, mother, and daughter, with the demands of her creativity. Early in her marriage she confided to a friend, "Patience at my household tasks leaves me forlorn, ugly, and horrid."[48] During the years of the salon on Appledore Island, she virtually managed the hotel. Ironically, Jane Vallier remarks that "the remote Isles of Shoals gave the second generation Transcendentalists a place to contemplate the glories of nature and escape the growing pressures of urban American life."[49] Ever attentive to her guests, Thaxter herself enjoyed little leisure for such contemplation.

The most telling comment on her domestic labor comes in a letter to her friend Annie Adams Fields. Exhausted with nursing her beloved mother she writes, "No sister, daughters, aunts, cousins, nothing but a howling wilderness of men! So it all comes on my shoulders."[50] In echoing Mary Rowlandson's captivity narrative, Thaxter underscores not only her sense of being held hostage, but also the brutality of her male "captors." Her angry vision here transforms white men into "Indians." That is, Thaxter takes the image of nature as Indian and male that white patriarchy allowed women writers and subverts it to include all men. In so doing she affirms that it is patriarchy itself, not nature, and not woman, that embodies and engenders—literally—the savage.[51]

In her later, idealistic (and not surprisingly more popular) book *An Island Garden,* and in the garden it describes (fig. 5.9), Thaxter attempts to recreate an Eden detached from a "howling wilderness of men." Her garden represents not, as Kolodny affirms of pioneer women, a space of family and community, but a space apart that allowed her to escape from the pressures of her family and distinguished guests. Yet even this "ideal" garden had its slugs, both literal and figurative: gardening was an acceptable form of women's artistry and self-expression in white middle-class Victorian America, and hence, this escape from patriarchal ideology is a contingent one.[52] It is as a writer that she is able to map out a more subversive and more sustaining space.

Nevertheless, in spite of a complex exploration of the affiliation between women and nature, an understanding of class as a determining factor in the perception of nature, an awareness of the flexible boundaries between nature and culture, and a powerful critique of patriarchy, Thaxter was not without the racism of the dominant society and ultimately, of the colonial revival spirit as we have seen it in certain works by Howells, Aldrich, and Jewett. If her cannibals, drunks, and captors were white men, they were also savage. All four writers attempt to create, in imagination or in reality, a space apart, a deep haven from the conflicts of the time. For Howells, that haven is a summer community away from the city; for Aldrich, a privileged childhood; for Jewett, a feminized rural community; and for Thaxter, an island garden. Although these spaces have different boundaries, they all have a sign at the gate: No Indians Admitted.

1 Sarah Orne Jewett, *Deephaven* (Boston: James R. Osgood, 1877), 74. All references are to this edition.

2 On colonial white male Americans and the land, see Annette Kolodny, *The Lay of the Land, Metaphor as Experience and History in American Life and Letters* (Chapel Hill: University of North Carolina Press, 1975).

3 See John Smith, *A True Relation of Such Occurrences and Accidents of Noate as Hath Happened in Virginia* (1608); Roger Williams, *A Key into the Language of America* (1643); Benjamin Franklin, "Remarks Concerning the Savages of North America" (1784); Thomas Jefferson, "Aborigines, Original Condition and Origin," *Notes on the State of Virginia* (1785); J. Hector St. John de Crevecoeur, *Letters From an American Farmer* (1782, 1793); and Herman Melville, *The Confidence-Man* (1857).

Roy Harvey Pearce, *Savagism and Civilization, A Study of the Indian and the American Mind* (Baltimore: Johns Hopkins University Press, 1965), 150. Pearce's study ends at 1851; nevertheless, many of his concepts point forward into the latter half of the nineteenth century.

Nathaniel Hawthorne, *The Scarlet Letter and Other Tales of the Puritans,* ed. Harry Levin (Boston: Houghton Mifflin, 1961), 181–212.

4 See Mary E. Wilkins, *Madelon* (New York: Harper Brothers, 1896); Wilkins, "Silence," in *Silence and Other Stories* (New York: Harper and Brothers, 1899); Helen Hunt Jackson, *A Century of Dishonor* (New York, 1881); Helen Hunt Jackson, *Ramona* (Boston: Roberts Brothers, 1884).

5 Thomas Nelson Page, untitled address, in *Agamenticus, Bristol, Gorgeana, York: An Oration Delivered by the Hon. James Phinney Baxter . . . on the Two Hundred and Fiftieth Anniversary of the Town* (York, Me.: Old York Historical and Improvement Society, 1904), 114; see Samuel Adams Drake, *Nooks and Corners of the New England Coast* (New York: Harper Brothers, 1875), 139–40, cited in Richard M. Candee's entry (cat. 5) in this volume; Maine Writers Research Club, *Maine Past and Present* (Boston: D.C. Heath, 1929), 34–35; David H. Watters, "Maine at Statehood: The Search for a National Style," in *Maine in the Early Republic, From Revolution to Statehood,* ed. Charles E. Clark, James S. Leamon, and Karen Bowden (Hanover, N.H.: University Press of New England, 1988).

6 Emma Lewis Coleman, *New England Captives Carried to Canada Between 1677 and 1760 during the French and Indian Wars* (Portland, Me.: Southworth Press, 1925).

7 Charles Edward Banks, ed., *History of York, Maine* (1931; reprint, Baltimore: Regional Publishing Company, 1967), 1:289; see also chap. 24, "The First and Second Indian Wars, 1675–1677, 1689–1692," 1:279–86, and 1:291, 293.

8 For examples of the work of another area writer who was deeply concerned with the relationship between humans and nature, see Alice Brown, "A Last Assembling," "The Way of Peace," and "A Second Marriage," in *Tiverton Tales* (Ridgewood, N.J.: Gregg Press, 1967). *Tiverton Tales* was originally published in 1899. Brown's personal history includes an Indian grandmother, Judith Runnels. See Dorothea Walker, *Alice Brown* (New York: Twayne, 1974), 22.

At this point I am assuming that the reader will be aware of the problematic and contingent nature of such terms as "savage" and "civilized" and hence will supply the quotation marks I have removed (except for direct quotations). Among the many people I would like to thank are Carolyn Eastman, PA, and Greg Colati, SB.

9 W.D. Howells, "Confessions of a Summer Colonist" in *Literature and Life: Studies* (New York: Harper and Brothers, 1902), 49; 54ff. See also his "From New York into New England" and "Stacatto Notes of a Vanished Summer" in the same volume, and Aldrich, *An Old Town by the Sea* (Boston: Houghton Mifflin, 1894).

10 Howells, "Confessions of a Summer Colonist," 53. "'St. Aspinquid, The Christian Indian,' based on an address by the Hon. E.C. Moody in the 1800s, rpt. 1912" (typescript, OYHS, 1912), 1; see also the following four typescripts in the vertical file, OYHS: "St. Aspinquid"; "St. Aspenquid (sic) of Agamenticus" (essays); anonymous, "York, Me, Agamenticus" (poem); John Albee, "St Aspenquid" (sic) (poem).

11 Pearce, Savagism and Civilization, 195. For a contrasting view of Story of a Bad Boy, see W.D. Howells, The Atlantic Monthly 25 (Jan. 1870): 124. See also David Watters, "Introduction," in Thomas Bailey Aldrich, The Story of a Bad Boy (1894; reprint, Hanover, N.H.: University Press of New England with SB Museum, 1990). On the relationship between Howells and Aldrich, see Kenneth S. Lynn, William Dean Howells, An American Life (New York: Harcourt Brace Jovanovich, 1971), 161–62.

12 John W. Crowley, The Mask of Fiction, Essays on W.D. Howells (Amherst: University of Massachusetts Press, 1989), 157–58. Thomas Bailey Aldrich, The Story of a Bad Boy (Boston: Houghton Mifflin, 1894), 7.

13 Aldrich, Story of a Bad Boy, 10. See James S. Olson and Raymond Wilson, Native Americans in the Twentieth Century (Urbana: University of Illinois Press, 1984), 40.

14 Aldrich, Story of a Bad Boy, 141ff.

15 Aldrich, Story of a Bad Boy, 160ff, 194.

16 Aldrich, Story of a Bad Boy, 249.

17 Aldrich, Story of a Bad Boy, 246.

18 Aldrich, Story of a Bad Boy, 233 (my emphasis).

19 Aldrich, Story of a Bad Boy, 22.

20 Crowley, The Mask of Fiction, 158.

21 Annette Kolodny, The Land Before Her, Fantasy and Experience of the American Frontiers, 1630–1860 (Chapel Hill: University of North Carolina Press, 1984). Kolodny focuses on the experience of the white middle and upper-middle class, who were much more likely to read and write than their Black, Indian, or working-class counterparts; hence her work is certainly applicable to the writers in this study.

22 Mary White Rowlandson, A True History of the Captivity and Restoration of Mrs. Mary Rowlandson, a Minister's Wife in New-England (London: Joseph Poole, 1682), 10; see Kolodny, Land Before Her, 17ff.

Phyllis Rogers, "Captivity, Transculturation and Puritan Society" (unpublished essay, Santa Cruz, Cal., Group for the Critical Study of Colonial Discourse, 1989), 13. Rogers discusses the Iroquois. See John D'Emilio and Estelle B. Freedman, Intimate Matters, A History of Sexuality in America (New York: Harper and Row, 1988), 3, 6–9, 31, 63, 86–93, 107–8, 187.

23 Rogers, "Captivity," 15–16. See also Kolodny, Land Before Her, 68–81; Frederick Turner, Beyond Geography: The Western Spirit Against the Wilderness (New York: Viking Press, 1980), 244; Pearce, Savagism and Civilization, 214. James E. Seaver, ed., A Narrative of the Life of Mrs. Mary Jemison (Syracuse, N.Y.: Syracuse University Press, 1990). The Seneca was a member tribe of the Iroquois Confederacy. George Abrams (in his "Preface," viii) disagrees with Kolodny about Jemison's age when she was taken captive. I am following what Jemison's account seems to indicate.

24 On the sexual politics of white-Indian relations and on the transformation of the captivity narrative and its reception over time, see Kolodny, Land Before Her, 17–89. That sexual prowess was at issue in white-Indian relations is clear in early white accounts of interracial marriage. James Axtell, ed., The Indian Peoples of Eastern America, A Documentary History of the Sexes (New York: Oxford University Press, 1981), 93–96.

25 Sometimes misguidedly, women reformers, mostly middle-class whites, promoted government services and missionary work to the Indians as a way of atoning for the atrocities of the past. See Mrs. Mary C. Todd, "Education of Indian Girls in the West," The Congress of Women, ed. Mary Kavanaugh Oldham Eagle (Boston: George M. Smith, 1894), 40. I am grateful to Cheryl Smith for directing me to this source.

26 Francis Otto Matthiessen, Sarah Orne Jewett (Boston: Houghton Mifflin, 1929), 47–48, 54, 118. On Jewett, nature, and industrialization, see Matthiessen, Sarah Orne Jewett, 20, 23, 149; and Sarah Way Sherman, Sarah Orne Jewett, an American Persephone (Hanover, N.H.: University Press of New England, 1989), 48.

27 Jewett, Deephaven, 203, 193. See also Sherman, Sarah Orne Jewett, 70, 118–53. Josephine Donovan, Sarah Orne Jewett (New York: Ungar, 1981), 33.

28 Kolodny, Land Before Her, 55ff; Jewett, Deephaven, 195.

29 Jewett, Deephaven, 202–3; for use of tobacco by native Americans, see Colin G. Calloway, Dawnland Encounters, Indians and Europeans in Northern New England (Hanover, N.H.: University Press of New England, 1991), 41; Howard S. Russell, Indian New England Before the Mayflower (Hanover, N.H.: University Press of New England, 1980), 158–61.

30 See Sherman, Sarah Orne Jewett, 137–39.

31 Jewett, Deephaven, 227–28.

32 Jewett, Deephaven, 232.

33 Sarah Orne Jewett, "York Garrison, 1640," Wide Awake 23, no. 1 (June 1886): 18–22. I am in debt to Jessie Ravage for locating this poem in manuscript and sharing her ideas on it, to Kevin Murphy for directing me to it, and especially to Special Collections Librarian P.A. Lenk of Colby College for supplying the reference for the published version.

34 For my earlier thoughts on Jewett's "mixing," see Karen Oakes, "'All that lay deepest in her heart': Reflections on Jewett, Gender, and Genre," Colby Library Quarterly 26, no. 1 (Sept. 1990): 152–60. Sarah Orne Jewett, The Country of the Pointed Firs and Other Stories (New York: W.W. Norton, 1981), 3, 4. Gwen L. Nagel, "'This prim corner of land where she was queen': Sarah Orne Jewett's New England Gardens," Colby Library Quarterly 22, no. 1 (Mar. 1986): 43–62.

35 Jewett, Country of the Pointed Firs, 63.

36 Jewett, Country of the Pointed Firs, 63.

37 Jewett, Country of the Pointed Firs, 64.

38 I am deeply grateful to Elizabeth Ammons for her generosity in sharing her work in progress and for reading a draft of this manuscript. Elizabeth Ammons, "Material Culture, Empire, and Jewett's Country of the Pointed Firs," forthcoming in New Essays on Country of the Pointed Firs, ed. June Howard (Cambridge: Cambridge University Press).

39 Jewett, Country of the Pointed Firs, 75.

40 William Dean Howells, Literary Friends and Acquaintance (New York: Harper and Brothers, 1901), 124.

41 Although Thaxter was ostensibly a member of the middle class by virtue of her education and family connections, the shape of her life suggests to me her affinity with working-class women.

42 Celia Thaxter, Among the Isles of Shoals (1873; reprint, Sanbornville, N.H.: Wake-Brook House, 1962), 96.

43 Thaxter, Among the Isles of Shoals, 98. Pauline Woodward, "Celia Thaxter's Love Poems," Colby Library Quarterly 23, no. 3 (Sept. 1987): 144–53.

44 Thaxter, Among the Isles of Shoals, 152, 52–53. See also Jewett, Deephaven, 66, 212.

45 Seaver, Narrative of the Life of Mrs. Mary Jemison, 48, 83.

46 Thaxter, Among the Isles of Shoals, 61–62.

47 Thaxter, Among the Isles of Shoals, 66.

48 Celia Thaxter, The Letters of Celia Thaxter, ed. Annie Fields and Rose Lamb (Boston: Houghton Mifflin, 1895), 4, cited in Jane E. Vallier, Poet on Demand: The Life, Letters, and Works of Celia Thaxter (Camden, Me.: Down East Books, 1982), 40.

49 Vallier, Poet on Demand, 18.

50 Thaxter, Letters, 49–50.

51 Vallier, Poet on Demand, 62ff., 84; see also Barbara White's "Foreword" to Vallier, Poet on Demand, xivff.

52 Celia Thaxter, An Island Garden (1894; reprint, Boston: Houghton Mifflin, 1988).

⊰ 45 ⊱

Thomas Bailey Aldrich (1836–1907)
The Story of a Bad Boy (1869)

Thomas Bailey Aldrich's wife, Lilian, wrote in her memoirs that *The Story of a Bad Boy* was told to her husband by the house of his school days when they summered there in 1868. She said, "the happy days of his boyhood spoke to him from every timber of that old home."[1] Rivermouth, the setting of the story, was Portsmouth; the "Nutter house" was his boyhood home (cat. 45); Tom Bailey was Aldrich himself. Aldrich's longtime friend and fellow editor, William Dean Howells, praised the story for its realism. At a time when boys' fiction depicted either the unlikely adventures of "youthful Natty Bumpos" or "impossible little prigs," Aldrich's memories of being a "not so very bad boy" provided him with an unusually realistic plot. Howells, while summering at Kittery Point in 1902, wrote to Aldrich, "You have no idea how your personality peoples Portsmouth for me with the young Aldrich. We are boys together there."[2]

Today we read *The Adventures of Tom Sawyer* and *Huckleberry Finn* as the epitome of real stories of American boyhood. But Aldrich's *Bad Boy* predates both books and was widely popular for many years after its publication in 1869. Not only did it go through multiple editions, but it was translated into several languages. When the author was traveling in Russia, he spotted a boy reading a book and asked what it was. Aldrich's interpreter reported it was *The Story of a Bad Boy*.[3]

The Story of a Bad Boy provides its reader with the optimistic tale of growing up in an older time in New England, not without occasional irreverence for Tom Bailey's elders and their traditions. For Tom Bailey, Sundays in the home of Grandfather Nutter are excruciating. Aldrich describes in hilarious detail his discomfort in observing two church services and eating the cold midday meal set out Saturday evening. In describing the venerable houses of Rivermouth he begins by saying, "Our ancestors were very worthy people, but their wall-papers were abominable."[4] Fifteen years later, however, when Aldrich wrote *An Old Town by the Sea* (cat. 49), he described the eighteenth-century wall decoration in Warner house in awed tones. By 1883 reverence had joined reminiscence to create a more somber style. Though the tone of *The Story of a Bad Boy* might be attributed to a younger intended audience, the tenor of each book strongly parallels that of his other work at each date. Aldrich in 1883 was more concerned about the loss of tradition than he had been in 1868.

Even in 1868, though, Aldrich tells his readers that Rivermouth is "the prettiest place in the world." He provides a description of Rivermouth touching on the landmarks and people of the colonial and Revolutionary periods. In his boy's imagination we meet the marquis de LaFayette, both as a young soldier and as an old man whose

Cat. 45. Thomas Bailey Aldrich house, Portsmouth, New Hampshire. Postcard, ca. 1910. Old York Historical Society.

heart still "holds its young love for liberty." John Hancock alights from his coach and climbs the steps of a Rivermouth mansion. Aldrich also makes sure his reader knows the author's own pedigree. He begins his description of the Nutter house by saying it has been in the family for nearly a century. Expanding upon the Nutter family's roots in Rivermouth, Aldrich describes the garrett of the family home:

> I need not tell a New England boy what a museum of curiosities is the garrett of a well-regulated New England house of fifty or sixty years' standing. Here meet together, as if by some preconcerted arrangement, all the broken-down chairs of the household, all the spavined tables . . . — who may hope to make an inventory of the numberless odds and ends collected in this bewildering lumber-room?[5]

The Nutter house became a house museum, the Thomas Bailey Aldrich Memorial, in June 1908 (cat. 54).

JR

1 Lilian Woodman Aldrich, *Crowding Memories* (New York: Houghton Mifflin, 1920), 110.

2 Ferris Greenslet, *The Life of Thomas Bailey Aldrich* (Boston and New York: Houghton Mifflin, 1908), 92. William Dean Howells to Thomas Bailey Aldrich, 1902, quoted in *Life in Letters of William Dean Howells*, ed. Mildred Howells (Garden City, N.Y.: Doubleday, Doran and Co., 1928), 2:159.

3 C.A. Hazlett, "Reminiscences of Portsmouth Authors," *Granite Monthly* 47, no. 4 (Apr. 1915): 37.

4 The manuscript for *The Story of a Bad Boy* was completed in 1868 and the work was first issued in serial form in 1869 in *Our Young Folks*, a children's magazine, beginning in the January issue (5, no. 1). The quotations here are from Thomas Bailey Aldrich, *The Story of a Bad Boy* (Boston: Houghton Mifflin, 1894), 35.

5 Aldrich, *Story of a Bad Boy*, 35–36.

Cat. 46. "Trap Dike, Appledore." From Among the Isles of Shoals *(1873). Old York Historical Society.*

CELIA THAXTER (1835–94)
Among the Isles of Shoals (1873)

Celia Thaxter's *Among the Isles of Shoals,* published in 1873, is a collection of four essays that appeared first in *The Atlantic Monthly* beginning in August 1869. John Greenleaf Whittier encouraged Thaxter to write about the Isles of Shoals because she was best equipped to write knowledgeably about every aspect of them as they had been before the advent of the hotels. He said, "It is thy Kismet. Thee must do it."[1] The book broadened the public's awareness of the Shoals. Perhaps its publication contributed to the startling growth in popularity of the Laighton hotels on both Appledore (cat. 46) and Star islands from the 1870s to the turn of the century.

Celia Thaxter's name first became tied to the Isles of Shoals in the 1860s when Nathaniel Hawthorne, in his *American Notebooks,* called her the "Miranda of the Isles," a reference to the island-bound maiden in Shakespeare's *Tempest.* Indeed her father, Thomas Laighton, was a suitable Prospero: like Miranda's father, he was a man discontented with society. Laighton moved his family to the remote White Island light in 1839 when Celia was just four years old. Before the family's exodus, however, he had bought four of the nine islands of the group with the intent of trying to revive the island fisheries and to begin developing the Shoals as a resort. His plans took nearly a decade to implement, and Celia with her younger brothers grew up on the Shoals with little knowledge of the larger world.

At sixteen, Celia married Levi Thaxter, her tutor and one of her father's early business associates, and the couple moved to the Boston suburbs. Her husband proved unable to support her and their three children so she performed a number of different acceptable forms of creative piece work within their home. Her work was often confined by the need to get a poem done quickly, a china bowl painted for a customer, or a quota of botanical drawings met.

Celia Thaxter became one of the best-loved poets of her era. In the 1860s, Houghton Mifflin refused Emily Dickinson's poetry on the grounds that they already had a female poet; Thaxter's first volume of poems was then in its sixteenth edition.[2]

Thaxter discovered her identity in the roles of poet, conversationalist, artist, and naturalist she played at the Shoals rather than in her marriage and life in the Boston suburbs. In her famous parlor at the Isles of Shoals Thaxter performed poetry readings for extra income. The oral, informal tone of *Among the Isles of Shoals* is reminiscent of a poetry reading, or perhaps an afternoon's walk with Thaxter leading the reader over the terrain of her beloved home, pointing out the sights and telling stories about them as they come to mind. The narrative flows easily from natural history to geology to history to architecture. Her descriptions are almost verbal pictures of the famous island views painted by Hassam and Brown.

Thaxter shows the reader the cellar holes of houses long gone, thus establishing the lengthy period of habitation on the Shoals and affirming their place in New England's history. Thaxter describes these cellar holes as if they are gardens of hedgerow plants sheltering in the lee of the walls. In these places where evidence of settlement lingers, however tenuously, the semblance of a garden remains as well. Thaxter gardened passionately all her life, fighting a combination of harsh weather and a lack of soil on Appledore. In *An Island Garden* (1893), she described her ordered garden as a place to find peace, to feel the turn of the season and the cycle of the day without external complications. She planted her famous plot mostly with old-fashioned plants like those she imagined New England settlers would have brought from old England. Like Jewett, the Tysons at Hamilton house, Alice Morse Earle, and countless other women of the era, Thaxter believed she was carrying on the colonial and matrilineal tradition of gardening into a new and confusing era. Not only did she find peace; she created meaningful simplicity with her choice of plants and their arrangement.

Change confused and unsettled Thaxter, like so many of her time. Despite uncertainty, she was unwilling to condemn change out of hand. Thaxter assessed the benefits of change when she discussed the Shoals. She observed that seasonal fluctuation had caused great hardship and isolation on the islands. In *Among the Isles of Shoals,* she describes the prematurely aged women on Star Island. Thaxter also relates child-rearing practices to poverty on the islands, and is certain that more harm is done for children than good. In the winter, some Shoalers get cabin fever and, in drunken frenzy, set fire to older houses. Though she regrets the loss of these antiquated buildings, they are replaced with white painted, green shuttered buildings whose "external smartness is indicative of bettering among the people."[3] Throughout her description of Shoaler habits, Thaxter's tone suggests that much might be improved in their material well-being through change of behavior.

The tenor of her discussion of time-honored customs differs greatly. Customs, the traditions that define the Shoaler personality, were threatened by the changes brought in part by her family's hotels. In an effort to preserve these invaluable parts of Shoaler heritage, she describes them, thus fixing them in time and defining their meaning, even though they may not persist in practice. At a time when folklore and anthropology were nascent disciplines, *Among the Isles of Shoals* earned her a reputation as an early practitioner in these fields.[4] She describes the unusual speech of the Shoalers, liberally sprinkled with obscenity and peculiarly accented. Thaxter tells how a young man who is courting hides in a hedge and showers his intended with stones to tell her he wishes to marry her. Cabbage parties, another Shoaler custom, are winter potlucks where each visitor brings ingredients for a communal meal. It is these behaviors that Thaxter hopes the Shoalers will not discard. These are the traditions upon which the islands' individual character is built.

Thaxter assumes that this individuality was originally fostered by the requirements of living in such a remote and rigorous location. *Among the Isles of Shoals* closes with a strong allusion to the colonization, both past and present, of the islands. She hopes that the Scandinavian settlers who have taken up the fishing industry on some of the smaller islands will create a successful settlement, "finally peopl[ing] the unoccupied portions of the Shoals with a colony that will be a credit to New England."[5] In this way, Thaxter finally connects the settlement activity of the 1870s with that of two centuries before.

JR

1 Quoted in Lyman Rutledge, *Lore and Legend of the Isles of Shoals* (Boston: The Star Island Corporation, 1971), 129.

2 Jane E. Vallier, *Poet on Demand: The Life, Letters, and Works of Celia Thaxter* (Camden, Me.: Down East Books, 1982), 101.

3 Celia Thaxter, *Among the Isles of Shoals* (Boston: Houghton Mifflin, 1873), 54–55.

4 Vallier, *Poet on Demand*, 77.

5 Thaxter, *Among the Isles of Shoals*, 184.

✧ 47 ✧

Sarah Orne Jewett (1849–1909)
Deephaven (1877)

Spending the summer away from the heat and complications of city life became increasingly popular among the Eastern middle and upper classes throughout the mid nineteenth century. Explaining the phenomenon of the summer movement, Harriet Beecher Stowe wrote in 1872:

> City people come to the country, not to sit in the best-parlor, and to see the nearest imitation of city-life, but to lie on the haymow, to swing in the barn, to form intimacy with the pigs, chickens, and ducks.[1]

Sarah Orne Jewett published a story in *The Atlantic Monthly* called "The Shore House" in 1873 about two young women who spend a summer in coastal Maine. This piece became "Kate Lancaster's Plan," the first part of *Deephaven*. In the story, Kate proposes to her friend Helen Denis that they spend the summer in Deephaven in her family's ancestral home rather than at a modish resort. Though in 1873 Jewett still lived in South Berwick, she had visited Newport,

Rhode Island, with friends and family, and knew the differences between such a place and the undeveloped Piscataqua region. Her narrator, Helen Denis, remarks, "Deephaven is utterly out of fashion."[2] Initially, Kate's family thinks the idea of going to Deephaven is outlandish because it isn't a fashionable summer destination, but after listening to the young women's arguments, they conclude with a hint of jealousy that "nothing could be pleasanter."[3]

William Dean Howells, Jewett's editor at *The Atlantic Monthly,* admired this sketch and urged her to write more. By 1876, he had proposed collecting them into a book. Jewett found the effort of reworking a number of discrete pieces into a whole tiring, and the editing took her nearly a year. In its final form, *Deephaven* provides a detailed picture of summering in rural New England in the 1870s. It chronicles the two young women's meetings with numerous country characters. They encounter rural poverty and pride, and discover a simpler existence than their own Boston lives. But when the weather chills and the autumn storms come up, they pack their belongings and head for the warm grates and social whirl of a Boston winter, not only rested, but also fortified with a broadened perspective of their heritage.

Houghton Mifflin published the first edition of *Deephaven* in 1877, and it was greeted with praise. John Greenleaf Whittier wrote to Jewett:

> I must thank thee for thy admirable book *Deephaven*. I have given several copies to friends, all of whom appreciate it highly, and I have just been reading it over for the *third* time. I know nothing better in our literature of the kind.[4]

Of the numerous editions of *Deephaven* published through the turn of the century, at least two were illustrated with scenes of the Yorks, South Berwick, and Portsmouth. James R. Osgood and Company published one with forty photographs taken by Emma Coleman (cat. 47). Houghton Mifflin produced an 1893 edition with drawings by Boston artists Charles and Marcia Oakes Woodbury (cat. 32).

Perhaps partly due to these illustrated editions, readers have sometimes assumed that Deephaven and York are one and the same. Indeed, during the summer of 1876, when Jewett was getting the manuscript ready, she wrote that though she associated York more and more with the village in her book, Deephaven had been "'made up' before [she] had ever stayed overnight in York, or knew and loved it as [she did] now."[5] Jewett thought that although fiction should closely follow real events and locations, it ought not to be identical. For her, fiction realized its ability to teach through representative rather than imitative illustrations of life. *Deephaven* so strongly suggests particular places that she felt it necessary to say that the book's setting was not one place but a culling from different Piscataqua region locales.

Deephaven's maritime past rather than its impoverished present rests heavily upon it. Kate and Helen look wistfully

Cat. 47. Emma Coleman, Sewall's Bridge, York River, ca. 1883–84. Photograph; 6¾ in. x 9¼ in. Published in Sarah Orne Jewett,
Deephaven (1885). Courtesy, Society for the Preservation of New England Antiquities.

at warehouses on the river and grand homes like the Brandon house where nothing was ever discarded. They like listening to the people talk of the past as if it were more real than the present day. One of Jewett's characters, Miss Chauncey, the mad but harmless daughter of a ruined West Indies merchant, bridges the gap between the two eras. With her elegant manners and fine diction, she stands for the proud old merchant aristocracy, but she has been broken by the economic changes of the region (cat. 47a).

The traditional ways speak of permanence and tradition. Helen, a Navy child with no roots, and Kate, a Brandon descendant who lives in the city where change is most profound, are searching for stability; Deephaven's rooted existence charms them both. Helen finds a past to latch onto; Kate discovers her heritage. By setting up housekeeping in Deephaven however temporarily, the two young women carry on ways of their maternal forebears. They carry the traditions of the New England past into their own generation, and come away from Deephaven with an enhanced sense of self through having identified and internalized their heritage.

This essentially optimistic framework conflicts with Jewett's clearly enunciated fear that all evidence of the Piscataqua region's past would be swept away in the path of the railway and the mills, such as those in Berwick. Like York in 1877, Deephaven is twelve miles from the iron road, and preserves its past through isolation. She concludes the book on a low note, saying:

Cat. 47a. Marcia Oakes Woodbury, Miss Sally Chauncey, ca. 1893.
From Sarah Orne Jewett, Deephaven (1893). Private collection.

By and by the Deephaven warehouses will fall and be used for firewood by the fisher-people, and the wharves will be worn away by the tides. The few old gentlefolks who still linger will be dead then; and I wonder if some day Kate Lancaster and I will go down to Deephaven for the sake of old times, and read the epitaphs in the burying-ground, look out to sea, and talk quietly about the girls who were so happy there one summer long before.[6]

Jewett said in the introduction to the 1893 edition that she had written *Deephaven* to encourage better understanding between city and country folk. She wanted summer people to know more about the territories they invaded seasonally. She wished that country dwellers would not use the income derived from the tourist trade to destroy the picturesque reminders of their maritime heritage. Not only did they remove the material evidence of this past, but they also removed what attracted the city dweller in the first place.

By 1893, Jewett had concluded that the summer movement had contributed greatly to the preservation of the artifacts of the New England past and a better understanding between urban and rural people.[7] She said that though some people would always be willing to dispense with their heritage, there would always remain a core of country people who would "preserve the best traditions of culture and of manners, from some divine inborn instinct toward what is simplest and best and purest."[8] For Jewett, this core stabilized the changing New England environment by becoming the keepers of tradition. Sarah Orne Jewett, a member of the rural aristocracy, a class threatened by the economic shifts of the post–Civil War era, perceived herself as a member of that group, and assigned herself a preservationist's role. Through her writing she described and fixed meaning to her heritage of New England customs and artifacts.

JR

1 Harriet Beecher Stowe, "The Lady Who Does Her Own Work," *House and Home Papers* (Boston, 1872), reprinted in Alan Trachtenberg, *Democratic Vistas* (New York: George Braziller, n.d.), 141.

2 Sarah Orne Jewett, *Deephaven* (Boston: Houghton Mifflin, 1893), 82.

3 Jewett, *Deephaven*, 14.

4 John Greenleaf Whittier to Sarah Orne Jewett, 1877, quoted in Francis Otto Matthiessen, *Sarah Orne Jewett* (Boston and New York: Houghton Mifflin, 1929), 56.

5 Sarah Orne Jewett to Horace Scudder, 1876, quoted in Matthiessen, *Sarah Orne Jewett*, 53.

6 Jewett, *Deephaven*, 304.

7 Sarah Orne Jewett to F.M. Hopkins, May 22, 1893, quoted in Carl J. Weber, ed., *Letters of Sarah Orne Jewett now in the Colby College Library* (Waterville, Me.: Colby College Press, 1947), 31–32.

8 Jewett, *Deephaven*, 5.

⟡ 48 ⟡

Sarah Orne Jewett (1849–1909)
"River Driftwood" (1881)

Sarah Orne Jewett's sketch, "River Driftwood," published first in 1881 in *The Atlantic Monthly*, discusses New England's proud traditions and the changes wrought by industrialization. These issues became recurrent themes throughout her work (cat. 48).

Jewett took the early advice of her father to write about what she knew and often used the Piscataqua region as a setting or inspiration. "River Driftwood" describes Jewett's home village of South Berwick using a formula Josephine Donovan calls a "village sketch." In the village sketch, the author takes the reader on a verbal tour of a locale, documenting its history through its landmarks and legends, its natural history, and possibly also its local characters.[1] The author hopes to preserve and fix meaning to these aspects of the place before they are irrevocably lost through change. The sketch provides not only a momentary view of the locale, but also a window on the author's mind and concerns.

Jewett was not the only writer to use the form—Celia Thaxter in *Among the Isles of Shoals* (cat. 46), Thomas Bailey Aldrich in *An Old Town by the Sea* (cat. 49), and to a lesser degree, William Dean Howells in studies published first in *The Atlantic Monthly*, and later collected in *Literature and Life: Studies* (cat. 51)—did as well. All of these examples are about Piscataqua region locales, and were first published either in *The Atlantic Monthly* or by Houghton Mifflin. Howells, an editor at *The Atlantic Monthly* from 1866 to 1881, encouraged his authors to write from experience rather than imagination. His "affirmative vision of country society and the importance of the commonplace" meshed well with the sensibilities of Aldrich, Jewett, and Thaxter.[2] Howells's able editorship encouraged these New England writers to write about what they considered best and most important from the places they lived.

Cat. 48. Sarah Orne Jewett. Photograph, ca. 1870. Courtesy, Society for the Preservation of New England Antiquities.

Cat. 48a. Portsmouth Manufacturing Company, South Berwick, Maine. Photograph, ca. 1870. Courtesy, Old Berwick Historical Society.

Jewett conducts her tour of South Berwick from a small rowboat on the eastern branch of the Piscataqua River. Her waterborne transport recalls in miniature the proud days of Berwick's maritime heritage when merchants and seamen derived their wealth from the West Indies trade. In those days the river was the highway of the inland village. Jewett's tour, however, begins in the part of the river now dammed above and below to power the Berwick mills. Her boat is trapped symbolically in its course by industrial change.

Jewett reminisces about scenes no longer to be found on the river. Once warehouses lined South Berwick's Lower Landing and many gundalows plied the tidal rivers of the Piscataqua region. Buildings personify history, providing tangible reminders of South Berwick's maritime past. Of the packet warehouse, a building once used for storing packet-boat shipments but demolished by 1881, Jewett writes, "It was like a little old woman who belonged to good family, now dead save herself; and who could remember a great many valuable people and events which everybody else had forgotten."[3]

Jewett finishes the sketch lamenting that South Berwick is no longer a seafaring town. Instead it has mills situated on the falls (cat. 48a). The railway, one of the most potent symbols of industrial and social change for the nineteenth century, has come to South Berwick. Jewett writes:

> [Berwick] is only a station on the railways, and it has after all these years, grown so little that it is hardly worth while for all the trains to stop. It is busy and it earns its living and enjoys itself, but it seems to me that its old days were its better days.[4]

While "River Driftwood" has the idiosyncratic feel of personal reminiscence, an article Jewett wrote in 1895 for the *New England Magazine* called "The Old Town of Berwick" (Jewett preferred to call South Berwick "Berwick" because it was the oldest of the Berwicks) has the air of documented history that robs her writing of much of its color. Nevertheless, this later piece illustrates how her concern with the New England traditions and industrial change developed during her career. Again, she discusses buildings and their importance as landmarks, and describes several in detail. By this time the facade of Berwick's meetinghouse had been modernized. The alteration caused Jewett to lament that:

> Changes are often made in good faith and with the best of intentions; but we must add to our inheri-

tance whatever will best represent our own time, without taking away anything which has the power to speak of old associations which are beyond all price . . . we Americans are only just beginning to value properly what has belonged to the past.[5]

By 1895, Jewett's interest in the past had become a national one with the blossoming of the colonial revival. Jewett thus concluded "The Old Town of Berwick" in a decidedly less pessimistic vein than she had "River Driftwood" fourteen years earlier. She wrote that not only had the standard of living risen, but "we are returning to some of the old standards of good taste and wider interest which we had at one time too hastily flung aside."[6]

JR

1 Josephine Donovan, "A Way of One's Own: The Writings of Sarah Orne Jewett," introduction to *The Best Short Stories of Sarah Orne Jewett* (Augusta, Me.: Lance Tapley Publishers, 1988), viii.

2 Jane Morrison, *Master Smart Woman* (Unity, Me.: North Country Press, 1988), 78.

3 Sarah Orne Jewett, "River Driftwood," *Atlantic Monthly* 48 (Oct. 1881): 504–5.

4 Jewett, "River Driftwood," 510.

5 Sarah Orne Jewett, "The Old Town of Berwick," *New England Magazine* 10 (July 1895): 606.

6 Jewett, "The Old Town of Berwick," 603.

❧ 49 ❧

THOMAS BAILEY ALDRICH (1836–1907)
An Old Town by the Sea (1883)

Thomas Bailey Aldrich's village sketch of his birthplace, Portsmouth (cat. 49), entitled *An Old Town by the Sea,* was first published in 1883 by Houghton Mifflin and flatteringly reviewed in the press. His slender volume is divided into chapters that describe a walk about Portsmouth—including the city's landmarks, buildings, and historic events—and a closing chapter on the death of local character. *Scribners' Magazine* published this last chapter as "Odd Sticks and Other Reflections" in January 1889. It opens with an allegorical tale:

The running of the first train over the Eastern Road from Boston to Portsmouth—it took place somewhat more than forty years ago—was attended by a serious accident. The accident occurred in the crowded station at the Portsmouth terminus, and was unobserved at the time. The catastrophe was followed, though not immediately, by death, and that also, curiously enough, was unobserved. Nevertheless, this initial train, freighted with so many hopes and the Directors of the Road, ran over and killed—LOCAL CHARACTER.[1]

Cat. 49. Puddle Dock, Portsmouth, New Hampshire. Photograph, ca. 1870. Courtesy, Historic Photograph Collection, Strawbery Banke Museum.

For Aldrich and his contemporaries, the railway was a potent symbol of industrial change. It brought places closer together, and encouraged homogenization of culture and custom while also being the product of industrial development. He claimed that the individual character of rural New England towns and villages grew more diluted with each passing decade as a result of the iron road. Therefore, Aldrich attempted to chronicle the venerable traditions and folk of places like Portsmouth and the effect change had upon them. Aldrich says:

> Everywhere in New England the impress of the past is fading out. The few old-fashioned men and women—quaint, shrewd, and racy of the soil—who linger in little, silvery-gray old homesteads strung along the New England roads and by-ways will shortly cease to exist as a class, save in the record of some such charming chronicler as Sarah Jewett, or Mary Wilkins, on whose sympathetic page they have already taken to themselves a remote air, an atmosphere of long-kept lavender and pennyroyal.[2]

As a native who left Portsmouth in the 1850s and returned for summers throughout the next two decades, Aldrich was acutely aware of the changes occurring in Portsmouth. He blamed the increasing immigration into America for the dilution of the New England character. Ethnic variety was no substitute for the prized quality of Yankee individuality. In 1880 he published *The Stillwater Tragedy,* the story of a stonecutting yard where an Italian organizes the laborers of northern European stock. Aldrich's prejudice against the Italian organizer clearly emerges as he condemns him for trying to effect change. In a similar vein, Aldrich's best-remembered poem today is "Unguarded Gates," written to support the institution of quotas barring immigration from southern and eastern Europe. In *An Old Town by the Sea* he says with a sense of doom that he expects in his time to see in Portsmouth a "Chinese policeman with a sandalwood club and a rice paper handkerchief, patroling Congress Street."[3] Clearly, he perceived immigration and industrialization as threats to New England traditions and individuality.

In part, Aldrich wrote *An Old Town by the Sea* to establish the details of Portsmouth's individuality. He describes its landmarks and historical attributes in loving detail, saying that enough eighteenth-century houses remained to "satisfy a moderate appetite for antiquity." Aldrich points out buildings with histories connected to the American Revolution rather than artistically significant examples of colonial architecture. He reminds the reader that though as venerable a patriot as George Washington found little to distinguish Portsmouth architecture, Aldrich's own century should venerate buildings with relationships to important events. To this end he chronicles not only where Washington slept while staying in Portsmouth, but also several members of the French nobility and lesser American patriots. For him some buildings even smell colonial. In a corner of the council chamber of the Wentworth mansion at Little Harbor he catches a hint of "colonial" punch. At Strawbery Banke, he is reminded of the stench of burning hayricks as he thinks of early settlers under Indian attack.

In this way Aldrich affirms his early association with his native city much as many Portsmouth natives did at the reunions and Old Home Weeks that grew increasingly popular in New England by the 1880s (see cat. 3). These events brought together natives of particular locales to reminisce and remind themselves of the importance of their heritage. Aldrich mentioned two such reunions in Portsmouth, in 1852 and 1873, in *An Old Town by the Sea.* The year the book was published, Aldrich wrote regretfully that he was unable to go to Portsmouth for the Return of the Sons. Of these gatherings, he said:

> What a strong sentiment it is that periodically impels us to flock back to [Portsmouth] from every point of the compass—making her the mecca of loving pilgrimages! We who are Portsmouth born and bred never get wholly away from the glamour of early association.[4]

Being a Portsmouth native enchants Aldrich with a sense of heritage. The place has a magnetism that draws him back periodically to renew the spell. Indeed, *An Old Town by the Sea* may be read as a reunion of the writer with his birthplace, providing him an opportunity to extoll and renew the special virtues of his New England background.

JR

1 Thomas Bailey Aldrich, *An Old Town by the Sea* (Boston: Houghton Mifflin, 1883), 105. Aldrich's work remained popular enough that in 1910, the Boston *Sunday Herald Magazine* reused the title "An Old Town by the Sea" for a travel piece on Portsmouth. The journalist relied heavily upon quotations from both this book and from *The Story of a Bad Boy* to describe the town, as if not trusting his own pen where Aldrich had already drawn the pictures so well.

2 Aldrich, *An Old Town by the Sea,* 122.

3 Aldrich, *An Old Town by the Sea,* 111–12.

4 Thomas Bailey Aldrich to unidentified recipient, 1883, quoted in Ferris Greenslet, *The Life of Thomas Bailey Aldrich* (Boston and New York: Houghton Mifflin, 1908), 16–17.

50

Sarah Orne Jewett (1849–1909)
The Tory Lover (1901)

For Sarah Orne Jewett, Hamilton house upon its eminence on the Piscataqua River embodied the spirit of her region's colonial past (cat. 50). She wrote about it in these terms as early as 1881 in her essay "River Driftwood"; by 1894 she was eagerly seeking some friend among her Boston social circle

Cat. 50. Charles Woodbury, Hamilton House, *South Berwick, Maine, ca. 1900.*
From Sarah Orne Jewett, The Tory Lover *(1901). Old York Historical Society.*

to purchase and preserve the place. Her friends Emily Tyson and Elise Tyson Vaughan bought the house in 1898 and began the process of turning it into a summer house replete with lattice covered wings and large colonial-style gardens.[1] Hamilton house and its gardens became a gathering place for many members of the Boston intellectual circle and the stage for many of Elise Tyson Vaughn's photographs. It also became the setting for Sarah Orne Jewett's historical ro-

mance about the American Revolution, *The Tory Lover,* published in 1901 by Houghton Mifflin.

For those who condemn Jewett as a romantic and minor female author, *The Tory Lover,* by contrast with her other work, clearly demonstrates how modern, real, and sure most of her writing is. She found writing the book hard, and it took her nearly a year to finish. She offered it to her longtime friend and erstwhile editor Horace Scudder, saying she felt very unsure of its quality though she was cautiously pleased with the result.[2] Early in her career Jewett had told Scudder she had difficulty with the novel form—she could visualize the setting and the plot, but had trouble bringing imagined characters to life.[3] In this, practically her last work, these problems overwhelmed her devoted but labored reworking of many of the legends and locales she knew and loved better than any other.

The Tory Lover was Jewett's only foray into the genre of historical romance. In 1895 she wrote, "There is no better way of learning American history than to find out what one can of the story of an old New England town."[4] Perhaps she felt this to be the most evocative genre to teach about the colonial past of the Piscataqua region. Beyond its evocative possibilities, romance also allows considerable freedom in manipulating history. Under Jewett's pen, the characters of the Piscataqua's colonial past assumed mythical proportions that amplified her profound belief in the historical importance of America's great men of the Revolution. Both John Paul Jones, the Piscataqua's local hero, and Benjamin Franklin play important parts in *The Tory Lover*'s denouement. Jones, in addition to acting the role of Revolutionary hero, also competes for the hand of the heroine, Mary Hamilton.

By introducing a fictional heroine native to South Berwick, Jewett devised a way to draw local players in the nation's history through Mary's network of friendships. In her article, "The Old Town of Berwick," Jewett provided simple biographies and the local lore for the two most prominent: Major Tilly Haggens, who built the Jewett house in South Berwick in 1774, and John Sullivan, veteran of both French and Irish conflicts. In *The Tory Lover* each becomes a caricature providing political views necessary to setting the colonial revival stage upon which the novel is set.

The stock patriotic sentiment of the colonial revival expressed in *The Tory Lover* seems out of place in Jewett because she did not approve of stating moral viewpoints explicitly in her work. She felt that plot, characterization, and style ought to inherently provide the writer's view. In this work, she violated this dictum in the interest of driving home the moral correctness of the American Revolution. Jewett describes the men gathered at the meal that opens the novel, saying "The faces gathered about the table were serious and full of character. They wore the look of men who would lay down their lives for the young country whose sons they were."[5] Master Sullivan tells Mary Hamilton that though he has been involved in great affairs in both France and Ireland, those of the American Revolution are the most stirring in his experience.[6] Mary Hamilton explains to British listeners that:

T'was not the loss of our tea or any trumpery tax; we have never been wanting in generosity, or hung back when we should play our part. We remembered all the old wrongs: our own timber rotting in our woods that we might not cut; our own waterfalls running to waste by your English law, lest we cripple the home manufactures. We were hurt to the heart, and were provoked to fight; we have turned now against such tyranny.[7]

Roger Wallingford, the title character, converts to the American cause because he admires his captain, Jones, and loves Mary Hamilton, both staunch patriots.

Beyond her characters, Jewett looked to the artifacts of the eighteenth century still visible in her time for confirmation of her vision of the events of the American Revolution. Hamilton house provided inspiration for the novel though it was built two years after the Treaty of Paris. She opened the novel by describing the legendary dinner held at Hamilton house to send off John Paul Jones on his first naval commission. Her own home and its first owner, Major Haggens, figure in the story, thus providing Jewett with her own piece of Piscataqua Revolutionary heritage. Like many intellectuals of the 1890s, Jewett discussed building preservation, architectural quality, and the preservation of traditional New England folkways in her letters and published writings. Preserving the artifacts of the past provided America with a memory. For Jewett, the past also furnished inspiration. *The Tory Lover* was her contribution to the effort to preserve the Revolutionary heritage of the Piscataqua region.

JR

1 Alan Emmet, "Hamilton House and its Gardens" (typescript, SPNEA, 1981), 5.

2 Sarah Orne Jewett to Horace Scudder, 1901?, quoted in Francis Otto Matthiessen, *Sarah Orne Jewett* (Boston and New York: Houghton Mifflin, 1919), 116–17.

3 Sarah Orne Jewett to Horace Scudder, July 13, 1873, quoted in Marjorie Pryse, "Introduction to the Norton Edition," in Sarah Orne Jewett, *The Country of the Pointed Firs* (New York and London: W.W. Norton, 1981), vii.

4 Sarah Orne Jewett, "The Old Town of Berwick," *New England Magazine* 10, no. 5 (July 1894): 606.

5 Sarah Orne Jewett, *The Tory Lover* (Boston: Houghton Mifflin, 1901), 7.

6 Jewett, *The Tory Lover*, 149.

7 Jewett, *The Tory Lover*, 314.

51

WILLIAM DEAN HOWELLS (1837–1920)
"Confessions of a Summer Colonist"
"Staccato Notes of a Vanished Summer"
"From New York into New England"
From *Literature and Life: Studies* (1902)

In June 1899 the *Old York Transcript* reminded its readers of the "splendid characterization of a typical Maine coast resort" William Dean Howells (cat. 51) had published in

The Atlantic Monthly the previous December. This study was "Confessions of a Summer Colonist," later collected in *Literature and Life: Studies* (1902), along with "Staccato Notes of a Vanished Summer" (1900), written about Kittery Point, and "From New York into New England." The *Transcript* noted with pleasure that the unnamed resort in "Confessions" was unmistakably York Harbor. At the same time, the newspaper lamented that Charles Dudley Warner, editor of New York's *Century Magazine* and also a summer visitor in the region, had not "found York sufficiently deserving for some such recognition of his pen."[1] The editorship at the *Transcript* celebrated the increasing tourist trade in York in the early years of the century, and Howells's contributions to the widely circulated *Atlantic Monthly* furnished wonderful advertisements for the Yorks.

From the 1860s, the Howells family summered in a number of New England locales, both hilly and coastal. "The Problem of Summer," another piece collected in *Literature and Life: Studies,* archly described the annual problem among Eastern middle-class families of choosing from the growing selection of summer resorts. Howells's tone suggested that his own family had had similar debates. In the late 1890s, the Howellses began summering in hotels in York Harbor. In 1902, they rented a house in Kittery Point belonging to George Wasson, an artist and author of

Cat. 51. *William Dean Howells. From Mrs. Thomas Bailey Aldrich,* Crowding Memories *(1920). Private collection.*

seafaring stories often published in *The Atlantic Monthly*. In October 1902, Howells wrote to his good friend Samuel Clemens, "On Saturday I went to Boston and got the deed of this place [house in Kittery Point]. I ought to have done it twenty-five years ago. But you can't think of everything."[2] He was so pleased with Kittery Point that he wrote a year later to Charles Eliot Norton, "I should like to spend the rest of my winters at Florence or Rome, and my summers at Kittery Point."[3]

By the time he purchased the Kittery Point property, Howells had lived in New York twenty years. Nevertheless, he and his family returned to New England each summer rather than shifting their summer base of operations to the Middle Atlantic's Long Island or Jersey Shore. Howells relished the sense of stability that New England's remote regions with their undiluted native tradition provided. In "From New York into New England," a third piece collected in *Literature and Life: Studies,* he advocated going to New England by overnight ferry, thus going to sleep in one land and waking up in another, and gaining the full effect of the difference between the two American regions.

Howells once wrote that New York was a "lighter minded civilization" than New England. It occupied itself with journalism while Boston was literary; New York looked to the future while New England maintained strong ties with its past. He described a young woman from New York who refused to see "the shy charm" of the houses and villages of the North Shore of Boston. She said they were "terrible, and she knew that in each of them was one of those dreary old women, or disappointed girls, or unhappy wives, or bereaved mothers, she had read of in Miss Wilkins' stories."[4] Although Howells admired the work of Mary Wilkins Freeman, he preferred to see New England's rural culture from Sarah Orne Jewett's window. Her more optimistic stories reflected the stern virtue, stable traditions, delicate humor, and optimism of rural New England that Howells found reassuring.

He found this culture in Kittery Point and wrote about it in "Staccato Notes of a Vanished Summer." This study depicts a community peopled by sturdy New England stock, proud and entrenched in their inherited traditions. He says:

> [Kittery Point] is quite untainted as yet by the summer cottages which have covered so much of the coast, and made it look as if the aesthetic suburbs of New York and Boston had gone ashore upon it. There are two or three old-fashioned summer hotels; but the summer life distinctly fails to characterize the place. The people live where their forefathers have lived for two hundred and fifty years.[5]

Howells sought this sort of locale rather than one like York Harbor where the new cottage architecture prevailed and the local people catered very much to the tourists. In "Confessions" he finds himself reflecting upon the effect the summer residents had upon the local populace, the architecture, and the economics of York. He describes the summer community of York Harbor, saying, "In a certain sort *fragile* is written all over our colony; as far as the visible body is concerned it is inexpressibly perishable; a fire and a high wind could sweep it all away."[6] If New York is light minded, York Harbor seems transient.

By using the word "colony" to describe York, Howells suggests a connection between summering away from the city and the tradition of the seventeenth-century New England settlers. Summer colonists sought a temporary change from the bustle of city schedules and reminders of the problems of industrialized America. For Howells, summers at Kittery Point represented uninterrupted periods of writing in his studio and digging in his vegetable garden. But he also participated in the social round of the Piscataqua summer season. He presented lectures in Portsmouth, and along with several other literary lights he performed a benefit reading in York Harbor in 1902. He visited the Spanish inmates at the prison in Portsmouth harbor and watched their mock bullfight. Howells was also credited with playing a major role in the campaign to save York's Old Gaol. Nevertheless, he writes in "Confessions" that he fears the day when someone would invite people for dinner at eight o'clock rather than the more informal hour of seven o'clock. He valued the less formal aspect of summer life away from the city, and wished not to see it disappear with increasing numbers of tourists. Writing in "Confessions," he says, "our summer colony is in that happy hour when the rudeness of the first summer conditions has been left far behind, and vulgar luxury has not yet cumbrously succeeded to a sort of sylvan distinction."[7]

For Howells, as with most of his contemporaries, even the most permanent-feeling rural New England community was a place for summers only. As with the young women in Sarah Orne Jewett's *Deephaven*, the city pulls the summer colonists at both Kittery Point and York Harbor back to their work and formal winter social round. By October only a few hardy souls, including Howells, remain, and though they regard the defectors with a "pity tinged with contempt" they know they too will soon leave. The casual, quaint atmosphere of summer's sociability has worn thin; its usefulness in restoring the city-weary has run its course for the year.

JR

1 "Summer People" *Old York Transcript,* June 1, 1899, 2.

2 *Life in Letters of William Dean Howells,* ed. Mildred Howells (Garden City, N.Y.: Doubleday, Doran, and Co., 1928), 2:162–63.

3 *Life in Letters of William Dean Howells,* 2:178.

4 William Dean Howells, "Puritanism in American Fiction," *Literature and Life: Studies* (New York: Harper and Brothers, 1902), 278–79.

5 William Dean Howells, "Staccato Notes of a Vanished Summer," *Literature and Life,* 256.

6 William Dean Howells, "Confessions of a Summer Colonist," *Literature and Life,* 45.

7 Howells, "Confessions of a Summer Colonist," 46.

⊰ 52 ⊱

ELIZABETH BISHOP PERKINS (1879–1952)
"The Codfish Ghost: The Biography of a House from the Seventeenth Century to the Present Day"
Unpublished manuscript, 1933
Old York Historical Society

In 1933, Elizabeth Bishop Perkins completed a manuscript called "The Codfish Ghost: The Biography of a House from the Seventeenth Century to the Present Day."[1] Perkins wrote the story as a romantic history of her summer home in York (cat. 52). By combining documentary evidence and local legends, she hoped to generate interest in her house as a historic landmark and tourist attraction, much as Nathaniel Hawthorne had done for the Old Gaol in York with *The Scarlet Letter* (1850) and Sarah Orne Jewett had done for Hamilton house in South Berwick with *The Tory Lover* (cat. 50). Although the story was never published, the manuscript documents her twin interests in preserving and publicizing the past.

As a young woman, Elizabeth Perkins wrote and published travel articles, society gossip columns, and a few short stories, with only limited success. Her interest in writing about historical subjects was spurred by a brief collaboration in 1924 with Mary Harrod Northend, the author of nineteen books and many articles on colonial homes and furnishings. Northend combined her love and knowledge of

Cat. 52. Cigar-store Indian guarding entrance to "tunnel," Elizabeth Perkins house, York, Maine. Photograph by Elizabeth B. Perkins, 1924. Old York Historical Society.

the past with a writing career, turning out articles "crammed with facts" on old jewelry, glass, figureheads, and doorways for magazines such as *Ladies' Home Journal* and *Good Housekeeping* at up to $250 each. Aging and unable to manage the business end of her work, Northend turned to Perkins for advice, assistance, and an occasional loan.[2]

In 1926, the year Northend died, Elizabeth Perkins sold a syndicated newspaper series called "Thumb Nail Sketches of Real Romance." Each piece was a 500–1,000 word biography of an historical figure. Twenty-six newspapers around the country bought at least one series, or four vignettes. Only the *Omaha Bee* bought more, running the series for four months.[3] Unlike Mary Harrod Northend, however, Elizabeth Perkins did not depend on writing for an income. Thus she was able to turn her attention to restoring her house in York and becoming increasingly active in the historical society there.

"The Codfish Ghost" is the history of the Perkins house, written in the style Perkins later characterized as "founded on fact, but woven with imagination."[4] The manuscript is divided into four parts, or four episodes in the life history of the house. In the seventeenth century, a man named Timothy murders his wife by hitting her with a salted codfish, then buries her in the cellar (cat. 52). Timothy flees, but the smell of salted cod—the "codfish ghost"—remains to plague later inhabitants. In the eighteenth century, a sea captain builds a smuggler's tunnel and stores his loot in a secret room in the cellar. In the nineteenth century, a young girl uses the secret room to hide a fugitive slave. Finally, a young woman buys the now-decrepit old house as a place to keep her family heirlooms. While restoring the house, she finds hand-beveled pine boards, small windows with greenish bubbled glass, a crane hook in the old fireplace, and ancient beams. With the help of a mysterious old man called "Grampy Baldwin," she also finds a diary, some gold watches, traces of the secret tunnel, and a treasure chart made by Captain Kidd that crumbles into dust before it can be read.

Most of these incidents have some basis in fact or local legend. The story of a man who lived on the site of the Perkins house and murdered his wife by beating her with a salted codfish first appeared in print in 1873.[5] It is a fact that one Timothy Yeales, who had a history of disorderly conduct, lived on the land from 1682 to 1689. However, he could not have murdered his wife, Naomi, since he predeceased her.[6] The house was later owned by a sea captain named John Pell, who was a privateer during the American Revolution.[7] Elizabeth Perkins herself exposed the beams in the dining room, which she believed to be the original part of the house, shortly before writing "The Codfish Ghost." And the nearby York River still gives off a suitably fishy smell when the winds and the tides are just right.

In writing "The Codfish Ghost," Elizabeth Perkins borrowed literary devices from Hawthorne's *Scarlet Letter,* as well as a character, the adulterous Hester Prynne, who appears as an inmate in the local jail. Hawthorne linked past and present in *The Scarlet Letter* by creating a narrative frame for the story. Working in the Old Customs House in Salem, the story's narrator finds an old parchment and a mysterious scarlet letter, elaborately embroidered in gold thread. The letter seems to burn as he holds it to his breast, and the brittle parchment tells Hester Prynne's tale. In similar fashion, the narrator of "The Codfish Ghost" finds a diary and four gold watches sealed up inside a brick oven. However, the main source of information for Perkins's narrator is Grampy Baldwin—possibly the spirit of the house itself—who guides her in recovering the past.

In 1938, Perkins asked to have the house listed as an historic site in the publicity materials used to bring tourists to York. Unable to claim any links with documented heroes or a literary muse, as the Tysons at Hamilton house could, Perkins argued that her house was still noteworthy because "there is unlimited material for stories, for the place is full of romance and history."[8] Earlier that year, she sent a copy of "The Codfish Ghost" to Florence Paul of York Village. Perkins admitted the fictional nature of the piece but emphasized that the story was part of the history of the house, saying, "It's the story told me many years ago which of course I have elaborated, but it's as accurate as any ghost story ever is."[9]

The tendency to embellish and romanticize, which was exaggerated in Elizabeth Perkins's historical writings, influenced her decorating and renovation choices at the Perkins house. The individual pieces of furniture and her dramatic arrangement of the dining room offer a visual representation of how Perkins sought to balance fact and fiction in her preservation efforts. The ghost story and the legendary smuggler's tunnel she attributed to the house were as much a part of her decorating scheme as the furnishings and room arrangements.

According to Elizabeth Perkins, facts and authenticity mattered less than making history come alive. She wanted people to care about history and about preserving artifacts and landmarks. Beneath the lurid surface of "The Codfish Ghost" is the message that old houses have a story to tell, and that history is waiting to be found, if you only look for it.

ANN

1   The manuscript is in the Perkins Coll., OYHS.

2   Mary Harrod Northend to Elizabeth Perkins, seventeen letters, Perkins Coll.

3   Elizabeth Perkins, notebook, Perkins Coll.

4   Elizabeth Perkins, "The Story of Lola Montez: Founded on Fact, but Woven with Imagination" (manuscript, Perkins Coll.).

5   G. Alex Emery, *Ancient City of Gorgeana and Modern Town of York (Me.), from its Earliest Settlement to the Present Time* (Boston: G. Alex Emery, 1873), 125.

6   Robert E. Moody, ed., *Province and Court Records of Maine* (Portland: Maine Historical Society, 1947), 3:306.

7   Charles Banks to Elizabeth Perkins, Aug. 14, 1927, Perkins Coll.

8   Elizabeth Perkins to Miss McClary, May 25, 1938, Perkins Coll.

9   Elizabeth Perkins to Florence Paul, Jan. 30, 1938, Perkins Coll.

VI
Exhibiting the Colonial

Fig. 6.1. "Sophia Turner, Curator and Jessamine Brooks at the Old Gaol Museum,"
York, Maine. Photograph by Marvin Breckinridge Patterson, ca. 1920.
Old York Historical Society.

Preceding page: "Old Gaol Vignette," York, Maine. Photograph, 1907. Old York
Historical Society; gift of Miss Dorothy M. Vaughan in memory of
Misses Jane and Vera Perkins.

The Politics of Preservation:
Historic House Museums in the Piscataqua Region

Kevin D. Murphy

In a 1933 publication of the American Association of Museums, Laurence Vail Coleman reflected that "our generation, naturally, has worked the territory it has claimed. Having taken over old houses for public education, the people are now administering them as agencies of instruction and inspiration—agencies of a new kind: *historic house museums*."[1] The development to which Coleman alludes began with early scattered projects like the preservation of George Washington's Virginia home by Ann Pamela Cunningham and the Mount Vernon Ladies' Association of the Union in the 1850s and gained momentum after the celebration of the centennial of American independence in 1876. From the vantage point of the early 1930s and the establishment of Colonial Williamsburg, Coleman could look back on an evolution of historic house museums that saw their numbers increase along with their professionalism and concern with accuracy.

As an institution, the historic house museum occupied a position where the public and private spheres overlapped. The house museum illustrated and memorialized a conception of history that emphasized domestic life and set aside more public dimensions of history. Although women had been construed as the moral and aesthetic guardians of the domestic environment during the nineteenth century and relegated to that domain, the growing association of the house museum with education and politics during the first three decades of the twentieth century saw women gradually parted from their initial control over these homelike institutions. The utility of the house museum for "instruction and inspiration" ultimately made it relevant to public issues, particularly the maintenance of Anglo-Saxon cultural dominance in the face of waves of immigration. And as the fields of architecture and history became increasingly professionalized through the early twentieth century, some historic house museums—which stood at the intersection of these two disciplines—became the purview of male professionals who displaced the authority of female amateurs.

Anne Higonnet has argued that the formation of house museums represented for women a socially sanctioned arena for the development and application of aesthetic discernment and administrative skills, calling the Isabella Stewart Gardner Museum in Boston "one of the 19th century's most outstanding examples of a brilliantly successful cultural strategy devised and executed by a woman."[2] Although Higonnet is most concerned with art museums established within domestic settings, her discussion of house museums as spheres in which women possessed a degree of authority that was denied them in other cultural, social, and political institutions can serve as an interpretive paradigm for the history of the Piscataqua region historic house museums.

In the field of historic preservation, a parallel debate on the role of women also informs the discussion. Charles B. Hosmer, Jr., writing in the 1960s, suggested that women abandoned the field of preservation as its emphasis shifted during the early twentieth century from sites of historical significance to buildings of architectural distinction. More recently, Gail Lee Dubrow has argued against Hosmer's interpretation of this issue:

> Evaluating the architectural significance of buildings, and then carrying out technically accurate restoration, required skills that architects alone claimed to possess. Yet for the most part, women found formal architectural education denied to them . . . By the 1930s, women had lost the organizational power that once had allowed them to define the content of preservation. Women in the preservation movement underwent much the same experience as women in medicine, law, and other fields in the process of professionalization. Institutional barriers effectively marginalized and eventually disempowered them.[3]

The difference of interpretation between Hosmer and Dubrow turns on the question of whether women "abandoned" the preservation field or whether they were forced out of it by male "experts." The institutional histories of the historic house museums in the Piscataqua region corroborate Dubrow's view, although they also show that women continued to play an important role in preservation through the 1940s. Women were entirely responsible for amassing and installing the collections of the Old Gaol in York between 1899 and 1900, but by the early 1930s their counterparts regularly called upon the advice of male architects and historians in restoring and furnishing the Macpheadris-Warner house in Portsmouth, although women continued to do most of the actual work (fig. 6.1).

Dubrow argues that the historic house museum provided a showcase for both women's skills and women's history. The content of the historic house museums of the Piscataqua region certainly drew attention to traditional women's roles in the home, yet the historical perspective presented in the houses also embodied many attitudes widely held by men during the same period. In particular, the house museums disseminated a view of history that tended to erase differences between members of the colonial community, to privilege the patriotic activities of men in the Revolutionary period, and to sanction the dominance of a handful of founding families. Such historical formulations were particularly useful to twentieth-century museum founders who felt their social and cultural authority to be at risk.

The address given by author Thomas Nelson Page on the occasion of the two-hundred-and-fiftieth anniversary of York in 1902 is shot through with expressions of such fears. He contrasts eighteenth-century colonists and their twentieth-century descendants who are "all of the same race" and all share "the same history" with immigrant populations elsewhere in the country:

> [These] large numbers of people of other races and with other traditions . . . have not the past that we have, but . . . bred under tyranny, have suddenly found themselves in a liberty which they know not how to appreciate or to preserve. They have become part of our body politic, but are alien as yet to its principles. They must either be absorbed into it or must be held aloof from it.[4]

The lessons of history were thus intended to inculcate the new arrivals with the values of the dominant culture. When such fear of political and cultural opposition escalated during the cold war era, Elizabeth Perkins asserted even more baldly the role that history could play in maintaining the social order. Looking back to the colonial period when "no atomic bomb disturbed the atmosphere," Perkins wrote in 1950: "At least we can hold on to history and landmarks [and] pray the generations of foreigners, hoodlums, and crack brain communists, do not destroy everything that stands for our American inheritance."[5]

Historical research and its physical manifestation in preservation projects in the Piscataqua region, as in the United States as a whole, thus served an ideological function for the members of the middle and upper classes who banded together for the purposes of saving old buildings. The historical institutions these groups formed differed in character from preservation organizations in Europe where, during the mid nineteenth century, strong central governments had taken the lead in restoring architectural monuments. Nonetheless, there was a degree of consistency between early preservation institutions throughout the West in how they used history to shore up the authority of the dominant culture while undercutting the legitimacy of those groups that challenged the status quo. Moreover, the emergence of a society comprised of heterogeneous elements was depicted in historic sites throughout the West as a peculiarly modern development; in the Piscataqua region the colonial period was portrayed as one in which

unchallenged agreement had prevailed among all members of the community. This misrepresentation of history corresponds to the model of institutional thinking proposed by Mary Douglas:

> That there was once a period of unquestioned legitimacy is the idea that our institutions use for stigmatizing subversive elements. By this astute ploy, the idea is given that incoherence and doubt are new arrivals, along with tramcars and electric light, unnatural intruders upon primeval trust in the idyllic small community. Whereas it is more plausible that human history is studded all the way from the beginning with nails driven into local coffins of authority.[6]

In the Piscataqua region there were prominent architectural expressions of social disorder—the York jail and the so-called "garrison" houses in York and Eliot, Maine, and Dover, New Hampshire—but early preservationists turned these buildings to their advantage and used them to demonstrate how resistance to the dominant culture had been effectively contained during the colonial period. Correspondingly, the inability to maintain a self-sufficient and homogeneous community was seen as the problem posed by modernity.

The promotion of colonial buildings as representations of a romanticized past began at least a quarter century before the designation of "museum" could be applied to any officially constituted institution in the Piscataqua region. The preservation movement began as the owners of the area's historic buildings opened their doors to travelers on an informal basis. When Arthur Little journeyed to Portsmouth and surrounding towns during the summer of 1877 he was able to gain access to the Moffatt-Ladd house and Sparhawk house in Kittery Point (which had recently been "restored" by its private owner), as well as to the Wentworth-Coolidge mansion in Little Harbor whose owner used broadsides to attract visiting tourists. Both of these houses were popularized on the bases of connection with colonial political figures, while the Wentworth-Coolidge mansion also had as part of its history a torrid love affair between the colonial governor and his maid. The Sayward-Wheeler house in York (cat. 14), although it had belonged to an important merchant rather than a political figure during the colonial period, was claimed by a correspondent of the Newburyport, Massachusetts, *Herald* in 1878 to be "as interesting as a visit to the residence of one of the old Colonial governors restored to its former splendor." Maintained by two aged sisters as a shrine to their forebears, the Sayward-Wheeler house and its grounds were described as being "as fresh as white paint could make them, everything indicating thrift, neatness, substantial antiquity and good taste."[7] The journalist could also have visited the nearby jail in York, where a tenant provided tours of the building to paying visitors. Undoubtedly, these early guides spread folktales about the imprisonment of witches and dramatic escapes that provided the foundations for the

Fig. 6.2. Emma Coleman, Old Jail in York, Maine with Old Church Spire, *1882. Photograph; 4¾ in x 7⁹⁄₁₆ in. Old York Historical Society.*

stories the Old Gaol was made to tell after its establishment as a museum.

The "rescue" or "restoration" of the Old Gaol (fig. 6.2) in 1900 thus signaled less a change in the interpretation of the building—although a collection of objects with local provenance was added—than a modification of its institutional status. The fact that the building was inhabited prior to 1900 suggests that its condition was not as dire as its preservers liked to assert, and that by preservation they meant not so much structural repair as institutional transformation: what the early preservationists gave to the Old Gaol was museum status and a governing committee to perpetuate the growing historical collections and seasonal displays.[8]

The effort to formalize the Old Gaol as an historic site was led by Mary Sowles Perkins, in 1899 a newcomer to the York summer community, and S. Elizabeth Burleigh Davidson, a year-round resident of the town. The two animators of the preservation project represented different segments of a socially and spatially stratified community, yet they shared membership in the upper-middle class and the interests that such a position would have entailed. Both women had a vested interest in the promotion of York's identity as a once important and prosperous seaport of the colonial period. In 1898 Mary Perkins and her daughter Elizabeth had purchased a house located on the York River,

removed from the more fashionable summer resort at York Harbor. The Perkinses boasted that theirs was the oldest residence in town and hoped that historical distinction would compensate for a less socially advantageous address. They assumed that history would confer prestige, and the celebration of the Old Gaol in the elaborate pageants that surrounded its opening as a museum could only have confirmed that equation. Elizabeth Davidson, whose husband owned a bank adjacent to the Old Gaol, and whose residence was also next door, benefitted from any physical improvements that might have been made to the building. Moreover, the establishment of the Old Gaol Museum signaled a degree of cultural attainment in the town of York which its prominent residents could only have welcomed.

After its opening as a museum during the summer of 1900, the Old Gaol continued to enjoy notoriety on the basis of its evocation of colonial techniques of punishment. However, during the 1907 season the institution's founders also appeared in the Gaol in old costumes to enact what were purported to be authentic colonial domestic rituals. By the turn of the century, spinning thread was viewed as the quintessential occupation of the virtuous colonial housewife and as such it found its way into the interpretation of the Old Gaol (fig. 6.3), as did a tea party (fig. 6.4). But women's history did not entirely displace male-dominated pursuits in the Old Gaol since displays of

Fig. 6.3. Old Gaol, York, Maine, built ca. 1719. Photograph, 1907. Old York Historical Society.

heraldry and firearms were also set up. Nor did the two women whom everyone acknowledged had done the bulk of the work in the project take prominent public roles in the ceremonies surrounding the opening of the Old Gaol. Praise for the efforts of Perkins and Davidson came from the male authors who gave speeches on the occasion, like William Dean Howells and Thomas Nelson Page, and from James T. Davidson who also addressed the crowd on opening day. A 1901 article on the Old Gaol portrays the women as having carried out ideas provided by the male leader of the local literary community:

It was Mr. William Dean Howells who suggested that the old jail ought to be saved . . .

"This is the oldest public building in this part of the world," remarked Mr. Howells, "and it is a very interesting place. Why can't something be done about it?"

One of the ladies of York, Mrs. Davidson, the banker's wife, was so impressed by these words that she induced her husband to hire the jail, and then, in co-operation with Mrs. Newton Perkins (who owns and lives in the oldest private house in the town),

Mrs. Davidson undertook to get up some entertainment to secure money for repairs.

"Let's have a lawn party at my house," said Mrs. Perkins. "Well," said Mr. Howells, slipping a bill into her hand, "I want to be your first patron."[9]

This final image encapsulates the point of the story. In establishing a museum in the Old Gaol, Mary Sowles Perkins and Elizabeth Burleigh Davidson were doing more than simply following through on concepts provided by men; they gained access to the economic capital controlled by men in order to advance their own cultural project. Following her husband's death, and perhaps as a result of having built skills and confidence in the field of preservation, Elizabeth Davidson became the first woman bank president in Maine.

A quarter century before Elizabeth Davidson's widowhood, another banker's wife, Annie E. Woodman of Dover, New Hampshire, had conceived of an institute for instruction in "literature, science and art" to be founded in her name with the proceeds of her estate. Her husband, Charles Woodman, had been the treasurer of the Strafford Savings Bank in Dover until his death in 1885. After that time, Annie

Fig. 6.4. Old Gaol, York, Maine, built ca. 1719. Photograph, 1907. Old York Historical Society.

Woodman used her "more than common capacity in business investments" to add to the $150,000 she had been left by her husband. Writing her will in 1886 she recommended "especially the study of the early history of Dover and of New Hampshire as a fitting object to be promoted by the operation of the Institute" and ordered that "its ministrations shall be made to conduce to the education, enlightenment, and entertainment of as many of the poor as possible."[10] Although museum founders in York were insulated from the social effects of industrialization, Woodman could have observed in Dover the growth of mills and factories and a corresponding influx of immigrant workers. Thus the Woodman Institute was intended to use local colonial history as a means of socializing the working class who threatened to destabilize the values for which Woodman and the members of her class stood.

The belief that by educating the working class the managerial class could preserve the social order was a central tenet of the turn-of-the-century reformers. Annie Woodman seems to have willed the resources for such efforts in 1885 but refrained from taking concrete measures to bring them about during her lifetime. Woodman "had no taste for social activities, and much less for social display, or any sort of demonstrative living."[11] Her death brought about the public articulation of her social and political intentions, as well as the institutional means by which she intended to have them implemented.

Woodman's posthumous reform initiative led Ellen Peavey Rounds to donate to the institute the William Dam garrison (cat. 5), claimed to be the oldest house in Dover, which she had "preserved" and "restored" as a private project. As part of this process she had amassed a collection of eight hundred objects which she arranged in the garrison to illustrate colonial domestic life (fig. 6.5). Consisting mainly of household furnishings, the collection was evidently important to Rounds who, in giving the garrison to the Woodman Institute, reserved the right to arrange the objects in the building for as long as she lived. The ability to shape this display of colonial domesticity provided Rounds with an important public role in the historical education of the community.

The "apartments" of the Dam garrison were a bastion of female control within the male-run Woodman Institute. The three men who served as executors of Annie Woodman's will, Col. Daniel Hall, Elisha R. Brown, and Judge Robert G. Pike, appropriated Ellen Rounds's

Fig. 6.5. *"Interior of the Garrison House, Dover, N.H." Photograph, ca. 1916. Courtesy, Woodman Institute Museum.*

preservation project as an integral component of the institute. Enshrined in an "artistic building" between two federal-period houses purchased by the Woodman trustees, the garrison was intended to dramatize the virtues of Dover's eighteenth-century inhabitants. In his address at the dedication of the Woodman Institute in 1916, Daniel Hall underscored the important socializing role which the garrison could play. Hall acknowledged that Dover had been "outstripped in growth and prosperity" by many cities, but he maintained that it was "typical of the best municipal life in New England" and projected that:

> If we could reconstruct that life, as in a large degree we can from the implements, utensils, and ordinary things of daily life, what a word picture they would show of what our ancestors did and thought, and how they lived one hundred, two hundred, and three hundred years ago. These souvenirs would show this town in its every-day clothes, as well as in its Sunday best, the plain living and high thinking that are the foundation of our New England life.[12]

Hall's speech is an acknowledgment of the cultural authority which the period room was perceived to possess by 1916. By that time, it would seem, domestic settings represented life in the "idyllic small community" of the past, which stood in diametrical opposition to the industrial city of the twentieth century.

Garrison houses were used during the nineteenth and early twentieth centuries to demonstrate how "plain living and high thinking" persisted among the colonists despite conflict with the Indians. The Dam garrison had "loopholes" in its exterior walls that were used to fire on advancing attackers, while the overhanging second story that is typical of the garrison-house type was believed to have provided a vantage point from which to pour water on burning arrows. The architectural features of the garrison thus provided an opportunity to show the superiority of colonists over the Native American population. At the time of the opening of the Dam garrison one observer suggested that

male colonists, in addition to sequestering women and children in garrisons, were themselves "compelled to pass much of their own time in inactivity, while perhaps the cattle were being killed in the pastures nearby, and the crops remained unharvested or were being destroyed by the Indians."[13] Their forced confinement in the garrison (the domestic, feminine sphere) suggested the symbolic emasculation of the male colonists in the eyes of this early twentieth-century writer. The reduction of the male settler to a state of passivity was not interpreted as evidence of the superiority of the Native American; instead, the defeat of the colonists showed the brutality of their opponents.

The incorporation of the William Dam garrison into Annie Woodman's reform project coincided with other preservation efforts in the Piscataqua region that likewise confirmed the growing recognition of the significance of historic house museums. Men came to play increasingly central roles in these projects as the institutions changed in character. Vernacular buildings like the Old Gaol or the Dam garrison that had been saved for their associations with a materially impoverished but morally superior colonial way of life became of less interest than the elaborate eighteenth-century residences of the mercantile elite of the Piscataqua region, "discovered" by architect-antiquarians during the 1870s. By the time that Wallace Nutting restored the Wentworth-Gardner house (cat. 56) in Portsmouth as part of his "Chain of Colonial Houses" in 1912–13, the history of American architecture had developed to the point where certain buildings could be preserved solely on the basis of aesthetic merit. Nutting's project, which as a money-making proposition is perhaps an anomaly in the history of historic house museums in the Piscataqua region, drew the attention of the Metropolitan Museum of Art to the elaborate carving found in the building. It is an indication of how little historical context mattered by 1918 that the Metropolitan could contemplate purchasing the Wentworth-Gardner house to remove its woodwork to New York.

The situation in the Piscataqua region prior to the First World War corroborates Dubrow's analysis of how the increasing importance attached to architectural significance in restored buildings brought about the marginalization of women preservationists. A clear illustration of this process can be seen in the preservation of the Moffatt-Ladd house (cat. 55) in Portsmouth which began when the Society of Colonial Dames leased the building in 1912. Built in 1764 by Captain John Moffatt for his son Samuel, the three-story Georgian mansion possesses elaborately carved interior detailing and an unusually large first-story stair hall.[14] Not only was the Moffatt-Ladd house distinguished by the fineness of its details, but it was also unique because of its nearly original condition; architect Philip Dana Orcutt commented in 1935 that "Until they entrusted it to the care of the Colonial Dames, the House has been continually enjoyed and kept up by the descendants of the man who built it."[15]

Fig. 6.6. Parlor, Moffatt-Ladd house, Portsmouth, New Hampshire, built 1764. Photograph, ca. 1914. Courtesy, Society for the Preservation of New England Antiquities.

The National Society of The Colonial Dames of America began in the 1890s and from the outset focused on preservation projects as a means of "Americanizing" immigrants and children. Among their early efforts was the restoration of the Van Cortlandt mansion in New York City which opened to the public in 1897.[16] Unlike the group of women who had organized to preserve the Old Gaol a decade earlier, the New Hampshire Dames who sought to make the Moffatt-Ladd house into an historic house museum operated under the aegis of a national women's organization which had proven abilities in the field of historic preservation. Yet the professionalization of the preservation field in the interim meant that the Colonial Dames used more outside advisors than their York counterparts. In 1900 it had been acceptable to furnish the Old Gaol in a way that suggested the colonial period, and nobody commented upon the accuracy of the effort. However, when the Moffatt-Ladd house was restored, the Colonial Dames consulted with Luke Vincent Lockwood, a lawyer and writer on American decorative arts. Between December 1912 and May 1913

Lockwood responded assuredly to a series of questions posed by the Dames concerning the interior treatment of the Moffatt-Ladd house, although he acknowledged that he was "advising simply from memory of the house" which he had "only seen two or three times." Many of Lockwood's recommendations were based more on aesthetic preferences than on documented historic treatments; for example, he advised "covering the furniture in the parlor with the blue. As your walls will be yellow, the contrast will be very good" (fig. 6.6).[17]

Although the Dames did not take all of his advice, Lockwood's involvement in the restoration of the Moffatt-Ladd house demonstrates the extent to which the shift in the preservation field from historical to aesthetic values had brought about the participation of male authorities by the second decade of the twentieth century. Yet these men did not do the real work of establishing historic house museums which continued to be founded and operated largely by women. The institutional history of the John Paul Jones house (fig. 6.7; see also cat. 57) in Portsmouth shows

Fig. 6.7. Stairhall, John Paul Jones house, Portsmouth, New Hampshire, built ca. 1758. Photograph, before 1920. Courtesy, Portsmouth Athenaeum.

how the period room persisted as a female domain. Led by restoration architect Joseph Everett Chandler and Woodbury Langdon, the movement to save the house from demolition or from the removal of some of its rooms to the Metropolitan Museum of Art culminated in Langdon's gift of the property to the Portsmouth Historical Society in 1919.

The John Paul Jones house was intended to serve as the headquarters of the Portsmouth Historical Society rather than as an illustration of colonial domestic life. The male organizers of the society hoped to assemble a collection of objects with local provenance, but never proposed to arrange them in ensembles representative of their use in the past, as had been done in historic house museums set up by women in the Piscataqua region. In 1920 the Reverend Alfred Gooding, president of the Portsmouth Historical Society, proposed that "Here [at the John Paul Jones house] we hope in the course of time to get together a most interesting and valuable collection of furniture, portraits, books, documents, china and silver connected with the history and the people of Portsmouth's long and significant past."[18] George Francis Dow, who had installed a series of period

rooms at the Essex Institute in Salem, Massachusetts, beginning in 1907,[19] addressed the Portsmouth Chamber of Commerce on behalf of the historical society and summarized: "the Jones House will be an administration house with a type [of] room display of furniture."[20]

Artifacts were used differently in the John Paul Jones house because the history they were supposed to represent was of a different order than that evoked by the Old Gaol or the Dam garrison. The perspective of the Portsmouth Historical Society paralleled more closely the outlook of other all-male organizations like the Maine Historical Society than it did the interpretation of the past that was presented by women in period rooms. Dow predicted in 1920: "You are going to have meetings during the year where papers will be read relating to Portsmouth— Portsmouth of the past, Portsmouth men, and very likely there will be light refreshments, and the ladies of your family will want to go."[21] The deeds of famous men, like John Paul Jones, were to be featured in lectures and memorialized in a proposed separate museum building dedicated to the veterans of the recent world war. Activities traditionally associated with women were not part of the history that would emerge in these contexts. The John Paul Jones house was instead conceived of as "a building architecturally of great interest and merit . . . and historically associated not only with the famous admiral by whose name it is now commonly known but also with noted Portsmouth families who have lived there."[22] Women would take interest in the monument to the extent that it occasioned social interaction.

The fact that the men of the Portsmouth Historical Society refrained from setting up period rooms in the John Paul Jones house suggests that this type of display was relegated to women preservationists carrying out the advice of professional architects, decorators, and historians, most of whom were male. It cannot be assumed, however, that women accepted their marginalization in the preservation field without a struggle. The preservation of the Macpheadris-Warner house (cat. 58) in Portsmouth shows the field in the process of being contested by women amateurs and men professionals. The project was initiated in 1931 by Edith Greenough Wendell, whose husband was Harvard literature professor Barrett Wendell, and grew out of the widespread recognition of the architectural importance of the house as well as its association with illustrious visitors like the marquis de Lafayette and, again, John Paul Jones. Wendell was successful in winning the financial support of established Portsmouth families and the volunteer work of women who were already experienced in the preservation of their own homes: Elizabeth Perkins of York and Elise Tyson Vaughan of South Berwick, among others.[23]

When Edith Wendell undertook this project, the reconstruction of Williamsburg had been under way for nearly five years. That highly publicized effort established a standard for restoration or reconstruction based on what was then considered the most thorough documentation possible. One Colonial Williamsburg publication described an almost obsessive research process, explaining that while post-Revolutionary buildings were demolished,

> a staff of research workers was exploring libraries, archives and museums all over the country, and in England and France, to discover the data needed to rebuild, and in some cases to refurnish, with meticulous authenticity the missing 18th century buildings. At the same time, skilled architects and builders were making the detailed studies required to repair and restore the remaining colonial structures, and archaeologists were examining, spadeful by spadeful, the ground upon which the original buildings stood.[24]

The result of such exacting study by "skilled" professionals would be the plausible recreation of the eighteenth century. With this model doubtless in mind, Edith Wendell named an Advisory Committee for the Warner House Association in 1934 which included professional architect-historians Norman Isham, Joseph E. Chandler, John Mead Howells, and Philip Dana Orcutt. All eleven members of the Advisory Committee were men.[25]

The validation of architects may have been desirable by the early thirties, but that did not mean that women organizers were no longer essential to the establishment of historic house museums. Edith Wendell knew the contemporary climate well enough to hire professional expertise, but did not completely abdicate responsibility for decisions that would be made as the Macpheadris-Warner house was restored. Elizabeth Perkins noted in her diary in 1933 that "Mrs. Wendell has given all orders to paint and to furnish as she likes and [is] making many mistakes. Mr. Orcutt and Mrs. Patterson from the Society for the Preservation of New England Antiquities are trying to guide her, but she won't listen."[26] William Sumner Appleton recognized that Wendell was "a tremendous asset but otherwise a dangerous woman . . . perhaps her greatest failing is her inability to appreciate anything that isn't spic and span, neat and clean, and lovely and beautiful according to her own ideas of what she would like to live with" (fig. 6.8).[27] Although she was roundly criticized for flouting standards of historical accuracy and for resisting the deferential attitude she was expected to display toward preservation professionals, Edith Wendell was central to the restoration of the Warner house. When she failed to return to Portsmouth for the summer of 1935, attendance dropped from around 1,000 the previous year to between 650 and 700 for the 1935 season. When Wendell returned the following year, the Secretary's report began in a tone of relief: "The Governors of the Warner House are glad to have Mrs. Wendell with them once more after her absence in Europe in 1935." With Edith Wendell once again promoting the organization, attendance surpassed earlier levels to reach 1,325 visitors for 1936.[28]

If resistance to the professionalization of historic preservation was only scattered, and it was no longer sufficient after Williamsburg to create pleasing period-room settings that evoked the colonial in an impressionistic way, women nonetheless continued to play important roles in the founding of historic house museums. They possessed organizational skills and innovative ideas for what might now be called "adaptive reuse projects." Elizabeth Perkins planned the removal of Jefferds Tavern from Kennebunk to York around 1940 and explained: "We want to open it to the public as a museum of what a tavern was in 1750 and to be able to earn some money for its upkeep by serving tea . . . and also some of the old time drinks instead of the everlasting road side 'tonics.'"[29] Even if she did feel compelled to seek the advise of York architect Howard Peck, it was Elizabeth Perkins who conceived of the educational purposes of her museum and the economic arrangements that would make them feasible.

The establishment of Colonial Williamsburg signaled the enstatement of architectural significance and new standards of historical authenticity as the criteria by which preservation projects were judged by the early 1930s. But John D. Rockefeller, Jr.'s massive undertaking did not overturn the ideological premises on which historic house

Fig. 6.8. Dining room, Macpheadris-Warner house, Portsmouth, New Hampshire, built 1716. Photograph by Douglas Armsden, ca. 1940. Courtesy, Warner House Association.

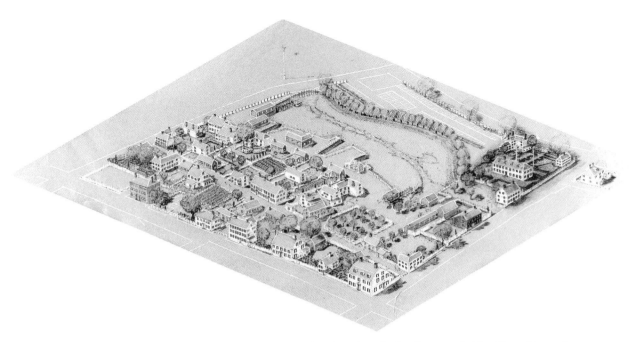

Fig. 6.9. Perry, Shaw, Hepburn, and Dean, Site Plan, Strawbery Banke, *Portsmouth, New Hampshire, 1963. Pencil on paper; 22 in. x 34 in. Courtesy, Strawbery Banke Museum.*

museums had previously been founded. In a publication subtitled "How the restoration of the historic city of Williamsburg to its 18th century appearance is helping to keep Americans 'Americans,'" Colonial Williamsburg anticipated visits by "many of America's naturalized citizens" and patriotic veterans.[30] By viewing the reconstruction, newcomers would be inculcated with the ideals associated with the colonial period and war heroes would find affirmation of their own beliefs. Historical importance and architectural significance were therefore not mutually exclusive categories; in fact, the discourses of both served to separate "real" Americans from new arrivals. If at first cultural authority had been based on a genealogical connection with well-known historic personages, by the 1920s that distinction had also been projected onto the field of aesthetics. Superior architectural examples were seen as the products of outstanding individuals.

Colonial Williamsburg brought to the Piscataqua region more than just a new appreciation for architectural quality and a desire to make preservation into a dispassionate science; it also provided a model for the establishment of a "colonial village" that eventually became Strawbery Banke Museum (fig. 6.9). The concept of an outdoor museum that would comprise the most architecturally distinguished but most dismally blighted neighborhood of Portsmouth was advanced by the National Park Service as a Works Progress Administration project during the 1930s in response to studies by architects John Mead Howells and Fiske Kimball that had brought attention to the wealth of historic buildings in the area. However, the project did not

actually get off the ground until 1957 when, after a proposal by the Department of Housing and Urban Development to demolish the entire area, Portsmouth librarian Dorothy M. Vaughan addressed the Rotary Club on "The History of Portsmouth and Its Potential as a Tourist Attraction." While Vaughan encouraged local concern over the loss of historic Portsmouth buildings, Jeremy R. Waldron and James B. Smith prepared a report which proposed a museum village as a solution to the preservation problem and substituted a village of restored buildings for a group of "garden" apartments which the Urban Renewal Administration intended to build in the Puddle Dock neighborhood.[31]

The example of Williamsburg as a well-attended large-scale restoration was undoubtedly in the minds of Vaughan, Waldron, and Smith when they proposed the establishment of a museum at Strawbery Banke. The museum's lineage was also clear in the choice of the firm of Perry, Shaw, Hepburn, and Dean, architects of Colonial Williamsburg, as planners for Strawbery Banke. While Dorothy Vaughan had been responsible for drawing attention to the architectural significance of the neighborhood, a professional architect, William G. Perry, was employed to actually point out which buildings were significant enough to be restored.[32] This division of responsibility follows the pattern observed in earlier Piscataqua-area preservation projects. Moreover, Strawbery Banke performed the same functions as had earlier restoration efforts in the area: the museum was promoted on the grounds of the tourism it would stimulate. Not only was Strawbery Banke intended to present a picture of the past that would mitigate the problems of the present as earlier historic houses had, the sanitized "colonial village" physically displaced the working-class Puddle Dock neighborhood which was perceived as ugly and dangerous.

The origin of Strawbery Banke Museum confirms the pattern of ideological intentions held by early preservationists in the Piscataqua region. Between 1900 and the 1950s groups formed in the area to control buildings belonging to famous people or to the canon of American architecture, and established institutions that promoted the dominance of an elite Anglo-Saxon culture. The accomplishment of this work was consistently dependent upon the efforts of women, despite the erosion of their authority that came with the professionalization of preservation. In this way, preservation provided a field in which women could play active roles in the community. But at the same time, the institutions founded by women preservationists also served to reinforce the relations of power established by men in social, political, and economic realms.

1 Laurence Vail Coleman, *Historic House Museums* (Washington, D.C.: American Association of Museums, 1933), 20. Marina Moskowitz brought this source to my attention.

2 Anne Higonnet, "Museums: Where There's a Will . . . ," *Art in America* 77, no. 5 (May 1989): 69. Higonnet also discussed these themes in a paper entitled "Women's House-Museums: Founders, Spaces and Strategies" presented at the forty-third annual meeting of the Society of Architectural Historians, Boston, Mar. 28–Apr. 1, 1990.

3 Gail Lee Dubrow, "Restoring a Female Presence, New Goals in Historic Preservation," in *Architecture, A Place for Women,* ed. Ellen Perry Berkeley (Washington and London: Smithsonian Institution Press, 1989), 163–64.

4 "Thomas Nelson Page's Address" in *Agamenticus, Bristol, Gorgeana, York: An Oration Delivered by the Hon. James Phinney Baxter . . . on the Two Hundred and Fiftieth Anniversary of the Town* (York, Me.: Old York Historical and Improvement Society, 1904), 116–17.

5 Elizabeth Perkins to William Wendell, June 8, 1950, William Wendell Correspondence, PA. I would like to thank Kari Federer and Kevin Shupe for making this correspondence known to me.

6 Mary Douglas, *How Institutions Think* (Syracuse, N.Y.: Syracuse University Press, 1986), 94–95.

7 The account from the Newburyport *Herald* is quoted at length in *The Union and Journal* (Biddeford, Me.), Aug. 9, 1878, 2. The Dam garrison was reportedly visited by many people during its last twenty years of private ownership by Ellen Peavey Rounds, between the mid-1880s and its donation to the Woodman Institute in 1915. See *Catalogue of Articles in Ye William Dam Garrison at the Woodman Institute, Dover, N.H., 1917* (Dover, N.H.: Charles F. Whitehouse, 1917), 5.

8 The Old Gaol Museum was run by the Old Gaol Committee of the Old York Historical and Improvement Society until the consolidation of York's three historical organizations in 1984.

9 Pauline Carrington Bouvé, "Women Welcome Visitors Where Witches Were Confined," *The Sunday Herald* (Boston), Aug. 25, 1901, 37.

10 "Address of Daniel Hall" in *Dedication Ceremonies on July 26, 1916: The Annie E. Woodman Institute* (Concord, N.H.: Rumford Press, 1916), 14–17.

11 "Address of Daniel Hall," 13–14.

12 "Address of Daniel Hall," 23.

13 "Account of the Will and a Description of the Institute," from the *Dover Democrat,* Aug. 10, 1916, reprinted in *Dedication Ceremonies on July 26, 1916: The Annie E. Woodman Institute,* 6–7.

14 See Jane C. Giffen, "The Moffatt-Ladd House," Parts 1 and 2, *Connoisseur* 175, nos. 704–5 (Oct. and Nov. 1970): 113–22, 201–7.

15 Philip Dana Orcutt, *The Moffatt-Ladd House: Its Garden and Its Period, 1763, Portsmouth, New Hampshire* (Norwood, Mass.: Plimpton Press for the New Hampshire Society of Colonial Dames of America, 1935), 37.

16 Charles B. Hosmer, Jr., *Presence of the Past: A History of the Preservation Movement in the United States Before Williamsburg* (New York: G.P. Putnam's, 1965), 131–39.

17 Luke Vincent Lockwood to Mrs. James R. May, Jan. 27, 1913, Moffatt-Ladd House Archives. Also see Lockwood's letters to Mrs. James F. May of Dec. 18, 1912, and May 5, 1913, in the same collection.

18 Quoted in "Facts about the Historical Society," *Portsmouth Chronicle,* Jan. 30, 1920, clippings file, PA.

19 On Dow, see Hosmer, *Presence of the Past,* 213–15.

20 Quoted in "Facts about the Historical Society."

21 Quoted in "Facts about the Historical Society." Elizabeth J. Miller has pointed out that the Maine Historical Society enlisted the help of women's organizations like the D.A.R. and the Colonial Dames when it was left the Wadsworth-Longfellow house by Anne Longfellow Pierce in 1901. Women were first admitted as members of the society in 1909. See Elizabeth J. Miller, "The First 100 Years of the Maine Historical Society, 1822–1922," *Maine Historical Society Quarterly* 26, no. 4 (Spring 1987): 199–200.

22 The Rev. Alfred Gooding, quoted in "Society Opens New Exhibition Room," *Portsmouth Herald,* Sept. 18, 1924, clippings file, PA.

23 Kari Federer, "It's a Small World: Elizabeth Perkins in the Historic Preservation Movement" (typescript, OYHS, 1989).

24 Colonial Williamsburg, *Preserving the Design for Americans* (Williamsburg, Va.: Colonial Williamsburg, [ca. 1945]), 9.

25 "Warner House Records, Sept. 1931 to June 24, 1954," 49, PA. The minutes of a meeting held Sept. 13, 1933, state: "Mrs. Wendell read the report of Mr. Norman M. Isham on what he considered the correct restoration of the house, and Mrs. Wendell also read a letter from Mr. Fletcher Steel [*sic*] on the subject of old paint on woodwork and walls and the manner in which they should be treated" (35).

26 Diary entry, Elizabeth Perkins, June 27, 1933, Perkins Coll., OYHS.

27 Quoted in Charles B. Hosmer, Jr., *Preservation Comes of Age* (Charlottesville, Va.: Preservation Press, 1981), 1:134.

28 "Warner House Records," 47, 57, 69.

29 Elizabeth Perkins to Lucius Knowles Thayer, [1940], Perkins Coll.

30 Colonial Williamsburg, *Preserving the Design for Americans,* 20.

31 Strawbery Banke, Inc., *Strawbery Banke in Portsmouth, New Hampshire* (Portsmouth, N.H.: Strawbery Banke, Inc., 1971), xviii, and "Chronology Goes Back to 1953," *Portsmouth Herald,* May 28, 1965, 20-A.

32 *Strawbery Banke in Portsmouth, New Hampshire,* xix.

53

OLD GAOL MUSEUM
York, Maine, 1719
Opened 1900

Research by antiquarians at the turn of the century into town and court records revealed that a prison had been ordered built in York in 1653; the existing structure—referred to variously as the "jail," the "King's Prison," and ultimately the "Old Gaol"—was assumed to date from that period. More recent research has shown, however, that the Old Gaol is the result of a series of building campaigns that began with the construction of two stone cells in 1719 and continued through the first decade of the nineteenth century. The most significant addition came in 1729 when living quarters for the jailer and his family were built in the form of a one-and-one-half story, hall-and-parlor house appended to the east side of the cells.[1]

The Old Gaol was undoubtedly a well-known local landmark from the time of its construction due to its public function and location at the center of York Village. Yet the notoriety of the building grew after 1860 as it fell into disuse as a jail and as its associations with macabre disciplinary practices of the colonial period became increasingly well known. The building seemed to excite in the imaginations of late nineteenth-century viewers visions of brutal punishments which made the treatment received by criminals in the modern period seem permissive.

One of the earliest widely published accounts of the Gaol as an historic landmark appeared in the centennial year, 1876. In *Nooks and Corners of the New England Coast,* Samuel Adams Drake wrote of the Gaol that:

It is a quaint old structure, and has held many culprits in former times, when York was the seat of justice for the county, though it would not keep your modern burglar an hour. It is perched, like a bird of ill omen, on a rocky ledge, where all might see it passing over the high-road. Thus, in the early day, the traveler on entering the county town encountered, first, the stocks and whipping-post; continuing on his route, he in due time came to the gallows at the town's end. The exterior of the jail is not especially repulsive, now that it is no longer a prison; but the inside is a relic of barbarism—just such a place as I have often imagined the miserable witchcraft prisoners might have been confined in. The back wall is of stone. The doors are six inches of solid oak, studded with heavy nails; the gratings secured with the blades of mill saws, having the jagged teeth upward; the sills, locks, and bolts are ponderous, and unlike any thing the present century has produced.[2]

Drake's account set the tone for many later articles about the Gaol by focusing on those elements of the building that

Cat. 53. Old Gaol, York, Maine, built ca. 1719. Photograph, ca. 1890. Old York Historical Society.

made its history seem particularly grisly and by comparing the historic structure with its less secure modern counterpart in Alfred.

On September 19, 1890, the *Eastern Star,* a Kennebunk, Maine, newspaper, confirmed that:

The old jail [cat. 53] at York . . . stands today practically unchanged, with its massive oaken doors, creaking hinges, and locks and mill-saw gratings. A correspondent says:—It has held evil doers of all classes, and many true and amusing stories of incidents and escapes can be related. It is eminently the duty of the town of York, whose property it is, to see that this venerable landmark is for all time kept in its original form and in good repair.

Evidently such press coverage of its most well-known landmark prompted the town to make repairs. Three months later, on December 26, 1890, the same paper reported that "[the Old Gaol] is in a good state of repair, part of it now being used for a dwelling house."[3]

By 1896 the York Bureau of Information could boast that the Old Gaol had been "preserved by the town," and by this time it appears to have functioned in an informal way as a museum. While there was no official institution to operate the Gaol as an historic site, tenants seem to have conducted tours for the public on a paying basis.[4] When in 1897 the Maine Historical Society held its annual field day in York, Moses A. Safford reported in the organization's *Collections and Proceedings* that the group had been shown around the Old Gaol "by the present occupants who admit visitors for a consideration."[5]

Despite Safford's positive assessment of the Gaol's condition under the care of the town and its tenant, the members of the York Historical Society who organized legally in 1896 were not satisfied, and many of them became leaders in the initiative to preserve the building as a museum. The effort was apparently spurred on by the local literary community and led by S. Elizabeth Burleigh Davidson (Mrs. James T. Davidson) and Mary Sowles Perkins (Mrs. J. Newton Perkins).

Cat. 53a. Garden party, York, Maine. Photograph, 1899. Old York Historical Society.

On August 15, 1899, Mary Sowles Perkins and her daughter Elizabeth hosted a garden party on the grounds of their house on the York River to benefit the restoration of the Old Gaol (cat. 53a). The endorsement provided by well-known writers in attendance was undoubtedly important in arousing enthusiasm for the Old Gaol. Yet equally significant was the collection of locally collected portraits, books, manuscripts, glass, ceramics, and household utensils which was displayed in two rooms of the Perkins house during the garden party.[6] Two days after the event, on August 17, the *Old York Transcript* praised the loan collection as an authentic and material representation of local history:

> That "Old York" is historically wonderful is a fact recognized for years past by historians, authors, visitors and, best of all, by our village folk. It has been felt rather in the atmosphere, and in a few tangible old landmarks, than by any concerted action in bringing relics to the light of modern days. But such negative recognition of the old-time grandeur and wonders of "ye ancient city of Georgiana" is not soul satisfying. It is so easy to fabricate tales of the unknown past that one wishes something substantial, ancient and historic beyond the shadow of a doubt. For the first time all York has been infused with the spirit of research, and has for two weeks been burrowing into the depths of old chests and trunks. The life of former days has been revealed: the costumes, books, utensils

of our grandfathers, have appeared as the wonder and delight of this closing nineteenth century.[7]

During the following winter (1899–1900) the Old York Historical and Improvement Society was organized and incorporated, with one of its principal objectives being the preservation of the Old Gaol; presumably the Society drew its members from two preexisting organizations, the Improvement and Historical societies. In May 1900 "many plans were made for immediately beginning the work of fitting up this ancient landmark in such a manner as to illustrate the mode of living in Colonial times" and to provide display space for the objects collected for the previous summer's garden party. It was hoped that the Old Gaol would be for York what the Essex Institute in Salem, the Old South Church in Boston, and Independence Hall in Philadelphia were for their communities. The group planned an immediate house-to-house search of the town for articles of historic interest to be put on loan in the Gaol for the summer season. Again, the museum's organizers emphasized the authenticity and local provenances of the objects to be exhibited.[8]

The Old Gaol Museum opened to the public on the Fourth of July, 1900. The opening-day festivities began at ten o'clock in the morning and featured addresses by James T. Davidson and Thomas Nelson Page. Davidson "laid particular stress upon the energy and ability of Mrs. Perkins, saying that too much praise could not be given her for the magnificent efforts she had made in behalf of the society in the achievement of the splendid work so auspiciously inaugurated."[9] The *Boston Globe* reported that "the old jail has been carefully restored and the place entirely fixed up and turned into a veritable museum." Although little or no structural work was done on the Gaol, the project was consistently referred to as a "restoration."[10]

The appearance of the interior of the Old Gaol at the time of the inception of the museum is known through published catalogues of its contents, as well as through annual reports made by the first curator, Sophia Turner. Her 1903 assessment provides a detailed description of the Gaol collection, as well as of the responses of visitors. The parlor, dining room, and kitchen provided an opportunity to display objects associated with domestic life—such as cooking utensils, glass, and ceramics—while the so-called "court room" featured historic documents and other "colonial relics." Elsewhere were displays of heraldry, firearms, costumes, and "industrial implements."[11] Thus the assembled objects appealed to a variety of historical interests: in daily life, in antique objects, in genealogy, in the military, and in industry. In bridging all of these historical pursuits, the organizers of the Old Gaol Museum assured their success.

As the first museum to be officially organized in the Piscataqua area, the Old Gaol was an important model for later preservation efforts in the region. Although its character as part public building and part private home distinguished it from neighboring house museums, the Old Gaol collected objects with local provenance that served to a large degree to illustrate domestic life in the "colonial" period. Moreover, the attention that the opening of the Museum of Colonial Relics drew in the press must have shown that historic buildings could be significant attractions for towns that were then developing as summer watering places.

KDM

1 The structural evolution of the Old Gaol is detailed in John Hecker, "Historical and Structural Analysis, Old Gaol, York, Maine" (typescript, OYHS, 1976), and Tom Jester, "Structural Analysis and Documentation Prepared . . . for the Old York Historical Society" (typescript, OYHS, 1988).

2 Samuel Adams Drake, *Nooks and Corners of the New England Coast* (New York: Harper and Brothers, 1876), 137.

3 *Eastern Star*, Sept. 19, 1890, 2; Dec. 26, 1890, 3.

4 *York, Maine Bureau of Information and Illustrated History of the Most Famous Summer Resort on the Atlantic Coast* (York, Me.: Bureau of Information, 1896), n.p. A photograph of the Old Gaol appears on the cover of this pamphlet.

5 Moses A. Safford, Esq., "Annual Field Day, 1897," *Collections and Proceedings of the Maine Historical Society*, second series, 9 (1897): 313.

6 "The 'Old York' Historical Village Party," *Old York Transcript*, Aug. 3, 1899, 4.

7 "Old York Garden Party," *Old York Transcript*, Aug. 17, 1899, 1.

8 These activities are described in an article entitled "For the Sake of Old York," *Old York Transcript*, May 3, 1900, 2.

9 "The Old Jail Museum," *Old York Transcript*, July 5, 1900, 1.

10 *Boston Globe*, July 8, 1900, 20. Although the opening of the Old Gaol was covered in this Boston newspaper, a search of the Portland, Me., newspapers did not reveal any mention of the event.

11 "Report of Miss Sophia S. Turner, Curator" (manuscript, OYHS, Aug. 15, 1903).

Cat. 54. Interior of Memorial Room, Thomas Bailey Aldrich Memorial, Portsmouth, New Hampshire. Photograph, ca. 1908. Courtesy, Historic Photograph Collection, Strawbery Banke Museum.

❋ 54 ❋

THOMAS BAILEY ALDRICH MEMORIAL
Portsmouth, New Hampshire, ca. 1797
Opened 1908

On Thursday, July 9, 1908, the *Portsmouth Daily Chronicle* announced that the trustees of the Thomas Bailey Aldrich Memorial Association had acquired the boyhood home of the noted author.[1] According to the newspaper, the association paid "much more than it could possibly have brought in the open market, but . . . had to have this building and the trustees of the Chase Home for children set a good figure on it and held at that."[2] Such an accomplishment is remarkable. The noted poet, author, and Portsmouth native, Thomas Bailey Aldrich, had died barely a year earlier in the spring of 1907, and the Memorial Association was founded within months of his death.

In the Articles of Association the objectives of purchasing the Aldrich house and establishing a "literary association" were clearly stated.[3] A committee of Portsmouth citizens, primarily local business and professional men led by Mayor Wallace Hackett, formed the core of the association which also included, among others, Charles Eliot Norton, Henry Cabot Lodge, George H. Mifflin, Thomas Wentworth Higginson, Samuel L. Clemens, Edmund Clarence Stedman, William Dean Howells, and Henry Van Dyke. In addition to serving on the committee, Lilian Woodman Aldrich and Talbot Aldrich, the author's widow and surviving son, agreed to deposit his collection of first editions, manuscript material, autographs, and other "literary relics of the first interest" at the memorial. They also promised to restore the house as nearly as possible to its appearance during the years that Aldrich lived there. Members of the Bailey family offered to replace many furnishings original to the house. The house was to give to the "American people a literary memorial of the greatest historic interest and of rich personal association."[4]

The house, known to readers of *The Story of a Bad Boy* as the "Nutter House," stands at 45 Court Street in Portsmouth. Built at the close of the eighteenth century, it is substantial in size with a wide central hall flanked by two rooms on either side. The Georgian architectural details are conservative in taste and similar to those in other houses built in Portsmouth in the latter half of the century. Thomas D. and Daniel Bailey purchased the house in 1823, Thomas Bailey became the sole owner in 1835, and it was sold by the Bailey heirs in 1870.[5] During the 1880s, the house served as Portsmouth's first hospital and subsequently was owned by the trustees of the Chase Home for Children, from whom the Aldrich Memorial Association purchased it.

Lilian Aldrich undertook the restoration of the "memorial home" with enthusiasm. Guided by descriptions in the autobiographical *Story of a Bad Boy* and memories of conversations with her husband about the years from 1849 to 1852 when he lived in the house, she injected a large dose of the colonial revival into the mix, and the house and adjacent museum opened to rave reviews. Many of the newspaper articles describing the memorial cited the contributions of the Aldriches to a $7,000 fund, and one account singled out Lilian Aldrich's "unremitting zeal" on behalf of the project, stating that she would "delegate to no one," and

> worked practically alone, until the finished product was ready for public inspection. From the full rigged ship on its high shelf in the hall to Aunt Abigail's sewing table, every detail is perfect in place and period. The effect sought for and wonderfully achieved is of a residence in actual use. The family may be out, but they obviously intend to return.[6]

Lilian Aldrich was quite pleased with the end result of her work. In 1911 she remarked that the house had been "restored with the utmost fidelity," adding that:

> There to-day the visitor may gaze in the very mirror that reflected Tom Bailey's blithe features, or turn the pages of the books that entranced him on rainy afternoons. In the quaint Colonial garden may be found every flower mentioned in his poetry, while in the fireproof room [cat. 54] that has been erected may be seen his priceless collection of autograph manuscripts, first editions, and literary relics. A visit here will better acquaint the reader with the background of the poet's youth than many pages of biographical rhetoric.[7]

The memorial was officially dedicated on June 30, 1908, and 1,100 people attended the public exercises held at the Portsmouth Music Hall and listened to speakers including

Governor Curtis Guild of Massachusetts, Page, Howells, and Clemens. After the ceremony, guests were taken to the Aldrich Memorial to see for themselves what William Sumner Appleton proclaimed eleven years later "about the most successful period house in America."[8]

When *The Story of a Bad Boy* was written in 1868, Aldrich emphasized the antiquity of Portsmouth for it was important to him to place his childhood in a setting evocative of a "respectable" past.[9] The rise of the colonial revival movement during the forty years that intervened between the publication of the book and the establishment of the memorial, as well as Lilian Aldrich's desire to keep her late husband's past "respectable," inspired the composition of her period interiors. Her fluency in the language and symbols of the colonial revival helped her fill in the inevitable furnishing gaps that existed where the book was silent and to create interior spaces that would appeal to, educate, and be understood by many visitors.[10]

The character of Grandfather Nutter in *The Story of a Bad Boy* embodied a conservative outlook or resistance to change and innovation championed during the colonial revival, and provided a rationale for opening the large kitchen fireplace and spreading an array of cooking equipment across the broad hearth (cat. 54a). The implements placed there—tin kitchens, peels, trivets, skillets, and pots designed for open-hearth cooking—were obsolete in middle-class urban Portsmouth households by 1850. Their appearance in the Aldrich Memorial was in the tradition of the New England or old-time kitchens at nineteenth-century fairs and foreshadowed numerous museum installations across the country. In the book, Aldrich described the products of the kitchen and the socializing that took place in the room, not the technical aspects of food preparation. Open-hearth cooking was not mentioned in the book, and it was undoubtedly an assumption on the part of Lilian Aldrich and her contemporaries that the household did not enjoy the benefits of a kitchen range.[11]

Elsewhere in the kitchen, the influence of the "colonial" was noticeable in the array of lighting devices on the mantel shelf and in the small braided rugs scattered randomly across the floor; the latter grew out of a turn-of-the-century interest in early American crafts. Produced by various methods including knitting, crocheting, braiding, and hooking, small rugs appear in quantity throughout the house. They were likely new or nearly new when the house opened in 1908, but were considered part of the desired old-time "look."

In the dining room, the dinner service, "Asiatic Palaces," manufactured by William Ridgway, Son & Co. about 1836–48, was appropriate for the restored interior. The service happened to be the blue transfer-printed "Staffordshire china" so dear to the hearts of early collectors, making it perfect for Lilian Aldrich's purposes. For the chambers, white dimity bed and window curtains of indeterminate styles and netted canopies were installed, sometimes in combination with later wooden valances. The

Cat. 54a. Kitchen, Thomas Bailey Aldrich house, Portsmouth, New Hampshire, built ca. 1797. Photograph by Boston Photo News Co., 1908. Courtesy, Society for the Preservation of New England Antiquities.

textile treatments were meant to complement period quilts and counterpanes and were elements of the colonial revival design scheme. Today, they would not be considered correct for the period of the restoration.[12]

Although the Bailey family donated furnishings to the cause, it is likely that several sources contributed to the furnishing of the building and that after the initial opening, family-owned and other artifacts may have trickled in over a period of years. However, many objects in the collection do have an Aldrich family history. The brick memorial building contains a jumble of artifacts whose value is chiefly derived from association with Thomas Bailey Aldrich and his literary career. Here, Lilian Aldrich installed her husband's collection of literary memorabilia as well as souvenirs of their travels and gifts from family friends. On the walls were hung illustrated poems, honorary degrees, and works of art, including three examples of china decorated by Celia Thaxter for the Aldriches. Thaxter's work was usually characterized by likenesses of old-fashioned flowers that seem to have been picked from typical New England gardens and often includes a few lines of verse. One of the examples in the Aldrich collection survives with a note from Thaxter to Lilian Aldrich asking her

"to accept this little milk jug which I have decorated with Shoals marigolds for your breakfast table, to remind you of your friend."[13] Glass tumblers and a pitcher said to have been owned by George Washington and a covered urn once belonging to Benjamin Franklin are also displayed in the museum, in honor of two of colonial America's most notable figures rather than for any connection with Aldrich.

The Aldrich Memorial was also a monument to a Portsmouth of an earlier era, a seemingly sleepy town comfortable in its genteel poverty and unthreatened by the social changes of the early twentieth century. Portsmouth citizens were proud of their town's historic past but at the same time they could see "their" history slipping away. In his address to the guests attending the opening of the memorial, Mayor Hackett spoke for many inhabitants when he noted that if Aldrich

were to wander about the town he could identify here and there a familiar landmark but he would be constantly impressed with the changed conditions which now prevail, particularly in the manners and customs of the people. When, however, he reached 45 Court Street, his eyes would be delighted to recognize the old Bailey house restored just as it was when as a lad he lived there . . . absolutely unchanged . . . Here is one spot where the world has stood still. Here is home! . . . What more appropriate memorial could we possibly prepare than to restore the "Nutter House" to its former condition, and leave it as a treasured legacy to future generations! As time goes on here is where we shall think of Aldrich most naturally. He will continue to live in the minds of countless pilgrims to this shrine, surrounded by the familiar scenes of the "Nutter House" in his beloved old town by the sea.[14]

CPR

1 "Have Paid for Memorial," *Portsmouth Daily Chronicle*, July 9, 1908, Thomas Bailey Aldrich Association Records, SB. The final payment was made possible by a $1,000 contribution from Andrew Carnegie.

2 "Have Paid for Memorial."

3 Articles of Association of the Thomas Bailey Aldrich Memorial were recorded in "Records of Voluntary Corporations," 14:126, Concord, N.H., July 5, 1907, Thomas Bailey Aldrich Memorial Association Minutes, SB.

4 *Portsmouth Herald*, Sept. 7, 1907.

5 Thomas Darling Bailey was Aldrich's maternal grandfather. John W. Durel, "From Strawbery Banke to Puddle Dock: The Evolution of a Neighborhood, 1630–1850" (Ph.D. diss., University of New Hampshire, 1984), 160.

6 *Women's Edition of the Manchester Union* (Manchester, N.H.), n.d., Aldrich Collection, SB.

7 Mrs. Thomas Bailey Aldrich, "The House Where the Bad Boy Lived," *The Outlook* 98, no. 4 (May 27, 1911): 205.

8 William Sumner Appleton, "Destruction and Preservation," *Art and Archaeology* 8 (May 1919): 164.

9 The childhood that Aldrich was writing about took place in the years around 1850. The Thomas Bailey Aldrich Memorial was perhaps the first house museum restored and refurnished to the Victorian period in the United States. John W. Durel, "'Historic' Portsmouth: The Role of the Past in the Formation of a Community's Identity," *Historical New Hampshire* 41, nos. 3/4 (Fall/Winter 1986): 103, 109.

10 For more on colonial revival period rooms, especially those designed by New Hampshire native Charles P. Wilcomb, see Melinda Young Frye, "The Beginnings of the Period Room in American Museums: Charles P. Wilcomb's Colonial Kitchens, 1896, 1906, 1910" in Axelrod, *Colonial Revival*, 217–40. Such strong similarities exist between Mrs. Aldrich's bedchambers and Wilcomb's 1910 installation of a colonial bedroom at the Oakland Public Museum illustrated in the article, that they could almost be interchangeable.

11 Cookstoves or ranges for the kitchen were readily available and advertised in Portsmouth papers during the 1840s.

12 Most of the quilts and counterpanes used in the Aldrich Memorial are examples of early nineteenth-century work, either the hand-embroidered "candlewick" type or those with loom-controlled raised patterns. One quilt, that dates to the mid eighteenth century, is a rare example of corded work in an all-over design which was created by inserting cording through the back of the quilt into tiny, previously stitched channels.

13 For more information on Celia Thaxter's china painting and her relationship with the Aldrich family, see Doreen Bolger Burke et al., *In Pursuit of Beauty: Americans and the Aesthetic Movement* (New York: Rizzoli International Publications in association with the Metropolitan Museum of Art, 1986), 471–72.

14 *Portsmouth Times*, June 30, 1908.

MOFFATT-LADD HOUSE
Portsmouth, New Hampshire, 1764
Opened 1912

In 1912, The National Society of The Colonial Dames of America in the State of New Hampshire opened Portsmouth's second historic house museum, known then as the Ladd house (cat. 55) and considered at the time "most famous among many famous old houses" in the city, one which "no student of colonial architecture can afford to miss."[1] This magnificent house was built between 1760 and 1764 by master craftsmen including housewright Michael Whidden, turner Richard Mills, and carver Ebenezer Deering.[2] Although the bills were paid and the title retained by the wealthy merchant, John Moffatt, the first occupants were his son Samuel Moffatt and his bride, Sarah Catherine Mason, who were married in 1764. After Samuel's bankruptcy in 1768, John Moffatt, through agents, purchased the contents of the house at auction and thereafter occupied the house until his own death in 1786. The house remained in the hands of his direct descendants until it was taken over by the Colonial Dames.[3]

Few changes were made in the house until about 1815, when the house was occupied by Samuel Moffatt's granddaughter Maria Tufton Haven and her husband Alexander Ladd. At this time, the front parlor was transformed into a dining room with an arch for a sideboard, a fireplace mantel in the neoclassical style was added, and the Dufour wallpaper illustrating "*Vues d'Italie*" was hung in the great stairhall. A generation later Alexander Hamilton Ladd made much more drastic alterations when he took title to the house in 1862. His wife insisted on a thorough renovation which involved removing wallpapers in the chambers, installing gas lighting and a furnace, modernizing the kitchen and pantry, and replacing the parlor mantel with a white marble fireplace arch. Fortunately Ladd preserved the Dufour paper in the great hall and kept samples of the original decorative elements of the "yellow chamber" including both the yellow damask and the eighteenth-century wallpaper with its unusual hunting prints. So extensive was this work that the *Portsmouth Journal* declared that Ladd had made "it really a new house in which all the rich outlines of a superb mansion of eighty years ago have been carefully preserved."[4]

The New Hampshire Society of the Colonial Dames was founded in 1892 for "patriotic, historical, literary, benevolent and social" purposes. Eligibility was based on lineage and the members were characterized as "a fitting representation of the wealth and culture" of New Hampshire.[5] The early meetings featured speeches, dramatic presentations, exhibitions of historic relics, patriotic songs, visits to historic sites, costumed garden parties, and old-fashioned refreshments. The first building owned by the society was the

Cat. 55. Moffatt-Ladd house, Portsmouth, New Hampshire. Engraving; 8 in. x 10 in. Courtesy, The National Society of The Colonial Dames of America in the State of New Hampshire.

Cilley house in Exeter, which the Dames named "Colonial Manor" and used for meetings, parties, and occasional overnight visits.

Colonial Manor lost its appeal to the Dames in 1911 when the heirs of Alexander Hamilton Ladd offered to lease their family home to the society. At a meeting on December 9, the Board of Managers unanimously accepted the offer and a thirty-year lease was signed.[6] The house was described as "magnificent. About it cluster historic memories, making of it a fitting home for a society whose object is to inspire patriotism in the new generation by recalling the virtues of the old." Even then the house was "known throughout the country as a model of the best architecture of its period, with stately hall and staircase, and panelling of rare excellence," and it was "understood that many of the beautiful and historical portraits which adorn the walls of the mansion and much of the furnishings will become a permanent loan."[7]

Mrs. James R. May of Portsmouth was named chairman of the House Committee and immediately turned her attention to the restoration and furnishing of the house. She had become acquainted with Luke Vincent Lockwood through his studies of antique furniture and did not hesitate to seek his advice. She consulted him several times on questions of appropriate paint colors, wall coverings, floor finishes, and lighting devices. As early as December 18, 1912, she had a let-

ter from Lockwood recommending that the gas chandeliers be removed, the woodwork painted dead white, the floors stripped, the original door from the parlor to the garden reopened, and the parlor painted yellow and blue, "a beautiful combination . . . much used in Colonial days" (see cats. 8a, b).[8] Mrs. May sent Lockwood a sample of the blue worsted draperies with yellow fringes which had long been in the house that she proposed to hang in the back parlor. On January 27, 1913, he wrote to her enthusiastically, "I like the color of the material very much. It is a pure Colonial combination . . . I would most assuredly advise re-hanging the old curtains, if they are in good enough condition to be used. They are a beautiful color and will greatly improve the looks of the room." In the same letter Lockwood suggested that furniture to be used in the room should be upholstered in the same blue as the curtains and the floor be waxed. He also offered advice about wall treatment, cautioning against stenciling and suggesting "painting it in the yellow color which appears in the fringe of the hangings, getting that yellow at its best, and not in its faded portions. It will make a very beautiful room."[9]

On the suggestion of Mrs. Hovey, the house was named the Moffatt-Ladd house in September 1914 and the Board of Managers agreed with the Ladd family that "it should always be kept as a historical museum and a dignified residence of the Colonial Dames."[10] The mansion was visited by 1,224 paying visitors in 1915.[11]

Cat. 55a. Stairhall, Moffatt-Ladd house. Photograph, 1912. Courtesy, Society for the Preservation of New England Antiquities.

At the time of the lease, the Ladd heirs left much of their family furniture and furnishings in the house either as individual loans or as undivided residue of the estate of Alexander Hamilton Ladd. These included furniture, ceramics and glass, fireplace furniture, engravings, manuscripts, gas fixtures, antlers, trunks, Franklin stoves, wallpaper and textile samples, curtain fixtures, fire buckets, oriental rugs, and a host of minor acccessories. Most of the furniture which remained in the house was of nineteenth-century date, although several early pieces were included, such as the "Flemish" chairs associated with Sir William Pepperrell and the Chinese Chippendale-style settee and chairs thought by Maria Tufton Haven Ladd to have been purchased by her father at an auction of the estate of Mark Hunking Wentworth in 1794 and given to her by her mother in 1842. Some of the loans, including the Chinese Chippendale-style pieces and many of the portraits, were later withdrawn by members of the family but have been returned in recent years.

When the house was first opened to the public, there was some concern that the furnishings were not all of a period. One reviewer reported "It has been objected by some visitors that the furnishings . . . are not altogether in harmony with their surroundings. In the hall, for instance, is a hair-cloth sofa (fig. 55a). In one of the chambers is a bedstead of the early Victorian period. If these things strike a false note, as undoubtedly they do, it must be remembered that the house has been occupied by generations of brides, who naturally wanted the fashionable furniture of the period. It is probable that with increased means, the Society of Colonial Dames will gradually replace some of the more modern furniture with that of the period of the house itself."[12]

To enhance the feeling of a colonial house, furniture and historic relics were brought from Colonial Manor and other pieces were borrowed, purchased, or rented from members, friends, or antique dealers. A netted tester was ordered in 1915 from L.E. Henry in Deerfield, Massachusetts, for $25 and a dimity canopy was ordered by Mrs. Arthur Rice and made up by Mrs. Emily A. Wiggin for $20.[13]

By 1920, President Mrs. Arthur Clarke was able to write glowingly on the "stately mansion" filled with evidence of the members' "profuse generosity and love" where "the larger part of the furnishings was presented by members, in memory of the brilliant and distinguished women of their families . . . or of beloved husbands and sons whose names stand for all that is best in our State . . . memorials of the elegance and dignity of our pioneer ancestry." Each piece had been "approved by connoisseurs in Antique furnishings."[14]

In 1936, while searching for evidence of the date of construction of Alexander Ladd's counting house, Miss Edith Shepard Freeman discovered the original inventories of the contents of the house which were taken at the time of Samuel Moffatt's bankruptcy in 1768 and after the death of his father John Moffatt in 1786. Although Miss Freeman recognized that these documents permitted one to see "each room (re)furnished as of 1768," it was not until these documents were rediscovered in the late 1950s by the House Committee Chairman, Mrs. G. Allen Huggins, that they became the basic guidelines for acquisitions and refurnishing schemes for the Moffatt-Ladd house.[15]

JCN

1 George Sargent, "The House that Ladd Built," 1912, newspaper clipping in Colonial Dames' Scrapbook, Moffatt-Ladd house. Sargent recommended that tourists arriving at Portsmouth en route to Maine and the White Mountains would "find this a very convenient lunching place and tarry at the Rockingham, they should take an hour more and visit not only the Thomas Bailey Aldrich memorial, but the Ladd House, both of which are only a few minutes walk from the hotel."

2 See James Leo Garvin, "Academic Architecture and the Building Trades in the Piscataqua Region of New Hampshire and Maine, 1775–1815" (Ph.D. diss., Boston University, 1983), 172–94.

3 Jane C. Giffen (Nylander), "The Moffatt-Ladd House," Connoisseur 175, nos. 704–5 (Oct. and Nov. 1970): 113–22, 201–7.

4 Portsmouth Journal, Nov. 15, 1862. I am grateful to Richard M. Candee for bringing this article to my attention.

5 Daily Mirror American, June 1, 1904.

6 The lease was extended to ninety-nine years in 1915 and title was transferred by the remaining Ladd heirs to the National Society of the Colonial Dames in the State of New Hampshire in 1969.

7 Boston Journal, Dec. 8, 1911.

8 Luke Vincent Lockwood to Mrs. James R. May, New York, Dec. 18, 1912, N.H. Dames Archives, Moffatt-Ladd house.

9 Lockwood to May, New York, Jan. 27, 1913, N.H. Dames Archives.

10 Agnes Rowell Hunt, A History of the New Hampshire Society of the Colonial Dames of America from 1892 to September 1936 (n.p., n.d.), 24.

11 Hunt, History of the New Hampshire Society, 25.

12 Sargent, "The House that Ladd Built."

13 Mrs. Rice served on the Dame's House Committee and was active in other historical activities in Portsmouth. She lived in the 1815 Larkin-Rice house on Middle Street, not far from Mrs. May.

14 Martha Bouton Cilley Clarke, Annual Meeting Address, June 19, 1920, N.H. Dames Archives.

15 A member of the society, Miss Freeman was a professional historian, serving as librarian of the New Hampshire Historical Society from 1908 until her death in 1943. The papers were found "among the early Court Files which are in the State Archives but placed in the Library of the N.H. Historical Society." They are now filed in the N.H. State Archives, Concord. Edith Shepard Freeman to Mrs. Dudley, Concord, n.d. [ca. 1936], N.H. Dames Archives. I am grateful to Nancy Goss for her research in preparation for this entry.

❧ 56 ❧

WENTWORTH-GARDNER HOUSE
Portsmouth, New Hampshire, 1760
Opened 1915

Standing in what had by the early twentieth century become a rundown waterfront neighborhood in the south end of Portsmouth, the Wentworth-Gardner house (cat. 56) had seen only minor changes since it was constructed in 1760 for Thomas Wentworth, the younger brother of the last royal governor of the Province of New Hampshire, John Wentworth. Georgian in form, the interiors are notable for a wealth of elaborate trim and spacious proportions, attributes that played a large part in the purchase of the house by Wallace Nutting in 1915 for inclusion in "The Wallace Nutting Colonial Chain of Houses." This business venture was Nutting's attempt to assemble a collection of houses throughout New England that would represent what he considered the finest in craftsmanship and decoration from the early settlement through the federal periods. Located within a day's drive from the Boston metropolitan area, they were marketed by Nutting as places of interest to an increasingly mobile public. At a time when most other formalized preservation efforts in the region originated in altruistic organizations such as the Society for the Preservation of New England Antiquities and the Historic and Improvement Society in York, Nutting attempted to integrate history and preservation with a capitalistic enterprise. His aggressive marketing of historic houses was buttressed by his concurrent business activities in creating and selling hand-tinted photographs of romanticized historic scenes that used their interiors as settings. Several of Nutting's photographs of interiors were staged in the rooms of the Wentworth-Gardner house.

Nutting restored the physical fabric of the house and furnished it with appropriate antiques to present to the public a picture of "a perfect Georgian type of the very acme of the colonial period."[1] He described his work on the house:

> The exterior of the main house is fully restored. The blocked front was discovered beneath a layer of clapboards. The handsome door head, by Mr. Charles Henry Dean, who also superintended the work on all houses of the chain, is a scroll or broken arch, with fluted pilasters, and Corinthian capitals similar to those in the interior. The fine green and gold pineapple, the emblem of hospitality, is like that preserved in the Essex Institute. The old door head had disappeared in decay, owing to the exposed position of the house.
>
> The interior required no restoration except the return to their proper places of the stair spindles, newel, and the under mantel carving of the parlor, which had been removed in 1871 to another house.[2]

Cat. 56. Parlor, Wentworth-Gardner house, Portsmouth, New Hampshire, built 1760. Photograph by Wallace Nutting, ca. 1915.
Courtesy, Society for the Preservation of New England Antiquities.

In his autobiography (1936), Wallace Nutting penned a somewhat anticlimactic axiom to his involvement with more than one historic house: "Nothing awakes the community to the values of its antiquities like the readiness of an outsider to acquire them."[3] Certainly in the case of the Wentworth-Gardner house, he served as an outsider who preserved a local landmark and awakened the Portsmouth community to its historic and artistic value. Yet it is also Nutting who was vilified when in 1918 he sold the house for its interior fittings to the Metropolitan Museum of Art. The woodwork that had been the primary attraction to preserve the house three years before was now responsible for its sale to an organization that would virtually assure the destruction of the building for its parts, for in early 1919 the Metropolitan announced its intentions of using the Wentworth-Gardner woodwork in the period-room settings of its planned American Wing in New York.[4] Through his dual roles as preservationist and entrepreneur, Nutting assumed the consecutive mantles of both hero and villain to the people of Portsmouth and in the process assured the public perception of the Wentworth-Gardner house as an out of the ordinary, and therefore valuable, local "antiquity."

The sale of the house by Nutting came at a time of financial reversals as a result of World War I. He tried to interest the SPNEA in acquiring his entire chain of houses; when that failed, he offered up the buildings to the public on an individual basis.[5] The sale of the Wentworth-Gardner house to the Metropolitan for its woodwork came about, quite simply, because the museum happened to show primary interest and had the financial capacity to buy it. Although its sale to the Metropolitan appeared to assure the removal of the house from Portsmouth, Nutting evidently did take some pains to see that the house would remain in the public domain: the only other offer for the house had come from a private party on Long Island who initially planned to float it on a barge to his estate there and remodel it as a summer home.[6] Even William Sumner Appleton, who strenuously resisted the removal of the house from Portsmouth for any reason, agreed that it was better that the rooms be available to the public at the museum in New York than forever closed on a remote estate.[7]

When the purchase of the house by the Metropolitan was publicly announced in 1919, the city of Portsmouth was entering a period of considerable activity in regards to the preservation of three major historic houses located there. Besides the Wentworth-Gardner house on the waterfront, there was activity on State Street as the Portsmouth Historical Society attempted to rescue the Purcell-Langdon-Lord (John Paul Jones) house from impending destruction, and on Daniel Street, in 1920, the Boston Museum of Fine Arts was securing the removal of the carved woodwork from the Jaffrey house at the instigation of Barrett Wendell and John Templeman Coolidge III. The latter house, an imposingly sited mansion of circa 1730 with finely crafted interiors, never received the publicity the other two houses did because of an advanced state of decay, and the removal of its features caused little stir. The house was replaced by an automobile garage.[8] In fact, in one of the few published accounts of the loss of the Jaffrey house, Elise Lathrop confuses it with the Wentworth-Gardner house:

> The Wentworth-Gardner House, built in 1760, is now a mere shell, for its fittings, fireplaces, mantels and doors, including the old front one, were purchased by the Boston Museum and practically nothing but the four walls remain of the old.[9]

Although Lathrop garbled both houses and museums, the important point remains that while destruction of other historic resources continued apace in this period, the Wentworth-Gardner house maintained an important place in Portsmouth's historic consciousness, in no small way attributable to Nutting's earlier marketing strategies for it. The Jaffrey house, a building of considerable architectural importance, never benefitted from similar fame in the public eye, and its demise never received the scrutiny or debate that centered on the anticipated removal of the Wentworth-Gardner house.

For three years the Metropolitan maintained the house on its original site in anticipation of its removal, either wholly or in parts, to New York. Plans during this period ranged from using the rooms as individual installations in the American Wing, to moving the house as a whole and re-erecting it in the interior courtyard of the museum.[10] In 1922, however, the trustees of the museum abruptly reversed their intentions (apparently due to financial considerations) and decided to leave the house in Portsmouth. When the new American Wing opened in 1924, Portsmouth was represented with finely paneled rooms taken from the seventeenth-century Samuel Wentworth house, removed from the Puddle Dock neighborhood by antique dealer Charles "Cappy" Stewart with little public notice or fanfare and sold to the museum.[11]

With the decision made to leave the Wentworth-Gardner house in Portsmouth, the Metropolitan assumed the role of landlord to an historic site removed from its center of operations. The house served as an exhibition facility in much the same vein it had when owned by Nutting: during the summer months it was furnished with items from the museum's collections in a style considered appropriately grand for its interiors. In 1930 a loan exhibition brought to the house examples of regional art and antiques from local collections. Elizabeth Bishop Perkins of York furnished one of the front parlors entirely with a collection of "early maple" (cat. 56a).[12] In 1933 the Metropolitan entered into an agreement with the SPNEA giving it a five-year option to purchase the house for $15,000. Because of financial difficulties caused by the Depression, the SPNEA was not able to raise the funds within that time. The option was extended and the pur-

Cat. 56a. Parlor, Wentworth-Gardner house. Photograph, 1930. Old York Historical Society.

chase price lowered to $10,000.[13] In 1940 the Wentworth-Gardner house and the neighboring Tobias Lear house were acquired by the Wentworth-Gardner and Tobias Lear Houses Association, which continues to maintain the houses today.

TBJ

1 Wallace Nutting, "The Wentworth-Gardner House," promotional brochure, ca. 1915.

2 Nutting, "Wentworth-Gardner House."

3 Wallace Nutting, *Wallace Nutting's Biography* (Framingham, Mass.: Old America Company, 1936), 150.

4 Charles B. Hosmer, Jr., *Presence of the Past: A History of the Preservation Movement in the United States Before Williamsburg* (New York: G.P. Putnam's Sons, 1965), 225.

5 William Sumner Appleton, "Report of the Secretary," OTNE 9, no. 1 (Nov. 1918): 33.

6 Hosmer, *Presence of the Past*, 226.

7 OTNE 10, no. 1 (Oct. 1919): 16.

8 "Facts About the Historical Society," *Portsmouth Chronicle*, June 30, 1920, 3.

9 Elise Lathrop, *Historic Houses of Early America* (New York: Tudor Publishing Co., 1916), 270.

10 Hosmer, *Presence of the Past*, 229.

11 "Famed Wentworth Gardner House Intact Here," *Portsmouth Herald*, Dec. 23, 1938, 23.

12 Thomas B. Johnson, "The Feel of the Colonial: Interiors of the Perkins House" (typescript, OYHS, 1989), app. 7.

13 "Wentworth-Gardner house," OTNE 29, no. 4 (Apr. 1939): 142–43.

Cat. 57. John Paul Jones house, Portsmouth, New Hampshire, built 1758. Photograph, 1920. Courtesy, Portsmouth Athenaeum.

❧ 57 ❧

JOHN PAUL JONES HOUSE
Portsmouth, New Hampshire, 1758
Opened 1920

Although it is an architecturally important Georgian mansion in its own right, the Purcell-Langdon-Lord house is equally noted for its historical connections with the brief tenancy of naval hero John Paul Jones, and today it bears his name (cat. 57). Jones never owned the house but he boarded there in 1781 and 1782 while overseeing the construction of the seventy-four-gun *America* on nearby Badger's Island.[1] While the house received recognition for its architectural merit and prominent location early in the colonial revival period, it was the connection with Jones that ultimately captured the public's imagination when it was opened as a museum by the Portsmouth Historical Society in 1920.

Built in 1758, the house was owned by several prominent Portsmouth families. The first owner, Captain Gregory Purcell, was a brother-in-law of the Wentworth clan, and in 1783 the house passed from his widow into the hands of the Woodbury Langdon family, whose own brick mansion stood next door. Other early occupants included members

of the Ladd family and John F. Parrott, a United States Senator. In 1826 Samuel Lord of South Berwick purchased the property and added the large garden lot at the front of the grounds; his heirs sold the property in 1912 to Gertrude E. Blaisdell, and it was she who sold it to the Granite State Insurance Company as the site of a planned office building in 1917.[2]

Although the Granite State Insurance Company was chiefly interested in the land, it was not entirely indifferent to the fate of the house. Instead of demolishing the house right away, the company attempted to locate parties interested in moving the building to another location. When this attempt failed, the Metropolitan Museum of Art in New York City showed interest in the piecemeal removal of interior architectural elements.[3] Although it is unclear how the museum first became aware of the possible availability of the woodwork, it is likely that they became involved through Charles H. "Cappy" Stewart, a local antiques dealer with a somewhat notorious reputation in the Portsmouth area for demolishing early buildings for the sale of their woodwork and building materials. It was he who obtained for the Metropolitan the outstanding seventeenth-century woodwork of the Samuel Wentworth "Great House" at Puddle Dock.[4] Evidently Stewart had an agreement with the Metropolitan to remove the Purcell-Langdon-Lord house woodwork for shipment to New York

Cat. 57a. Interior, John Paul Jones house. Photograph, ca. 1920. Courtesy, Historic Photograph Collection, Strawbery Banke Museum.

should it become available.[5] It was one building Stewart lost out on, however, for the actions of two other Portsmouth men eventually secured the building and grounds intact.

The threat of the probable loss of the building finally engendered a local movement to keep the "Jones House," as it increasingly came to be identified during this period, in Portsmouth. Architect Joseph E. Chandler and the Honorable Woodbury Langdon, a descendent of the

second family to own the house and an owner of a significant eighteenth-century mansion on Pleasant Street himself, joined forces to save the Purcell house. While their first intention was to move the house to another site, when it became known that the lot on which it stood could be purchased from the insurance company, Langdon donated $10,000 toward the $15,000 needed to buy the land and secure the location.[6] At the same time, Chandler persuaded Secretary Henry Kent of the Metropolitan to have the museum withdraw from the project in order to assist in the local preservation of the house.[7] By August 1919 Woodbury Langdon was able to donate the recently purchased land to the Portsmouth Historical Society, a group formed by himself and other prominent local citizens that was active in saving the house.[8] A campaign to raise $10,000 to repair and upgrade the building was immediately commenced, and plans were made for a "magnificent stone building" to be erected on the property for use as a fireproof museum and local memorial to the brave men "who fought and won" the First World War.[9]

In July 1920, the house then secure, William Sumner Appleton observed:

> The saving of this house is particularly welcome on account of the contemporaneous loss of the Wentworth-Gardner and Jaffrey houses, to which Portsmouth will have to reconcile itself, and it is pleasant to see that people continue to be alive to the importance of saving some at least of the best local work, which is so good that the museums of New York and Boston have secured fine examples. To the Moffatt-Ladd house and the Aldrich Memorial can now be added the Purcell-Langdon-Lord house as another building open to the public and forever safeguarded. Although this fails to reconcile us to the loss of the Wentworth-Gardner and Jaffrey houses, it is nevertheless another welcome step in the right direction. The Jaffrey house was never restored and furnished, as was the Wentworth-Gardner, and its dismantling will make less impression on the public, but now that Portsmouth has taken this additional stride on the right path let us hope that several more of its best houses may eventually be safeguarded.[10]

Opened to the public on July 23, 1920 (cat. 57a), the "Historic John Paul Jones House" showed "many interesting relics" and "priceless heirlooms" throughout its newly painted and refurbished rooms.[11] Mostly loaned by local families, items ranged from what was purported to be the oldest piano in the country, dated 1765, to an 1866 rosewood baseball bat (suitably protected in a glass case) that had been a gift from President Franklin Pierce to James Dow, a player in the Rockingham Baseball Club.[12] From early records, it is clearly evident that the building was conceived of as a place in which to display local curiosities and heirlooms, with no intent to present the building as a period setting or as the home John Paul Jones might have known.

It is possible that if the stone building planned as a museum and war memorial had been erected, these displays of local ephemera would have been moved to that location and the rooms of the Purcell house restored to some semblance of their original appearance. Fundraising for the museum building lagged, however, and by 1924 members of the Historical Society voted to alter the interior of the old house to accommodate the growing collections. Although

the entrance hall and "formal" front rooms of the house were left essentially intact, the rear wing that had been the location of the kitchens, bedrooms, and stables was made over into a large meeting room upstairs and a spacious exhibition hall downstairs by the removal of interior partitions.[13] These areas were furnished with a number of glass cases in which the neatly labeled remnants of the past were exhibited. The front rooms became repositories for donated furniture and an attempt was made to present period settings here that consciously evoked an old-time atmosphere.

The story of the "saving" of the John Paul Jones house and its subsequent use by the Portsmouth Historical Society is a chronicle of a male-dominated upper-middle-class effort to preserve a house that served as a physical link to the romance and bravery of Portsmouth's eighteenth-century history. At a time when other important buildings were being lost in Portsmouth, notably the Jaffrey and Wentworth mansions, and the danger of the loss of the Wentworth-Gardner house was at its greatest, the elite of Portsmouth were able to save the John Paul Jones house. Arguably the Jaffrey, Wentworth, and Wentworth-Gardner houses could be considered more important than the John Paul Jones house from a purely architectural viewpoint, thus interesting the art museums. Yet each of these three houses was located in areas of the town then run down and stricken by poverty, while the Jones house stood close by still-fashionable State Street and Haymarket Square. Neither did the other three have any firm connections to the patriotic impulses of the American Revolution such as the Jones house could boast of. And in the end, none had a single wealthy benefactor such as Woodbury Langdon who could be stirred on both patriotic and familial impulses to step in and save them. It was only in the Jones house that history, architecture, and patriotism could be brought together to excite the residents of Portsmouth then willing, and able, to do something to preserve their past.

TBJ

1 *Portsmouth Herald,* Sept. 25, 1924.

2 *Portsmouth Herald,* Sept. 25, 1924.

3 *Portsmouth Chronicle,* Jan. 30, 1920.

4 James Garvin, *Historic Portsmouth: Early Photographs from the Collections of Strawbery Banke* (Portsmouth, N.H.: Strawbery Banke, 1974), 100.

5 Garvin, *Historic Portsmouth,* 100.

6 *Portsmouth Chronicle,* Jan. 30, 1920.

7 Joseph Chandler to Henry Kent, Apr. 17, 1917, Metropolitan Museum of Art Archives, New York, N.Y.

8 *Portsmouth Chronicle,* Jan. 30, 1920.

9 *Portsmouth Chronicle,* Jan. 30, 1920.

10 *OTNE* 11, no. 1 (July 1920): 28.

11 *Portsmouth Chronicle,* July 24, 1920.

12 *Portsmouth Chronicle,* July 20, 1920.

13 *Portsmouth Herald,* Sept. 18, 1924.

Cat. 58. Macpheadris-Warner house, Portsmouth, New Hampshire, built 1716. Photograph by Douglas Armsden, 1932. Courtesy, Portsmouth Athenaeum.

MACPHEADRIS-WARNER HOUSE
Portsmouth, New Hampshire, 1716
Opened 1932

The Macpheadris-Warner house (cat. 58) was recognized in the nineteenth century as one of the historic mansions of Portsmouth, although it did not become a public museum until 1932. By the 1870s the Warner house was noted in the region for its hallway murals and lightning rod, supposedly installed under the supervision of Benjamin Franklin. In 1914 Mary Northend described the charms of its "quaint cupola" and noted the local opinion that the house was "the most picturesque . . . in Portsmouth."[1]

The house takes part of its name from its builder, Captain Archibald Macpheadris, a wealthy merchant who was married to Sarah, the sister of Governor Benning Wentworth. Wentworth himself lived in the house in the 1750s when the Province of New Hampshire considered, but never approved, its purchase as the royal governor's mansion. In 1760, Jonathan Warner married the daughter of Captain Macpheadris and moved in; he remained until his death in 1814. Warner's long occupancy assured the connection of his name with the place. A niece, Mrs. Nathaniel Sherburne, inherited the property from Warner, and when her son John assumed ownership in the mid nineteenth century, the house ceased to be used as a year-round residence and became a family summer home. When John Sherburne's grandson Thomas Penhallow died in 1928, the surviving heirs showed no interest in taking up even seasonal residence in the old house and 212 years of family occupancy came to an end. In 1930 a local oil and service station company approached the Penhallow heirs about purchasing the house as a site for a filling station.[2]

It was at this crucial point that Edith Greenough Wendell headed an effort to raise $10,000 to purchase the house and secure it as a public museum. This activity engendered the founding of the Warner House Association, whose mission was "to preserve the property for the benefit of the public."[3] The money for its purchase was raised through subscription, coming mainly from descendants of old Portsmouth families. On March 26, 1932, title formally passed from the Penhallow heirs to the Warner House Association.[4]

The efforts to preserve the Macpheadris-Warner house centered on the historic associations of its early occupants and on the architectural and artistic importance of the structure, being at once a house where "great names figure largely in its history" and a "legacy of Portsmouth's early architectural grandeur."[5] Newspaper accounts of the period focus upon these attributes. The *Christian Science Monitor* recounted the reception for Lafayette held there in 1824 and earlier visits by local hero John Paul Jones.[6] In the *Portsmouth Herald*, architect Philip Dana Orcutt waxed

euphoric over the "earlier, purer period of building" that the house represented, the "easy tread" and murals of the stairway, and the old glass still surviving in its windows.[7] Yet no account expressed the prevailing sentiments about the Macpheadris-Warner house better than that of restoration architect Joseph E. Chandler of Boston:

It would be difficult to name in the North, another house of such outstanding merit as the MacPheadris-Warner House, viewed as an architectural background for picturing the political and social life of the early eighteenth century in one of our most important early maritime towns. It has fortunately been preserved to us thus far by the recent occupants who extended to our day the fortunate social atmosphere which still persists within its walls.[8]

In the first years after acquisition the association embarked on several efforts to restore the house. The exterior was cleaned of yellow paint applied in the nineteenth century, and a new fence was erected along the Chapel and Daniel street fronts, after a design by architect John Mead

Cat. 58a. *"Loan Exhibition of Family Heirlooms and Rare Antiques, Stairhall," Macpheadris-Warner house. Photograph, 1938. Courtesy, Warner House Association.*

Howells. Inside, work to halt the decay of the hallway murals and restoration of the marbleized finish on the dining room walls was accomplished. Edith Wendell engaged Luke Vincent Lockwood to give a well-attended fundraising lecture on old houses at Portsmouth's Masonic Hall in the summer of 1933, and also appears to have been responsible for retaining Norman Isham to perform an architectural inspection and report on correct methods for restoration in September of that year.[9]

The furnishing of the interior with appropriate objects also seems to have elicited her energies both in planning and in actual gifts. In 1934 Wendell arranged for nineteen pieces of furniture to be loaned to the house by the Metropolitan Museum of Art in New York and was able to strike a similar agreement with the Garvan Collection at Yale University.[10] In 1936 the Secretary's Report noted that Mrs. James Amory Sullivan, a Boston acquaintance of Edith Wendell's, had lent "a bed from 'Tuckahoe' Virginia and the old chintz used on it as a bed spread has been supplied by Mrs. Wendell from her attic, that storehouse of treasures."[11]

Appropriate gifts were also solicited from other local sources (cat. 58a). Elizabeth Perkins of York, an early member of the association, placed on loan two eighteenth-century needlepoint covered Continental armchairs and a fine Boston-area mahogany bonnet-top high chest of circa 1760 that had come down to her by inheritance; all were later converted to gifts.[12] Descendants of the Warner family were convinced to place on loan the original Joseph Blackburn portraits of the family, and these were later purchased for the house by Mrs. Woodbury Langdon.[13] Although the furnishings assembled were not required to have local provenance, authenticity and scholarship were considered the most important tenets of the preservation of the Macpheadris-Warner house.

TBJ

1 Mary Northend, *Historic Homes of New England* (Boston: Little, Brown and Company, 1914), 15.

2 William G. Wendell, "History in Houses: The Macpheadris-Warner House in Portsmouth, New Hampshire," *Antiques* 87, no. 6 (June 1965): 712.

3 "Record Book of the Warner House Association, September 1934–June 28, 1954," PA, Sept. 13, 1934.

4 "Buy Historic Warner House," *Portsmouth Herald*, Mar. 26, 1932.

5 "Warner House at Portsmouth to be Preserved," *Christian Science Monitor*, Mar. 26, 1932.

6 "Warner House at Portsmouth to be Preserved," *Christian Science Monitor*, Mar. 26, 1932.

7 "The Warner House," *Portsmouth Herald*, July 29, 1933.

8 "The Warner House," *Portsmouth Herald*, July 29, 1933.

9 Record Book of the Warner House Association, Sept. 13, 1934.

10 Record Book of the Warner House Association, June 14, 1934.

11 "Report of the Secretary," Record Book of the Warner House Association, 1936.

12 Thomas B. Johnson, "The Feel of the Colonial: Interiors of the Perkins House" (typescript, OYHS, 1989).

13 "Report of the Secretary," Record Book of the Warner House Association, 1936.

❦ 59 ❦

JEFFERDS TAVERN
York, Maine, 1750
Opened 1940

While restoring, moving, rebuilding, and furnishing Jefferds Tavern from 1939 to 1942, Elizabeth Perkins described the building's significance in the colonial period and its potential educational value to the community of the present day. Perkins's unpublished history of the Tavern followed the chatty model of Alice Morse Earle and other writers, describing both architectural elements and objects such as the fireplace crane, bar cage, and hearth to explain the role of the tavern in colonial life. By emphasizing York's connections with Revolutionary events like the "shot heard 'round the world" and a York tea party, Perkins could connect the spirit of 1776 with Allied support in 1940–42. Working through the Association for the Preservation of Historic Buildings, which she founded, Perkins brought about the completion of exterior preservation begun by local architect William E. Barry in 1925; together, the two projects illustrate two different approaches to preservation in southern Maine during the early twentieth century.

Barry's work on Jefferds Tavern was the product of his family connections to the building and his interest in colonial architecture as an expression of an earlier, harmonious American culture. Descended from prominent local families, Barry trained in a Boston architectural firm before returning to Kennebunk as a year-round resident in 1884 and purchasing the fine federal-period house known as "Wallingford Hall." Barry's 1909 publication on the Kennebunk area, *A Stroll by a Familiar River*, and his 1923 *Chronicles of Kennebunk* described local history and genealogies as well as homes owned by the gentry. After writing an unpublished history of the tavern and its owners, Barry leased Jefferds Tavern from his uncle, George Lord, in the early 1920s and began the restoration with his own funds. Exterior work—reclapboarding, replacing the sills and corner boards—was completed using materials salvaged from a nearby mill (cat. 59).[1]

While Barry's preservation work on Jefferds Tavern grew out of a personal interest in historic buildings, by the 1920s tourist literature on colonial buildings, decorative arts, and costumed pageants were also influential. Barry's model for the project, the Wayside Inn in Sudbury, Massachusetts, was a famous building and a commercial success made familiar by Henry Wadsworth Longfellow's collection of poems, "Tales of a Wayside Inn." Longfellow's poetry must have affected both Barry and Perkins, as well as many other readers, with its evocative nostalgia for a romanticized, rural domestic life. Barry commented in 1925 to William Sumner Appleton that the site in Wells compared favorably to the charm of Sudbury with its oak trees.[2]

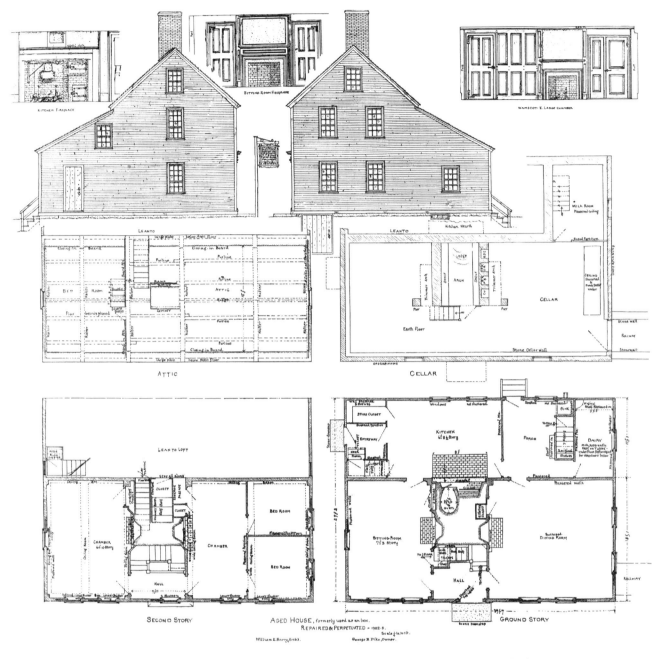

Cat. 59. William E. Barry, Measured Drawings of Jefferds Tavern, York, Maine, *ca. 1923. Pen and ink; 12 in. x 7½ in.*
Old York Historical Society.

Longfellow's earliest knowledge of the Wayside Inn was from 1862; his collection of patriotic verses later romanticized the history of the Howe family who had owned the tavern for 175 years. Alice Morse Earle, writing in 1900, described the tap-room at the Wayside Inn as a "typical example" of this kind of room; the featured photograph shows the bar cage, the hearth graced by brass andirons and a fender, and a collection of small tables and chairs.[3] Earle must have visited the inn during the period that it was operated as a paying attraction by a Salem, Massachusetts,

antique collector. In 1923, the Wayside Inn was purchased by Henry Ford who popularized the building as a combination museum, hotel, and restaurant.[4]

Henry Ford's project coincided historically with William Barry's restoration of Jefferds Tavern and was likely part of the impetus behind it. When Elizabeth Perkins purchased the tavern, she too was inspired by the Wayside Inn. Perkins hired local architect Howard Peck to negotiate the purchase and supervise the repairs to the building. In the ten years between Barry's restoration and

Cat. 59a. Taproom, Jefferds Tavern, York, Maine, built ca. 1750. Photograph by Douglas Armsden, ca. 1950. Old York Historical Society.

Perkins's purchase of the tavern, it had suffered extensive vandalism. Peck directed the dismantling of the building in the winter of 1939–40 while Perkins looked for land in York on which to reassemble it. From 1940 to 1941, the building remained in Peck's barn. In discussing possible sites for the tavern, Peck referred to the configuration of buildings in York Village as "symbolic with the old English courtyards adjacent to taverns"; initially both the old mill and coach house on the tavern site in Wells were considered as part of a proposed complex of restored buildings.[5] Peck's rendering of a grouping in York Village included Jefferds Tavern and a school house situated around an English-style courtyard garden. The tavern now stands on the former glebe land at the corner of York Street and Lindsay Road where it was moved in 1959, adjacent to a one-room school that Elizabeth Perkins relocated to the property by 1938.

Elizabeth Perkins's writings about the building omit the tavern's original location and obscure the colonial owner's history. Instead of focusing on architecture, Perkins publicized the building as an historic site for charity events. Anxious to promote the war-relief work carried on at the tavern, Perkins emphasized the tavern's connection to Revolutionary fervor, no doubt hoping for a similarly com-

mitted response to her Aid to All Allies functions, which included benefit auctions of Chinese imports and "attic treasures," and the operation of a tea-room in the tavern's tap-room (cat. 59a).[6]

To furnish Jefferds Tavern in the 1940s, Perkins drew on early travel books and historical studies by Alice Morse Earle and her contemporaries, and on her own experiences with the Little Picture House on Manhattan's upper east side (cat. 59b) from 1920 to around 1934.[7] An outgrowth of Perkins's work during World War I, the Little Picture House had offered the public carefully selected "clean" films and a pseudo-colonial tap-room. Many of the organizers, drawn from the surrounding upper-class neighborhood, like Perkins, summered in New England and could have had firsthand knowledge of the Wayside Inn. The theater's tea-room approximated the look of colonial period rooms, popularized in Sudbury and in New York at Fraunces Tavern Museum opened by the Sons of the American Revolution in 1907.[8]

The variety of "colonial" objects used by Perkins to furnish the Little Picture House included maps of colonial America, a print of "George and Lady Washington," a mid-nineteenth-century shelf clock, and a samovar among

Cat. 59b. Tea-room, Little Picture House, New York, New York. Photograph by Richard Averill Smith, ca. 1925. Old York Historical Society.

tables, chairs, and architectural fragments. Illustrations of the interior from the 1940s show that Jefferds Tavern shared several of the ubiquitous furnishings popularized at the Wayside Inn: bar cage, tall desk on stand, and assorted pewter and ceramic vessels. Many of the tavern furnishings in York had been used in the earlier tea-room in the Little Picture House.

The relocation of Jefferds Tavern complemented what Howard Peck called the "Atmosphere of 'Old York'" which had been cultivated since the turn of the century when the Historical and Improvement Society began its efforts to prettify the village center.[9] By the time that Elizabeth Perkins began to embellish the center of York, the development of modernism provided an alternative to historically inspired design that she perceived to be at odds with her own project. In 1940 Perkins expressed the hope that

> once we get going . . . we will be popular as a stopping place for motorists and that even the most modern enthusiast for steel chairs and indirect lighting may be interested in our old pine furniture made by our

forebears and in lanterns and Betty lamps with open fires and foot warmers on cold days.[10]

MAC

1 For a more detailed discussion of Barry's career, see Kevin Dean Murphy, "'A Stroll Thro' the Past': Three Architects of the Colonial Revival" (M.A. thesis, Boston University, 1985). A large collection of Barry's drawings is located at The Brick Store Museum, Kennebunk, Maine.

2 Murphy, "'A Stroll Thro' the Past,'" 52.

3 Alice Morse Earle, *Stage-Coach and Tavern Days* (New York: Macmillan, 1900), 15, 43.

4 For the Wayside Inn, see Karal Ann Marling, *George Washington Slept Here: Colonial Revivals and American Culture, 1876–1986* (Cambridge, Mass.: Harvard University Press, 1988), 162–64.

5 Howard Peck to Elizabeth Perkins, Jan. 15, 1940, Perkins Coll., OYHS.

6 Undated newspaper clipping, Perkins Coll.

7 Mary Caroline Crawford, Alice Van Leer Carrick, and Mary Harrod Northend were a few of the writers producing travel, decorating, and historical guides to early American culture from 1870 to 1940. Perkins's involvement with her mother, Mary Sowles Perkins, in restoring York's Old Gaol in 1899–1900, was possibly her introduction to this genre.

8 Marling, *George Washington Slept Here*, 209.

9 In a letter to Elizabeth Perkins, Jan. 15, 1940, Perkins Coll.

10 Elizabeth Perkins to Lucius Thayer Knowles, Nov. 2, 1940, Perkins Coll.

Elise Tyson Vaughan, Emily Tyson and Sarah Orne Jewett, *1905. Courtesy, Society for the Preservation of New England Antiquities.*

Selected Bibliography

This is a selective bibliography that includes secondary sources as well as primary materials published between 1860 and 1930. More detailed information appears in the notes. The listing of printed materials is divided into six sections: sources that provide background and context, local histories, popular histories in magazines, guidebooks to the region, architectural publications, and regional fiction and literature.

Unpubublished Materials

Several manuscript collections were used extensively in the project and are noted throughout the text. They include the Elizabeth Perkins papers, Old York Historical Society, York, Me.; the Wendell collection, Portsmouth Athenaeum, Portsmouth, N.H.; the Sayward family manuscript collections, and the Hamilton house and Sayward-Wheeler house records, Society for the Preservation of New England Antiquities, Boston, Mass.; Olmsted Archives, Frederick Law Olmsted National Historic Site, Brookline, Mass.; the Sarah Orne Jewett collection, Houghton Library, Harvard University, Cambridge, Mass.; the William E. Barry collection, The Brick Store Museum, Kennebunk, Me.; Portsmouth Public Library, Portsmouth, N.H.; New Hampshire Historical Society Library, Concord, N.H.; and Maine Historical Society archives, Portland, Me.

Photograph collections at the Old York Historical Society, Portsmouth Athenaeum, Society for the Preservation of New England Antiquities, and Strawbery Banke Museum provide rich sources for visual documentation of the region during the colonial revival period.

The institutional archives of the Moffatt-Ladd house, Old York Historical Society, Portsmouth Athenaeum, Strawbery Banke Museum, Warner House Association, and Wentworth-Gardner house are also laden with scrapbooks, letters, documents, and photographs.

Background and Context

This section includes works that provide a general overview of the colonial revival and related movements such as the arts and crafts movement. These works place the primary sources from the Piscataqua region into a more national context.

Axelrod, Alan, ed. *The Colonial Revival in America.* New York and London: W.W. Norton for the Henry Francis du Pont Winterthur Museum, 1985.

Barendsen, Joyce P. "Wallace Nutting, An American Tastemaker: The Pictures and Beyond." *Winterthur Portfolio* 17, no. 2/3 (Summer/Autumn 1983): 187–91.

Boris, Eileen. *Art and Labor: Ruskin, Morris, and the Craftsman Ideal in America.* Philadelphia: Temple University Press, 1986.

Brown, Dona, "The Tourist's New England." Ph.D. diss., University of Massachusetts, 1989.

Burke, Doreen Bolger, et al. *In Pursuit of Beauty: Americans and the Aesthetic Movement.* New York: Rizzoli International Publications in association with the Metropolitan Museum of Art, 1986.

Curry, David Park. *Childe Hassam: An Island Garden Revisited.* Denver: Denver Art Museum in association with W.W. Norton, 1990.

Dubrow, Gail Lee. "Restoring a Female Presence, New Goals in Historic Preservation." In *Architecture, A Place for Women,* ed. Ellen Perry Berkeley, 159–70. Washington, D.C., and London: Smithsonian Institution Press, 1989.

Durel, John W. "'Historic' Portsmouth: The Role of the Past in the Formation of a Community's Identity." *Historical New Hampshire* 41, no. 3/4 (Fall/Winter 1986): 97–117.

Fairbrother, Trevor J., et al. *The Bostonians: Painters of an Elegant Age, 1870–1930.* Boston: Museum of Fine Arts, 1986.

Faxon, Susan, et al. *A Stern and Lovely Scene.* Durham, N.H.: University of New Hampshire Art Galleries, 1978.

Glassberg, David. *American Historical Pageantry: The Uses of Tradition in the Early Twentieth Century.* Chapel Hill: University of North Carolina Press, 1990.

Green, Harvey. *The Light of the Home: An Intimate View of the Lives of Women in Victorian America.* New York: Pantheon Books, 1983.

Handlin, David P. *The American Home: Architecture and Society 1815–1915.* Boston: Little, Brown, 1979.

Hart, Patricia E., ed. *A Century of Color, 1886–1986.* Ogunquit, Me.: Barn Gallery Associates, 1987.

Haskell, Barbara. *Marsden Hartley.* New York: Whitney Museum of American Art in association with New York University Press, 1980.

Higonnet, Anne. "Museums: Where There's a Will . . ." *Art in America* 77, no. 5 (May 1989):65–75 .

Hosmer, Charles. *Presence of the Past: A History of the Preservation Movement in the United States Before Williamsburg*. New York: Putnam, 1965.

_____. *Preservation Comes of Age: From Williamsburg to the National Trust, 1926–1949*. 2 vols. Charlottesville: University Press of Virginia for the National Trust for Historic Preservation, 1981.

Judd, Richard W., ed. "Maine's Oldest Historical Societies." *Maine Historical Society Quarterly* 26, no. 4 (Spring, 1987).

Kammen, Michael. *Mystic Chords of Memory: The Transformation of Tradition in American Culture*. New York: Alfred A. Knopf, 1991.

Kaplan, Wendy, ed. *The Art That is Life: The Arts and Crafts Movement in America 1875–1900*. Boston: Museum of Fine Arts, 1987.

Lears, Jackson, *No Place of Grace: Antimodernism and the Transformation of American Culture, 1880–1920*. 2d ed. New York: Pantheon Books, 1981.

Leon, Warren, and Roy Rosenzweig, eds. *History Museums in the United States: A Critical Assessment*. Chicago: University of Illinois Press, 1989.

Luria, Joan, and Warren Seamans. *Earth, Sea, and Sky: Charles H. Woodbury, Artist and Teacher, 1864–1940*. Cambridge, Mass.: MIT Museum, 1988.

MacDougal, Elisabeth Blair, ed. *The Architectural Historian in America*. Washington, D.C.: National Gallery of Art, 1990.

Marling, Karal Ann. *George Washington Slept Here: Colonial Revivals and American Culture, 1876–1986*. Cambridge, Mass.: Harvard University Press, 1988.

May, Bridget A. "Progressivism and the Colonial Revival: The Modern Colonial House, 1900–1920." *Winterthur Portfolio* 26, nos. 2–3 (Summer/Autumn 1991): 107–22.

Openo, Woodard Dorr. "The Summer Colony at Little Harbor in Portsmouth, New Hampshire, and its Relation to the Colonial Revival Movement." Ph.D. diss., University of Michigan, 1990.

Pierce, Patricia Jobe, and Rolf H. Kristiansen. *John Joseph Enneking, American Impressionist Painter*. North Abingdon, Mass.: Pierce Galleries, 1972.

Reed, Roger G. *A Delight to All Who Know It: The Maine Summer Architecture of William R. Emerson*. Augusta, Me.: Maine Historic Preservation Commission, 1990.

Rhoads, William B. *The Colonial Revival*. 2 vols. New York and London: Garland Publishing, Inc., 1977.

Robinson, William F. *A Certain Slant of Light: The First Hundred Years of New England Photography*. Boston: New York Graphic Society, 1980.

Rossano, Geoffrey L., ed. *Creating a Dignified Past: Museums and the Colonial Revival*. Savage, Md.: Rowman & Littlefield Publishers, Inc., 1991.

Scully, Vincent J. *The Shingle Style*. New Haven: Yale University Press, 1955.

Sears, John F. *Sacred Places: American Tourist Attractions in the Nineteenth Century*. New York: Oxford University Press, 1989.

Sherman, Sarah Way. *Sarah Orne Jewett, an American Persephone*. Hanover: University Press of New England, 1989.

Stilgoe, John R. *Borderland: Origins of the American Suburb, 1820–1939*. New Haven: Yale University Press, 1988.

_____. *Metropolitan Corridor*. New Haven: Yale University Press, 1983.

Sturgis, Walter Knight. "Arthur Little and the Colonial Revival," *Journal of the Society of Architectural Historians* 32, no. 2 (May 1983): 147–63.

Weinberg, H. Barbara. *The Lure of Paris: Nineteenth-Century American Painters and Their French Teachers*. New York: Abbeville Press, 1991.

Westbrook, Perry D. *The New England Town in Fact and Fiction*. East Brunswick, N.J.: Associated University Presses, Inc., 1982.

LOCAL HISTORIES

Books on local history provide the most readily available sources for those primarily concerned with the stories of "colonial" buildings and their occupants. This chronological listing includes only those works published in the nineteenth century that deal exclusively with the Piscataqua region and its individual towns. It is largely from these works that popular and professional writers derived the "facts" about specific buildings to develop romantic tales of historical association. While better or more elaborate local histories appeared after 1900, their nineteenth-century predecessors formed the most available core of information to many later writers.

Adams, Nathaniel. *Annals of Portsmouth*. Portsmouth: Nathaniel Adams, 1825. Reprint. Hampton, N.H.: Peter Randall, 1971.

Agamenticus, Bristol, Gorgeana, York: An Oration Delivered by the Hon. James Phinney Baxter . . . on the Two Hundred and Fiftieth Anniversary of the Town. York, Me.: Old York Historical and Improvement Society, 1904.

Albee, John. *Newcastle, Historic and Picturesque.* Boston, 1884. Reprint. Hampton, N.H.: Peter Randall, 1974.

Banks, Charles Edward, ed. *History of York, Maine.* 1931. Reprint. Baltimore: Regional Publishing Company, 1967.

Brewster, Charles W. *Rambles About Portsmouth—First Series.* Portsmouth, N.H.: C.W. Brewster & Son, 1859. Reprint. Somersworth, N.H.: New Hampshire Publishing, 1971.

_____. *Rambles About Portsmouth—Second Series.* Portsmouth, N.H.: L.W. Brewster, 1869. Reprint. Somersworth, N.H.: New Hampshire Publishing, 1972.

POPULAR HISTORIES IN MAGAZINES

The increase of popular magazines of history and the creation of local historical societies with their own publications during the nineteenth century provided seemingly endless opportunities to tell and retell the stories of hardy pioneers and local elites, historic communities, and the buildings of the "colonial" past. For this region, the *Granite Monthly* published the greatest number of stories related to communities on both sides of the Piscataqua.

Baer, Annie Wentworth. "Stories of an Ancient City [York] by the Sea." *Granite Monthly* 11 (Apr. 1888): 143–48, 188–92.

Baxter, James Phinney. "Piscataqua and the Pepperrells." *Maine Historical Society Collections,* 2nd ser., 4 (1893): 426–30.

Bourne, Edward Emerson. "Garrison Houses in York County." *Maine Historical Society Collections* 7 (1876): 109–20.

Chadwick, John W. "The Isles of Shoals," and Clark, Sarah D. "A Summer at York." *Harper's New Monthly Magazine* 65 (Sept. 1882): 487–98.

Colby, Fred Myron. "A Day at Old Kittery." *Granite Monthly* 2 (July 1878): 68–71.

Martin, Stella. "The Captives of York." *Granite Monthly* 35 (Aug. 1849): 113–20.

Preble, George Henry. "The Garrison Houses of York, Maine." *New England Historic and Genealogical Register* 28 (1874): 268–72.

Safford, Moses. "Historic Homes of Kittery." *Maine Historical Society Collections,* 2nd ser., 5 (1894): 113–28, 387–407.

GUIDEBOOKS TO THE REGION

Guidebooks, travel literature, and reminiscences of travel provide a rich source of information about the natural and historic scenery of the Piscataqua region. They reveal a complex tourist business that often used the region's historical assets to attract tourists. These guidebooks, along with hotel directories, account books, and other ephemera, exist in quantity at the Portsmouth Athenaeum and the Old York Historical Society.

Appleton's Illustrated Handbook of American Summer Resorts. New York: Appleton, 1876.

Drake, Samuel Adams. *Nooks and Corners of the New England Coast.* New York: Harper and Brothers, 1875.

Drake, Samuel Adams. *The Pine-Tree Coast.* Boston: Estes and Lauriat, 1891.

Emery, George Alex. *Ancient City of Gorgeana and Modern Town of York.* 1873. Reprint. Boston: G. Alex Emery, 1894.

Foster, Sarah H. *The Portsmouth Guide Book.* Portsmouth, N.H.: Joseph H. Foster, 1879. 2d ed., 1884. 3d. ed., 1896.

Gurney, Caleb S. *Portsmouth Historic and Picturesque.* 1902. Reprint. Portsmouth, N.H.: Strawbery Banke, 1982.

Ingersoll, Ernest. *Down-East Latch Strings: or Seashore, Lakes, and Mountains.* Boston: Boston and Maine Railroad, 1887.

New England's Summer and America's Leading Winter Resorts. New York: G. Frederick Kalhoff, 1897.

Return of the Sons and Daughters of Portsmouth, 1873. Portsmouth, N.H.: Charles Gardner, 1873.

Sweetser, Moses F. *Here and There in New England and Canada: All Along Shore.* Boston: Passenger Department, Boston and Maine Railroad, 1889.

ARCHITECTURAL PUBLICATIONS

The architecture of the Piscataqua was widely published in books, folios, and journal articles in the forms of architectural photographs, measured drawings, and architects' sketches of early buildings in Portsmouth or other towns of the larger Piscataqua region.

Architects' Emergency Committee. *Great Georgian Houses of America.* N.Y.: Kalkoff Press, 1933.

Barry, William E. *Pen Sketches of Old Houses.* Boston: James R. Osgood & Co., [1874].

Brown, Frank Chouteau. "Three-Story Colonial Houses of New England." *White Pine Series of Architectural Monographs* 3, no. 1 (1917): 1–14.

Chandler, Joseph E. *The Colonial House.* New York: Robert McBride & Co., 1924.

Corner, James M., and Eric Ellis Soderholtz. *Examples of Domestic Colonial Architecture in New England.* Boston: Boston Architectural Club, 1891.

Dow, Joy Wheeler. *American Renaissance.* New York: William T. Comstock, 1914.

Howe, Lois Lilly, and Constance Fuller. *Details from Old New England Houses.* New York: Architectural Book Co., 1913.

Howells, John Mead. *Lost Examples of Colonial Architecture.* New York: William Helburn, Inc. 1931. Reprint. New York: Dover Publications, 1963.

Kimball, Fiske. *Domestic Architecture of the American Colonies and of the Early Republic.* New York: Charles Scribner's Sons, 1922. Reprint. New York: Dover Publications, 1966.

Litchfield, Electus D. "Portsmouth, N.H., an Early American Metropolis." *White Pine Series of Architectural Monographs* 7, no. 1 (Feb. 1921): 1–14.

Little, Arthur. *Early New England Interiors . . . Salem, Marblehead, Portsmouth, Kittery.* Boston: A. Williams & Co., 1878.

Porter, John Hutchinson. "A Survey of Existing Colonial Architecture in Maine." *Architectural Review* 7 (Aug.–Nov. 1918): 29–32, 47–51, 94–96; 11 (July–Dec. 1920): 13–15, 45–48, 83–88, 119–20, 155–56, 183–86; 12 (Feb.–June 1921): 41–46, 64, 92, 151–52. Continues in *American Architect* 120 (Aug. 1921): 149–50.

Walker, Howard C. "Some Old Houses on the Southern Coast of Maine." *White Pine Series of Architectural Monographs* 4, no. 2 (Apr. 1918): 1–14.

Whitefield, Edwin. *The Homes of Our Forefathers, Maine, New Hampshire, Vermont.* Reading, Mass.: By the author, 1886.

REGIONAL FICTION AND LITERATURE

Between 1860 and 1930, the Piscataqua region was a popular summer resort area for several members of the Boston literary circle. This group of writers wrote about the region in nationally distributed publications, especially *The Atlantic Monthly.*

Aldrich, Thomas Bailey. *An Old Town by the Sea.* Boston: Houghton Mifflin, 1894.

——————. *The Story of a Bad Boy.* 1869 and numerous later editions. Reprint. Hanover, N.H.: University Press of New England with Strawbery Banke Museum, 1990.

Howells, William Dean. "Confessions of a Summer Colonist," "From New York into New England," and "Stacatto Notes of a Vanished Summer." In *Literature and Life: Studies.* New York: Harper and Brothers, 1902.

Jewett, Sarah Orne. *Deephaven.* Boston: James R. Osgood, 1877.

——————. "River Driftwood." *Atlantic Monthly* 48 (Oct. 1881): 500–510.

——————. "The Old Town of Berwick." *New England Magazine* 10 (June 1894): 585–609.

——————. *The Tory Lover.* Boston: Houghton Mifflin, 1901.

——————. "York Garrison, 1640." *Wide Awake* 23, no. 1 (June 1886): 18–22.

Page, Thomas Nelson. "Miss Godwin's Inheritance." In *Under the Crust: The Novels, Stories, Sketches and Poems of Thomas Nelson Page.* New York: Charles Scribner's Sons, 1910.

Perkins, Elizabeth Bishop. "The Codfish Ghost: The Biography of a House from the Seventeenth Century to the Present Day." Unpublished manuscript, Old York Historical Society, 1933.

Thaxter, Celia. *Among the Isles of Shoals.* 1873. Reprint. Sanbornville, N.H.: Wake-Brook House, 1962.

——————. *An Island Garden.* 1894. Reprint. Boston: Houghton Mifflin, 1988.

Wasson, George. *The Green Shay.* Boston: Houghton Mifflin, 1908.

——————. *Cap'n Simeon's Store.* Boston: Houghton Mifflin, 1902.

Illustration Credits

Dust Jacket: David Bohl, Society for the Preservation of New England Antiquities

Endpapers: Old York Historical Society

Frontispiece: Society for the Preservation of New England Antiquities

Chapter dividers:

Chaps. 1, 2, Bibliography: Society for the Preservation of New England Antiquities

Chap. 3: The National Society of The Colonial Dames of America in the State of New Hampshire

Chap. 4: Strawbery Banke Museum

Chaps. 5, 6: Old York Historical Society

Color plates:

Pls. 1, 6, 7: Old York Historical Society

Pl. 2: The Mitchell Family

Pl. 3: Private Collection

Pl. 4: David Bohl, Society for the Preservation of New England Antiquities

Pl. 5: Nancy Flentje

Pl. 8: Mr. and Mrs. Arthur G. Altschul

Figures:

Fig. a: Drawing by Lisa Blinn

Figs. b, 1.5–1.7, 1.9–1.12, 1.14, 2.2, 2.4, 2.10, 3.4, 3.6, 3.8, 3.11, 4.5, 4.6, 5.1–5.3, 6.1–6.4: Old York Historical Society

Figs. c, 1.3, 1.13, 5a, 5b, 2.6–2.7a, 2.11a, 3.5, 3.7, 21-22a, 4.12, 4.13, 6.6: Society for the Preservation of New England Antiquities

Figs. 1.1, 6.7: Portsmouth Athenaeum

Fig. 1.2: Old Berwick Historical Society

Fig. 1.4: The B&O Railroad Museum

Fig. 1.8: Maine Historic Preservation Commission

Fig. 2.1: Frick Art Reference Library

Fig. 2.3: Boston Public Library

Figs. 2.5a, 2.5b: Mr. and Mrs. S. Thompson Viele

Figs. 2.8, 2.11b: Douglas Armsden, Portsmouth Athenaeum

Figs. 2.9, 5.6: University of New Hampshire

Fig. 3.1: The Lamont Gallery, Phillips Exeter Academy, gift of Thomas W. Lamont, class of 1888

Fig. 3.2: New Hampshire Historical Society

Figs. 3.3, 3.9, 3.10: Marvin Breckinridge Patterson, Piscataqua Garden Club

Figs. 4.1, 4.9, 5.4, 6.9: Strawbery Banke Museum

Fig. 4.2: Henry Parsons Coolidge

Fig. 4.3: Nancy Flentje

Fig. 4.4: Portland Museum of Art

Fig. 4.8: Smith College Museum of Art

Figs. 4.10, 4.14: Mrs. John B. Staley

Figs. 4.11, 5.7, 5.8: Portsmouth Public Library

Fig. 4.15: Woodard Openo

Fig. 4.16: Museum of Art of Ogunquit

Fig. 4.17: The Historical Society of Wells and Ogunquit

Fig. 5.9: National Museum of American Art, Smithsonian Institution, gift of John Gellatly

Fig. 6.5: The Woodman Institute Museum

Fig. 6.8: Douglas Armsden, The Warner House Association

Catalogue entries:

Cats. 1, 3a, 6–7, 9, 15, 15a, 18, 18a, 20, 36b, 38a, 41, 41a, 45, 46, 47, 50, 52, 53, 53a, 56a, 59, 59b: Old York Historical Society

Cats. 1a, 2c, 3, 4, 8a, 11, 12a, 13, 24, 27, 44, 44a, 57: Portsmouth Athenaeum

Cats. 2, 4a, 12, 23, 29, 29a, 49, 54, 57a: Strawbery Banke Museum

Cats. 2a: Earle G. Shettleworth, Jr.

Cat. 5: The Cooper-Hewitt Museum

Cats. 5a, 5b, 8, 9a, 10a, 13a–14a, 16–17, 17b, 21–22a, 31, 32, 38, 48, 54a, 55a, 56: Society for the Preservation of New England Antiquities

Cats. 8b, 19, 19a, 55: The National Society of The Colonial Dames of America in the State of New Hampshire

Cat. 10: Maine Historical Society

Cat. 58: Douglas Armsden, Portsmouth Athenaeum

Cat. 11a: The Historical Society of the Town of Greenwich, Connecticut

Cat. 15a, 59a: Douglas Armsden, Old York Historical Society

Cat. 17a: The Brick Store Museum

Cat. 20: Garden Club of America

Cat. 25: The National Museum of American Art, Smithsonian Institution, gift of John Gellatly

Cats. 25a, 42a: University of New Hampshire, Isles of Shoals Collection

Cats. 26, 26a: Marvin Breckinridge Patterson, Piscataqua Garden Club

Cat. 30b: Mr. and Mrs. Thomas Rosse; Vose Galleries

Cats. 32a, 36a: Estate of David O. Woodbury

Cat. 33a: The Brooklyn Museum, John B. Woodward Memorial Fund

Cat. 34: The Historical Society of Wells and Ogunquit

Cat. 35c: Paul S. Stevens

Cat. 39: Maine Historic Preservation Commission

Cat. 39a: Richard Cheek, Maine Historic Preservation Commission

Cats. 40, 40a: Kevin D. Murphy

Cat. 43: Philip H. Kendrick

Cat. 48a: Old Berwick Historical Society

Cat. 58a: Douglas Armsden, Warner House Association

Bruce Kennett produced the copy photographs of many of the items in the collections of the Old York Historical Society.

Index

N.B.: Page references for illustrations are set in bold type. Cross references and publication titles are set in italic type. Page numbers followed by an "n" refer to endnotes.

A

Abandoning an Adopted Farm (Sanborn), 39–40
Académie Julian (Paris, France), 135
Acme Portrait Company (Portsmouth, New Hampshire), 16
Adams, Frank C., 53
Adams, Henry, 116
Adams, John Howard, 61, 62 n. 7
Adopting an Abandoned Farm (Sanborn), 39–40
aesthetic modernism. *See* modernism, aesthetic
Agamenticus River (Woodbury), 145, **145**
Akerman, Benjamin, 106, 107 n. 1
Albee, John, 17, 62, 126
Aldis, Owen, 92
Aldrich, Lilian Woodman, 104, 207, 208–9
Aldrich, Talbot, 207
   Aldrich house garden photo by, **105**
Aldrich, Thomas Bailey, ix, 13, 84, 165, 170, 175, 182, 207
   childhood home of, 14
   on Portsmouth's decay, 4
   Portsmouth "village sketch" by, 184–85
   reactionary/exclusionist politics of, 11–12, 185
   on "the savage," 165, 166
Aldrich Memorial. *See* Thomas Bailey Aldrich Memorial
Alger garden (York, Maine), 89, **89**
Allen, Frances, 155
Allen, Mary, 155
Allen house (New Castle, New Hampshire). *See* Bos'n Allen house (New Castle, New Hampshire)
America (ship), 217
American Architect and Building News, The, 50, 122, 128
American Architecture, Decoration, and Furniture (Wallis), 48–49
American Notebooks (Hawthorne), 179
American Renaissance (Dow), 50
American Society of Landscape Architects, 88
Ames, Kenneth L., XII
   on "colonial," XIII n. 2

Ammons, Elizabeth, 172, 173
Among the Isles of Shoals (Thaxter), 14 n. 8, 172, 179–80, 182
   illustration from, **178**
Ancient City of Gorgeana and Modern Town of York (Emery), 16
Andrew, A. Piatt, 100
Annie B. Woodman Institute (Dover, New Hampshire), 28, **29**, 196–97, 198. *See also* Dam garrison house (Dover, New Hampshire)
Appledore Island, Isles of Shoals, 5, **178**
   artistic community on, 156–58
Appleton, William Sumner, 28, 45, 56–57, 67, 68, 73, 201, 215, 219, 222
Architectural Heritage of the Piscataqua, The (Howells), 45, 51–52
architecture, XII, 20, 48–54, 62, 103, 143. *See also* entries for individual architects and architectural styles
   women in, 88
Armory Show (1913), XI
Armsden, Douglas
   Boardman house photo by, **47**
   Jefferds Tavern taproom photo by, **224**
   Macpheadris-Warner house photo by, **202, 220**
   Perkins house dining room photo by, **69**
   Wendell house photo by, **44**
"Artists' Homes as They Paint Them" (Hamilton), 132
Arts and Crafts Exhibition Society (England), 128
Ashe, William A., 35
Association for the Preservation of Historic Buildings, 222
Astor, John Jacob, 127
Atlantic Gypsum Company, 160
Atlantic Heights (Portsmouth, New Hampshire), 160, 160–62
   bird's-eye drawing of, **161**
Atlantic Monthly, The, 166, 179, 180, 182, 188
Atlantic Ship Building Corporation, 158–60
Attractive Bits Along Shore, 13

B

Badger's Island, New Hampshire, 217
Baker, C. Alice, 27, 41–43, 91, 151, 152, 154
Baker, E.W., 66
Ball, Henry B., 58, 147

elevation of Portsmouth Athenaeum fireplace by, **59**
Barbizon school, 115, 124 n. 1, 152–54
Bar Harbor, Maine, 7
Barrell, Charles C., 35
Barrell, Elizabeth, 64–65, **65**
Barrell, George Octavious, 66
Barrell, Joseph, 67 n. 3
Barrell, Mary, 64–65, **65**
Barrell, Nathaniel, 35
Barrell, Sally (Mrs. Nathaniel)
   portrait of, 66, 67 n. 9
Barrell Grove (York, Maine), **34**, 35, **36**
   renovations to, 66–67.
Barrell Homestead (Monroe), **34**
Barrett, Samuel, 62
Barrott, Chauncey E., 61
Barry, William E., 28, 222
   Lady Pepperrell house watercolor by, **55**
Bartlett, George, 126
Basketmaker (Coleman), 152, **153**
"Bay of Naples, The" (wallpaper), 76
Beauport (Gloucester, Massachusetts), 100, 101–3
Beautiful Gardens in America (Shelton), 87
Beaux, Cecilia, 100, 131
Bellamy, Charles G., 53, 55 n. 6
Bellamy, John Haley, 38, 149
Benson, Frank, 130, 131
Berwick Academy (South Berwick, Maine), 88
Beyond New England Thresholds (Chamberlain), 51
Bigelow, William Sturgis, 128
Blackburn, Joseph, 67 n. 9, 222
Blackwell, Elizabeth, 31
Blaisdell, E.B., 31
Blaisdell, Gertrude E., 217
Blockhouse and Stockade Fort, The (Barry), 28
Boardman house (Portsmouth, New Hampshire). *See* Langley Boardman house (Portsmouth, New Hampshire)
Bonnat, Léon, 147
Bonny, Mrs. (*Deephaven*), 170, **170**
Bos'n Allen house (New Castle, New Hampshire), **122**
Boston, Massachusetts. *See also* Arts and Crafts Exhibition Society in Boston
   Barbizon school painters and, 115, 124 n. 1
Boston and Kennebunkport Seashore Company, 6, 7
Boston & Maine guidebook. *See Here and There in New England and Canada* (Sweetser)

Boston & Maine Railroad, 6, 17
    map ca. 1912, **5**
Boston Architectural Club, 49
"Boston School," 131
Boston Society of Architects, 149
Boudin, Eugène, 147
Bourne, Edward Emerson, 26–27
Boyd garden (Portsmouth, New
    Hampshire), 81
Brandon, Kate (*Deephaven*), 170, 180–82
Bray house (Kittery Point, Maine). *See*
    John Bray house (Kittery Point, Maine)
Brayton, George, 73
    Hamilton house parlor photo by, **73**
Brewster, Charles W., 9, 16, 26
British Architect, The (Swan), 60
Brooks, Jesamine, **192**
Brown, Frank C., 50
Brown, J. Appleton, 156
Brown, Walter R., 38, 53
Browne, Herbert W.C., 52, 53, 63, 71, 77, 97,
    103
Bryant, Gridley, 20 n. 2
Bryant and Rogers (architects), 17
Bulfinch, Charles, 57
Butler, Philip, 19

C

Caffin, Charles, 133
Cambridge School of Architecture and
    Landscape Architecture for Women, 88
Cape Ann, Massachusetts, 8
Cape Arundel (Kennebunkport, Maine), 6, 7
Cape Neddick, Maine, 30–31
captivity narratives, 169, 171, 173, 175
Carey, Alida Astor, 127
Carey, Arthur Astor, 116, 127–29
Carey, John, 127
Carey residence (Little Harbor, New Hamp-
    shire). *See* Arthur Astor Carey residence
    (Little Harbor, New Hampshire)
Casson, Charles P., 61
Century Illustrated Monthly Magazine
    (periodical), 145
Cézanne, Paul, 115
Chamberlain, Joshua, 22
Chamberlain, Samuel, 51
Champernowne, Captain Francis, 149
Champernowne Farm (Kittery Point,
    Maine). *See* John Thaxter residence
    (Kittery Point, Maine)
Chandler, Joseph Everett, 44–45, 50, 200,
    201, 218–19, 221
Chase, Daniel, 17
Chase Gallery (Boston, Massachusetts). *See*
    J. Eastman Chase Gallery (Boston,
    Massachusetts)
Chauncey, Miss Sally (*Deephaven*), 170–71,
    181, **181**

Cheever, Henry, 66
Chelsea (Massachusetts) Keramic Arts
    Works. *See* Dedham Pottery
Cheney, Russell
    Pepperrell Cove by, **120**
Chicago School, XII
Chicago Tribune Tower (Chicago, Illinois), 56
Children at Wentworth-Coolidge House
    (Perkins), **113**
Chippendale-style furniture, 24, 26 n. 12,
    136, **136**, 212
Choate, Mabel, 107
Chronicles of Kennebunk (Barry), 222
Church, Frank S., 27
Church Point, Portsmouth New Hampshire
    (Hassam), 119, **121**
Cilley house (Exeter, New Hampshire),
    210–11
Clark, Sarah D., 118
Clemens, Samuel Langhorne, 22, 188, 207
Cleveland, H.W.S., 82
Cliff House (York, Maine), 6, 31 n. 1, 32
Coast of Maine, The (Chamberlain), 51
"Codfish Ghost: A Biography of a House
    from the Seventeenth Century to the
    Present Day" (Perkins), 69, 189–90
Codman, Ogden, Jr., 75–76, 103
Coffin, Marion, 88
Cogswell house (Essex, Massachusetts), 101,
    102
Cole, W.B.
    "Surf Side" cottage owned by, 7
Coleman, Emma, 13, 27, 87, 151, 165
    The Basketmaker by, **153**
    Chases Pond by, VI
    Deephaven photographs by, 180, **181**
    haying photo by, **118**
    Old Gaol photo by, **195**
    as photographer, 152–55
    By the Third Bridge, York River by,
    ENDPAPERS
    The Woman with Faggots by, **154**
Coleman, Vail, 193
"colonial"
    defined, xi n. 2
Colonial Dames, Society of. *See* Society of
    Colonial Dames
Colonial Furniture in America (Lockwood),
    25
Colonial House, The (Chandler), 44, 50
*Colonial Houses of Maryland, Pennsylvania
    and Virginia* (Chandler), 44
Colonial Interiors (French), 51
Colonial Manor (Exeter, New Hampshire).
    See Cilley house (Exeter, New
    Hampshire)
colonial revival, VII
    architects, 103
    in architecture, XII, 20, 48–54, 62, 103, 143
    artistic and literary works and, 13–14
    material culture interests of, XI

at the national level, XIII n. 3
    and Native Americans, 167–69
    in painting, 131
    photo documentation and, 152–55
    and reactionary politics, 11–12, 194
    in the second generation, 129
    Thomas Bailey Aldrich Memorial and,
    208–9
colonial revival style (architecture), 143,
    147, 162. *See also* colonial revival
"colonial trinity," 103
Colonial Williamsburg (Williamsburg,
    Virginia), 45, 193
    as historic preservation model and
    standard, 201–3
Columbian Exposition of 1893. *See* World's
    Columbian Exposition of 1893
    (Chicago, Illinois)
Company International de Belles Artes
    (Portsmouth, New Hampshire), 16
"Confessions of a Summer Colonist"
    (Howells), 165, 188, 189
Connarroe, George M.
    Cragmere cottage owned by, 7
Cook, Clarence, 38
cookstoves, 208, 210 n. 11
Coolidge, J. Templeman, III, 39, 100, 116,
    128, 130
Copley, John Singleton, 67 n. 9
Corcoran School of Art (Washington,
    D.C.), 131
Cornish, New Hampshire, 115
Cottage Hospital (Portsmouth, New
    Hampshire), 58
Country House, The (Hooper), 40
Country of the Pointed Firs, The (Jewett),
    172
Coventry Hall (York, Maine), 39
Cragmere cottage (York Cliffs, Maine), 7
Craigie house (Cambridge, Massachusetts).
    See Vassall-Craigie-Longfellow house
    (Cambridge, Massachusetts)
Cram, Ralph Adams, XII
Crandon, Anne Lawton, 141
Crane house (Portsmouth, New Hamp-
    shire). *See* Elisha Crane house
    (Portsmouth, New Hampshire)
Creek farm (Little Harbor, New Hamp-
    shire). *See* Arthur Astor Carey residence
    (Little Harbor, New Hampshire)
Crosby, Raymond Moreau, 43
Crowley, John, 167, 168
Cunningham, Ann Pamela, 193
Cunningham, Johnny, 81
Curry, David Park, 108, 119, 156
Curtis, Greely, 103
Cutt farm. *See* Ursula Cutt farm (Ports-
    mouth, New Hampshire)
Cutts, Oliver, 38, 56
Cutts, Sally, 56
Cutts Farm (Kittery Point, Maine), 149

D

Dabney, William H., Jr., 147–48
Dame, Luther
  Kittery Point photo by, **119**
  Pepperrell tomb photo by, **11**
  Sparhawk house photo by, **52**
Dam garrison house (Dover, New Hampshire). *See* William Dam garrison house (Dover, New Hampshire)
Daubigny, Charles François, 147
Daughters of Edward D. Boit (Sargent), 131
Davenport Company, 58
Davidson, Elizabeth Burleigh, 92, 195–96, 205
Davidson, James T., 196, 206
Davis, Elizabeth Jacobs, 97
Davol, Joseph
  Josias River by, **125**
Davol, Ralph, 147
Davol cottage (Ogunquit, Maine), **143**
De Camp, Joseph, 131
Decorator and Furnisher, **18**
Dedham Pottery, 128
Deephaven (Jewett), 118, 165, 180–82, 189
  illustrated editions of, 135–37, 137 n. 8, 152, 180
  Native Americans, savagery, and the feminine in, 170–71
  Whittier on, 180
Deerfield Academy, 151
Deering, Ebenezer, 210
DeHaven, Frank, 31
Denis, Helen (*Deephaven*), 170–71, 180–82
Dennett, Hartley, 129
Dennett, Mary Ware, 129
Details from Old New England Houses (Fuller), 50
Devens, Mary, 87
"Devil's Kitchen" (York, Maine), 16
Dickinson, Emily, 179
Domestic Architecture of the American Colonies (Kimball), 50
Donovan, Josephine, 182
Dorothy Quincy house (Exeter, New Hampshire), 25
Dover, New Hampshire, XI, 3
Dow, George Francis, 200
Dow, James, 219
Dow, Joy Wheeler, 50
Down East Latch-Strings (Ingersoll), 12
Downes, William Howe, 144
Downing, A.J., 35
Drake, Samuel Adams, 13, 15, 27, 115, 117, 118, 205
Dublin, New Hampshire, 115, 128
Dubrow, Gail Lee, 193, 198
Dufour and Leroy (wallpaper printing firm), 76
Dunelawn (Ogunquit, Maine). *See* George F. Smith residence (Ogunquit, Maine)

du Pont, Henry Francis, 25
Duran, Carolus, 131
Dwight, Timothy, 3

E

Eagles Rock (Prides Crossing, Massachusetts), 103
Earle, Alice Morse, 83, 87, 96, 108, 222, 224
Earle house (Cape Neddick, Maine). *See* James Earle house (Cape Neddick, Maine)
Early American Churches (Embury), 50
Early New England Interiors (Little), 39, 48, **49**, 50, 54
Ear of Corn (Hartley), 138–40
Eastern Railroad, 6, 17
Edwards, Jesse B., 19
Eldredge Brewery (Portsmouth, New Hampshire), 16
Eliot, Charles
  on coastal preservation, 82
Eliot, John, 167
Eliot, Maine
  historical exercises in, 23
Elisha Crane house (Portsmouth, New Hampshire), 107
Elizabeth Perkins house (York, Maine), 41, 67–70, **68**
  cigar-store Indian at, **189**
  dining room of, **69**
  gardens of, 84–85, **85**, **96**, 96–97
Elizabeth Perkins summer fellowship program, VII
Elwyn, Elizabeth Langdon, 61
Embargo Act of 1807, 3
Embury, Aymar, 50
Emergency Fleet Corporation. *See* United States Emergency Fleet Corporation
Emerson, Edward Octavius, 39
Emerson, William Ralph, 52, 120, 122, 149
Emerson house (York, Maine), 39, **40**, 41
Emery, Alex, 16
English cottage-style (architecture), 152
English garden city movement, 162
Enneking, John J., 146–47
Essex Country Club (Hamilton, Massachusetts), 78
Essex Institute (Salem, Massachusetts), 103, 200, 206
Evans, Henry E., 9
Examples of Domestic Colonial Architecture in New England (Corner & Soderholtz), 49

F

F.A. Whiting subdivision (Ogunquit, Maine), 88
Faneuil Hall (Boston, Massachusetts), 143

Farrand, Beatrix Jones, 88
federal style (architecture), 78, 122, 162
Fenway Court (Boston, Massachusetts), 103
Fernald, George Porter, 71, 76–77
  Essex Country Club murals by, 78
  Hamilton house gardens influenced by, 97
  Hamilton house murals by, 71–72, 74, **75**, 76–78
  Villa d'Este, Tivoli and, 77, **77**
Field, Hamilton Easter, 117, 118, 138
  self portrait by, **117**
  Washington Andirons by, **139**
Fields, Annie Adams, 149, 175
Fieldstone (Ogunquit, Maine), 141
First Parish Church (York, Maine), 92, **93**
First Sketch of Ogunquit (Woodbury), 144
Flemish glass, 24
Fogg Memorial (South Berwick, Maine), 88
Folsom, Nathan, 74 n. 4
Footman, Frederick N., 19, 20 n. 8
Ford, Henry, 223
Foster, Joseph, 16
Foster, Sarah Haven, 16, 122, 123
  Bos'n Allen house watercolor by, **122**
Four Acres (York Harbor, Maine), 45, **45**
Francis L. Stetson house (York Harbor, Maine), 88–89
Franklin, Benjamin, 187, 221
Frary house (Deerfield, Massachusetts), 27, 151
Fraunces Tavern Museum (New York, New York), 224
Freeman, Edith Shepard, 213, 213 n. 15
Freeman, Mary Wilkins, 188
French, Leigh, Jr., 51
Frink farmhouse (Newington, New Hampshire), 123
Frisbee, Jesse E., 6
"From New York to New England" (Howells), 188
Frostfields (New Castle, New Hampshire), 24, 122, **126**, 126–27
Frost garrison house (Eliot, Maine), 28–29
Fuller, Constance, 50

G

gambrel roof, 122, 162
Gaol Kitchen, The (Enneking), 146–47
garden city movement, 162
Garden in Its Glory, The (Hassam), **109**
Gardner, Isabella Stewart, 103, 130, 131. *See also* Isabella Stewart Gardner Museum (Boston, Massachusetts)
Garvan Collection (Yale University), 222
Gaugengigl, Ignaz Marcel, 156
Gauguin, Paul, 115
General John Sullivan house (Durham, New Hampshire), 39
George F. Smith residence (Ogunquit, Maine), **140**, 140–41

Georgian Period, The (Ware), 49–50
Georgian style (architecture), 49–50, 55–56, 60–61, 67, 78, 122, 148, **148**, 162, 208, 213
Gilder, Richard Watson, 156, 158 n. 9
Girl Crocheting (Tarbell), 131
Girl Reading (Tarbell), 132
Gloucester, Massachusetts, 115
Going to Ride (Tarbell), 132, **133**
Gooding, Reverend Alfred, 200
Goodwin, Alpheus, 74 n. 4, 97
Goodwin, General Ichabod, 97
gothic revival style (architecture), 37
Governor John Langdon mansion (Portsmouth, New Hampshire), 12, 17, 19, 37, 39, 60–61, 123
  dining room of, **60**
  garden of, **111**
Gowen, Angie
  York village photo by, **91**
Grace Morrill cottage and studio (Ogunquit, Maine), **141**, 141–43, **142**
Granite State Insurance Company, 217
Grant, John, 81
Graves, Abbott F., 62
Great Georgian Houses of America (Architects' Emergency Committee), 50, **86**
Great House (Portsmouth, New Hampshire). *See* Samuel Wentworth house (Portsmouth, New Hampshire)
Great Island Common (New Castle, New Hampshire), 122, 126
Greenough, Arthur T., 24
Gregory, Albert, 87
Gregory and Browne, 71
guidebooks. *See under* Piscataqua River region; Portsmouth, New Hampshire; York, Maine
Gurney, Caleb Stevens, 16, 24, 87

H

Hackett, Wallace, 58, 207, 209
Haggens, Major Tilly, 187
Haggins, John, 135
Hale, Philip Leslie, 131
Haley cottage (Smuttynose, Isles of Shoals, New Hampshire), **173**
Hall, Colonel Daniel, 197, 198
Halliday Historic Photograph Company
  Jaffrey cottage photo by, **62**
Hamilton, Francis, 132
Hamilton, Jonathan, 74 n. 4, 97
Hamilton, Mary, 187
Hamilton house (South Berwick, Maine), XII, **XIII**, 12, 13, **33**, 41, 63, 189
  as artistic enclave, 116–17
  colonial revival and, 70–71
  garden cottage, 100–103, **101**, **102**
  garden pergola, 98, **100**
  garden plan of, **86**, 87

gardens of, 97–100, **99**, **100**
hallway of, **11**
in *House Beautiful* magazine, XII, 74
interior decoration of, 71–74, **72**, **73**
murals in, 71–72, 74–78
parlor of, **72**, **73**
photographic documentation of, 134, 135
pinewood at, 98–99
during renovation, **43**
restoration and renovation of, 71–74
Sarah Orne Jewett and, 185–86
Sarah Orne Jewett photo of, **70**
sculptures at, 116
Hamilton house (Woodbury), **186**
Hancock house (Boston, Massachusetts). *See* John Hancock house (Boston, Massachusetts)
Hanson, Halfdan M., 101
Harold C. Richard house (York Harbor, Maine), 89
Harper's New Monthly Magazine, 115, 118, 119, 121, 145
  Woodbury's *Agamenticus* in, 145, **145**
Harrison, Paul, 55
Hart house (Newington, New Hampshire). *See* Sally Hart house (Newington, New Hampshire)
Hartley, Marsden, 138–40
Harvard Lampoon, 116
Haskell, Barbara, 138
Hassam, Childe, 87, 108, 119, 156–58
  Garden in Its Glory by, **109**
  In the Garden by, **174**
  Portsmouth Athenaeum etching by, **57**
  Portsmouth buildings depicted by, **57**, 119
  White Island Light by, **121**
Haven, Maria Tufton, 210
Hawthorne, Hildegarde, 73, 87
  on Hamilton house gardens, 98
Hawthorne, Nathaniel, 165, 179, 189, 190
Haying (Coleman), **118**
Henry, L.E., 121
Here and There in New England and Canada (Sweetser), 9, 10
Higginson, Thomas Wentworth, 207
Higonnet, Anne, 134, 193
Hill, Adams Sherman, 116
Hilton, Frank W., 17
Hilton, Martha, 115–16
Historic American Building Survey, 51
Historic and Improvement Society. *See* Old York Historic and Improvement Society
Historic and Present Day Guide to Old Deerfield (Baker and Coleman), 155
historic houses. *See also* names of individual houses
  amateur v. professional, 201
  historical significance v. architectural distinction and, 193, 198, 199
  as museums, 193–204
  women and, 193–204

"History of Portsmouth and Its Potential as a Tourist Attraction" (Vaughan), 203
History of York (ed. Banks), 165
Hodge, Virginia, 57
Homer, Winslow
  Junkins Garrison by, **27**
Homes of America, The (Lamb), 48
Hood, Raymond M., 56
hooked rugs, 143
Hooper, Charles Edward, 40
Hopkins, James C., 160
Horticulturist (periodical), 35, 37
Hosmer, Charles B., Jr., 193
hotels. *See* names of individual hotels
Houghton Mifflin, 179
House Beautiful (periodical), XII, 108
  Bray house renovations covered by, 43, **45**
  Hamilton house covered by, 74
  Stonecrop cottage/studio covered by, **141**, 141–43, **142**
houses, historic. *See* historic houses
Howe, Lois Lily, 50
Howe family (Sudbury, Massachusetts), 223
Howells, John Mead, 45, 55, 56–57, 201, 203, 221–22
  and historic photography, 51–52
  Lady Pepperrell House elevation by, 56
Howells, William Dean, 8, 11, 56, 165, 175, 182, **188**, 207
  on Aldrich's *Story of a Bad Boy*, 177
  on Celia Thaxter, 172
  in Kittery Point, Maine, **188**
  on Native Americans, 165, 166–67
  and the Old Gaol, 196
  and Sarah Orne Jewett, 180
Howells house (Kittery Point, Maine). *See* William Dean Howells house (Kittery Point, Maine)
Hoyt, Clarence Piper, 151
Hoyt, Merry Delle, 141
Huggins, Mrs. G. Allen, 213
Hunt, William Morris, 124 n. 1, 152–54
Hutchinson, Martha Brooks, 88

I

Independence Hall (Philadelphia), 206
Indians. *See* Native Americans
Industrial revolution, 165
In the Garden (Hassam), **174**
In the Orchard (Tarbell), 131
Irving and Casson (furniture manufacturer), 61
Isabella Stewart Gardner Museum (Boston, Massachusetts), 193
Isham, Norman, 201
Island Garden, An (Thaxter), 108, 110, 175
Island Garden Revisited, An (Curry), 108, 119
Island House, The (Woodbury), **144**

Isles of Shoals (Maine/New Hampshire), 3, **173**. *See also* Appledore Island; Star Island; White Island
  artistic community on, 119, 156–58
  and the resort industry, 5
  Thaxter's writing and, 179–80
Italianate style (architecture), 35–36, 74–75
  gardens, 87
Italian landscape murals/wallpapers, 74–78, **75, 76**, 210
Italian Villas and Their Gardens (Wharton), 75–76, 77

J

Jack, Eliza, and Louise Coolidge (Perkins), **129**
Jacob Wendell house (Portsmouth, New Hampshire), 23–26, **24, 25, 106**, 106–7
  photographs of, 14, 24, **24**, 26 n. 8, **44**
  "Wendell couch," 25
Jaffrey cottage (New Castle, New Hampshire), 41, **62**, 62–64, **63**
Jaffrey house (Portsmouth, New Hampshire), 215, 219
Jefferds Tavern (York, Maine), 112, 201, 222–25, **224**
  measured drawings of, **223**
Jefferson Hall (Portsmouth, New Hampshire), 36
Jemison, Mary, 169–70, 173
Jewett, Sarah Orne, 10, 11, 13, 41, 64, 77, 117, 118, 155, 175, **226**
  on front yards, 83
  Hamilton house and, 71
  Hamilton house photo by, **70**
  and Marcia Oakes Woodbury, 135–37
  and Native Americans, 170–72
  Piscataqua River described by, xi
  on South Berwick's decline, 4, 183
  on "the savage," 165, 166
  and Thomas Bailey Aldrich, 170, 171
  and William Dean Howells, 180
  on women's relationship to nature, 165–66
Jewett, Captain Theodore, 135
Jewett house (South Berwick, Maine). *See* Sarah Orne Jewett house (South Berwick, Maine)
Job Wells house (York Harbor, Maine), **84, 85**
John Bray house (Kittery Point, Maine), 43, 45
John Hancock house (Boston, Massachusetts), **123**
John Langdon house (Portsmouth, New Hampshire). *See* Governor John Langdon mansion (Portsmouth, New Hampshire)
John Paul Jones house (Portsmouth, New Hampshire), 84, 199–201, 215, **217**, 217–19

interior of, **218**
  stairhall of, **200**
Johnson, Bradbury, 57
John Sullivan house (Durham, New Hampshire). *See* General John Sullivan house (Durham, New Hampshire)
John Thaxter residence (Kittery Point, Maine), 149, **149**
Jones, E. Alfred, 25
Jones, Frank, 6, 17–20, 20 n. 8, 158
Jones, John Paul, 187
Josias River, 124, **125**
Juglaris, Tommaso, 135
Junkins Garrison, The (Lane), **164**
Junkins garrison house (York, Maine), 27, **27**, 118
  paintings of, 27, **27**

K

Katwijka (Woodbury), **137**
Kelp Rock cottage (New Castle, New Hampshire), 62
Kendrick, Philip H.
  White Mountain Paper Company Office drawing by, **159**
Kent, Henry, 218
Kilham, Walter H., 160–62
Kilham and Hopkins (architects), 160
Kimball, Fiske, 50, 203
Kingsbury, Edith, 98
Kinney, Joseph N., 31
Kitson, H.H., 151
Kittery, Maine, xi
  historical exercises in, 23
  population of, 14 n. 3
Kittery Point, Maine, 8, 118, **119**
  old historic houses of, **13**
  Pepperrell Cove in, **120**
Kolodny, Annette, 165, 168–69, 170, 172, 175

L

Ladd, Alexander Hamilton, 210, 212
Ladd house (Portsmouth, New Hampshire). *See* Moffatt-Ladd house (Portsmouth, New Hampshire)
Lady Pepperrell house (Kittery Point, Maine), 38, **55**, 55–57, **56**
Lady Pepperrell Mansion (Barry), **55**
"Lady Wentworth" (Longfellow), 115–16
Laighton, Thomas, 5, 119, 179
Lamb, Martha J., 48
Lamb, Professor Mortimer F., 19
Lancaster Building (York Harbor, Maine), 148, **148**
Landscape architecture, 88–90

Lane, Susan Minot, 27, 152–55
  The Junkins Garrison by, **164**
Langdon, Dr. Francis, 123
Langdon, John, 60
Langdon, Woodbury, 12–13, 17, 19, 39, 61, 200, 218, 219
Langdon house (Portsmouth, New Hampshire). *See* Governor John Langdon Mansion (Portsmouth, New Hampshire)
Langdon Room. *See under* Rockingham Hotel (Portsmouth, New Hampshire)
Langley Boardman house (Portsmouth, New Hampshire), 45, **46, 47**, 76
Lathrop, Elise, 215
Lathrop, Henry, 92, 93
Laurent, John, 138
Laurent, Robert, 138
Lay of the Land, The (Kolodny), 165
Lazar's School, 135
Ledgemere cottage (Sorrento, Maine), 20 n. 8
Leila Usher cottage (Kittery Point, Maine), **151**, 151–52
Lincoln's birthplace, 28
Literary Friends and Acquaintance (Howells), 172
Literature and Life: Studies (Howells), 182, 187–89
Little, Arthur, 39, 47 n. 7, 48, 103, 122, 194
  architectural illlustration by, **49**
  sketch of Sparhawk house by, **54**
  on Sparhawk house, 53
Little, J. Lovell, 140–41
Little, J. Lovell, Jr., 143
Little and Russell (architects), 143
Littlefield, Captain Charles, 144
Little Harbor, New Hampshire, 123, 129–31
  artistic community in, 128–29
Little Picture House (New York, New York), 224
Lockwood, Luke Vincent, 25, 199, 222
Lodge, Henry Cabot, 207
"logg" houses, 26–29
  construction and use of, 26–27
Long Branch, New Jersey, 7
Longfellow, Alexander Wadsworth, Jr., 116, 127, 128
Longfellow, Henry Wadsworth, 115, 222–23
Longfellow house (Cambridge, Massachusetts). *See* Vassall-Craigie-Longfellow house (Cambridge, Massachusetts)
Lord, George, 222
Lord, Samuel, 217
Lorimer, Rebecca, 136
Lost Examples of Colonial Architecture (Howells), 51
Louisiana Purchase Exposition (St. Louis, 1904), 28
Lowthorpe School of Landscape Architecture, Gardening, and Horticulture for Women, 88

M

Macpheadris, Captain Archibald, 221
Macpheadris-Warner house (Portsmouth, New Hampshire), 60, 76, 193, **220**
  dining room of, **202**
  stairhall of, **221**
Main Building, International Exhibition (Aubrun), XII
Maine Historical Society (Portland, Maine), 200, 204 n. 21, 205
Manning, Warren, 89
Mansfield, Erastus G., 17
Maplewood Farm estate (Portsmouth, New Hampshire), 19
maps
  Boston & Maine railroad in New England, ca. 1912 (detail), **5**
  Piscataqua River region, **x**
Market St. Portsmouth, N.H. (Bufford), **21**
Marshall, Frank, 22
Marshall, Nathaniel Grant, 6
Marshall house (York Harbor, Maine), 6, **6**
Martine cottage (Little Harbor, New Hampshire), 116
Mason, E.F., 128
Mason, George C., 37
Mason, Sarah Catherine, 210
Mason, William, 156
"Massacre of Candlemas Day," 165
Masterson, Polly ("York Garrison"), 171
McIntire garrison house (York, Maine), 27, 28, 118
McKim, Charles F., 38
McKim, Mead and White (architects), 61
Measured Drawings of Woodwork Displayed in the American Wing (Metropolitan Museum of Art), 50
Meinerth, Carl, 87
Metropolitan Museum of Art (New York, New York), 198, 217, 218–19, 222
  and Wentworth-Gardner house, 215–16
Mifflin, George H., 207
Miller, Frederick Roy, 146
Millet, Jean François, 152
Mills, Richard, 210
"Miss Godwin's Inheritance" (Page), 74 n. 5
Mission house (Stockbridge, Massachusetts), 107
Mitchell, Horace, 53–54
"Modern English Plaster Houses" (Little), 143
modernism, aesthetic
  colonial revival and, XI–XII
Moffatt, Captain John, 95, 210
Moffatt, Samuel, 210
Moffatt-Ladd house (Portsmouth, New Hampshire), 37, **50**, 76, 194, 198, 210–13, **211**
  gardens of, **79**, 93–95, **94**
  horse-chestnut tree, 95, **95**

  parlor of, **51**, **199**
  stairhall of, **212**
Monet, Claude, 118
Monograph Series, The, 51
Monroe, Sophia Sewall Wood
  Barrell Homestead by, **34**
"Monuments of Paris" (wallpaper), 78
Morning, New Castle Harbor (Tarbell), **132**
Morrill, Grace, 141
Morrill cottage and studio (Ogunquit, Maine). *See* Grace Morrill cottage and studio (Ogunquit, Maine)
Morris, William, 97, 108
Mother and Mary (Tarbell), 132
Moulton farmhouse (York, Maine). *See* Four Acres (York Harbor, Maine)
Mount Vernon Ladies' Association of the Union, 193
"Mr. Brooks in his Antique Shop," photo ca. 1930 (York, Maine), **9**
Mrs. Bonny at Home (Woodbury), 170
Murphy, Kevin D.
  Sea Hill photo by, **151**
  Usher Cottage photo by, **151**
My Family (Tarbell), 131–33, 146

N

Nantucket, Massachusetts, 8
Narrative of the Life of Mary Jemison, A (Jemison), 169–70
National Gypsum Company, 160
National Park Service, 203
Native Americans
  Piscataqua writers and, 165, 166–75
New Castle, New Hampshire, XI, 8
  artistic community in, 119–20
  harbor, **132**
New Castle Historic and Picturesque (Albee), 62
New Church (Swedenborgian) School (Waltham, Massachusetts), 129
Newell, Lafayette, 87
New England Captives Carried to Canada . . . (Baker and Coleman), 27, 154–55, 165
  illustration from, **164**
New England Doorways (Chamberlain), 51
New England Farmer's Home and Modern Kitchen (display), 146
New England Magazine, 145
New Hampshire Farms for Summer Homes, 39
New Homes Under Old Roofs (Seabury), 41
Newport, Rhode Island, 7
New York International Exhibition of Modern Art. *See* Armory Show (1913)
Niles, Edward G., 62–64, 64 n. 8
Nims, Frederick C., 155
Nooks and Corners of the New England Coast (Drake), 27, 115, 205

North Church (Portsmouth, New Hampshire), 36
Northend, Mary Harrod, 40–41, 189–90, 221
  Jacob Wendell house photo by, **24**
Northrup, Dr. Birdsley, 83
Norton, Charles Eliot, 116, 123, 128, 188, 207
Nova Scotian Homestead, A (Woodbury), 144
Nubble Lighthouse (York Beach), 16
Nutter, James, 58
Nutting, Wallace, 198
  autobiography of, 215
  "chain of colonial houses," 213–15
  Wentworth-Gardner house photos by, **2**, **214**

O

Oakes, Marcia. *See* Woodbury, Marcia Oakes
Ocean Bluff House (Kennebunkport, Maine), 6
Oceanic Hotel (Isles of Shoals), 5, 6, 17
"Odd Sticks and Other Reflections" (Aldrich), 184–85
Ogunquit, Maine, XI
  artistic community at, 117–18, 124, 138
  Perkins Cove area, **117**, 124, **125**
Ogunquit House, 144
Ogunquit School of Painting and Sculpture, 117–18, 138
"Old Berwick Day" (The Berwicks, Maine), 23
Old Colonial Architecture and Furniture (Wallis), 48
"Old Family Mansion in York, The" (anonymous poem), 65
Old Fence in Nova Scotia, An (Woodbury), 144
Old Fields (South Berwick, Maine), 97
Old Gaol, The (Woodbury), 144–45
Old Gaol (York, Maine), 10, 16, 84, 189, 193, 195
  as museum, 191, 192, 195, 205–7
  photographs of, **191**, **192**, **195**, **196**, **197**, 205
  and women's history, 195–96
"Old Historic Mansions, Kittery Point, Maine," photo ca. 1900, **13**
Old Homes Made New . . . Illustrating the Alteration and Remodeling of Several Suburban Residences (Woollett), 57–58
"Old Home Week," 9, 21–23
Old House Altered, The (Mason), 37
Old Kitchen, The (Enneking), 146
Old Lyme, Connecticut, 115
Old Salem House, An (Woodbury), 144
Old Ship Meetinghouse (Hingham, Massachusetts), 52
Old Silver of American Churches (Jones), 25
Old South Church (Boston, Massachusetts), 151, 206
Old Time Wall Papers: An Account of Pictorial Papers on our Forefather's Walls (Sanborn), 76, 78

"Old Town by the Sea, An" (Aldrich), 119
Old Town by the Sea, An (Aldrich), 177, 182, 184–85
"Old Town of Berwick, The" (Jewett), 183–84, 187
Old York Historical and Improvement Society, 82–83, 84, 91–93, 96, 206, 213
  trees planted by, 92
Olmsted, Frederick Law, 82, 88–89
Olmsted, Frederick Law, Jr., 88
Olmsted Brothers (landscape architects), 88–89
Open House in New England (Chamberlain), 51
Orcutt, Philip Dana, 93, 201, 221
Oriental painting, 138
Osgood, James R., 48

P

Page, Thomas Nelson, 11–12, 22, 93, 165, 194, 206
  and the Old Gaol, 196
Paine, John Knowles, 156
Paine Hall (Harvard University), 56
Paris, France, 115
Parker House Hotel (Boston, Massachusetts), 20 n. 2
Park Field Hotel (Kittery Point, Maine), 6
Parkman, Francis, 130
Parrish, Maxfield, 77
Parrott, John F., 217
Passaconaway Inn (Cape Neddick, Maine), 30, 30–31
Patterson, Marvin Breckinridge
  Alger garden photo by, 89
  Howells house garden photo by, 83
  Langdon mansion garden photo by, 111
  River house garden photo by, 89
Paul, Florence, 190
Peabody, Robert Swain, 37, 48, 122
Pearce, Roy Harvey, 165, 167
Pearl painting, 138
Peck, Howard, 201, 223–24, 225
Pell, John, 190
Pencil Points, 51
Penhallow, Pearce, 52
Penhallow, Thomas, 221
peonies, 108
Pepperrell, Lady Mary, 55
Pepperrell, Sir William, 39, 52, 53
  tomb of, 11
Pepperrell Cove (Cheney), 120
Perkins, Elizabeth Bishop, 41, 43, 87, 110, 163, 189–90, 201, 222, 223
  garden photos by, 85, 96
  Perkins house cigar-store Indian photo by, 189
  Wells house slide by, 84
Perkins, Rev. J. Newton, 70 n. 2

Perkins, Mary Sowles, 67, 68, 70, 195–96, 205–7
Perkins, Molly Coolidge, 114, 129–31
  photos by, 113, 129, 130
Perkins Cove (Woodbury), 117
Perkins house (York, Maine). *See* Elizabeth Perkins house (York, Maine)
Perkins summer fellowship. *See* Elizabeth Perkins summer fellowship program
Perry, Shaw, Hepburn, and Dean (architects), 203
  Strawbery Banke site plan by, 203, 203
Perry, William G., 203
Peterborough, New Hampshire, 143
Philadelphia Centennial Exhibition of 1876
  New England Farmer's Home and Modern Kitchen display, 146
phlox, 108
Phoebe Weare house (Cape Neddick, Maine), 68
photography
  colonial revival and, 51–52, 129–31, 152–55
  and gardens, 83, 85, 87, 89, 99, 100, 105
  and historical/architectural documentation, 49, 51–52, 118, 134–35, 152–55
Pierce, President Franklin, 219
Pierce, Herbert H.D., 62
Piggin house (York, Maine). *See* Elizabeth Perkins house (York, Maine)
Pike, Judge Robert G., 197
Pinehurst cottage (Cape Neddick, Maine), 31, 32, 32
Pine-Tree Coast, The (Drake), 15, 15, 22
Piscataqua Garden Club (York, Maine), 84, 96, 110–12
  roadside clean-up sponsored by, 110
Piscataqua River region, xi
  artistic and literary images of, 13–14
  guidebooks to, 15–17
  historical celebrations in, 21–23
  historic house museums in, 193–204
  landscape of, 3, 81
  map of, x
  photography and, 129–30
  population of, 14 n. 3
  transition from water to rail economy in, 4–5
Piscataqua writers
  and Native Americans, 165, 166–75
"Plan of Piscataqua Harbor, Town of Portsmouth, Ec." (Grant), 81, 82
Point of Graves (Portsmouth, New Hampshire), 169
Polley, George H., 48
Porter, Frederic Hutchinson, 53
Porter, John Hutchinson, 50
Porter, Rufus, 76
Portsmouth, New Hampshire, xi, 4, 121
  architecture, 35–36
  architecture documented, 48–49, 51–52
  Blunt's painting of the harbor of, 2

Childe Hassam and, 119, 158
cookstoves in, 208, 210 n. 11
Custom House, 36
early landscape painting of, 80, 81
economic decline of, 21
guidebooks to, 15–16, 123
Market Square renovations, 35–36
Market Street in, 21
new North Church in, 36
population of, 14 n. 3
Puddle Dock in, 184, 203, 204
tourism in, 16
West India trade and, 3
Portsmouth, N.H.: A Camera Impression (Chamberlain), 51
Portsmouth Athenaeum (Portsmouth, New Hampshire), 36, 57, 119
  fireplace of, 59
  reading room renovation, 57–58
Portsmouth Book, The, 49
Portsmouth & Dover Railroad, 6
Portsmouth Guide Book (Foster), 16, 123
Portsmouth Harbor, Portsmouth, New Hampshire (Blunt), 2
Portsmouth Historical Society, 84, 200–1, 215, 217
Portsmouth Historic and Picturesque (Gurney), 16, 16, 24
Portsmouth Manufacturing Company (South Berwick, Maine), 183
"Problem of Summer, The" (Howells), 188
Prynne, Hester (*Scarlet Letter*), 165, 190
Publisher's Paper Company, 158
Puddle Dock (Portsmouth, New Hampshire), 184, 203, 204, 215, 217
Purcell, Captain Gregory, 217
Purcell-Langdon-Lord house (Portsmouth, New Hampshire). *See* John Paul Jones house (Portsmouth, New Hampshire)
Purdon, James, 140–41, 143

Q

Quarterly, Arthur, 156
Queen Anne style (architecture), 36–37
Quimby, Frederick B., 87
Quincy house (Exeter, New Hampshire). *See* Dorothy Quincy house (Exeter, New Hampshire)

R

railroads, 4, 6, 17, 21
  map of Boston & Maine lines in New England ca. 1912, 5
  York Beach trolley, 6
Rambles About Portsmouth (Brewster), 9, 16, 17 n. 6, 26
Reclaiming the Old House (Hooper), 40

Redcote cottage (York Harbor, Maine), 147–48, **148**
Remodeled Farmhouses (Northend), 41
Renoir, Pierre-Auguste, 118
resort industry, 5–7
    and coastal access, 82–83
    historical/antiquarian interests and, 9–14
    and Isles of Shoals, 5
restoration and remodeling
    architects and historicism and, 36–38, 44–45
    of colonial homes, 40–46
    and the family farm, 39–40, 41
    total transformation and, 35–36
"Restoring Frary House" (Coleman), 151
"Return of the Sons" (Portsmouth, New Hampshire), 21–22, 24
Rice, Mrs. Arthur, 212, 213 n. 13
Richard house (York Harbor, Maine). *See* Harold C. Richard House (York Harbor, Maine)
Richardson, H.H., 128
Richardson, Harriet, 43
"River Driftwood" (Jewett), I, XI, 71, 77, 182–84, 185
River house (York, Maine)
    garden, **89**
Roberts, Kenneth, 112
Robertson, Hugh C., 128
Robie, Virginia, 54
Robinson, Frank T., 145
Robinson-Smith house (Newport, Rhode Island), 38
Rockefeller, John D., Jr., 201
Rockhaven cottage (Cape Neddick, Maine), 31
Rockingham Bank (Portsmouth, New Hampshire), 36
Rockingham Baseball Club, 219
Rockingham Hotel (Portsmouth, New Hampshire), 6, **17**, 17, **18**, 19–20, 45, 61
    Langdon Room of, **61**
Rogers, Phyllis, 169
Roland Thaxter house (Kittery Point, Maine), 149–50, **150**
Rollins, Governor Frank, 22
Room of Flowers, The (Hassam), 156–58
Roosevelt, Theodore, 28
Ross, W.F., 58
Rounds, Ellen Peavey, 197
Rounds, Mrs. Holmes B., 28
Rowlandson, Mary, 169, 175
rugs, 143
Ruskin, John, 108, 115, 119
Russell, Benjamin F.W., 143
Russo-Japanese Peace Conference, 20

S

Sacred Places: American Tourist Attractions in the Nineteenth Century (Sears), 15

Safford, Moses A., 53, 205
St. Aspinquid, 166–67, **167**
St. Aspinquid Park (York, Maine), 166–67, **167**
    advertisement for, **166**
St. George's Episcopal Church (York Harbor, Maine), 148 n. 4
St. John's Church (Portsmouth, New Hampshire), 50
Sally Hart house (Newington, New Hampshire), 100–1
Salter, Thomas P., 58
Samuel Haven house (Portsmouth, New Hampshire), 43
Samuel Wentworth house (Portsmouth, New Hampshire), 215, 217
Sanborn, Kate, 39–40, 76, 78
Sarah Orne Jewett house (South Berwick, Maine), **42**, 135
Sargent, John Singer, 87, 131
Sawyer, James C., 88
Sayward, Jonathan, 64
Sayward-Wheeler house (York, Maine), 64–67, **65**
    parlor of, 65–66, **66**
Scarlet Letter (Hawthorne), 165, 189, 190
School of the Museum of Fine Arts (Boston, Massachusetts), 130, 131
Scribner's Monthly Magazine, 108, 184
Scudder, Horace, 186–87
Seabury, Joseph Stowe, 41
Sea Hill (Kittery Point, Maine), 151, **151**
Sears, Jabez H., 17, 19, 20 n. 10
Seurat, Georges, 115
Seven Lamps of Architecture, The (Ruskin), 119
Sewall, Rev. and Mrs. David, 136
Sewall's Bridge, 112
Sewall's Bridge (Coleman), **181**
Shadow of the Flowers, The (Aldrich), 104
Sharksmouth (Manchester-by-the-Sea, Massachusetts), 103
Sheafe farmhouse (Little Harbor, New Hampshire), 116
Sheldon, George, 155
Shelton, Louise, 73, 85, 87
    on Hamilton house gardens, 98
Sherburne, John, 221
Sherburne family decanter, 24, 26 n. 12
Sherburne house (Portsmouth, New Hampshire), 35
Shingle style (architecture), 147
Shipman, Ellen Biddle, 88, 89
"Shore House, The" (Jewett), 180
Shurcliff, Arthur, 84, 89
Simonds, O.C., 93
Sleeper, Henry Davis, 100, 101–3
Small House in the Sun (Chamberlain), 51
Smibert, John, 58
Smith, George Ferguson, 140–41
Smith, James B., 203

Smith, John, 165
Smith, Richard Averill
    Little Picture House tea-room photo by, **225**
Smith and Dove Manufacturing Company, 141
Smith residence (Ogunquit, Maine). *See* George F. Smith residence (Ogunquit, Maine)
Society for the Preservation of Historic Landmarks in York County, 96
Society for the Preservation of New England Antiquities, 45, 64, 68, 73, 98, 201, 213
    Elise Tyson Vaughan photos collected by, 134
Society of Arts and Crafts in Boston, 128
Society of Colonial Dames
    in Massachusetts, 25
    the National, 199
    in New Hampshire, 84, 93, 198, 210–11
Society of Landscape Architects. *See* American Society of Landscape Architects
"Some Houses Along the Southern Coast of Maine" (Walker), 50
South Berwick, Maine, XI, 3
    artistic community at, 116–17
    decline of, 4, 183
    population of, 14 n. 3
South Berwick Square (photograph), **4**
Souther, Emeline Arnold, 133 n. 1
Southwest Prospect of the Seat of Colonel George Boyd at Portsmouth, New Hampshire, New England (painting), **80**, 81
Southwood (Brookline, Massachusetts), 154
Sparhawk, Nathaniel, 52
Sparhawk house (Kittery Point, Maine), 37, 38, 48, **52**, 52–55, 63, 123, 194
    stairhall at, **54**
Springchorn, Carl, 138
"Staccato Notes of a Vanished Summer" (Howells), 165, 188–89
Stackpole, Dr. Frederick Dabney, 147–48
Stackpole Block (York Harbor, Maine), 148
Staffordshire china, 208
Stanwood, James Rindge, 24, 58, 107
Staples, Walter Chesley, 87
Star Island, Isles of Shoals, New Hampshire, 3
    stone meetinghouse on, 119
Stedman, Clarence, 207
Stedman house (New Castle, New Hampshire), 62, 123–24, **124**
Steele, Fletcher, 87, 107
stenciling, wall
    Moses Eaton style, 69–70
Stetson house (York Harbor, Maine). *See* Francis L. Stetson house (York Harbor, Maine)
Stewart, Charles (Cappy), 215, 217
Stewart, John, 22

Stilgoe, John
   landscape defined by, 81
Stillwater Tragedy, The (Aldrich), 185
Stokes, I.N., 56
Stonecrop (Ogunquit, Maine). *See* Grace
   Morrill cottage and studio (Ogunquit,
   Maine)
Story of a Bad Boy, The (Aldrich), 3–4, 11,
   104, 165, 177, 208
   gender relations in, 168, 170
   Native Americans in, 167–68, 170
Stowe, Harriet Beecher, 180
Strafford Savings Bank (Dover, New
   Hampshire), 196–97
Strawbery Banke Museum (Portsmouth,
   New Hampshire), 185, 203, 204
   site plan for, 203, **203**
Street in Portsmouth (Hassam), 158
Stroll by a Familiar River, A (Barry), 222
Student-Days at Harvard (Tripp), 115–16
Sturgis, John Hubbard, 116, 128
Sturgis, R. Clipston, 35, 47 n. 11, 49, 116, 128
Sullivan, Mrs. James Amory, 222
Sullivan, John, 187
summer people, 10–14
summer resorts, 5–8. *See also* resort industry
   and coastal access, 82–83
   social stratification in, 7–9
Sunday Dinner, The (Woodbury), 135–37,
   136
Sunset cottage (York Harbor, Maine), **38**
Surf Side cottage (York Beach, Maine), **7**
Swampscott, Massachusetts, 7
Swampscott Shanty, A (Woodbury), 144
Swan, Abraham, 60
Sweetser, Moses, 9, 10

T

Taft, Joseph H., 31, 31 n. 7
Tales of a Wayside Inn (Longfellow), 115, 222
Tallmadge, Thomas E., xii
Tarbell, Edmund C., 13, 119–20, 130,
   131–33, 133 n. 3
   Going to Ride by, 132, **133**
   Morning, New Castle Harbor by, **132**
   Tarbell family photo by, **122**
Tarbell family (Little Harbor, New
   Hampshire), **122**
"Tarbellites," 131
Taylor, W.L.
   illustration for Jewett's "York Garrison"
   by, **171**
Tenney, U.D., 58
Thaxter, Celia, 14 n. 8, 84, 87, 119, 122, 149,
   175, 182
   china decorated by, 209
   gardens, 108–10, **109**, **110**
   life and writing of, 179–80
   parlor of, 156–58, **157**

on "the savage," 165, 166
   William Dean Howells on, 172
   on women and nature, 172–75
Thaxter, John, 122, 149, 151
Thaxter, Karl, 149
Thaxter, Levi Lincoln, 122, 149, 179
Thaxter, Roland, 122, 149
Thaxter, Rosamond, 151–52
Thaxter residence (Kittery Point, Maine).
   See John Thaxter residence (Kittery
   Point, Maine)
Thomas Bailey Aldrich Association, 104–5
Thomas Bailey Aldrich Memorial (Ports-
   mouth, New Hampshire), 14, 104–5, **105**,
   177, 207–9
   colonial revival and, 208–9
   kitchen of, **209**
   Memorial Room interior, **207**
   quilts and counterpanes used in, 209,
   210 n. 12
"Three-story Colonial Houses of New
   England," 50
"Thumb Nail Sketches of Real Romance"
   (Perkins), 190
Tinsel painting, 138
Todd, Mrs. (*Country of the Pointed Firs*), 172
Tory Lover, The (Jewett), 74 n. 4, 185–87, 189
   illustration from, **186**
tourism. *See* resort industry; summer resorts
Towle and Foster (architects), 36
"Trap Dike, Appledore" (*Among the Isles of
   Shoals*), **178**
Treadwell, E.P., 122, 126
Tripp, George Henry, 115
*True History of the Captivity & Restoration
   of Mrs. Mary Rowlandson . . .* (Rowland-
   son), 169
Tucker, William, 36
Tudor revival style (architecture), 141, 152
Turner, Ross, 156
Turner, Sophia, **192**, 207
Tyson, Elise, 13, 41, 73, 74–78, 97–98, 103,
   116, 186
   Emily Tyson and Sarah Orne Jewett
   photo by, **226**
   Hamilton house photos by, **11**, **43**, **72**, **134**
   Hamilton house mural, photo by, **75**
   Jewett house photo by, **42**
   Villa d'Este, Tivoli photo by, **77**
Tyson, Emily (Mrs. George), 71, 74–78, 97,
   100, 104, 116, 186, **226**

U

"Unguarded Gates, The" (Aldrich), 11–12,
   185
Union Chapel (North Hampton, New
   Hampshire), 89
Union Chapel and Library (York Harbor,
   Maine), 147–48, 148 n. 4

United States Custom House (Portsmouth,
   New Hampshire), 36
United States Emergency Fleet Corporation,
   158, 162
   bird's-eye drawing of Atlantic Heights by,
   161
Ursula Cutt farm (Portsmouth, New
   Hampshire), **16**
U.S. Shipping Board. *See* United States
   Emergency Fleet Corporation
Usher, Leila, 151–52
Usher cottage (Kittery Point, Maine). *See*
   Leila Usher cottage (Kittery Point, Maine)

V

Vallier, Jane, 175
Van Cortlandt mansion (New York, New
   York), 199
Van Dyke, Henry, 207
Vassall-Craigie-Longfellow house
   (Cambridge, Massachusetts), 55, 57
Vaughan, Dorothy M., 203
Vaughan, Elise Tyson (Mrs. Henry G.). *See*
   Tyson, Elise
Vaughan, Henry, 112
Vaughan's Woods (South Berwick, Maine),
   98
Vermeer, Jan, 131, 133 n. 5, 146, 147
Vermeule, Cornelius and John, 30, 32
"Views in the New Rockingham Hotel at
   Portsmouth, New Hampshire," 18
Villa d'Este, Tivoli (Fernald), 77, **77**
Village sketch(es), 182, 184–85
"Visitors at the tomb of Sir William
   Pepperrell at Kittery Point, Maine,"
   photo, 1902 (Dame), **11**
"*Vues d'Italie*" wallpaper. *See* Italian
   landscape murals/wallpapers

W

Waldron, Jeremy R., 203
Walker, C. Howard, 50
"Wallace Nutting Chain of Colonial
   Houses," 213
Wallingford, Roger, 187
Wallingford Hall (Kennebunk, Maine),
   222
   Les Vues d'Italie wallpaper in, 76, **76**, 77
Wallis, Frank E., 48, 50
wallpaper(s), 76–78
Walnut Hill (Ogunquit, Maine), 141
Ware, William Rotch, 49
Warner, Jonathan, 39, 221
Warner House Association (Portsmouth,
   New Hampshire), 25, 107, 221
   Advisory Committee for, 201
Warren, Peter, 58

Washington Andirons (Field), **139**
Wasson, George, 188
Wayside Inn (Sudbury, Massachusetts), 222–23, 225
Weare, Theodore, 6
Weare family (Cape Neddick, Maine), 30, 31 n. 1
 homestead (photo ca. 1860), 32, **32**
Weare house (Cape Neddick, Maine). *See* Phoebe Weare house (Cape Neddick, Maine)
Weber, Paul J., 74
 Hamilton house garden photos by, **99, 100, 101, 102**
 Hamilton house photograph by, **xiii**
Wells, Frank L., 124 n. 17
Wells Beach, Maine, 5
Wells house (York Harbor, Maine). *See* Job Wells house (York Harbor, Maine)
Wendell, Barrett, 10, 23–25, 39, 43, 62, 106, 107, 116, 126, 201
Wendell, Edith Greenough, 23–25, 201, 221–22, 222
Wendell, George Blunt, 107
Wendell, Jacob, 10, 24
 garden notes of, 106–7
Wendell, Jacob, II, 122, 126–27
Wendell, William Greenough, 24, 107
Wendell house (Portsmouth, New Hampshire). *See* Jacob Wendell house (Portsmouth, New Hampshire)
Wentworth, Governor Benning, 17, 39, 115–16, 221
Wentworth, John, 213
Wentworth, Mark Hunking, 212
Wentworth, Samuel, 115, 215
Wentworth, Thomas, 213
Wentworth-Coolidge Mansion, The (Coleman), 155
Wentworth-Coolidge mansion (Little Harbor, New Hampshire), 129–30, 194
Wentworth-Gardner and Tobias Lear House Association, 216
Wentworth-Gardner house (Portsmouth, New Hampshire), 1, 60, 198, 213–16
 parlor of, **214**, 216
 woodwork sold to Metropolitan Museum, 215–16, 217–18
Wentworth Hotel (New Castle, New Hampshire), 6, 17–20, **19**
 "Colonial Annex" of, **19**, 20
"Wentworth Mansion and the Mouth of the Piscataqua," **15**
Wentworth mansion (Little Harbor, New Hampshire), 37, 39, 48, 65, 122, 123, 185, 219
 colonial figure wood sculptures at, 116, **116**
 photos of, **113**, **114**
West India trade, 3, 183
Wharton, Edith, 75–76
Wheeler, Elizabeth Cheever, 66
Wheeler, Dr. and Mrs. Leonard, 66

Wheelwright, Edmund March, 116, 122, 126–27
Whidden, Michael, 60, 210
Whipple, General William, 95
Whipple garrison house (Kittery, Maine), 26
Whistler, James McNeill, 108
White, William L., 123
"White City." *See* World's Columbian Exposition of 1893 (Chicago, Illinois)
Whitefield, Edwin, 27
White Island, Isles of Shoals, New Hampshire, 119
White Island Light (Hassam), **121**
White Island lighthouse (White Island, Isles of Shoals, New Hampshire), 119, 121, 179
White Mountain Paper Company Office (Portsmouth, New Hampshire), 158–60, **159**
White Pine Series (architecture monographs), 50, 51, 123
Whiteside, Agnes, 128
Whiting subdivision (Ogunquit, Maine), 88
Whitman, Sarah W., 128
Whittier, John Greenleaf, 179
 on Jewett's *Deephaven*, 180
Wide Awake, 171, **171**
Wiggin, Emily A., 212
Wiggins, J. Gregory
 Wentworth mansion wood sculptures by, 116, **116**
William Dam garrison house (Dover, New Hampshire), 28, **28**, 197–98, **198**, 204 n. 7
William Dean Howells house (Kittery Point, Maine)
 garden of, **83**
William Ridgway, Son & Co., 208
Williams, Roger, 165
Williamsburg. *See* Colonial Williamsburg (Williamsburg, Virgina)
Winn, Ralph, 30–31
Winslow and Bigelow (architects), 66
Winthrop house (Plymouth, Massachusetts), 45
Woman with Faggots, The (Coleman), 152, **154**
women
 in architecture, 88
 changing status of, 83–84
 historic house museums and, 193–204
 and Native Americans, 169–75
 relation to nature, 165–66, 168–69, 172–75
 suffrage movement, 165
Wood, William M., III, 56
Woodbury, Charles H., 27, 117, 118–19, 122, 141, 143, 144–45
 Agamenticus River by, 145, **145**
 Island House by, **144**
 Perkins Cove by, **117**

Woodbury, Marcia Oakes, xi
 Deephaven illustrations by, 180, **181**
 Katwijka by, **137**
 Mrs. Bonny at Home by, **170**
 Sunday Dinner by, 135–37, **136**
Woodbury Langdon II farmhouse (Newington, New Hampshire), **124**
Woodcock, S.S., 36
Woodman, Annie E., 196–97
Woodman, Charles, 196
Woodman Institute. *See* Annie B. Woodman Institute (Dover, New Hampshire)
Wood Sprites (Perkins), **130**
Woollett, William M., 57–58
Woolrich, Norman, 55 n. 7
Works Progress Administration, 51, 203
World's Columbian Exposition of 1893 (Chicago, Illinois), 92, 123
Wright, Frank Lloyd, x

Y

Yale University, 222
Yeales, Naomi, 190
Yeales, Timothy, 190
Yellow House (New Castle, New Hampshire), 62
Yoch, Florence, 88
York, Maine, 3, **91**. *See also* Old York Historical and Impovement Society
 artistic community at, 118
 development and preservation in, 91–93
 guidebooks to, 16
 population of, 14 n. 3
 trees planted in, **92**
 two-hundred-and-fiftieth anniversary of, 194
 village green restoration, 91–93
 year-round residents v. summer visitors in, 22
York Beach, Maine, 5, 7, 8, **8**
York Bureau of Information (York, Maine), 16
York Cliffs (Cape Neddick, Maine), 30, 31
York Cliffs Improvement Company, 31, 32
York County Tercentenary, 1936, 22–23
"York Garrison" (Jewett), 171, 171–72
York Harbor, Maine, 6, 8, **8**, 188
 architecture of, 147
York Harbor Reading Room, 141
York Historical Society, 205
York Tercentenary, 1902, 22, **23**
Young, Ammi B., 36

OLD
YORK

HISTORICAL
SOCIETY

This book has been printed and casebound in an edition of 1000 copies by Thomson-Shore, Inc. The paper is 80-lb. Mohawk Vellum, an acid-free sheet that will not yellow or become brittle with age. The binding is smyth sewn, for easy reading and a long reference life. Penmor Lithographers produced the color plates, printing them on acid-free, 80-pound Potlatch Karma.

Monotype Centaur, the type used for the title page, chapter titles, and catalogue numbers, is recognized as one of the most beautiful typefaces ever designed. Created by New Englander Bruce Rogers toward the end of the colonial revival period, Centaur was meant to be a modern interpretation of the famous roman type made by French typefounder Nicholas Jenson in the 1470s. Rogers designed it for letterpress printing, and it has appeared in some of the finest books produced in the twentieth century. The Metropolitan Museum of Art in New York began to use the capitals as soon as they were available, and the complete font with lowercase letters first appeared in a lavish edition of Maurice de Guérin's *Centaur* (1915). Arrighi, the companion italic face, was designed ten years later by Frederick Warde, who named it for a famous Italian writing master.

The book's text has been set in Adobe Minion, which should soon be acknowledged as a modern masterpiece. Rather than using a particular type as his model, Robert Slimbach chose to emulate the spirit of several "old style" types from the late Renaissance, including those of Jenson, Garamond, Griffo, and Van Dijck. Released in 1990, Minion has great clarity and warmth, while paying full attention to the specific needs of electronic typesetting equipment. It also has a full complement of true small caps, ligatures, and other refinements that have been put to good use in composing this book.

Bruce Kennett designed and typeset the book using QuarkXPress software on a Macintosh IIcx platform. Lois Thompson ably proofread the pages; Paul D'Alessandro created the index; and B&W Typographers provided the Linotronic output. Special thanks to Sarah Giffen for her participation in the design of the book.

Bruce Kennett